THE FUTURE STARTS WITH US

THE FUTURE STARTS WITH US

GORDON BROWN

SIMON &
SCHUSTER

London · New York · Amsterdam/Antwerp · Sydney/Melbourne · Toronto · New Delhi

First published in Great Britain by Simon & Schuster UK Ltd, 2026

1 3 5 7 9 10 8 6 4 2

Simon & Schuster UK Ltd, 7th Floor,
199 Bishopsgate, London EC2M 3TY

www.simonandschuster.co.uk
www.simonandschuster.com.au
www.simonandschuster.co.in

Simon & Schuster Australia, Sydney
Simon & Schuster India, New Delhi

The authorised representative in the EEA is Simon & Schuster Netherlands BV, Herculesplein 96, 3584 AA Utrecht, Netherlands. info@simonandschuster.nl

A CIP catalogue record for this book is available from the British Library

Hardback ISBN: 978-1-3985-1418-8
eBook ISBN: 978-1-3985-1419-5

Typeset in Perpetua by M Rules
Printed and Bound in the UK using 100% Renewable Electricity at CPI Group (UK) Ltd

MIX
Paper | Supporting responsible forestry
FSC® C013604
www.fsc.org

To the people of Kirkcaldy and Fife who have supported and inspired me through the years

CONTENTS

PART TWO

Breakthrough: Values-led pragmatism and global order

PREFACE

In today's world, there are three stories that need telling.

First, the breakup. Globally, we are watching the highly visible fracturing of the world order we once took for granted. This rules-based order – with its support for the rule of law, human rights, democracy, international cooperation, humanitarian aid and environmental stewardship – that underpinned our lives for decades is collapsing in plain sight in what one writer speaks of as liberalism's 'Great Capitulation'.[1] Disorder, violence, bombings and wars fill our TV screens. From Russia's assault on Ukraine and the recent wars in Gaza and Iran, to apparently never-ending conflicts and civil wars in Sudan, Ethiopia, Myanmar and elsewhere, we are witnessing countless deaths, the displacement of millions and the worst levels of forced migration in modern history. Meanwhile, humanity faces droughts, firestorms, floods and the hottest temperatures in recorded history – and whether it be ending wars, tackling climate change or addressing the massive economic changes ahead arising from AI, governments seem unable to come together to confront the challenges facing our world.

Second, the breakdown. Side by side with the breakup of the world order, we are seeing another twenty-first-century phenomenon: the breakdown of local communities. It is a slow, grinding, at times almost invisible, erosion of civic life and with it the social contract on which democracy has long depended. It is the decline in the neighbourliness, networks and norms that once shaped the life of our villages, towns, cities and workplaces. And, across the Western world, it is reflected in the falling attendance at churches and faith groups, the halving of trade union memberships, and the decline of social clubs, working men's clubs and local associations such as Mothers' Unions, Women's Institutes and youth organisations, resulting in the hollowing out of what once constituted the public square. In a series of original polls conducted for this book – which I refer to throughout – I find that around half of adults across western Europe and North America do not now participate in any civic groups of any kind and they do not feel there is any organisation or support system to which they can turn in times of need. This latter point is, perhaps, the greatest casualty of all: the very idea that we are all in this together, that there are common causes worth fighting for, and that by coming together as a community we can make a difference.

If our physical infrastructure – our roads, railways and airports – broke down, there would be a public outcry and a demand for their immediate repair. If our financial infrastructure collapsed – if ATMs shut off and bank transfers failed – there would be panic. But the failure of our civic infrastructure – our clubs, associations, political parties and the public square itself – is happening in plain view and near silence.

Too often, however, we linger on what has gone wrong – the breakups and the breakdowns – and draw only the bleakest of conclusions. This book moves through them quickly – not to ignore or minimise their impact, but to make space for what matters most: the third story, of the close-at-hand breakthroughs that can rebuild community, renew the global order, and set us on a more hopeful, equitable and sustainable course, and the role that every one of us, as active and engaged citizens, can play in bringing that about.

The promise of deep and even fundamental change – from a failed status quo to a new beginning – has been the mantra of almost every public campaign of recent years, from American presidential campaign slogans such as Barack Obama's 'Change we can believe in' and 'Change you can trust' to the more recent and stark 'Change' pledged by the United Kingdom Labour Party. In today's world, no leader wins support, draws a crowd or secures election without promising change. From Australia to South Africa and from Indonesia to Latin America, it is a proven formula for electioneering, a well-worn path for would-be leaders and an all-too-familiar playbook known to the rest of us.

And for good reason. There is hardly a group of citizens anywhere who are not desperate to break with a recent past that has denied them the higher living standards they were promised and the better quality of life they believe they deserve. In both head and heart, millions of people now sense that something must give. This desire for change is often torn between a nostalgia for what has been lost and a realisation that there is no going back – but it seldom offers a concrete prospectus for a better future.

Change cannot mean a return to a discredited and patently unpopular recent status quo. Too much water has gone under the bridge. The future cannot and will not neatly mirror the past. By 2050, India's economy will likely be four times the size of the UK's, China's twice that of the European Union, and Asia's bigger than those of America and Europe combined. Four out of every five of the world's people will be living in Africa or Asia. By 2008, when the global financial crisis hit, the world's economic centre of gravity had already shifted, as Danny Quah has graphically portrayed, from its traditional twentieth-century point in the Atlantic Ocean, midway between the United States and western Europe, 5,000 kilometres eastward to somewhere between Europe and Asia.[2] By 2040 it will have moved another 5,000 kilometres eastward to somewhere between China and India. And as if to illustrate the shift, Quah himself has moved his professorship from London to Singapore.[3] And so we will all have to grapple with changing fundamentals: the shifting economic balance of power; the fallout from revolutionary new technologies such as AI and their transformative impact on employment, living standards and individual freedoms; the existential challenge of climate change; and the tensions created by unprecedented human mobility (almost one billion people globally say they would prefer to leave their own country for another if they could).[4] All of this is, as we shall discover, aggravated by three seismic global shifts now underway that will, unless we change things, most likely define the next decades: from a unipolar world order towards a multipolar one; from a dominant neoliberal economic ideology to a neo-mercantilist one; and from a rules-based to a power-based world – each of these shifts underscored by the rise of an aggressive and authoritarian ethno-nationalism.

The way this still-young twenty-first century unfolds in its second quarter will be – and must be – different from the quarter-century that preceded it. We must begin by asking: why is it that the breakup of the world order and the breakdown of civic life are happening at the same time? What, if anything, links the two?

There is no shortage of candidate causes for both the breakup and the breakdown, from the political to the economic to the cultural. Politically, not just the upsurge of an aggressive, anti-establishment ethno-nationalism, but the rise of polarising rhetoric, often now online, the fragmentation of political parties and the inroads of big money into decision-making have effectively privatised the public sphere. The once-crowded town squares of civic debate have been displaced by online silos where people speak past strangers they never meet. Economically, rising inequality and decades of neoliberalist policies have left millions without security, fairness or opportunity. Culturally, social and geographical mobility have not always brought integration; consumerism and individualism have eroded a unifying sense of social obligation; and identity politics has splintered common cause into competing grievances.

I wanted to unpick what is common to these differing

explanations and trace them back to discover the root causes, the key that will unlock solutions that might work. In order to do so, and to ground these ideas in the lived experiences of people across the globe, over the last two years I have worked with polling experts on three major surveys, covering nearly 100,000 people from forty-five countries across the Global North and South. Our objective was to hear what the general public have to say about their own lives and local community life and how this relates, if at all, to the breakup of the world order.

Some of the findings have surprised me, others have shocked me, and over the course of this book I will be unpacking what the responses mean for the prospects of community life at home and for international cooperation abroad. What people say and what they desire for the future might illuminate a route forward on both a local and a global scale.

What the polling makes clear is that we need, for this time of transformational change, an honest debate about who we are, who we want to be and, above all, where we are going. It is about focusing on a present and future that learn from history without romanticising a past that was far from perfect.

And so this is where our story begins: with the conviction that change cannot come soon enough. That is why my title is *The Future Starts With Us*. The change we seek starts here and now – at home and near to home. And it starts with us – with you and me. That is the crucial finding of this book. For in the end, despite what we might have once assumed, the future will not be decided by the declarations of presidents or prime ministers or by detailed communiqués from international summits. The future is not in the gift of leaders, governments or even blind economic forces, which may constrain what we can do today but must not determine what we do in times to come. The future is in our hands.

INTRODUCTION

This book is a child of crisis.

It was born amid the seismic shifts that have jolted the tectonic plates beneath our feet. These tumultuous transformations are changing our world beyond all recognition, affecting our jobs, our standards of living, the patterns of our daily lives and how our children will fare in the decades to come. I believe the shifts I identify below will prove more dramatic and be more consequential than any of the many changes that we have seen since the Second World War, no matter where you live or what your circumstances are. War, it has been said, is the locomotive of history and today's conflicts involving great powers – those in Ukraine and the Middle East – have turbocharged changes already in motion and fast-forwarded us to a different kind of world.

So – what are these changes?

The first is this: the world is moving from the certainties of unipolarity to the uncertainties of multipolarity. For almost all the years since 1945, but especially since the 1990s when the Cold War ended, the United States of America has worked with friends and allies in a world that it has dominated. In other words, it usually acted multilaterally in a unipolar world. Recently it has done the opposite – disregarding, and often insulting, its friends and allies in a world over which it no longer has unquestioned control. In other words, it has been acting unilaterally in what is becoming a multipolar world.

'The United States, not the United Nations,' Hal Brands has written, was 'the closest thing to world government'.[1] But while America may still think of itself as a benevolent hegemon bestriding a unipolar world with its massive military firepower by air, on land and at sea, events have repeatedly revealed its limits. The eclipse of the unipolar world, as Daniel Drezner of Tufts University has argued, cannot just be dismissed as scaremongering, as 'the latest hymn from the Church of Perpetual Worry'.[2]

If since 2022, in the first European war involving a great power since 1945 and in what will go down as perhaps the first AI war, America has been unable to decisively turn back Russian aggression, so too in 2026, in a war in which the weaponisation of the Strait of Hormuz by Iran has brought the biggest disruption of the world energy market in history and one of the biggest supply shocks ever seen, America has found it difficult to keep sea lanes open, even by force.

And it has not achieved the aim it set itself for what it considers its own sphere of influence: the takeover of Greenland. The US may well remain the most powerful and strongest, as well as the wealthiest, country that the world has known, with no rival equal to it, but the limits of American power – clear to the rest of the world for some time – are at last being laid bare to American leaders and the American public. The question for the decades ahead is not whether we can return to an era of single-power domination, with a unipolar world reborn, but how we manage the transition to our new multipolar world, one in which there are multiple centres of decision-making power. Not, let us be clear, powers of equal capacity and status – America remains the superpower with outsized influence above all others – but states sufficiently strong to create competing spheres of influence, each with the ability to determine in some way not just regional but global events and trends.

Ironically, as we will find, globalisation, which has been described by a number of writers as centripetal force bringing people together, has over time become a centrifugal force fragmenting the world and at times tearing it apart.[3] By expanding eastward and giving birth to strong rival economies in Asia, the speed and scale of globalisation undermined the unipolar order and with it the multilateralism of the day. A phenomenon which once promised to unite us can now be a major force for division. It may be that globalisation did not fail because cooperation across borders will always be impossible. It may be that it faltered because the political leaders who ran it failed to show that what was an open economy was also an inclusive economy. But for whatever reason, economic integration has, I will suggest, brought the political disintegration we currently see around us.[4]

Second, we are moving from a neoliberal economics built around free trade, open markets and the unimpeded flow of capital – once seen as the one route to prosperity – to a far more protectionist and indeed neo-mercantilist world characterised not only by more and higher tariffs on traded goods but also by import and export bans, new barriers to investment and the transfer of technology between countries, and the imposition of sanctions by countries on their competitors. Such measures are designed to protect native industries, achieve greater domestic self-sufficiency, enhance national power and, more often than not, directly harm competitors who have come to be seen as adversaries. It is a marked change from the 'open trade' policies pursued for most of the last eighty years, and it challenges, at root, the positive-sum mindset of mainstream economists that presumed that ever-increasing global trade was a win–win, and that all would benefit from the global expansion of commerce. That optimism has now been replaced not just by an inward-looking protectionism but also by a zero-sum mindset whereby the assumptions are that 'I can only do well if others do badly' and 'my country will only prosper at the expense of other countries failing'. Trade once brought people together and gave rise to the hope of a world at peace. Now trade blocs are driving people apart and causing conflict. And we should not underplay the threat that this fragmentation of the world poses to people's living standards. For a rise in protectionism, a disruption to global supply chains, as has been seen in the spring of 2026 in the Strait of Hormuz, and a breakdown in cooperation between countries could over time, as the International Monetary Fund has shown, reduce global economic activity by as much as 7 per cent, a loss of more than $7 trillion in national incomes. This is, as they say, the equivalent to losing the combined annual incomes of France and Germany. It represents a loss more than three times the output of the entire sub-Saharan African economy, with the most devastating effect to be felt in the poorest countries, where 250 million more people could, the IMF says, be thrust into poverty for an entire decade.[5] And even if the worst of these scenarios does not materialise, protectionism is, like other forces – war, the disruption of supply chains and the rising level of debt to 100 per cent of global income – one of the contributory factors to a world that is characterised by 'radical uncertainty': a world of known unknowns (things we know we don't know) and unknown unknowns (things we don't know we don't know). The world may be realigning but it is not stabilising, with countries feeling they have no choice but to de-risk, diversify or hedge to manage their heightened vulnerability to shocks. Only higher levels of productivity-led growth that can come from innovations like AI and other new technologies offer the prospect of escaping the likely consequences of lower trade, higher inflation, greater fiscal pressures and the threat to living standards.

And in the third seismic shift, we are moving from a relatively stable, rules-based order to a more volatile and far more violent power-based order; a might-is-right world where, as most recently in Ukraine and Gaza and Iran, and across sixty-one conflicts worldwide, the rule of law is being replaced by the law of the jungle.[6] 'Strategic managed cooperation' – the compromise mooted by China for describing the China–USA relationship in the Biden era – has, under Trump, been replaced by the less challenging term 'constructive strategic stability'.[7] But when the big powers are asserting their own values, seeking to impose their own rules and weaponising their own native technologies, they are also increasingly drawn into confrontation and even conflict. Insuperable barriers are erected, the world fragments and the space for meaningful cooperation narrows – and disorder becomes the norm when no one power has the combined economic or military might or the authority to guarantee peace and maintain stability.

A world increasingly dominated by raw power and brute force is also one where we are only as strong as our weakest link. From Bin Laden after 2000 to Isis after 2010 to, now, the militant supporters of Iran, the terrorist threat – and the fear it instils – has never gone away, with enemy agents capable of breaking through even the most elaborate security cordons and conducting assassinations in the streets of any of our cities, and able to strike any oil facility, any tanker, or any commercial port or hub, sometimes with a drone costing only £40,000. Vigilance against sleeper cells and terrorist networks will be called for in every place at all times, not least because the Islamic Revolutionary Guards' Quds Force has warned that its enemies 'will no longer be safe anywhere in the world', a threat confirmed by the US director of national intelligence, who states that extremists who do not believe coexistence is possible 'will seek to conduct terrorist activities against US targets worldwide'.[8]

The loudest expression of all these changes and what has become the dominant political force of our times is the rise of a new kind of 'my country first' ethnic nationalism – as seen in 'America First', 'India First', 'China First', 'Russia First' and many others; a new form of tribalism which asserts that what matters above all is the pursuit of national advantage over others, thereby inculcating an adversarial view of the world. In its modern form it is both authoritarian and populist, as illustrated by a new generation of leaders who have become adept at using social media to demonise immigrants, foreigners and any who do not share their views. This need come as no surprise: those leaders have been able, as we shall see, to exploit a void that has emerged from the very weakness of our local institutions and community associations, and from the breakdown of civic life. Through social media, they bypass what are already weakened local organisations and forge direct, manipulative links between themselves and voters who feel isolated: getting into people's heads and encouraging people to think that our societies are divided into warring, irreconcilable tribes for whom coexistence is impossible.

Whether you support one of these right-wing populist nationalist parties, one of their radical-left rivals or a mainstream and traditional political party, the atmosphere in which public debate now takes place has become overlaid by a polarisation between rival camps and by feelings of fear, and even loathing and outright anger, with all the unpleasant features we associate with an adversarial nationalism: the regular targeting of immigrants, foreigners, any who are considered to be 'others', and the regular application of the 'blame game' to make them convenient scapegoats when things go wrong. But the deeper question we will pose is whether the focus on targeting and even demonising 'outsiders' – whether defined by a different ethnicity, religion or ideology – is masking and often obscuring the underlying currents of a deeply felt economic disappointment or even a strong sense that society is broken.

As I write this book, far-right or radical-right parties have achieved their highest share of the vote across Europe ever – overtaking, in terms of popular support, even the levels achieved by extreme nationalist parties before they seized power in the period of Nazism and fascism in the 1930s. While support for particular political parties in individual countries will ebb and flow, the new wave of populist nationalism does not now look like just an anti-incumbent reaction, the predictable rejection of unpopular leaders and their administrations when they have been in power for some time. It appears to be more akin to an anti-system movement: the rejection of an entire political system that seems incapable of either delivering the basic goods of a decent life or bringing people together around a set of shared objectives and aspirations.

And these do not seem to be passing sentiments that can be written off as temporary reversals or setbacks, the result of the ups and downs of a local and national economy whose fortunes rise and fall with the cyclical nature of trade and industry. For at least two decades now, and particularly since the global financial crisis, millions of people – especially in large parts of Europe and North America – have increasingly expressed their feeling that instead of globalisation propelling us all forward, and lifting us up, it has let most of us down. Quite simply, globalisation is seen by millions as a free-for-all that has not been fair for all, and has left in its wake whole communities suffering from stagnant or declining living standards. All in all, this has created a common and widely shared belief, indeed the prevailing sense of the age, that the world is becoming dysfunctional, less fair, and increasingly out of control.

At the same time, as people witness a new and more volatile international environment, and wake up almost every day to threats of military aggression that we thought had been relegated to the history books, they are more aware than ever that they are living through a decade of global disorder. And if, when we look outward, we see the breakdown of world order, we also find that when we look inward, once-stable communities, faced with industrial collapse and economic and social disruption, no longer appear strong or resilient enough to come together to manage change and shape their own future.

It has been commonplace, now, to see the challenges that come from building communities, building nations and building a world order as so distinct and so different that we must formulate completely separate answers for what has been causing them. We leave community development to social workers and volunteers, nation-building to domestic politicians, and world governance to diplomats and international elites, as if the three are wholly different exercises demanding completely different skills and quite different approaches because they reflect very different challenges, as if to even comment on these three dimensions of public life in the same conversation makes no sense. And there is a whole industry of academic writing that suggests that we can be localists or globalists but cannot be both, suggesting a divide between what David Goodhart called 'people of somewhere', rooted in their communities, and 'people of nowhere', the cosmopolitan elite.[9]

But are we really forced to choose between the one and the other? What happens when we link the breakup of the world order to the breakdown of civic life? Does this recent rupture with the past in both spheres really arise from origins and causes that are completely separate? Of course, global changes can be attributed to the machinations of macho leaders and the realpolitik of international elites, whose interests are far from those of the ordinary public. Perhaps domestic discontents can be seen as primarily a story of individuals struggling to adjust to the inevitability of economic and social change. Or could we dare to glimpse some common ground, and perhaps a shared set of underlying causes, which have given rise to the breakup of global order and the breakdown of local communities at one and the same time? And, if this were to be the case, are there perhaps shared responses and even solutions to the huge challenges these two earthquakes have created?

'There is no such thing as society': the new world order undone

Beneath the bombastic rhetoric of politicians at home and abroad, and the pervasive sense of decline and precarity experienced by voters across the world, we need to ask whether there is a common cause and what, if anything, is the role played by changes in established ways of thinking about our world, in particular the neoliberal economic paradigm that has been dominant for four decades and the hyper-individualistic worldview that accompanies it.

It was a model built on the promise that markets alone could deliver prosperity but now, no longer able to explain how economic benefits can flow to working families, it has instead produced insecurity, inequality and civic fragmentation. The vacuum it has left in its wake – economic failure, social decline and, to some extent also, moral decay – has been filled, as I will show, by a politics of grievance nationally and globally.

This worldview began from the claim that 'there is no such thing as society'. If people are simply atomised individuals out for themselves, then government's role is reduced to guaranteeing the free play of impersonal market forces – or getting out of the way. For a time, this ideology claimed victories: inflation was brought under control, some monopolies were broken open, concentrations of economic power were challenged, and trade and capital flows expanded. But it stripped economics of any idea of the common good. People were recast as merely consumers rather than citizens, thought to be driven only by a selfish desire to maximise their own interests, with no responsibilities beyond acquiring as much as they can.

But the more profound question is whether these mainly economic phenomena are not all symptoms of something larger: the loss of a moral framework and an erosion of the sentiments and commitments that we shared with each other that once gave meaning to our lives. We want to ask: have widely held norms that traditionally placed emphasis on civic duty, solidarity and common purpose been undermined by a worldview that insists there is nothing but the individual and nothing beyond the individual? And yet does history not show us that people cannot live indefinitely as rootless individuals? Do we not also long to belong? Does community not matter? Do we not crave its presence and suffer greatly in its absence?

So throughout this book, I will ask you to join me in answering these questions: do we need to recover that sense of belonging, and with it, the conviction that we matter because we are part of something larger than ourselves? Might our civic life require something less passive than a cross on a ballot paper every few years? Might becoming a citizen mean taking on the work of citizenship as well as the title? And if we want our shared future to rest on common ground, should we not resist the temptation to demonise those with whom we disagree and instead engage in the more demanding task of listening to each other, cooperating across boundaries of ethnicity, religion and ideology and rebuilding that necessary but elusive key to communities living harmoniously together: trust? And where does this start, if not at home?

To help answer these questions, I will be drawing on original polling undertaken in 2025 and early 2026. One important fact stands out, which is worth emphasising at the outset: most of us see the world through the lens of our own everyday experience and that of the communities in which we live. We do not see the world in the abstract. This means that people cannot be expected to see themselves as global citizens unless they first experience citizenship close at hand. As the great economist Adam Smith perceived 250 years ago when he wrote of 'circles of sympathy', there is no crude dividing line that definitively separates the local and the global. Empathy – the capacity we all have to put ourselves in other people's shoes and see the world from their perspective – was, he thought, essential to the strength and resilience of communities. But, as he wrote, it radiates outward in circles of belonging: beginning with the intense loyalties we feel to each other as members of a family or a group of friends, but extending outward to our neighbourhood, then to the town or city, the nation and finally – far less intensely but present nonetheless – to humanity as a whole.

History books record laws, treaties and conferences, but might internationalism – like nationalism – begin in the ordinary life of towns and streets? Can it perhaps be practised, as Eleanor Roosevelt observed, 'in small places, close to home – so close and so small that they cannot be seen on any maps of the world. Yet they are the world of the individual person; the neighbourhood he lives in; the school or college he attends; the factory, farm, or office where he works.'[10] The road to peace and understanding may not start at summits or in foreign ministries, but in these small places – in acts of recognition, instances of cooperation and displays of trust that widen our circle of belonging outward from our immediate family. 'I am often asked: what can people do to become a good global citizen?' said former United Nations secretary-general Kofi Annan, 'I reply that it begins in your own community.'[11]

Such a discussion of the importance of belonging therefore raises a more personal challenge for each of us: are we as individuals simply victims of history, with little or no role to play in shaping the global environment around us? Are we mere spectators, watchers on the shore, as we observe the fate of our national democracies and the breakdown of global order? Or is what we do, and how we act in our communities, a crucial part in shaping what happens beyond our front door, our city limits and our national borders?

The evidence brought together from the opinion polls and presented in this book will suggest that there is something in common that links what we do locally in our own communities and in our own country to what happens globally. It will show that millions of us do not want, or need, to accept that events and forces beyond our garden gate are beyond our control; but in fact that none of us is totally powerless, even when battered by a turbulent and tumultuous world.

For one message becomes clear, a common thread in all the evidence we accumulate throughout the chapters of the book: change in the workplace, the community or in our wider democracies both nationally and internationally cannot be effective without the active engagement of citizens, of people like you and me. And if I return to this as a major theme in 2026, it is because the case for active citizenship is important: little acknowledged and often ignored, but a topic that is taken up in times of challenge and change by some of the most important political leaders in history. 'Whenever things get so far wrong as to attract their notice, they [the people] may be relied on to set them to rights,' wrote Thomas Jefferson, the author of the American Declaration of Independence, to a friend.[12] 'Do you want to know who you are?' he urged people on another occasion. 'Don't ask. Act! Action will delineate and define you.'

'I go for all sharing the privileges of the government who assist in bearing its burdens,' wrote Abraham Lincoln, arguing that national challenges could not be met without a 'people's contest'.[13] At times of crisis in the twentieth-century leaders like Franklin D. Roosevelt and Winston Churchill summoned up an active citizenship. And addressing students at the height of the Cold War, and after creating a Peace Corps of young public-spirited citizens, President John Kennedy sought to rouse US citizens to action by saying: 'This Nation was not founded solely on the principle of citizens' rights. Equally important . . . is the citizen's responsibility.'[14] 'For, in a democracy, every citizen,' he also explained, 'holds office: every one of us is in a position of responsibility.' If Kennedy, Lincoln and the rest are right, it is passivity, inactivity, complacency and opting out that will destroy our chances of a better future.

We are witnessing breakup on a global scale, and breakdown on a civic scale – but this is not the complete story, as our examination of public opinion reveals: even as disillusionment spreads, billions of us continue to live lives in search of meaning. We work, we give birth to and raise our children, attend baptisms, weddings and celebrations, and find satisfaction in what seem to some small joys – from family get-togethers to local successes shared by the whole community, such as sporting victories. And survey after survey shows that these everyday attachments underpin something more fundamental: that most of us do want to have stronger ties not only to our friends and family who share our sorrows and joys, but also to neighbours and wider communities.

Yes, we cooperate out of need. But do we not also have a human need to cooperate? Can this be the overlooked, often unrecognised and certainly undervalued key that could unlock a better world in the future – our longing for belonging?

Rebuilding for the twenty-first century

As I write, our world is changing fast. While events – from new bombings hitting hitherto safe havens to new alliances forming between once-sworn enemies – dominate the news, the underlying trends are my real focus. 'Events are 75 per cent negative for the world,' it has sometimes been said, 'trends are 75 per cent positive.'[15] In recent times, commentators may have been 75 per cent focused on events that come and go, when, if we are to make the right decisions, we need also to be 75 per cent focused on trends whose impact casts a long shadow. I hope to shift that balance a little – focusing less on immediate events, and less in particular on the negative news, and more on the huge underlying changes happening around us that are perhaps less noticeable but more consequential in shaping our destinies.

This book attempts to take the long view. In periods of peace and stability, when time seems to stand still, we tend to turn to policy specialists to address discrete problems. But in times of rapid change, when we are faced with massive, seemingly unmanageable challenges of strategic importance, we need to learn from the sweep of history as well as from contemporary thinkers. What one gains in breadth, however, one may lose in depth, and for reasons of space I have not covered in as much detail as I wanted astonishing developments like those in AI, quantum computing and cyber, or the consequences of the changing nature of warfare – such as the growing threat of nuclear proliferation, assaults on civilian populations by drones and cyberattacks.

But I believe our focus on public opinion – and what lessons we can draw from it – will stand the test of time. From listening to people express both their fears and their aspirations about the future, I have been able to assess what a future social contract and a new political economy might look like. I try to show how both our interests and our values matter, and how they are both important foundation stones for a better national and international order. And I suggest that it is only by combining, in a planned way, the benefits of the coming technological revolution with a commitment to human dignity that we will be able to deliver the security and prosperity that people seek.

If the first part of the book tries to understand the 'why' – why the current crises have emerged – the second half of this book focuses on the 'how' – how we might make a reality of a reinvigorated sense of belonging, and what that means for how we govern ourselves not just locally and nationally but as a global community.

We can start to glimpse an alternative to hyper-individualism at home and aggressive nationalism abroad by reaffirming that the goal of economic life is not simply to accumulate output, but to expand the range of choices each of us can freely make – to bridge the gap between what we are and what we have it in ourselves to become. That means the economy cannot be reduced to a marketplace of self-seekers out for themselves, nor simply to an exercise in production, consumption and distribution. We must redefine it as a joint effort in mutual cooperation, advancing a shared and sustained prosperity that delivers not just wealth but wellbeing – agreed, where possible, through citizens deliberating among themselves, and thus grounded in values we share in common.

Neoliberalism is characterised by five detrimental features: too little priority given to the five Es, as I will call them: Employment, Equality, Environment, Efficiency and Ethics. A programme for a better economic future must change this. In place of insecure, undervalued employment we must restore the dignity of work, with decent pay and recognition for all. In place of inequality, we must seek genuine opportunity for all, with unfair privilege for none: equality of opportunity leading to fairness of outcome. In place of environmental degradation, we must plan a future where we renew the natural world around us. In place of the blatant inefficiencies of a neoliberal economy – too often rigged in favour of the powerful – we must raise productivity and restore growth by realising the potential of all. And finally, we must recognise the importance of a benchmark of ethics, by which we judge value beyond the price mechanism: markets must be underpinned by morals.

If the economy is a joint effort in pursuit of agreed goals, then civil society is a joint effort in the attainment of a common good. Economic reforms will not be enough to build strong communities. Restoring faith in democracy also requires a renaissance of civic life, by honouring, and where possible resuscitating and revitalising, the institutions that lie between markets and the state and are far too often undervalued – family, schools, faith groups, charities, clubs and local civic associations.

It would be a mistake, however, to believe that renewal can be achieved just by looking inward. What good is it to invest in social clubs and jobs at home if, at the same time, our prosperity and security are undermined by the breakdown of order abroad, by the fires of climate change or by the spectre of war? We will be able to show from our polling that the single most convincing argument people offer for greater international cooperation is this: we need peace and stability abroad if we are to have the best chance of success at home. And, crucially, as we will find, ordinary people are open to and prepared to support international cooperation if it advances, globally, the very same rights they hope to secure at home – good jobs, a healthy environment, civic participation and a political voice.

We need to build a new world order based in a coalition of the responsible, united around shared values and mutually agreed rules that the vast majority of us can support and promote, and into which the superpowers of America and China are invited if they, too, meet the terms to join – a commitment to the rule of law, respect for human rights and democratic accountability. It should be an invitation to all countries as long as they will uphold these humane values even in the face of fierce economic competition and pressure from adversaries.

Events in Iran in early 2026 have made clear yet again – as they did in 1973, 1979, 2008, 2011 and 2022 – the role that fossil fuels play in translating geopolitical struggles into crises across the world. Even as our economies become less dependent on carbon-based energy, global consumption of oil and gas has doubled since the 1970s, sustaining our vulnerability to price shocks. In the 1970s, oil shocks brought not just inflation and recession, but the end of Keynesian economics and the birth of neoliberalism. A return to 'stagflation' in the West as in the 1970s, and genuine fuel and fertiliser shortages in the Global South as we saw in 2008 and 2011–12, could mark a decisive end to hopes for international cooperation. Or it could be a signal that the way we manage global warming and security needs to change. That is why I turn at the end of this book to the climate transition and argue for a new approach to North–South cooperation as key tests for a reinvigorated system of multilateral cooperation.

We have, therefore, two tasks: to revitalise our civic communities and to rebuild our international order. To achieve advances in international cooperation without rebuilding communities may still leave a vacuum and whole communities prey to populist xenophobic nationalists. To restore communities without renovating our global order will leave everyone still vulnerable to instability and insecurity.

The situation is perilous, but, as I have suggested, we are not powerless. Depressed as so many of us are about our present circumstances and future prospects, we are also, as I will show in the final chapter, eager to find seeds of hope, and can do so. Hope is not just the last thing to go when we are up against it; it is the first building block of a better world. And from our surveys we find that the worldview of so many commentators, which sees life as an endless struggle between 'us' and 'them', is not what most people believe. That, perhaps, is our most important discovery: contrary to the popular narrative of rising xenophobia and isolation, most people still feel something for those beyond their own communities and countries – even for those they will never meet or know. Millions feel the pain of others and believe in something bigger than themselves. Most of all, they feel that if they were empowered to do so, they could play their part in creating a better world and would want to do so. This means that the future starts with each of us: rebuilding our communities, one step and one connection at a time. It falls to each and every one of us to keep the flame alive – the flame of engagement, the flame of cooperation, the flame of mutual respect and the flame of hope.

PART ONE

Breakup:
The end of an order

I

THE RISE AND FALL OF FOUR WORLD ORDERS

On 7 April 2026, President Trump issued a threat that will be remembered in print as long as history books are written: 'A whole civilization will die tonight,' he wrote, 'never to be brought back again,' an ultimatum that threatened to destroy the entire infrastructure of Iran and inflict genocide on 90 million people.[1] His words echoed a statement made a few days earlier when he also threatened crimes against humanity: 'Over the next two to three weeks, we are going to bring them [Iran] back to the Stone Ages, where they belong.'[2] While, as I write, full-scale war has been averted, no attempt was made by the president to justify such actions by reference to the international rule of law. Indeed his disdain for a rules-based order was made explicit when in January of the same year he replied to a question put to him by a *New York Times* journalist who asked what might halt US military actions in Venezuela and the possible annexation of Greenland: 'Yeah, there is one thing,' he said. 'My own morality. My own mind. It's the only thing that can stop me.'[3] But what that means was made even more explicit by Stephen Miller, Trump's close White House aide, who explained: 'The real world is governed by strength, force, and power.' Treaties and universal norms, he said, amount to nothing more than 'international niceties'.[4] Or as James Traub has put it, the Trump administration believes that their ability to coerce people by force or the threat of force renders 'both institutions and allies superfluous'.[5] The question that recent events pose is whether might will now invariably mean right or whether a rules-based order can be re-established over one based on raw power and brute force.

For President Trump is not the only world leader who is prepared to abandon long-established precepts supporting a rules-based world order. Statements that range from those of autocratic leaders from Xi and Putin (Xi has declared that reunification with Taiwan 'cannot be stopped by any force or anyone', while Putin argues that 'no one is ready to play by rules set by someone far away'[6]) to the theocratic leadership of Iran favour rule *by* law, rather than the rule *of* law. And even leaders in democracies like Israel have recently asserted that might will always be right. 'History proves that, unfortunately and unhappily, Jesus Christ has no advantage over Genghis Khan,' Israel's Prime Minister Netanyahu announced in March 2026. 'Because if you are strong enough, ruthless enough, powerful enough, evil will overcome good. Aggression will overcome moderation.'[7] But if he later walked this remark back, he has not corrected the statement he made in August 2018 that 'the weak crumble, are slaughtered, and are erased from history, while the strong, for good or ill, survive'.[8] These statements are in the tradition that was perhaps best personified by Otto von Bismarck, who was to become the first German chancellor: in 1862, a few years before he used force against France and Austria to unite Germany, he said: 'Not through speeches and majority resolutions will the great questions of the time be decided – that was the great mistake of 1848 and 1849 – but by iron and blood.'[9]

The history books tell us where, by 1914, this resort to 'iron and blood' led. What we must now try to understand is: first, what has gone wrong to produce a return to such widespread insecurity that destroyed one world order; and second, as we consider what the shift to a new world order will entail for this era, what lessons, if any, we can learn from previous centuries at those times when rules gave way to the exercise of raw power.

For the best part of 500 years the West has been dominant. But no world order lasts forever, and no order ever anticipates its own collapse. A shorthand account of recent Western-led history might say that the fifteenth century belonged to the Portuguese, the sixteenth to the Spanish, the seventeenth to the Dutch, the eighteenth to the French, the nineteenth to the British and the twentieth to the Americans; indeed, when some commentators talk of the 'Long Twentieth Century', they mean that American leadership – first demonstrated by its intervention to end the First World War – remained dominant for at least two decades beyond 2000.[10] But today, just over twenty-five years into what has already been a surprisingly violent and yet still young twenty-first century, we face not just a moment of truth but a point of departure, as we start to move from a unipolar moment dominated by a single Western power to a multipolar future where power will inevitably have to be shared.

Four Western-led world orders have risen and fallen in the last two centuries alone. The first two, which between them lasted 125 years, were the post-1815 Concert of Europe, which sought to balance the power of the main imperial states – Russia, Germany, France and Britain – followed by the post-1918 attempt to guarantee peace through a League of Nations. Now, over a relatively brief eighty-year period, we are seeing the rise and fall of the two world orders that followed: the post-1945 international architecture built around the United Nations which was, for the first time, ambitiously focused on economic prosperity as well as geopolitical security; and the post-1990 new world order built around American hegemony, a state of affairs which has survived intact for little longer than the average marriage.

The rise and fall of each world order is a matter of historical interest but it is also of contemporary relevance, for it is important to understand how and why each order ended, and to learn lessons from their failings that can inform and perhaps provide answers to our own current predicament.

The first order, from 1815 to 1914, which emerged after the defeat of Napoleon, was an attempt to maintain the balance between the power held by each major imperial state. It succeeded in keeping the peace, perhaps for longer than could reasonably have been expected, and had notable successes, for example in preventing Russia from overpowering Turkey in the 1850s and again in the 1870s. But over time the faith that the Concert of Europe placed in the diplomacy of the Great Powers was undermined by their diverging economic and political interests abroad, by the rise of nationalism and, in the wake of a brutal, uneven industrialisation, by the rising social tensions at home that produced the failed revolutions of 1848 to which Bismarck, quoted earlier, referred. As a result of all these pressures, the post-1815 order was unable to prevent the Crimean War of the 1850s, the Franco-Prussian War of 1870 and, ultimately, the far more dangerous and eventually catastrophic thirty-year build-up of imperial competition before 1914 between Germany, Russia, France, Britain, Italy and Turkey. What seems now like a fanciful notion – that we could forever balance the interests of imperial powers, curb their chauvinistic ambitions as they aggressively pursued colonial expansion, and do so without agreed rules and procedures to which everyone subscribed – ended in the bloodbath and barbarity of trench warfare in the First World War, claiming the lives of 20 million people. Elite diplomacy, underpinned by slowly emerging agreements but only on the rules of conduct of war, and ultimately without any shared norms to underpin it, could only take us so far. In the end, no amount of solidarity between social classes across borders proved able to prevent the xenophobia and the aggressive nationalism that led to widespread public support among each country's populations for war. The events of 1914 proved that the appearance of order can easily unravel and at any time the façade of stability can crumble.

If the peace that was reached after the main dynastic empires collapsed was to be enduring, the post-1918 system had to be different. US president Woodrow Wilson set out his Fourteen Points, the objectives for a peaceful world to be achieved by a new set of rules that would replace the arbitrariness of the Concert of Europe's practices. Wilson was pivotal to the establishment of a wholly new global body, the League of Nations, that would outlaw war.[11] 'If it be only a struggle for a new balance of power,' he argued in his 'Peace Without Victory' speech, which rejected 'the old diplomacy' of the Concert, 'who will guarantee . . . the stable equilibrium of the new arrangement? Only a tranquil Europe can be a stable Europe. There must be . . . not a balance of power, but a community of power.'[12] But while forty-two nations initially signed up to the League in 1920, Wilson's own country refused to join (and later other major powers – Germany, Italy and Russia – also walked out), and the collective institutions that Wilson had proposed were found wanting when tested by fascist regimes seeking territorial gains in Africa, Asia and Europe.

The League of Nations suffered from many design faults that any future order must avoid. It was brought into existence to keep the peace but it denied itself any peacekeeping force of its own. Its decision-making process was founded on the impossible dream that, on major and inevitably divisive issues around which conflicts arose, the League could proceed by unanimity. The difficulties that the League faced were compounded by the two-decade-long argument over the scale and alleged vindictiveness of the reparations enforced on Germany as a result of the Treaty of Versailles, a running sore that was never healed and a resentment never removed even after changes were made in the payback clauses. What's more, an absence of international cooperation on the economy made for recession, high unemployment and widespread poverty – in turn exacerbating already deep social tensions, and fuelling support for protectionist trade policies (which a world trade conference failed abysmally to counteract) and extreme nationalist political parties.

And so, despite its foundation in clearly stated objectives and rules of procedure that marked a break from the old, the League of Nations proved unable to prevent or end the aggression of major powers. By the 1930s the world had once again succumbed to a bout of aggressive adversarial nationalism. What followed was even greater carnage than in the First World War as battles by land, sea and air spread from Europe worldwide and on this occasion hit the domestic fronts of most countries. At least 60 million lives (the very large number of Russian deaths have never fully been accounted for) were lost on the blood-strewn battlefields of Europe and Asia, in bombed-out towns and cities far from the trenches, in the horror of Nazi concentration camps designed to exterminate an entire Jewish people and ultimately in the burnt-out ruins of Hiroshima and Nagasaki, razed to the ground by the first nuclear bombs.

To avoid what President Truman later called the 'mistakes'[13] that had been made when creating the post-1918 world order – where country after country had ignored the peace treaties, defied the League of Nations and simply violated its rules with apparent impunity – the post-1945 architecture had to be different again. 'Practical necessity', not 'idealism', was how its principal author, Franklin D. Roosevelt, explained his proposed United Nations, warning that without US involvement, it would become a 'new Holy Alliance' dominated by Europe and by the old unanimity rules that, as he said, allowed 'one or two recalcitrant nations' to block the majority's will.[14] So in 1945, at America's instigation, fifty nation-states came together in San Francisco to form the United Nations; with Poland's later signature, the UN had fifty-one founding members. The UN was to be built around a commitment that countries would act together through a single executive body which would, where necessary, impose peace by military means. To this end the United Nations Security Council was created with provision under Article 43 of the UN Charter for a Military Staff Committee and a UN military force.[15] The Council was, however, now dominated not by the League's need for unanimity but by the veto-wielding power of the five major states – the USA, Russia, France, the UK and China – that had emerged victorious from the Second World War.

What was also novel about the new order was the emphasis, reflected in the convening of the Bretton Woods conference of 1944, on creating new overarching economic institutions; their intervention was thought to be the key to avoiding war by making trade and commerce between nations the driver of a shared peace achieved through a common prosperity. However, the world was still assumed to be one of separate nations operating like islands – and there was no sense at the time that a globally integrated economy would emerge with such complicated global supply chains and such extensive global flows of capital as we have today. And so, while the International Monetary Fund (IMF) was set up, it was, in essence, a bank created to smooth over the national balance-of-payments problems faced by individual countries, on the grounds that large deficits could endanger peaceful trade between countries. At the same time the World Bank was created, which was initially seen as the agency that would ensure reconstruction of a bombed-out Europe, but at the last minute of the negotiations the Indian delegate added 'development' to its remit as well as 'reconstruction'. It was many years before it became the primary agency for dealing with global poverty. The IMF and World Bank were meant to work alongside a new trade body that would avoid the protectionism of the 1930s, but the International Trade Organization was never created as planned. Instead we saw the General Agreement on Tariffs and Trade (GATT) of 1947, which secured seven tariff-reducing world trade agreements, the most significant being the Kennedy Round of 1964, the Tokyo Round of 1973 and the Uruguay Round of 1986. This lasted until the World Trade Organization was eventually set up in 1995, since when no further world trade agreement has been secured.

Alongside these economic bodies there was to be a network of international agencies, covering health, humanitarian aid, peacekeeping and human rights, each of which sought to elevate global cooperation above tribal nationalism. The creation of the United Nations was followed by and linked to the later adoption of the Universal Declaration of Human Rights on what were considered to be the inalienable rights of every human being – a charter conceived in the wake not just of the war but of the shocking revelations of the extent of the Holocaust.

All these new bodies had to operate for a third of a century in the shadow of a Cold War during which trade between its two blocs was virtually non-existent. The Security Council – originally intended as a NATO-style collective command and security body via Article 43 – instead became an arena for great-power politics and posturing, with the largest number – 59 – of the total number of 500 vetoes over its eighty years issued in the 1950s at the height of the Cold War, 57 of them by the USSR. If violence and conflicts were at least contained, it was probably more by the threat of mutually assured destruction than by any authority exercised by the Security Council.

The 1990s saw the breakup of the Soviet Union and the Warsaw Pact, alongside what was then called a democratic revolution but which now seems more like a collection of nationalist revolutions against an exhausted Russian imperialism that had imposed itself on once-independent nations. This inaugurated an era of American hegemony, labelled 'the new world order' – a term the first President Bush is said to have dreamed up while fishing. It was, he told the US Congress, a 'world order' in which 'the principles of justice and fair play [would] protect the weak against the strong – a world where the United Nations, freed from Cold War stalemate, is poised to fulfil the historic vision of its founders. A world in which freedom and respect for human rights find a home.'[16]

For a time after 1990, as the Cold War ended, people talked not just of the end of ideology but of 'the end of history', as famously stated by Francis Fukuyama.[17] Fukuyama's use of the word 'end' has been much misunderstood and was meant by him to signify the completion of the 'objective' of history as achieving an open liberal society – but was taken to signify that we had progressed to a comfortable and comforting future that would always be free of conflict. And even though the liberal world order was never fully liberal, never embraced the whole world and was not always orderly, we in the West nonetheless talked of the realisation of an open society with a governing philosophy and guiding framework in which democracy was expanding, freedom advancing, tolerance spreading, prosperity rising and poverty falling. Indeed, the world economy grew fifteenfold as population trebled, and global life expectancy rose from just forty-five years to seventy-three.

We did not reach the end of history. The year 1990 was the critical turning point where ultimately history did not fully turn. It was the moment when international cooperation was expected to take on a wholly new lease of life, building upon and renewing the international architecture designed in 1945 that had been undermined by the now-ended Cold War. Surprisingly perhaps, President George H. W. Bush resisted any formal charter setting out the new order's objectives, and there was no serious attempt to update the architecture to recognise a changing world, and the failure to do this may be at the root of our current problems.

While GATT was transformed in the 1990s into, as we have charted, the more neoliberal World Trade Organization with powers to overrule individual member states, the IMF and World Bank remained under-resourced to accommodate the impact of rapid changes and the risks that flowed from the growing global supply chains, the growth of globally significant financial institutions and the emergence of a category of goods – like climate change and pandemics – that could be deemed global public goods and which required a globally coordinated approach. Nor was there an agreement on new laws or rules to define how the world would respond to some of the new challenges that were emerging, such as the growth of non-state terrorism that would come to characterise the early 2000s. The most relevant model for such a new order – the Helsinki Declaration of 1975,[18] which thirty-five countries with an interest in Western stability had signed, including the Soviet Union – was not taken further by successive American administrations. They agreed to an enhanced role for the Conference on Security and Co-operation in Europe – including Russia (in 1995 it became the Organization for Security and Co-operation in Europe), but successive American presidents preferred to continue acting primarily through Cold War institutions the US itself dominated, most of all NATO.

Within a decade, this American-dominated, rules-based order had morphed into what some called a 'hyper-globalised' free-for-all that, as I have said, turned out not to be fair to all. It was, perhaps unfairly, called the Washington Consensus, after work by an American economist who suggested that America was exporting to the rest of the world a model of economic management whose main features were liberalisation, deregulation, privatisation and a focus in macroeconomic policy on low inflation even if at the expense of high unemployment.

For years the IMF and World Bank promoted with renewed fervour this model under a policy of 'structural adjustment', which required stricter fiscal and monetary discipline than often the US itself achieved, and open capital accounts alongside global free trade. There was, for a period, a confidence that – with nation after nation opening up their markets, and integrating into the world economy – globalisation would make us all better off, that global output would rise substantially, and that the gains from free trade would be widely diffused.

Indeed, few could have predicted the scale and speed of global economic integration. World trade grew by around 7 per cent a year during the 1990s and 2000s, twice the rate of overall global economic growth. According to the UN trade and development body UNCTAD, foreign direct investment, once modest and overwhelmingly from the Global North, surged tenfold between

1990 and 2007 and the share of investment going to developing countries rose from around a quarter of funds in the 1990s to around half by the mid-2010s, with capital beginning to flow in new directions and at new volumes, reshaping patterns of production and investment.[19]

As a result, developed economies saw their once-dominant share of world trade gradually eroded as lower-middle-income developing economies like China multiplied their role in global commerce. China's share of world exports rose from around 2 per cent in 1990 to more than 12 per cent by the 2010s, while developing economies as a group (including China) came to account for nearly half of global trade. This is just one of many shifts, which I will return to in detail in Chapter 4, that has created a new reality of economic multipolarity in the world. These developments were not an accident but the direct consequence of a post-1990 order built around liberalisation, openness and the assumption that markets, if freed, would allocate resources efficiently around the world.

Of course, a globalisation that was open-ended but insufficiently inclusive was bound to run into trouble. The early years were marked by the relocation of manufacturing from the West to the East, a switch of production that was justified by the expectation that displaced Western workers would be compensated through new domestic opportunities. But the result was that, instead of being broad-based, the gains from trade were heavily skewed. By replacing high-paid jobs in the West with lower-paid jobs in the East, with over 2 million manufacturing jobs lost in the US alone in the 2000s as a result of the 'China Shock',[20] globalisation was hurting Westerners on middle and low incomes, the very people who had been promised that the opening up of trade would make them better off. At the same time, while the middle classes of emerging Asia saw incomes rise by 70–80 per cent in the 1990s and 2000s, working- and lower-middle-class incomes in advanced economies stagnated.[21] As a result, the very order America had created eventually fell foul of an American public opinion which felt its industrial communities were being hollowed out as a result of the shift of global economic activity towards Asia. The results make familiar reading: exposure to trade competition pushed up the Trump vote by an electorally significant four points in key US swing counties, and directly boosted support for protectionist, more ideologically extreme candidates.[22] Within a few years the so-called Washington Consensus had lost support, even in Washington. A market economy that fails large parts of the population causes problems far beyond economics: it not only breaks the implicit social contract that binds citizens together but also undermines trust in the institutions of democracy.

Alongside the erosion of popular support, the fate of the old world order was also decided by the growing scepticism of American politicians who started to believe that the order they had created was not working for them at a geopolitical level either, and that their post-war commitment to free trade and the free movement of capital was now working to their disadvantage and to the benefit of others, in particular China. And so while during the long twentieth century America had played the role of a sure and steadfast anchor, its ambivalence towards and – under President Trump 2.0 – its rejection of the very world order that it had created has turned America itself, as many commentators have concluded, into more of a destabilising than stabilising global force.

Yet the remarkable fact remains: the post-1990 order succeeded in one of its central aims – the rapid expansion of global markets, production and wealth – even as it failed to manage the consequences. It accelerated the rise of new Asian competitors, most of all China, and later India and the rest of Asia. It integrated developing economies into the heart of the world system. It created a world in which capital, goods and increasingly people moved at a speed and scale never before imagined. In doing so it also created the conditions in which economic power would inevitably shift – and sooner or later, as history suggests, that economic power would equally inevitably come to be matched by geopolitical power. The post-1990 order unleashed forces that could not be contained by the institutions designed to manage them, and thereby created the economic preconditions for its own downfall, as economic integration led to political disintegration.

Everything that has followed, which we explore throughout this book – the backlash against economic change, the rise in protectionism, the fracturing of trust, the return of great-power rivalry – took root in a world shaped by the spread of globalisation on a scale that, as we have suggested, its architects neither anticipated nor, perhaps, ever fully understood. But there was also a direct correlation between what was happening to the world order as it was transformed and the impact on local communities hurt by profound industrial change. And, as we shall see in the next chapter, much of the fallout from these destabilising changes remains unaddressed to this day.

2
A FIFTH WORLD ORDER?

One of the first and most important decisions I had to make in 2007, as an incoming prime minister, was to issue a set of instructions to the military setting out our country's response, in the event of a doomsday scenario, to a nuclear attack. These instructions are written down in the aptly named 'letter of last resort'.

Every new incumbent faces a choice of whether to instruct a nuclear response at all, and if so whether to retaliate against the aggressor with nuclear weapons targeted on civilian centres of population or on military targets, and at which locations. What makes the decision even more complicated is that there is always a risk that the contents of that letter of last resort might fall into enemy hands. Prime Minister Callaghan later talked of how he would have authorised retaliation if necessary, but admitted: 'I've had terrible doubts . . . if I had lived after having pressed that button, I could never ever have forgiven myself.'[1] It is said of another prime minister that he 'went white' and fell 'quite quiet' when briefed on what was expected of him.

No one making that decision can fail to recall, as they grapple with their conscience and the realities of power politics, the tragic loss of life that followed President Truman's fateful decision to drop two nuclear bombs on the civilian populations of Hiroshima and Nagasaki – nor, while aware of the power of deterrence, can they ignore the fact that each nuclear bomb today has a destructive power at least thirty-three times more deadly than those detonated by America in 1945.

Today the breakup of the old world order is being accelerated not just by the absence now, for the first time for sixty years, of any nuclear weapon reduction treaties between the major powers but also by the militarisation of new technologies, which is changing the nature of conflict. The legacy of the wars of the 2000s is that 'boots on the ground' in land battles are likely to prove unacceptable to public opinion in most countries, regime change from the air is deemed unlikely to succeed, and naval vessels are more vulnerable than ever to missile attacks and even to low-cost drone strikes. As a result, in many capitals around the world, debates are again centring on the acquisition of nuclear weapons.

In the 1960s, President Kennedy prophesied there would be up to twenty-five nuclear-weapon states within two decades.[2] But countries from Sweden to South Africa, which had access to the necessary technology, explicitly chose not to become nuclear-weapon powers, and the success of deterrence and of efforts at non-proliferation worked until recently to restrict the number of nuclear-weapon states to nine.

One testimony to our current disorder, however, is the rise in the number of countries now considering the 'ultimate insurance policy'. In at least six – Germany, Poland, the UAE, Saudi Arabia, South Korea and Japan – some consideration has been given to acquisition, and some European countries are seeking to extend or supplement the American nuclear umbrella. They do so as North Korea proclaims to the world that its ownership of nuclear weapons is its protective shield, and as Iranian leaders argue that the absence of them has left Iran vulnerable to attack. Now we not only face what has been called an 'axis of upheaval' – China, Russia, Iran and North Korea – but, as the International Atomic Energy Authority has warned, 'a crack in the system' of non-proliferation that could cause 'a domino effect', with the possibility of twenty countries pursuing a nuclear weapons programme.[3]

Even more disconcerting is the attempt – like the plot of the satire *Dr Strangelove* – to automate nuclear systems in order to increase their deterrence effect. Recent war games run through AI, led by Professor Kenneth Payne of King's College, London, have shown that across twenty-one simulated crises, AI chose to use nuclear weapons 95 per cent of the time. As Payne observed, the nuclear taboo does not appear to be as powerful for machines as for humans – so as AI becomes increasingly embedded in our systems, it is more important than ever that we have human cooperation between states to reduce the scope for miscalculations as well as misunderstandings.[4] These new risks are one reason why the Bulletin of the Atomic Scientists – in existence since 1945 – has moved its famous Doomsday Clock closer to midnight than at any point in its history: from seven minutes to midnight when it was first set in 1947, to eighty-nine seconds in January 2025, and to eighty-five seconds in January 2026.[5]

If current trends persist, the UN secretary-general has warned, global military spending could more than double from $2.7 trillion in 2024 to as much as $6.6 trillion by 2035.[6] In this new context – a lower nuclear threshold, a likely proliferation of weapons, and an almost unstoppable resort to automated systems – we have to ask whether better ways of cooperating to avoid such catastrophic outcomes can urgently be found.

If we do not find our way to a new, stable and peaceful world order, the Doomsday Clock will move ever closer to midnight. This is the environment in which the world order into which this generation was born is drawing to a close. The post-1945 order was not simply an economic order but also, as we have seen, intended to be a rules-based one. The question we have been asking is whether the order is beyond repair and what, if anything, can be put in its place. For it is not just one of the established pillars of the American-led order – nuclear deterrence and the prevention of nuclear proliferation – that is now under pressure and crumbling. It is all of them: support for the rule of law, democracy, human rights and multilateral cooperation, including the shared responsibility for humanitarian aid and (more recently) for environmental stewardship.

By the mid-2010s we were witnessing not only the emergence of a new coterie of nationalist leaders but the normalisation of democratic backsliding as a governing strategy, upending the assumption that with the expansion of trade and commerce, the spread of democracy would follow. The empirical evidence cannot be ignored. At the last count there were ninety-one autocracies but now only eighty-eight countries that can be called democracies.[7] Nearly three quarters of humanity now exist under autocratic rule, more than at any time since the 1970s.[8] Freedom House's most recent annual 'state of democracy' finds that we have lived through the eighteenth straight year in which more countries saw reductions in the political rights and civil liberties of their citizens than improvements.[9] The number of fully liberal democracies worldwide – countries that meet not just some but all the conditions for a free accountable democracy – has fallen to just twenty-nine, the lowest in over three decades.

The way breakdowns in the democratic processes happen has changed too. Whereas, during the Cold War, military coups accounted for the majority of the collapses in democratic rule, since 2000 the dominant mode has been the executive takeover – democracy hollowed out from within. Of the 197 democratic breakdowns recorded between 1973 and 2018, 88 were executive-led coups or incumbent-driven dismantlings of institutions.[10] And this shift is accelerating: in the 1990s, these internal takeovers were only marginally more common than military coups; in the twenty-first century, they have accounted for four out of every five.

The features of this democratic backsliding are consistent across countries. Judicial independence is weakened – global risk data consultancy Verisk Maplecroft finds that government interference in legal systems has increased in forty-five countries over the past decade.[11] Legislative oversight erodes – fifteen countries show statistically significant declines in the power of legislatures. Media freedom falls dramatically – forty-four countries have experienced worsening state censorship; and freedom of expression has declined in the same number, making it one of the most fragile elements of our democracies. Civic space is shrinking and the public square is being emptied – eighty-one states now restrict or close civic space, with protest criminalised, dissent suppressed and independent NGOs silenced. According to CIVICUS, over 72 per cent of the global population now lives in such hostile environments, and nearly 30 per cent reside in countries where civic space is 'completely closed' and effectively government-dominated.[12]

Take the most basic requirements of a stable global order: the prevention of war and, where war is unavoidable, the adherence to rules for its conduct – and how such rules are now being ignored, circumvented or simply violated. For more than a century and a half, states have sought to cooperate to prevent the worst excesses of war, even when unsuccessful as in 1914 and 1939. For several decades after 1945, supporters of international cooperation could take some comfort in the apparent decline of wars between states. From the end of the Second World War until around 2010, such wars receded in number. By one measure land grabs – the amount of territory conquered by foreign states each year – fell to less than 6 per cent of what it had been during the century before the 1928 agreement to formally outlaw war.[13]

That pattern has now reversed. The war between Russia and Ukraine – the most devastating conflict in Europe since 1945 and the only European one in recent decades directly involving a great power – has shattered assumptions about the likelihood of restraint. The Israel–Gaza and the more recent American–Iranian wars, alongside less reported but equally brutal conflicts in Myanmar, Sudan and the Democratic Republic of Congo, reinforce the view that armed violence is once again becoming a routine instrument of politics. And these much-publicised conflicts are only the visible tip of a much larger iceberg. In

2024, one in eight of the world's population – nearly one billion people – were exposed to armed conflict, and more than fifty countries – one quarter of the world's states – were suffering extremely high levels of violence. War, persecution or violence had forcibly displaced more than 120 million people – more than double the number a decade earlier and the highest level recorded outside the world wars.[14]

The 2020s now rival the violence of the 1990s, as data from the Uppsala Conflict Data Program confirms. In 2023 alone, 59 conflicts were recorded across 34 countries, leading to over 120,000 deaths. And in 2024, this rose to 61 conflicts across 36 countries, with a recorded 76,000 battle deaths that year in the Ukraine war and 26,000 confirmed in Gaza.[15] While civil wars remain the most common form of conflict, a most alarming development has been the resurgence of what are called 'internationalised civil conflicts' – that is, internal wars that draw in major external powers. Twenty-three such conflicts were recorded in 2023.

What is also worrying is the disappointing outcome of the debates which led to over 170 heads of state agreeing in 2005 to a declaration, the Responsibility to Protect.[16] Under international law there is no right to invade another country to protect civilians, even if that country's government is the one harming them. But partly as a result of the American-led intervention in Kosovo – which an international commission declared 'illegal but legitimate'[17] – the Responsibility to Protect declaration proclaimed that if a state failed to meet its obligations to protect its own citizens, the international community should act out of humanitarian concern. 'Imagine for one moment, in those dark days and hours leading up to the genocide,' said the then secretary-general, Kofi Annan, in 1999, referring to the failure to prevent the Rwandan genocide, 'there had been a coalition of states ready and willing to act in defence of the Tutsi population, but the [UN Security] Council had refused or delayed giving the green light. Should such a coalition then have stood idly by while the horror unfolded?'[18] But of course, a similar logic – in this case self-defence against a possible 'unprovoked attack' – has been used by President Putin to invade Ukraine and by President Trump to strike Iran.

The historian Odd Arne Westad does not expect 'agreement nor convergence, nor moral equivalence' between the great powers but simply 'compromise', though he is concerned that with nationalism, 'mutual suspicions' and 'jingoism, fatalism and fear' on the rise we are currently revisiting the conditions that led to the First World War.[19] Others fear we are approaching a moment comparable to the run-up to the Second World War, when repeated failures to agree collective action to combat the rise of aggressive nationalisms made war increasingly difficult to prevent.

Beyond failing to prevent wars, the breakdown of world order is such that when wars do break out, we are failing to follow the clear rules that have been agreed for their conduct. It is now more than 160 years since the first Geneva Convention of 1864 prohibited attacks by invading armies on hospitals, medical personnel and their patients.[20] From the late nineteenth century onward, laws were passed, conventions agreed and treaties signed to separate the civilian from the military and to shield non-combatants from attack. Eighty years ago, the Geneva Conventions – later supplemented by three Additional Protocols – went further, prohibiting the targeting of civilian sites even in pursuit of military objectives.[21] Yet today this distinction between 'military' and 'civilian' is being steadily erased. It is also more than a century since the Hague Conventions prohibited the execution of prisoners of war[22] and attacks on undefended towns, villages, dwellings or buildings.[23] These prohibitions, ratified by all major states, are now systematically ignored.

The St Petersburg Declaration of 1868 banned the use of explosive, fragmenting and small-arms munitions,[24] a prohibition reinforced in later global treaties, including one I was involved in negotiating in 2009. Today, these restrictions are disregarded at will. A series of conventions, culminating in the 1925 Geneva Protocol, prohibited the use of 'asphyxiating, poisonous or other gases, and bacteriological methods of warfare'.[25] That ban did not prevent the stockpiling of chemical weapons, nor their use by the Assad regime in Syria and, according to recent reports, by Russia in Ukraine.

Even the most celebrated recent efforts to eliminate particularly indiscriminate weapons have begun to unravel. The 1997 Ottawa Convention was intended to end the use of anti-personnel landmines.[26] Yet mines have been used extensively by both sides in the Russo-Ukrainian war, to the point that several NATO countries bordering Russia have withdrawn from the convention, unwilling to deny themselves what they now describe as an essential form of defence.

The tragedy is not just that these laws are broken, but that they are broken routinely, openly, without embarrassment and with impunity. In the conflicts of recent years – from Gaza to Ukraine, Iran to Myanmar, the Democratic Republic of Congo and the other ongoing fifty-plus civil wars and inter-state conflicts – such violations are no longer rare or exceptional. They are a daily occurrence.

This backward slide is not limited to violating established, often century-long, protections; it extends to the abuse of the legal concepts on which those protections depend. Alongside the erosion of civilian safeguards has come a steady distortion of the legal justifications for war. The principle of legitimate self-defence was once applied narrowly, to cases in which one state defended itself against an armed attack by another. This became commonplace after war itself was renounced as a policy for solving international controversies in 1928 – a treaty commitment still technically in place today.[27] But today, that definition of self-defence has been expanded to justify repeated, sustained – and what might reasonably be considered disproportionate – actions against civilians who simply live near, or among, those judged to be combatants. At the same time, by stretching the concept of 'dual use', states increasingly claim that whole sectors of a domestic economy may be treated as legitimate military targets if they are alleged, even indirectly, to contribute to a war effort. As the Israel–Gaza war has shown, this elastic reasoning allows civilian infrastructure – housing, food systems, energy supplies and communications – to be reclassified as lawful targets. When the category of 'dual use' expands without limit, the civilian protections painstakingly built into international humanitarian law collapse from within. Compliance is claimed in form, even as substance is emptied out. This is not the breakdown of law through neglect, it is the hollowing out of it through reinterpretation. In response to President Trump's and Defense Secretary Pete Hegseth's statements referring to 'stupid rules of engagement',[28] 100 American legal experts stated that they were 'seriously concerned' about the threats to international human rights and humanitarian law from tactics pursued by America, Iran and Israel in the Iranian war of 2026. Among these were 'intentionally directed attacks against civilians'. The experts' letter points out that Rule 10 of the customary rules of international humanitarian law explicitly states: 'Civilian objects are protected against attack, unless and for such time as they are military objectives.'[29]

Innocent and vulnerable children are bearing the brunt of these failures. The consequences are visible in the horrific images of malnutrition and shootings in Gaza in 2025, and in the abduction of children from Ukraine to Russia from 2022 onward – both now the subject of investigations by the International Criminal Court. Casualties among children and women in armed conflicts have quadrupled in the past two years.[30] The laws designed to protect children in war are among the most developed and least ambiguous in international law. They outlaw the use of child militias, prohibit the abduction of children and ban the targeting of schools. Yet these protections are now being removed with impunity. Children are routinely drawn into conflict and used as soldiers, sex slaves, human shields and, more broadly, as weapons of war.

The rising violations against children were first systematically recorded by Graça Machel in a landmark UN report in 1996,[31] and later documented in detail by Shaheed Fatima KC in her 2020 report for Save the Children and Theirworld.[32] The warnings were clear. Despite early progress in expanding rights, the pattern has not been reversed but entrenched as we witnessed in the spring of 2026 with the bombing of more than 100 children who died while being taught in their school classrooms in Iran. Children are not collateral to the breakdown of the international order. They are its clearest evidence.

The post-1945 international order did not rely on humanitarian law alone. It was reinforced by institutions created to ensure that violations would not simply be recorded but judged. Chief among them were international judicial bodies designed to uphold the rule of law beyond the reach of any single state. The International Court of Justice, established in 1945 with all United Nations members automatically subject to its jurisdiction, was created to settle legal disputes between states and to provide advisory opinions on international legal questions. It was never intended to hold individuals to account – that task fell instead to the International Criminal Court, established as a court of last resort to indict individuals responsible for genocide, crimes against humanity, war crimes and, since 2018, the crime of aggression.

From the outset, however, the reach of the ICC has been constrained by the reluctance of powerful states to submit themselves to its authority. China, India, Turkey, Saudi Arabia, Indonesia, Egypt, Ethiopia and others never signed the Rome Statute and the United States and Russia signed but did not ratify. Russia later withdrew its signature altogether. A number of states similarly signed but failed to ratify, while recent withdrawals have included Burundi, the Philippines and Hungary, the first member of the European Union to leave the court, a decision which may now be reversed. In total, only 125 of the world's 195 states are currently parties to the ICC,[33] and compliance with ICC rulings has now fallen from 80 per cent to 50 per cent.

This pattern is not accidental. States have repeatedly withdrawn from, or threatened to sanction, the court precisely when its investigations have come close to their own conduct or that of their allies. Accountability is accepted in principle but resisted in practice. The gravest crimes are acknowledged, yet the mechanisms designed to prosecute them are deliberately weakened. Law, stripped of enforcement against the powerful, becomes selective – and law if selective ceases to function as law altogether.

The international institutions designed to create the conditions in which all can thrive, and to neutralise the sources of conflict in the first place, have been weakened – and some say beyond repair. These global institutions once created by the United States in the wake of the Second World War are now at risk from the Trump administration's withdrawal or threat of impending withdrawal – from the United Nations Human Rights Council, the World Health Organization and UNESCO to the many bodies dedicated to the protection and advancement of human rights that were among the forty international organisations from which America withdrew in January 2026. And then there is the relegation of the United Nations itself – not least in the Trump administration's unwillingness to ever pay the $3 billion the USA owes to it.[34]

Taken together, these changes in the status of international laws and institutions amount to more than a collection of isolated failures. 'We are not in a world without law . . . the vast majority of the rules of international law continue to be respected,' writes Philippe Sands, who points to the record number – twenty-three – of cases being brought before the International Court of Justice, the recent judgement on climate change and the convention now being discussed outlawing crimes against humanity.[35] The eminent Yale Law School Professor Harold Koh also suggests international law, while entering a period of severe stress, is fragmenting but not disappearing. Despite what he called Trump's first 'one hundred days of lawlessness',[36] he urges us to focus less on unevenly enforced and politically contested formal treaties and more on the networks of courts, civil society and democratic states and what he has termed the 'transnational legal process'.[37] At all times we must be vigilant. In her book *Hypocrisy and Human Rights*, Professor Kate Cronin-Furman writes of 'zombie norms' – norms of international law that are hollowed out but still linger in common parlance, even though they no longer meaningfully constrain anyone's behaviour.[38] This represents not merely the failure of individual institutions and treaties, but an assault on the very idea of the rule of law itself: the principle that power is subordinate to law and that the powerful and the powerless are both bound by the same legal foundations.

This danger has been recognised beyond the traditional centres of global power. In a joint statement, South Africa's President Cyril Ramaphosa, Malaysia's Prime Minister Anwar Ibrahim and Colombia's President Gustavo Petro warned that 'just as the international community once united to dismantle apartheid in South Africa – through similarly coordinated legal, economic and diplomatic pressure – we must now unite to enforce international law'.[39]

We do not say that medicine has failed because someone got cancer. The question now is not whether the international order has been and is being violated, but how deep the disorder now is – and why it has come to this? So we have to look beyond the law itself to more fundamental causes: the failings of the world order itself.

The world order reassessed

Why is the current world order falling apart so soon after the end of the Cold War, having lasted no more than thirty years? This failure has not come out of the blue. The unipolar American-led world order has been on life support for the better part of the last decade.

Twenty years ago President Putin would not have dared invade Ukraine, but Russia first entered Georgia in 2008 and then Crimea in 2014 – and even the might of a thirty-two-country NATO could not push him back. Less than twenty years ago, in 2009, America demanded that Israeli forces who had entered Gaza leave immediately, successfully vetoing their occupation. Now Israel appears to make its own decisions, and many are made without prior American approval or even, at times, forewarning. Not long ago, Arab leaders would have rushed to meet any American president arriving in their region, but when President Biden sought to convene them during his 2023 visit, none would meet him – yet another sign that the unipolar era has been drawing to a close in a way that not even the hegemonic ambitions of President Trump can forestall for long.[40] While America retains massive strike power, as demonstrated in the Iran war in early 2026, and huge economic and financial leverage, its hegemony – taken for granted two decades ago and broadly intact even ten years ago – no longer applies. This can be seen in the attendance of fifty-three African countries at the most recent Forum on China–Africa Cooperation summit in Beijing in 2024; the hundred-country turnout at the inauguration of the China-led Global Development Initiative; and the twenty new applications to join BRICS, an organisation whose principal *raison d'être* is standing up to American power, and which now stands at eleven members following the recent admission of six new states.

The order was first weakened by the 'War on Terror'. The US-led intervention in Iraq exposed the gap between an order that presented itself as liberal and rules-based and the reality of pre-emptive war. America's moral authority, on which so much of the post-1990 architecture depended, was badly damaged. Yet US hegemony was not yet displaced; there was still no near-peer rival able to shape the system from the outside.

Then came the crash of 2008–9. A financial crisis made in the West shook confidence in the entire neoliberal model. The idea that 'the market knows best' – that technocratic management of globalisation would deliver prosperity if governments only stood back – was decisively punctured. For three decades governments had been told to obey the dictates of markets: open up, deregulate, privatise, liberalise or be punished. After 2008, the direction of causality began to reverse. While in the initial stages of the global financial crisis trade restrictions were averted, the decade after 2010 brought a rapid retreat into tariff and non-tariff protectionism. Governments intervened, sheltered, subsidised and weaponised their interdependence, and justified it by reference not to the goal of greater economic efficiency but to national interest and self-sufficiency. Economic cooperation was no longer assumed; it had to be negotiated, often grudgingly, between governments that were themselves under siege from angry publics.

The new mood was summed up by the once left-leaning friend of the Open Society foundation, Viktor Orbán, who ruled Hungary from 1998 to 2002 and 2010 to 2026. He freely admitted that it was the lessons he drew from the 2008 global financial crisis that made him an authoritarian populist nationalist – and the European leader most admired by President Trump. 'The global financial crisis of 2008 proved that the system built on liberal ideology is unable to protect national economies,' he explained. Elected in 2010, he claimed, four years into his leadership, that 'the 2008 financial crisis showed that the liberal model of organising society has reached the end of the road'. And he declared unequivocally in words that travelled the world – a message that challenged all European countries to now look beyond Western liberal models – that 'the new state that we are building in Hungary is an illiberal state'.[41]

In 2008–9, the G20 became a summit of the heads of all major governments, a recognition that a crisis made in the West could no longer be solved by the West alone. Emerging economies, not just China but also Indonesia, India and Brazil, had to be brought into the room. But if for a brief moment it seemed we might be able to rebuild globalisation on a broader, more co-operative and more representative basis that took into account and reflected the changing balance of economic power, these hopes were dashed by the growing retreat into protectionism over the next decade.

What we see in this period, from 2008 to 2015, is the fragmentation of the global economic order. And yet, in these same years, there were also serious attempts to resurrect the old order and renew the promise of multilateralism. The Sustainable Development Goals, agreed unanimously in 2015 by every member country of the United Nations, represented the most ambitious effort yet to set out a shared agenda for ending extreme poverty, advancing health and education, and protecting the environment – an attempt to give globalisation a more human face.[42] The Paris climate agreement that followed, though a compromise in ensuring that any climate action would be grounded in nationally determined contributions, was another highly aspirational effort to prove that collective action – in this case an agreement on global carbon reduction targets – on an existential threat was still possible.[43] These initiatives showed that the desire for rules-based cooperation had not vanished. But they were layered on top of, and would soon be undermined by, an economic order whose foundations were already cracking.

Yet all the institutions, treaties and habits of cooperation built since 1945 still stood, and there remained a choice: to attempt, probably in vain, to patch up a fraying status quo, or to move consciously towards a new settlement that acknowledged the realities of a multipolar, interdependent world in which the centre of economic gravity had moved. In the referendums and elections of 2016, as the UK voted for Brexit and President Trump secured his first term, much of the West did not vote to reform the old order but appeared in open revolt against it. Instead of renewing multilateralism and updating global rules, what had been anti-incumbent protests became an anti-system movement, as electorates turned to those who promised 'to take back national control', to re-erect borders and to pursue national self-interest even at the expense of global cooperation.

What followed as we shifted economically from a neoliberal order to a neo-mercantilist order was in hindsight predictable: a move from unipolarity towards multipolarity, from a single dominant rule setter towards a world that we discuss later where rules are bent, challenged or ignored, and where the institutions created in 1945 and repurposed in 1990 no longer command automatic authority.

By the middle of the 2010s, the world was in an uneasy interregnum. Its centre of economic gravity had shifted decisively, but the political architecture lagged behind. Year after year, borders were being psychologically re-erected even as goods, capital and people continued to move. Countries increasingly viewed the world through a zero-sum lens – guided by 'I win, you lose' policies – not only assuming cut-throat economic competition with their neighbours but now prepared to circumvent the international system to pursue narrow national advantage.

This was the world that emerged in the years after 2016: not simply a fractured and fragmented international system, but the ascendancy of movements headed by leaders who saw the world in zero-sum terms, who treated multilateralism as the enemy of freedom, and who elevated the nation and national supremacy to the supreme object of political life. What had begun as a crisis of globalisation had become a crisis of democracy itself. And underlying it all was an ideological force that would structure the politics of the decade to come. It meant finding enemies even where none existed, casting pluralism as weakness rather than strength, and recasting interdependence as a descent into vulnerability – the result, so the argument ran, of lost border control and the erosion of national independence at the hands of global elites.

What is clear is that the rules-based world this generation inherited will not be the one we bequeath to our children. Not only has the material distribution of power changed recently but so has the ideological landscape. If the liberal world order was under attack at the turn of the century from religious extremists including anti-Western terrorists, as witnessed in the events of 9/11, the more recent attack from leaders like Putin, Xi, Kim Jong Un, Erdoğan and Orbán, but particularly from heads of countries which profess to be democracies, is far more fundamental. And what now sets the 2020s apart from the 2010s is the scale of the attack from within – akin to an autoimmune disorder – where the liberal world order is currently being challenged by its erstwhile greatest supporter, the United States. Under President Trump, the US has abruptly shifted from championing liberal democracy and an open society to being explicit in its downgrading of democracy, the rule of law and human rights as stated American objectives. At the same time, America has led the way in pursuing hyper-protectionist policies, has supported illiberal regimes and has stated in its National Security Strategy that far-right parties in Europe 'can count on America's backing'.[44]

The increasing willingness of the Trump administration to use military force to advance US national interests led in December 2025 to airstrikes against Islamic State in Nigeria and strikes at sea against drug-trafficking small craft in the Pacific and the Caribbean. The administration has already attempted to extract profit from Ukraine's natural resources as payment for military assistance; and some of the oil wealth of Venezuela, Trump said, 'goes also to the United States of America in the form of reimbursement'.[45] Washington conducted airstrikes in 2025 against Iran's nuclear preparations, and the 2026 Iran war has seen America engage in assassination and the destruction of the country's air force, army bases and battleships – even when at sea in international waters – with considerable loss of life to civilians, including in the bombing of a school that killed 168, of whom 110 were girl pupils.

Trump's new Board of Peace, which largely comprises authoritarian regimes, is ostensibly designed to act as an alternative to the UN peacekeeping agency, but is a unilateral instrument under his personal control, a corporate body. Its founding document states that Trump has the capacity to 'enter into contracts, acquire and dispose of immovable and movable property, institute legal proceedings, open bank accounts, receive and disburse private and public funds' in terms more akin to an international property developer under the guise of making peace.[46] So under his administration longstanding norms have been ignored, treaties abandoned, peacekeeping mandates vetoed, international courts dismissed as illegitimate. The guiding assumption is no longer that the supranational institutions we have built since 1945 could solve shared problems, an argument about their ineffectiveness, but that they constrain national ambition, an argument that focuses on their illegitimacy.

The Trump administration is explicitly critical of its predecessors. The National Security Strategy argues that former presidents 'lashed American policy to a network of international institutions, some of which are driven by outright anti-Americanism and many by a transnationalism that explicitly seeks to dissolve individual state sovereignty'.[47] With the series of executive orders in early 2026 that withdrew the US from almost all multilateral bodies dealing with economic, social, educational, environmental or climate issues the US is moving 'from withdrawal to confrontation' with global institutions,[48] and seeks to destroy the World Health Organization (by leaving and persuading others to leave and defund it), disable the World Trade Organization (by rejecting its basic principles of equality of treatment between nations) and end the Paris climate accord. Meanwhile the US has expanded its campaign of strikes against alleged narcotic smuggler boats across the Caribbean; the Russians are making extensive use of 'black fleet' vessels; and drones are becoming more widely weaponised against ships, undermining the 1899 Hague Convention on laws of war at sea and the freedom of the seas, which underpins the interdependence of the global economy.

Nevertheless, there has been some progress in discrete areas. In 2025 the International Maritime Organization oversaw a new agreement to tax maritime emissions and the so-called 'High Seas Treaty' came into effect, while the WHO was able to adopt a binding pandemic treaty even as the Trump administration chose to withdraw from the body.

We may see a new president in Washington in 2029, but a new administration will not be able to quickly restore confidence in the reliability of American support for democracy, the rule of law and human rights. Trust, once broken, is difficult to rebuild. If America is no longer to be considered reliable, the world is inevitably a more dangerous place, with an increased risk of conflict leading at its most extreme to nuclear proliferation.

The globalisation that the old order promoted has created a new economic landscape, but it is one that can no longer support its continuing existence. The post-1990 order thus planted the seeds of its own unravelling. The political scientist Kenneth Waltz argued that war has always been unlikely when there is only one dominant great power.[49] And so there may be a good reason why this decade has been unable to sustain a stable world order. No sufficiently authoritative higher body – neither the US nor the UN – is able to police the world. But the alternative to international rules is not freedom, but an unruly free-for-all. When long-established rules are no longer upheld, let alone monitored, a world without order drifts towards the anarchic. And when competing national interests take precedence over international norms, anything goes.

There is one alternative way forward: a coalition of the responsible, which I return to in Chapter 9. Latin America, Africa and Europe may be forming closer bonds. What were once American-led organisations are now linking up with other regional blocs – such as ASEAN and the Gulf Cooperation

Council[50] – without now expecting or waiting for American leadership. In other words, there is now a race between what America does – and, to a certain extent, what China does – and what the rest of the world does in response. The participants in this race are, on the one hand, those countries striving to maintain multilateralism but in new forms – finding solace in a global solidarity that might for at least a time have to exclude America and China – and, on the other, an aggressive group of populist nationalist leaders who agree on nothing other than their desire to replace that world order with their own versions.

But before we can turn to those questions about the future of the world order, there is another story we need to tell if we are really to grapple with the scale and breadth of the societal dilemmas facing the West in particular. From the broad sweep of geopolitics, we now turn to the most familiar and intimate parts of our lives and communities, and ask what the significance of these changes is in our everyday lives – beginning with my own experiences in my country of Scotland.

3

THE BREAKDOWN OF COMMUNITY?

The town of Kirkcaldy in Fife is not only where I grew up but the place that shaped my view of the world. It sits on the water, its extensive one-mile promenade marking it out as a unique coastal conurbation. The town's centuries-old port looks out on the North Sea to Europe and beyond to the wider world. As one of Scotland's biggest trading entrepots in the eighteenth century, it was the inspiration for the argument put forward 250 years ago by Adam Smith in his *Wealth of Nations*, that trade – and with it economic specialisation and the division of labour – had become the modern engine of growth. Well into the twentieth century, Kirkcaldy was exporting grain to every continent and importing from India linseed oil, the raw material for the town's staple industry and biggest employer: the manufacture of linoleum. For a time, until fitted carpets replaced lino as the fashionable floor covering, it was the 'linoleum capital of the world'[1] – an impressive feat for a town that is even now home to only just over 50,000 people. Coupled with a significant mining presence – at one point the county of Fife was home to sixty-six pits and 30,000 of Scotland's 138,000 miners[2] – Kirkcaldy was one of Scotland's industrial heartlands. Like so many other towns across Britain and the West, industry supported relatively good-quality jobs and rising prosperity.

Living two streets away from the linoleum factory, we could look out of the window in the morning and watch a community walking to work. The strength of that community is what I remember most: a rich network of locally led organisations and associations which brought children and families together across social divides. Growing up I was a member of a score of local organisations, many of which were tied to school, from sports to music. Outside school there was everything from the St Andrew's Ambulance Society, where I learned first aid in the station waiting room, and the philately society (I had been given a stamp collection by a friend of my parents) to the local fundraising charity my brother created around the local newspaper that he and our friends produced. And of course there were churches, youth fellowship programmes, the LifeBoys (in whose football team I played), the Boy Scouts, the local rugby club, the tennis club, and all the football supporters' activities in support of our local professional team, Raith Rovers, whose 140-year-old stadium still stands close to the centre of the town. I have fond memories of my first venture into enterprise – joining the group of young people selling match-day programmes, a job that came with free entry to the team's games.

We may not have described it as such, but an implicitly understood social compact bound us together: on offer were secure jobs and the benefits of mutual support; the concomitant responsibilities were to work hard and, where able to do so, play your part in community life whether as an active member of local organisations, holding local office or simply offering a helping hand.

The post-war years are often identified as the high point of economic progress and civic solidarity across the West. While the 'upswing' towards greater income equality, a pluralistic public square and a more cohesive social fabric began in many developed countries at the beginning of the twentieth century, it was the Second World War which probably did the most to cement the dominance of social democracy.[3] 'The war experience had motivated a fortunate alignment of economic forces, government policies, and enlightened behaviour by social institutions and businesses,' Martin Sandbu writes, in sync with the pioneering historical studies of Angus Calder and Paul Addison (who was my brilliant history tutor), 'which had ensured a post-war economy of belonging.'[4] In Britain between 1950 and 1970, real household disposable income roughly doubled as the economy grew by 2.9 per cent per year on average.[5]

The post-war settlement was never only about paid employment. There was, indisputably, a togetherness in that period that signalled a strong collectivist norm: an expectation that prosperity would be broadly shared, that each person's contribution would be recognised, and that the institutions of everyday life – workplaces, unions, churches, clubs and local public services – would bring people together into a common social milieu.

One can of course exaggerate the spread of prosperity and equality during this period. Low wages, unemployment and poverty were never eradicated and at times even got worse. In Britain, between 1953 and 1960, the proportion of households in poverty rose from 10 per cent to 17 per cent despite real GDP growing at the same time by nearly a third.[6] But it is true that industrial jobs were plentiful. In 1951, nearly 9 million jobs, 36 per cent of the entire workforce, were in manufacturing or mining.[7] Work was not simply a means to private consumption. It was an organising institution: a source of identity, and routine, which helped build community.

Spinning out of workplaces were a whole host of other civic organisations and sports teams, not just for the workers themselves but also for their families. The union branch, the workplace committee, the cooperative movement, the working men's club, the works football team were all part of a wider ecosystem of reciprocity: the shared rituals, the regular encounters and the steady accumulation of trust and obligation that makes a neighbourhood resilient. So much of this was the work of women, who, far more than the men, were the main community builders and caregivers. Throughout the 1950s and 1960s, many women balanced their family responsibilities with informal care, running voluntary associations, committee rooms and parish groups, and local fundraising – the everyday work of holding a community together. Their contribution was indispensable, but more often than not undertaken without pay or formal recognition. The post-war industrial settlement, while conducive to strong and cohesive community life, was not a fair or equal one. Like every preceding settlement, it was patriarchal in nature: the power within the family unit was firmly centred on the man, the breadwinner and often the only one.

Women were all too often excluded from the workforce. In the immediate post-war years just 17 per cent of married women in Scotland were employed,[8] and prior to the 1970 Equal Pay Act those who did work earned at least one third less.[9] Leadership of local communities, such as town councils, was dominated by men. LGBTQ+ people and minority ethnic groups also lacked adequate representation, protection and recognition. Many of the norms and expectations that shaped the economy of belonging were, in important respects, exclusionary. The cohesion of the period was real, but it was not evenly experienced and it rested, too often, on hierarchies that later for the very best of reasons would be challenged.

Changes that have taken place, albeit too slowly, in recent decades mean our societies are now for the most part far more tolerant and inclusive. Not before time the civil rights and liberation movements of the 1960s, 1970s and 1980s challenged some of the outdated presumptions and prejudices that defined the years of my childhood. Our communities and societies became less deferential, old hierarchies were challenged and new rights recognised. But when individuals demanded more autonomy, it need not have been at the expense of our obligations to each other. A duty-free world need not have replaced a dutiful world.

So the post-war settlement did not merely deliver a particular model of growth; it fostered a particular pattern of social life.

It linked economic contribution to social recognition, and it embedded people in institutions that were capable, at their best, of nurturing mutual responsibility and a shared sense of destiny. Whatever its injustices – and they were real and damaging – 'the economy of belonging' helped sustain an everyday solidarity. The question is not whether we should return to that settlement – we should not, and in any case we cannot. The question is why the institutions of solidarity proved so fragile when the economic foundations that underpinned them began to erode – and what we can do about it.

If the post-war settlement fostered solidarity, the following half-century has steadily unwound it. The industrial jobs that supported economic security and sustained prosperity in towns like Kirkcaldy have largely disappeared. Between them at their peak, mining and linoleum provided thousands of jobs in Kirkcaldy of which just 100 now exist in a town which has become, like so many others, dependent on service and whose biggest employer is the National Health Service. Gone is the Seafield colliery to the west of the town, which at one time employed close to 2,000 miners[10] and whose undersea reserves were once heralded as guaranteeing the future of the Scottish coal-mining industry. For a time, there were seven linoleum factories employing over 4,000 workers. Now there is only one small workplace with few employees.[11] In Scotland's industrial heyday, manual workers represented more than 75 per cent of its employees but by the turn of the twenty-first century, service workers accounted for the same percentage.[12] Since 1950, 6 million manufacturing and mining jobs have been lost in the UK alone,[13] while many tens of millions have been lost across the West.

The decline of mining is not in itself a source of unadulterated regret. Few parents would wish their child a life down the pits, and Kirkcaldy was not immune to the tragedies that come with precarious industrial work. I can recall the roof collapse at Seafield in 1973, which claimed the lives of five men – the youngest of whom was just twenty.[14] But I also remember the community rallying round in support of the families of the dead and injured. What has been lost with the decline of the mining industry is not only the jobs but the strength of the solidarity between working families that was at the heart of every mining community. 'The closure of pits, steel mills and factories fundamentally alters livelihoods and associations,' concludes Ewan Gibbs in his study of deindustrialisation in Scotland, 'by challenging a strongly held social order in towns and villages which had developed around coalmining.'[15]

So perhaps the most profound transformation I have observed since the 1960s is cultural: the hollowing out of so many of the clubs and community events that once brought neighbours closer together. The organisations which survive, from the churches and faith groups to the local trade union branch, now have smaller memberships and even smaller active memberships. Trade union membership in Britain stood at its peak in 1979 with over 13 million members, representing around half of the employed population, but it has since declined to just over 6 million, less than half the 1979 level, despite a rise in the overall workforce from 25 million to 33 million.[16] The pattern is repeated in many other Western industrial communities. And while once spread across the whole economy, the majority of organised workers today, 3.5 million, are in the public sector, which accounts for only 20 per cent of the workforce. Less than 10 per cent of the 28 million private sector workers are unionised.[17]

Religious life tells a similar story of decline. In the 1950s more than 1.2 million people were communicant members of the Church of Scotland. Today, there are now only 245,000 recorded members and a recent audit found only 60,000 people now attend Church of Scotland services each Sunday.[18] The church where my father was a minister once had two services on a Sunday, but has now amalgamated with other churches not once but twice.

Organisations such as the Rotary Club, the Women's Institute and the Mothers' Union once boasted millions of members in thousands of chapters across the world. In the UK, for instance, membership of the Women's Institute once stood at close to half a million. Today, that number has nearly halved to 235,000.[19] Youth organisations likewise once flourished. British membership of the Scouts, Guides, and Boys' and Girls' Brigades at their combined peak was 1.7 million but now stands at around 770,000, having more than halved.

Many civic meeting places have also disappeared. The number of working men's clubs – once the beating heart of many industrial communities' social life – has since 1970 fallen from 4,500 to 1,175,[20] with their membership dwindling from 4 million to under one million.[21] Meanwhile, the number of pubs in Britain has almost halved from 75,000 to below 39,000.[22] Today's civic associations are more likely to be focused on leisure and sporting activities, more oriented towards personal than community development. Volunteering, for example, has fallen sharply in Britain. Ten years ago, 27 per cent of adults in Britain reported formal volunteering at least once a month,[23] but in the polling carried out for this book we found that just 13 per cent reported volunteering at any point in the last year.*

While time spent being active in community life has declined, the time we spend looking at screens has increased. At the start of the 1950s only 350,000 households (2 per cent) in the UK had a television set. By the early 2000s, the average time spent watching TV every day was 3½ hours in the UK and just over 4 hours in the US. Today, we are grappling with an even more addictive form of technology – phones and social media. In 2025 for the first time, people aged over fifteen in Britain spent more time each day on their phone (3 hours 21 minutes) than watching TV (3 hours 16 minutes). One estimate suggests if trends continue, at least fifteen

* Further details about the methodology and full country sample can be found in Chapter 6.

years of our lives will be spent on just our phone. When laptops, games consoles and tablets are also taken into consideration, the total average screen time for UK adults is 7 hours 27 minutes – an increase of almost a full hour since 2015.[24]

Of course, community life remains vibrant in many areas. In Kirkcaldy I recently attended the 160th anniversary celebration of Seescape, a brilliant and thriving visual impairment charity that used to be called Fife Society for the Blind. I visited the YMCA's impressive new headquarters near the town centre, redesigned to cater for the needs of teenagers in new ways in the digital age. Many of the youth organisations are still active, though some time ago the local Boys' Brigade platoon was forced to sell its central hall. There are also flourishing civic groups that are new to the town since I was young – like Inspire, a disability drama club run by the local theatre, the Saturday morning Parkrun which brings together scores of people every week, and the Warm Welcome Group, which started off as a temporary space for people unable to afford to heat their homes over winter but has become a permanent institution, with the realisation that, as people come together to combat loneliness, the welcome was equally or even more important than the warmth.

Some of these civic projects have flourished, adapting to the shifting tides in society. The innovative Cottage Family Centre started in the 1970s in a run-down cottage and has since expanded to occupy two sites in the town. It offers a range of services to locals in the lowest-income areas, well beyond the traditional crèches, breakfast clubs and school-holiday entertainments, innovating with, for example, a dads' club to develop parenting skills, a grannies' club and mental health counselling. Raith Rovers FC, too, have proved adaptable, operating community hubs and boosting season ticket holders to nearly 2,500 thanks to an innovative policy where under-twelves go free and under-sixteens pay just £60 for the whole season. The local rugby club has similarly gone from strength to strength, and after struggling for many years the Fife Flyers ice hockey team is now in the premier British league. What marks a change from my youth is the new importance of the local radio stations and newspapers to help bring the community together, and one vital point of connection for people is the astoundingly successful Love Kirkcaldy! Facebook group, which boasts over 50,000 members, from current residents to those who have emigrated far away but who still think of the town as home.

My successor as MP, Melanie Ward, conducted a study which asked locals what made them proud of their town. The standout answer was community spirit.[25] Local residents are proud of the collective identity that has to a large extent survived in spite of the economic and social headwinds that have made life increasingly difficult for so many. But they also know their community is under pressure. The very existence of two town centre regeneration groups illustrates how Kirkcaldy is symptomatic of what we see up and down the country, as high streets decline, many now dominated by betting shops, vape sellers and barbers, as well as charity shops, the major retail stores having moved to out-of-town sites. They are shells of the once vibrant town centres which sculpted a shared pride and sense of belonging. In fact, three in five British citizens say their high street has worsened in recent years, according to a poll by More in Common.[26] 'If I were to sum up what most typifies people's sense of "broken Britain" on a personal level,' Luke Tryl, its director, said, 'it is declining local high streets and antisocial behaviour.'[27] And not surprisingly, in the Kirkcaldy study, as many as 93 per cent felt the town centre looked worse than of old. This disappointment is reflected in the town's politics. From before I was born until I stepped down from Parliament, Kirkcaldy was among the safest Labour seats in the country, but in the last twenty years it has veered between Labour and nationalism – the latter a sign of people's frustration at a status quo that is no longer felt to deliver.

The social cost

The decline in active participation in community life, and the subsequent erosion of what Robert Putnam termed 'social capital', has profound consequences for both communities and individuals. Loneliness has risen from a fringe issue to becoming a significant public concern: an estimated 20 per cent of people worldwide have reported being lonely, while the figure for adults in Britain is even higher at 27 per cent.[28] In America, the outgoing surgeon-general of the Biden administration categorised the rising levels of loneliness as 'a public health emergency'[29] with, he said, consequences as harmful to life chances as smoking fifteen cigarettes a day. The risk of heart disease, dementia and stroke, as well as the directly related mental conditions of depression and anxiety disorders, are all known to increase with loneliness.[30] The physical effect of loneliness is such that it is estimated to reduce life expectancy by up to fifteen years.

Loneliness has also been shown to carry harm beyond ill health, as it leads to higher levels of distrust, fear of others and 'a hypervigilance to threats'[31] – which researchers have connected to greater support for populist nationalist parties.[32] Disconnection from community life changes how we relate to people whom we see as different from ourselves. The Council of Europe defines 'social cohesion' as 'the capacity of society to ensure the well-being of all its members, minimising disparities and avoiding marginalisation' and states that it 'is built upon trust and respect between groups, on a shared sense of belonging, and a commitment to equality and fairness'.[33] This trust in turn is built up through meaningful, positive contact with others, rooted, when I was growing up, in the civic organisations which built a strong sense of solidarity.

Without question, the Kirkcaldy of today is far more diverse than it was fifty years ago. Some like to point to our increasing diversity as a reason for the decline in community. This claim turns upon a false and divisive story. We know from decades of research into what is called contact theory that meaningful and positive contact, bringing people together across lines of difference, whether religious, ethnic or ideological, reduces prejudice and increases understanding and tolerance. The logic of these findings is that we need to build institutions that provide opportunities for people of diverse backgrounds to meet, by investing in, for example, public parks, public libraries, public transport, swimming pools and sports facilities – amenities that offer services that people can afford. But it is not proximity to others that is itself decisive in building community cohesion: it is positive interaction with others. Being a member of just one civic group, as our own research, which I will discuss in detail in Chapter 6, finds, cuts the likelihood of having no close friends by more than half. People who don't participate at all in civic groups are three times more likely never to interact with someone of a different social class, religion or ethnicity than active community participants. Thus clearly, without a vibrant civic square, the opportunities for positive and meaningful interaction are reduced, and suspicion and prejudice can take hold.

The political cost

The fallout from economic and civic decline – what people, when asked in polls, now refer to as a 'broken economy' and a 'broken society' – is not confined to these two spheres but is also political in its consequences. All across the West, trust in government has declined markedly. This loss of trust is mirrored by a decline in formal participation in politics. Turnout at elections has fallen globally in sixty years from 77 per cent to 67 per cent and in Britain it is even lower, with only 59.7 per cent voting in 2024's general election – the worst turnout for twenty years.[34]

Underlying this downturn in participation is something more profound than general distrust; it links back, once again, to the hollowing out of the local organisations that traditionally connected people with politics and trained them in the skills needed for democracy to flourish. Political parties themselves were once built from and thrived on widespread grassroots engagement. In almost every town, local parties were, at their best, important civic institutions offering residents the opportunity to discuss and debate what seemed best for their communities. The idea was that these views would then be aggregated up to a national level at party conferences which fed into political manifestos. In Britain, membership of the two major parties, Labour and the Conservatives, once stood in the millions. Individual constituency parties could count membership into the thousands and meetings were often attended by hundreds. Thirty years ago when my local constituency had 1,500 Labour members, the monthly meetings were composed of more than fifty attendees and there was often competition from within the branches to be nominated as delegates to the constituency-wide body which would debate all the great issues of the day. Today, delegates are no longer the basis of representation as a far smaller number turn up to meetings. In Germany, since 1990, membership of the six main parties has halved from 2.4 million to only 1.2 million – less than 2 per cent of the population.[35] In the US, where party membership has never existed in the same form as in Europe, we can instead consider formal party identification. In 1988, two-thirds of American adults considered themselves to be either a Republican or Democrat, but by 2025 this had fallen to just over half.[36] The direction of political engagement has reversed. Political parties are now run more in the manner of electoral machines, from the top downward, with the result that the public square has been emptying out.

Political alignment was once inextricably bound up with class. That link has also eroded. We are in the age of what polling expert Sir John Curtice calls 'multidimensional politics'.[37] White working-class men without a degree, once the bedrock of the social democratic Labour movement, have now moved in large numbers to the populist nationalist right. In the UK, the 2019 general election saw the collapse of the Red Wall[38] – the collection of working-class-dominated constituencies of the Midlands and northern England that traditionally voted for the Labour Party. Once defined by its heavy industry, today this region has the most frayed social fabric in the UK.[39] It is perhaps unsurprising that just three years earlier, in 2016, these constituencies voted overwhelmingly for Brexit.

Similarly, in the US, the equivalent Rust Belt, an area famous for its labour activism and support for the Democratic Party, played a pivotal role in both of Trump's election successes. Where once every proud 'union man' would be expected to support the Democrats, today, as a major study records, the parking lot of a Rust Belt factory is filled with cars which proudly display MAGA and TRUMP stickers.[40] Unions have given way to National Rifle Association (NRA) gun clubs as the most important source of community activity for many workers.[41]

So the profile – the membership and activism – of local political parties has dropped almost in sync with the decline we have described in participation in other civic organisations. These institutions when taken together did more than provide solidarity, collective bargaining, shared worship and social outlets. They created what Alexis de Tocqueville called 'schools of democracy'[42] in which people learned how to live together: how to conduct social relationships, negotiate, argue their case and compromise.[43] And something important has been lost in the process. For there is a distinction between civic organisations and civic opportunities, as described by political scientist Hahrie Han.

Civic organisations are groups which lie between the state and the commercial marketplace, and which the public can join. Civic opportunities are the 'experiences necessary to cultivate the capacities for collective life in pluralistic societies'.[44] Not all civic organisations provide civic opportunities, but it is the ones that do that are becoming less prevalent in our everyday lives. While undoubtedly sports and exercise clubs offer health and other personal benefits, they do not necessarily require members to become involved in the running of their organisations or in the work of the wider community, although of course some do. Those organisations that regularly demand more of their members, including those that represent causes rather than only activities, have lost ground in recent decades. So, as citizens, we are not only less connected, we are also less engaged and less experienced in the practice of an active citizenship, which is so important for a vibrant and resilient public life.

The retreat from regular and meaningful civic participation into the silos of social media has led to the privatisation of the public square.[45] When social media first emerged, it was heralded as a tool that would break down barriers to connection. It is of course a great technological marvel that physical space is no longer a barrier to connection. But it is also true that the benefits of online connection do not match those of face-to-face interactions.[46] Misinformation on social media is a growing concern and made worse when traditional local media has been hollowed out.[47] Instead of a community coming together in a town hall or getting news from a trusted local newspaper, we are instead admitted into a digital domain that more often than not directs us into echo chambers. In-person contact through local groups and civic associations, on the other hand, is far more likely to connect us to people with different views and open us to new ideas.[48]

The emptying of the public square has also changed who we look to for leadership. The populist nationalist leaders who seem ever present on social media are now taking the place of community leaders, who even if they have not vanished into thin air often lack a social media presence. These mainly right-wing populists encourage, exploit and exacerbate the anti-pluralist, anti-government, anti-culture, anti-system sentiments of people from all generations and classes. In fact, they do more than that. Even when they are speaking from a distance, the social media output of these populist leaders lends a false intimacy, coming directly into people's devices and feeds, and telling them that they understand them better than local leaders, and indeed understand the causes of the cultural pessimism they feel, accelerating the loss of trust in institutions.

It is important to note, however, that our investigations mapping the erosion of civic life and the public square demonstrate that populist nationalist leaders such as Trump, Farage and Le Pen are better understood as surface symptoms rather than the root cause of the changes we are experiencing. Rather than being the architects of change, as they claim, they are opportunists who are taking advantage of fifty years of economic and social transformation and the ever-widening gap between winners and losers that this has created.

Future historians may well point to 2016 as the trigger for our new age of populism.[49] Within just five months the two seismic, generation-defining events that we mentioned earlier took place – Brexit in the United Kingdom and the election of President Trump in the United States. Very easily, both of these results could have gone the other way. In this parallel universe, it would be simple to conclude that the global populist surge would have been avoided. But this would be to mistake symptoms for causes. While it might have lain dormant in the political arena for five or ten more years, the undercurrent of anger and disappointment would not have disappeared. The social and economic foundations had already eroded over the preceding decades, and if 2016 had not brought a nationalist populist breakthrough, another year, crisis or leader almost certainly would have appeared. It was never a case of 'if' but of 'when'.

But the political upheaval of recent times is almost certainly not the product of any individual populist leader, however charismatic or disruptive. It appears to be the cumulative result of the everyday experience of change and decline for millions of citizens in Western democracies: the disappearance of dignified work that brought security and status, the thinning of community life, the rise of loneliness and mistrust, and the weakening and in some cases the withering away of institutions that once taught citizens how to work together. The most important consequence of all this has been the creation of a vacuum which populist nationalist politicians can enter and exploit – but it is a consequence, not a cause. And we must look to causes if we are to reverse the trend.

A democracy can survive low enthusiasm for its politicians. It cannot survive the long-term disappearance of active citizens. When people are no longer part of organisations which create the space and opportunity for them to debate, deliberate and decide on action, when the public square is replaced by a digital domain that screens out alternative views, the foundations upon which liberal democracies rest are weakened.

In my lifetime, I have witnessed the once-strong pillars of community life – social networks, civic responsibility, faith groups and town centres – decline in significance. What has replaced them are, to a large extent, TV, mobile phones and social media, which now dictate the rhythm of life. The result is a more individualised society composed of people who are encouraged to think of themselves as consumers rather than citizens, who are less likely to be active locally and engaged nationally. We are aware of the impact that increased loneliness and isolation is having. What we are maybe less prepared for is the impact on our democratic way of life.

There is, however, nothing inevitable about our current trajectory. For all the fractures in our society, our polling shows that people *want* to participate, and long to be part of a fair economy and a connected community. Had this desire been lost then our situation would be far bleaker. But as the conclusions of our transnational poll demonstrate, the longing for belonging is still there, and it is visible in new community-organised initiatives springing up, and in people's aspirations to connect with their neighbours. To break out of our current malaise we need a new generation of active citizens. The task ahead is not to return to the past, but to build forms of civic life that can flourish in a diverse, mobile and digital world – ones that bridge divides rather than deepen them, and that make participation and belonging possible for all. I will set out proposals to achieve this in Chapter 13. But before we can turn to solutions, we need to understand how experiences of civic decline have coincided with experiences of economic decline, and how both together have helped bring about the rise of populist nationalism.

4

NEOLIBERALISM: FREE FOR ALL, BUT NOT FAIR TO ALL?

During the 1970s, a time of great upheaval and dissent in America, Gore Vidal and John Kenneth Galbraith toured their country speaking together on the state of the nation. Vidal would introduce himself to the huge audiences by saying that Galbraith would talk about the economy: 'That's 99 per cent of America's problems.'

I met Galbraith only once. He told me how he had spoken at an anniversary event for the Austrian Republic attended by many of the great Austrian neoliberal economists, led by Friedrich von Hayek. He had congratulated the republic on the decades of progress it had seen since the end of the Second World War. In particular, he said, he had wanted to thank Hayek and his fellow neoliberals for the contribution they had made to the success of Austria. For, as he said, if they had not left the country for America in 1945, Austria could never have enjoyed the combination of economic prosperity and social justice that marked it out as a social democratic success story for the next forty years.

The acidity of this remark reminds us that in the last seventy-five years verbal battles that have been fought over economic theory have been among the fiercest, bitterest and most contested of all. In its heyday, the neoliberal doctrine was pursued with dogmatic certainty by Hayek and its other leading apostles, to the exclusion of all other opinions branded as heresy. At one point in the 1970s, Hayek planned a debate between himself and those he believed were his enemies. So dismissive and intolerant was he of any views that deviated even slightly from his that his list of enemies included Alexander Solzhenitsyn, Daniel Bell and Iris Murdoch – all well-known anti-communists but whom he considered to have failed his purity tests. This reminds us that neoliberalism was advocated, followed and implemented in such an extreme way – and with such success for a time – that it washed away in its wake many commonsense propositions. Neoliberalism championed the entirely rational and self-interested 'economic man' (*Homo economicus*) against the more cooperative 'social man' (*Homo reciprocans*), an idea that has now to be rescued and rehabilitated.

Over the last seventy-five years, the world has moved from its post-war embrace of Keynesianism to the enthronement and then the rejection of its successor ideology, neoliberalism. You do not need to be a determinist to acknowledge the historical fact that when the economic fundamentals of a society shift, almost everything else starts to shift with them: the level of prosperity people enjoy, the kinds of jobs they do, where they live, what status they hold, what they can expect for their children, and how they feel about the future. The combined forces of deindustrialisation and neoliberal-driven globalisation have profoundly restructured advanced economies and their societies. If the post-war settlement fostered solidarity that helped sustain communities like Kirkcaldy, the following half-century saw it steadily, but sometimes violently unwind: from the 1960s, plants closed, pits were sealed, and the industries which had given many towns their distinctive identity started to disappear. Western countries such as Britain began the difficult transition to knowledge-based service economies as the world opened up and the majority of manufacturing moved abroad. In 1980, 25 per cent of UK jobs were in manufacturing. By 2010, that share had fallen to 8.2 per cent.[1] What had once been stable, broad-based employment was replaced by more footloose forms, often concentrated in a small number of cities and regions, with the good jobs increasingly dependent on educational credentials that large sections of the population did not possess. In just seven years between 2012 and 2019, the average number of jobs held over a working life in the OECD rose from six to seven.[2]

At the same time, the rising prosperity of the second half of the twentieth century had given ordinary families far greater choice in how they lived their lives. More young people began attending university and entering higher-paid service-sector jobs, leading to a significant expansion of the middle class. (Under the New Labour governments I was a member of, university attendance at eighteen rose from around 30 per cent in 1997 to 45 per cent in 2010.)[3]

Suburbanisation – the decision to move outside city centres in search of more space and better living conditions – became increasingly popular. Greater geographic mobility allowed people to seek better jobs and lifestyles. But this led once-tight family units and friendship groups to be dispersed across wider geographical areas, and the dense, place-based relationships that had previously sustained community life were thinned out.

The costs of this transition were not evenly distributed. Among those who lost most were non-university-educated, working-class men – a group that had previously commanded a higher social status and formed the bedrock of the labour movement. The share of young men entering low-paying, low-progression jobs such as customer services more than doubled from 17 per cent to 36 per cent as manual occupation employment fell from 41 per cent to 26 per cent when we compare those born in the 1950s to those born in the late 1980s.[4]

The new knowledge economy placed a much higher premium on formal education; gone were the days when it was possible to leave school unqualified and find a job that provided security, solidarity and status. It is therefore not surprising that it is this group – white working-class men without a degree whose partners may be in better-paid jobs than they are – who have, in large numbers, felt their status diminished and have shifted towards the populist right in recent decades.[5]

While the move towards a knowledge economy was always going to present challenges, political choices played a decisive role in widening the economic divide. During the 1980s, Margaret Thatcher in the UK and Ronald Reagan in the US led a neoliberal agenda of tax cuts, deregulation and union-busting that by the early 1990s had cemented steep economic inequality and severed the post-war cross-class compromise. In the UK, the Gini coefficient, a measure of inequality, rose from 26.1 to 36.6 under Thatcher; in Reagan's America, the bottom 20 per cent saw annual income growth of just 0.1 per cent, while the top 20 per cent saw incomes grow thirty times faster by 3.2 per cent each year. By the 2020s, according to the United Nations, three-quarters of the world's population lived in countries in which income inequality had deteriorated in the previous thirty years.[6] During the deindustrialisation of the 1970s and 1980s, right-wing populism did at times threaten to become a strong political force across Europe, but the centre held, and populists such as Jean-Marie Le Pen in France were kept to the margins of political life.[7]

The fall of the Berlin Wall ushered in nearly two decades of what many felt to be the golden period of globalisation. In the early 2000s, steady economic growth in Western democracies, alongside the cheapening of consumer goods now being imported from the East, allowed living standards to rise for the majority of workers. Typical consumption levels in the UK rose by 20–25 per cent between 2000 and 2008. However, this had unforeseen consequences. Consumption, not civic participation, increasingly became the dominant means of engagement in society. This rise of consumerism further reinforced the shift towards a greater individualism. For much of history, as Jon Alexander explains, the vast majority of humans were 'subjects', who largely accepted what they were given.[8] This changed in the twentieth century, when people became 'consumers', gaining greater freedom of choice and new rights. But in defining individuals primarily as consumers, rather than as active citizens, something vital is being lost, as we saw in the previous chapter.

For a time, the apparent rise in living standards masked the deeper structural problems that were being created by the scale of deindustrialisation and the polarisation of the labour market, but any illusion that the changes underway were not profound was shattered by the global financial crisis of 2008–9.

As Branko Milanovic has shown in his famous 'elephant curve', and as became clear to all after 2008, the neoliberal era had reshaped our world: looking at all income growth across the world from 1988 and 2018, he saw an elephant, with little growth for those at the bottom or for those in upper-working-class jobs in North America in Europe, while the bulk of the emerging middle class – the elephant's body – in the Global South saw incomes rise by 70–80 per cent and the global 1 per cent, the wealthiest members of Western economies, saw their incomes rise by 60 per cent – the elephant's trunk.[9] Workers in the West saw everyone else – their bosses or their counterparts abroad – get better off, while their own incomes stagnated.

In the aftermath of the global financial crisis, governments faced a choice. Historically low interest rates offered the opportunity to invest our way out of recession: to rebuild infrastructure, support employment and renew the social fabric that had been fraying under the pressures of deindustrialisation and globalisation. Instead, across much of the West – and certainly in Britain – fiscal austerity prevailed.

These cuts hit hardest at the local level. In England, public services funding fell by 24 per cent, and the cuts were concentrated in areas already scarred with a history of industrial decline,[10] deepening local communities' sense of disenfranchisement and injustice. These economic changes actively amplified the sense of political discord, measured in a direct connection between the intensity of austerity cuts in Britain and subsequent support for leaving the European Union. Estimates suggest that without austerity, support for the Leave vote could have been as much as 9.51 percentage points lower, leading to a 58–42 vote to Remain (instead of 52–48 to Leave).[11] Similarly, surveys of decline on British high streets in the run-up to Brexit directly link the erosion of local retail and increased support for Reform UK's predecessor UKIP,[12] evidencing the impact place-based economic decay can have on the appeal of right-wing populism.

Austerity was therefore not only a fiscal strategy, but a social one, although perhaps unintentionally. By cutting back the institutions that underpinned everyday community life, national governments exacerbated the decline of community spaces. In many towns, places that were once the heart of local social interaction – youth clubs, libraries, community centres – were among the first to go. This impacted not only the provision of local services but the shared routines and everyday encounters that sustained civic life.

At the same time, new technologies stepped in to fill the void left by the retreat of public provision. Digital platforms offered convenience and choice, but at the cost of further weakening face-to-face interaction or the expectation of it. Online services meant that people no longer needed to go to the supermarket, or leave their homes for entertainment or, increasingly, for work. Twelve per cent of workers fully or partially worked from home in the UK in 2019, a rate which more than tripled to 40 per cent by 2024. Internet shopping, streaming services and remote working further reduced the number of shared physical spaces in which people routinely encountered others unlike themselves. The Covid pandemic dramatically accelerated these trends, normalising patterns of isolation, even as people rallied to help each other.

But the disruption of community life cannot be attributed solely to deindustrialisation. Neoliberal thinking shifted responsibility for the social security safety net from the welfare state to charities and food banks. In countries like the United Kingdom, social mobility, which had been on an upward trajectory, first stalled then started to fall. As noted by Minouche Shafik, it takes, on average, only two generations for a Danish citizen to move from a lower-income family to an upper-income one, but four generations for a British one.[13]

This undermining of an implicit social contract was the result of a set of neoliberalist views that, as we suggested at the outset of this chapter, were advocated with semi-religious zeal by a few true believers, but whose dogma eventually fell out of favour when they, ultimately, failed to deliver on their promises. And so we turn, now, to the rise and fall of an idea: neoliberalism.

From social democracy to neoliberal order

In 1971, the US Republican president, Richard Nixon, was reluctantly forced to concede that 'we are all Keynesians now'.[14] For three decades after the Second World War, the broadly social democratic settlement had been dominant across much of the advanced industrial world: a market economy tempered by state intervention, committed to full employment, rising living standards and expanding public provision. This settlement – forged as a result of the shared experience of depression and war – endured, with national variations, from the 1940s until the late 1970s and early 1980s.

At its outset neoliberalism emerged as a critique of that settlement. At its core, it asserted that government intervention distorted markets, constrained growth and prevented capitalism from unleashing its full potential for innovation and production. 'The goal of the neoliberalism', as historian Gary Gerstle puts it, was 'to get the government out of the economy'.[15] But what started as an alternative set of ideas became something far more consequential once it was translated into a governing paradigm under Margaret Thatcher in the UK and Ronald Reagan in the US.

An ideology becomes an order when it is accepted not only by one political faction, but by most of the political establishment and, in turn, large sections of the electorate. And this is precisely what happened, first in the United States and then across much of the Western world. A bipartisan consensus formed around neoliberal ideas, to the point that, by the 1990s, as Gerstle records in *The Rise and Fall of the Neoliberal Order*, 'a new generation of American Democrats [was] adopting neoliberal principles as their own – a sure sign of this ideology's ascent'.[16]

With echoes across Europe and far beyond it, from Argentina to India, neoliberalism became 'the very rationality of our time':[17] a way of thinking that reshaped not only economic policy but the purposes of government and the language of politics, and became the common sense of the age, representing the expectations citizens held of themselves and others. Markets were treated as self-correcting mechanisms, privatisation, deregulation and competition as the primary source of efficiency, and private choice as the highest expression of freedom.

For a time, this framework appeared to deliver: inflation was brought under control, consumer choice expanded, and global integration reduced the price of many goods. But as the years passed – and particularly in the wake of the global financial crisis of 2008–9 – the answers neoliberals offered to the advanced Western economies in crisis became steadily less convincing and no longer credible. The global financial crisis exposed not only technical weaknesses in financial regulation but deep flaws in the neoliberal worldview itself. Markets did not self-correct, risks were not necessarily efficiently priced, and the costs of failure were not borne by those who created them. Instead, losses, such as the cost of the banking collapse, were socialised, public trust was eroded, and the legitimacy of economic institutions was profoundly damaged. What had once been presented as a neutral, technocratic system of allocation increasingly appeared as a political project – one that distributed risks and rewards in deeply uneven ways. Across virtually every sphere of public concern, the promises of the neoliberal order fell short.

The failure of neoliberalism: the five Es

For neoliberals, society is simply the sum of the individual choices of self-seeking consumers maximising their economic self-interest in a marketplace (*Homo economicus*). National success is measured in terms of wealth rather than wellbeing, and the principal role of government is to establish and protect free markets. Economics, in this framework, is presented as a value-neutral, technical science concerned with efficiency rather than purpose. But this claim to neutrality has always been misleading. The neoliberal order did not remove ethics from economics; it smuggled in a particular ethical vision while denying that it was doing so.

The incompleteness of this framework becomes clear when judged against the 'five Es' that I raised earlier, the metrics by which the general public tend to evaluate a legitimate and successful economic order: the quality and availability of **employment**; the attainment of **equality**; appropriate stewardship of the **environment**; **efficiency** in how resources are used; and, crucially, an alignment between production and our broader **ethics**. Under neoliberalism, the first four Es were repeatedly promised but rarely delivered, while the fifth was largely ignored. Over time, this imbalance produced not only a malfunctioning economy but a deeper sense that our society was divided and in disarray.

The abandonment of economics as the more intersectional study of political economy and as an ethical pursuit has a long intellectual history. In an influential essay of 1932, 'The Nature and Significance of Economic Science', Lionel Robbins defined economics as 'the science which studies human behaviour as a relationship between ends and scarce means which have alternative uses'.[18] By stripping economics of any concern with a moral and collective purpose, and by making it agnostic about ends, Robbins reduced the discipline to a branch of logic: the optimisation of choice under conditions of scarcity. Moral questions were reclassified as external to economics and left to politics or philosophy, while the older tradition of political economy – associated with Adam Smith – was consigned to history.

Yet as Smith made clear in *The Theory of Moral Sentiments*, markets are always underpinned by moral judgements. Because they are founded in shared norms and expectations, markets do not merely reflect preferences; they actively shape them. 'Putting a price on every human activity erodes certain moral and civic goods worth caring about,' Michael Sandel has written. 'Once we see everything in economic terms, there's a danger that we value only what can be priced.'[19] For decades, GDP has stood as the dominant measure of progress, despite its well-known limitations. As Robert F. Kennedy observed in 1968, 'The Gross National Product counts air pollution and cigarette advertising . . . Yet it does not allow for the health of our children, the quality of their education, or the joy of their play . . . It measures everything, in short, except that which makes life worthwhile.'[20]

How we define, measure and talk about 'the economy' therefore reflects our priorities and our moral judgements. If we focus narrowly on output and consumption, we should not be surprised when other values – dignity, contribution, stewardship – are crowded out and our economy looks values-free. With this ethical concern moved to the foreground, we are better placed to evaluate the failure of neoliberalism against the other four Es – understood not as technical objectives, but as expressions of an ethical commitment to a shared life.

Employment is central. Good jobs for all should be at the heart of economic policy, with well-paid, secure employment that is widely geographically spread. Neoliberalism's obsession with free markets concentrated decision-making power in the hands of owners and investors, at the expense of employees and to the exclusion of the wider public. Average mark-ups by firms – the multiple of the prices they sell at compared to the cost of production – rose from 1.2 in 1980 to 1.6 in 2019 in the US,[21] and from 1.2 in 1996 to 1.6 by the mid-2010s in the UK.[22] At the same time as profits rose, the relationship between workers' productivity growth and their wages halved in the US between the 1970s and the 2000s.[23] With its focus on reducing inflation at the expense of employment, neoliberalism could never guarantee 'good' work. As a result, precarious work has proliferated, with 7 per cent of UK workers reporting uncertain and insecure work and 1.1 million stuck in 'zero hours' contracts with no guarantee of work.[24]

Employment matters not only because of what people earn, but because of what they contribute – what is sometimes called contributive justice.[25] A former manufacturing worker who becomes a warehouse worker has neither the earnings nor the status of the steelworker, shipbuilder or coalminer. Nor are they as likely to have the pride and satisfaction in the skill required to carry out their trade. A few who are dependent on welfare transfers may, if disabled, receive the same income as someone in work, but not, perhaps, the same sense of dignity or social recognition. When work ceases to confer status or meaning, resentment and withdrawal follow. By ignoring the hollowing out of manufacturing employment and forcing workers into a race to the bottom on wages, neoliberalism not only downgraded their relative earnings but undermined the status and pride they derived from their work.

Nor did neoliberalism meet the challenge of the environment. Because it treated externalities as peripheral, its focus on privatisation, deregulation and liberalisation ignored the damage caused by the ruthless exploitation of natural resources. Current policies across the world have a 62 per cent chance of triggering catastrophic climate 'tipping points', where the Amazon and permafrost ice sheets both retreat;[26] and the average decline of species' population since 1970 has been 73 per cent.[27] Our stewardship of the environment is the clearest test of our sense of obligation to future generations, and I will return to this in the penultimate chapter of this book. Climate change, biodiversity loss and environmental degradation are not to be dismissed as technical side-effects; they are moral failures rooted in an economic system that discounts the future.

Equality, too, was sacrificed in the pursuit of efficiency – and neoliberalism delivered neither. Freedom was on offer to those who had the money to buy it. The inequalities that now characterise advanced economies are not only unjust, they are inefficient and corrosive. As Thomas Piketty, Emmanuel Saez and Branko Milanovic have shown, excessive concentration of wealth – with inequality levels returning to rates last seen in the 1920s – allows a small elite to bend the rules of the game, perpetuate privilege and exercise undue influence over democratic institutions.[28] As inequality has risen, it has been justified as the fair reward for talent and effort, ignoring the vast advantages conferred on those fortunate enough to be born into the upper echelons of society. Meanwhile, those at the bottom have been disciplined (by those at the top) with sticks rather than encouraged by carrots. For millions, the 'American Dream' is in tatters, with children born in the bottom fifth having just an 8 per cent chance of making it to the top fifth, embedding inherited class status.[29] As a new survey by *The Times* commemorating the 250th anniversary of the American Declaration of Independence revealed, only 38 per cent of US citizens believe the American Dream is alive. In 1976, 70 per cent thought their children would be better off than them but today only 17 per cent do.[30]

'To focus on the production of wealth without regard for its distribution,' Larry Kramer, president of the London School of Economics, has argued with impressive erudition and eloquence, 'is to overlook that real-world markets do not naturally allocate according to morally defensible criteria – not to mention that excessive concentrations of wealth eventually and inevitably provoke social unrest.'[31] His conclusion is that it is not enough merely to compensate those disadvantaged by market outcomes. The task is not just ending the violation of their rights but righting the wrongs that produce injustice in the first place, sometimes requiring a level of intervention that is almost antithetical to the stated tenets of neoliberalism.

Finally, there is growth and economic efficiency itself. Some argue that we must abandon growth altogether, pursuing zero or even negative growth to protect the planet. They often call for large-scale redistribution to create parity from what we already produce. But even then, hard choices would remain. Norway, for example, may be wealthy enough to divide its income equally and still ensure high living standards. Most of the world is not. Equalising global income today would give each person around $22,000 in purchasing power – less than 70 per cent of what a full-time UK worker on the minimum wage earns. That figure falls well short of the $75,000 (at 2010 prices) often cited as the threshold beyond which additional income no longer improves wellbeing.[32] This reality reminds us of the continuing importance of growth to raise the standards of living globally, independent of reforms to boost equality. But we can deliver growth of a different sort, with different goals, practices and outcomes, to that delivered by neoliberalism.

And to bring the story up to date, while the hubris of neoliberalism was most clearly manifested in so many of the decisions leading up to the global financial crisis, the inefficiency of neoliberalism has been plain to see in the years that followed. Since 2007/8, the rate of economic growth in advanced economies has fallen by 0.8 percentage points on average, according to the OECD – almost all of which is explained by a fall in innovation and efficiency (so-called total factor productivity), which fell by 0.7 points in the US in the 2010s compared to the 2000s.

As neoliberalism's promise has been exposed as hollow, but with no clear alternative yet taking its place, the response has been to fall back on allowing public debt to rise to close the gap in living standards. US public debt – which fell from 106 per cent of GDP at the end of the Second World War to 21.6 per cent by 1990 – is now at 120 per cent and forecast to rise to 155 per cent over the next three decades. Even as AI delivers on its promise of restoring innovation-led growth, that will most likely just slow rather than reverse the accumulation of public debt in the US.[33] According to the IMF, eighteen countries are now estimated to have debt at more than 100 per cent of their national incomes, with one of the poorest (Sudan) and one of the richest (Japan) both at over 270 per cent. Total global public sector debt now comes to around $100 trillion.

Already the Bank of International Settlements – often dubbed 'the central bank for central banks' – is sounding the alarm,[34] noting that the new faultlines in the global financial system are sovereign debt and the liabilities of the non-banking sector, much more so than the running up of risky household debts and the overleveraging of banks – capitalism running without capital – that we saw in the 2000s. The dying days of neoliberalism and the upsurge of populism may be a combustible combination, potentially providing the tinder needed for the next global financial crisis, which could look very different in a world where the economic centre has shifted and the challenges multiplied.

Neoliberal globalisation's legacy: multipolarity and the shift of power

Sooner or later, economic power is matched by geopolitical power. As Britain discovered, manufacturing power feeds through into military power; and the influence that rising economies can exercise gives them leverage over others, reshaping diplomatic alliances and enabling them, with new confidence in their capacity to lead, to project soft power. What we are witnessing today is not simply a shift downward in growth rates, but a structural recalibrating of the global economy away from the advanced industrial democracies that dominated the twentieth century and towards a more geographically balanced position where the global economy is composed of countries with very different systems of government. It is this reorientation that is triggering the current backlash of protectionism, polarisation, politicisation and populism – and challenging the very basis of the post-1945 international settlement. This profound change in attitudes and behaviour cannot be blamed on one country alone. It is the result of seismic shifts in the world economy that have affected all countries, albeit in very different ways.

The rise of China to become the second-largest economy in the world, and of Asia more broadly to become the world's largest producer and consumer, represents the core underlying shift in global power. Measured by purchasing power, the combined output of the G7 – Canada, France, Germany, Italy, Japan, the UK and the US – accounted for 45.9 per cent of the world economy in 1900. It rose to 50.9 per cent in 1950 and remained almost as high – 44.9 per cent – as recently as 2000.[35] Today, the G7's share of world output is shrinking rapidly to below 30 per cent in purchasing power terms. China and India together now account for around 23 per cent of world economic activity, and by 2030 are likely to reach 35 per cent, thereby overtaking the G7, with Asia rising further still and China at its centre. Fifty years ago, in 1970, developed economies accounted, as Dani Rodrik has recorded, for 82 per cent of world trade in goods. By 2022, that figure had fallen to 57 per cent. Meanwhile the share of the higher-income developing economies increased from 12 per cent to 33 per cent.[36]

The same pattern can be seen in investment, where the share taken by developed countries fell from four-fifths of global foreign direct investment outflows to around half, with China now accounting for around 20 per cent.[37] These figures show that it is not the growth rates of developed countries – which have recently averaged 1 to 2 per cent per annum – that have transformed the world economy, but the explosive growth of China, India and other developing nations like Indonesia, whose output in 2000 was similar to that of the Netherlands, but is now more than three times larger. On one projection, by the turn of the next century China and India together will represent nearly half (44 per cent) of the world economy, while Europe and the United States combined will account for just one quarter, around 24 per cent: a reversal of the position only a decade ago, when Europe and the US accounted for 36 per cent of world output and China and India, as mentioned above, just 23 per cent.[38]

The eastward shift is also being reflected in patterns of consumption. Asia will soon account for around 40 per cent of all global consumer spending.[39] China's share of global consumption has risen from just 3 per cent in 2000 to a projected 20 per cent by 2030, as the Asian consumer comes to rival the American consumer in the overall calculations of global exporters. With this shift in consumption is coming a redistribution of wealth and income – and, increasingly, of cultural influence and soft power.

China is no longer simply the world's factory. It has become a leading consumer market in its own right and is now the lead trading partner for around sixty countries, roughly equal to the EU (as a single bloc) and double the thirty countries where the United States leads trade relations.[40] While Europe and China have maintained or even increased their mutual reliance across most categories of goods (China's trade with the EU surged by 20 per cent in the first two months of 2026 alone),[41] the relationship between China and the United States has changed markedly since 2018. China's share of US imports has fallen from a peak of 22 per cent in 2017 to 13.4 per cent in 2023,[42] while US investment flows into China have declined by more than 90 per cent.[43] Chinese investment into the United States has also dropped by more than 95 per cent from its peak in 2016, a trend likely to intensify following the imposition of further tariffs and investment restrictions under the second Trump administration.

But a narrow focus on US–China trade obscures the more significant shift underway. The deeper transformation lies in the redirection of Chinese trade from the Global North to the Global South. Over the past decade, the share of Chinese exports going to the Global South has risen from just 8 per cent to around 30 per cent. By 2023, ASEAN countries had overtaken both the United States and the European Union as the single largest destination for Chinese exports.[44] Seven of the ten fastest-growing trade routes in the world now link China to its regional partners. Africa–China trade reached almost £300 billion in 2024, and today fifty-two of Africa's fifty-four countries trade more with China than with the United States – up from just eighteen two decades ago.[45]

This remaking of global trade flows has helped to accelerate a return of protectionism. It is not only the standoff between the United States and China, or the rise of European industrial policy, that marks this shift. We are witnessing a four-way protectionism. Asian countries, and now Mexico, are taking action to shield their domestic economies from a flood of Chinese imports. Mexico has raised tariffs on Chinese textile imports to as much as 35 per cent. Malaysia, Thailand and Vietnam have introduced protective measures for similar industries and have recently banned the presence of Chinese e-commerce platforms. Brazil has raised tariffs on steel in an effort to protect its domestic producers. Amid the emergence of trade blocs and revived national anti-dumping policies, this wave of protectionism has further undermined the authority of the World Trade Organization and other multilateral institutions. The deeper truth beneath all this surface change is that the shift underway is structural. It begins with productivity and manufacturing power; it moves through trade, investment and consumption; it extends to soft power and diplomacy; and it ultimately reshapes the geopolitical architecture. The old balance of power is giving way to a world in which Asia – led by China and joined increasingly by India and the ASEAN economies – is no longer peripheral to the global economy but central to it. As the economic gravity of the world has moved, so too the political gravity will follow.

Following Antonio Gramsci in emphasising the blend of force and consent that constitutes hegemony,[46] the late Joseph Nye defined soft power as 'the ability to get what you want through attraction rather than coercion or payments. It arises from the attractiveness of a country's culture, political ideals, and policies. When our policies are seen as legitimate in the eyes of others, our soft power is enhanced.'[47] Economic power, on this account, does not translate automatically into influence; it does so only when it is accompanied by a set of values, institutions and practices that others find compelling or legitimate.

Despite growing suspicions about Chinese protectionism, the combined impact of Chinese consumer imports and China's expanding presence around the world – through foreign direct investment, tourism and a rapidly growing overseas student population, alongside the internationalisation of national brands such as BYD – has contributed to a steady rise in Chinese cultural influence. On one measure, the 2025 Global Soft Power Index, China surpassed the United Kingdom to become second only to the United States.[48] On a more direct measure of public sentiment, the 2025 Democracy Perception Index found that China now enjoys a more positive reputation than President Trump's United States among 110,000 respondents across 100 countries.[49]

China's growing overall power reflects not only its economic weight but its capacity to present itself as an alternative pole in a more plural world. Chinese leaders have sought to frame their country as a champion of open trade and the United Nations Charter, even as they promote a distinctive model of state-directed capitalism and centralised political control. Through initiatives such as the Global Development Initiative, the Global Security Initiative, the Global Civilization Initiative and most recently the Global Governance Initiative, China has aimed to draw partners into its orbit and to weaken the claim that Western liberalism represents a universal set of values rather than one tradition among many.[50]

The result is not the replacement of one hegemonic order with another, but something more fragmented. The intensifying ideological competition between China and the United States has created a world in which other countries are increasingly empowered to pick and choose from a menu of possible values, institutions and alignments. Instead of a shared global framework, there is growing evidence of selective adaptation, and the adoption of hybrid models or simply pragmatic accommodation by smaller countries, all visible signs of the growing fragmentation of a world in which American leadership is being challenged.

Neoliberalism's other legacy: a new nationalism

If nineteenth-century nationalism began as a reaction to the uneven and inequitable development of industrialisation in Europe, twenty-first-century nationalism came about as a response to the uneven and inequitable development of globalisation across the world. The cruel irony is that the very openness of our hyper-connected world – and the growing feeling among millions that they have lost out – may have contributed to the spread of contemporary nationalism. While globalisation has helped drive global economic convergence, with remarkable impact – reducing poverty especially in China and enabling a rising Asian middle class – it has also been instrumental in destabilising a geopolitical order that could not keep up with the pace of change.

But there is no mechanical relationship between economic hardship and nationalism. The same material conditions can give rise to very different political responses, as was briefly experienced in the rise of left populist movements like Occupy in America and Syriza and Podemos in Europe in the immediate wake of the global financial crisis.

Nor do high rates of growth necessarily defuse the timebomb

of populist nationalism, for if low growth alone explained nationalism's upsurge, we would need to account for the strength of populist movements in the relatively robust economies of the US or Spain as well as the consolidation of authoritarian nationalism in the fastest-growing emerging economies, not least India and China. Some communities have become radicalised even where income and job growth remains strong and inequality low, as in the more rural parts of Sweden.

A purely economistic account of populist nationalism will always prove inadequate. The economy shapes opportunities and imposes constraints, but it does not necessarily determine how people respond. Seen from the perspective of today's rise of neo-nationalist parties, a strong sense of a national consciousness appears to appeal to hearts more than minds. Nationalist politics may gain traction not just because people are more financially insecure, but because they feel forgotten, neglected, ignored, disrespected and even invisible, excluded from a shared story of progress, which leads to a widely held sense of injustice when their expectations are not matched by their experience. The appeal of zero-sum narratives rests on more than material concerns, drawing on cultural grievances and strong feelings about what is just and fair.

Over the last two centuries the appeal of nationalism has undermined the idea that economics determines history and class struggle is its motor. Nationalism may be such a powerful ideology today that there appears to be less likelihood of the West revisiting or recreating the struggles of the twentieth century between capital and labour. But it may also be the case that, at every point where conflicts between nations loom, the more powerful emotional pull is with nationalism, and appeals to international solidarity, as in 1914, fall on deaf ears. It is to the visceral appeal of an aggressive us-versus-them nationalism that we now turn.

5

NATIONALISM: THE DOMINANT IDEOLOGY OF THE AGE?

Inventing the 'other'

On his nomination in 2022 to become president of the World Bank, Ajay Banga visited every continent and addressed audiences across the globe. When asked what was the biggest problem he would face, he said that what worried him most as he woke up each morning was not war, famine or energy crises – nor economic uncertainty or even a worsening climate emergency – but rather 'xenophobic nationalism'.[1] All other problems were solvable, he said, if countries cooperated – but with xenophobic nationalism it was the law of the jungle.

His fears are well founded. In the spring of 2026, as I write, radical – and mainly right-wing – populist nationalist parties lead in opinion polls across every continent from the Americas to Europe – and President Trump has now announced he is prepared to fund a right-wing nationalist coalition.[2] It is a nationalist timebomb and it is detonating now.

It is an aggressive ethno-nationalism that lies behind the Russian invasion of Ukraine, the Israel–Gaza conflict, what many observers have called out as 'genocides' in Sudan, the Democratic Republic of Congo, Myanmar and Ethiopia, and the rising tensions over China's ambitions to control Taiwan. It is also the competition between ethnic nationalisms that lies behind the long-running Kurdish struggle in Turkey, the Caucasian conflicts that have emerged since the dissolution of the Soviet Union and the growing exclusion of Muslims by Hindu leaders in India.

Nationalism's ability to attach itself to, and appear to provide an answer to, a multiplicity of diverse grievances – economic, cultural, demographic and racial – gives it its extraordinary reach, but it usually does so by demonising others. If your economy is doing badly, someone else is always to blame. If jobs are at risk, it is the fault of another country stealing your industries. If your child's school is crumbling and you can't find a home at a price you can afford, it's the fault of incomers. If your pay is stagnant, it's because an immigrant is poised to take your job. This ethnic nationalism thrives by reducing every issue to a single answer centring on the alien, non-national 'other'.

By stigmatising 'others' at home and manufacturing suspicions that lead to blaming 'others' abroad, this us-versus-them rhetoric is playing a huge part in reshaping geopolitics.

The great paradox is that nationalism is resurgent even in a world marked by unprecedented mobility and contact between people, either face to face or remotely, of different ethnicities and religions. While in 1900, an estimated 50 million people lived outside the land of their birth, the figure now exceeds 260 million. In 1991, just 5 million people – 0.1 per cent of the world's population – had access to technologies allowing instantaneous communication across borders; at the latest count 6 billion – nearly three quarters of the world – do. But rather than breaking down barriers, this very openness appears to have intensified the nationalist resurgence, as millions of people become aware of the inequalities that exist within and between countries, and feel that they have been left behind by a globalisation that may have delivered benefits to other people but has not kept its promises and done so for them, even in a hyper-connected world.

The once-hopeful and idealistic vision of an 'open society' in a post-national age is crumbling in the face of inward-looking nationalism. Barely mentioned today is what was commonplace talk fifty years ago: the idea of the 'global village'.[3] This utopian sentiment, which does not fit well with what some have called 'dystopian times', has fallen victim to the seductive power of an aggressive ethno-nationalism that assumes an unbridgeable divide between different groups who will always, it suggests, find it difficult to live alongside each other. By setting people against people, traditional alliances fracture and the world becomes more fragmented, with the result that, as we have seen, our geopolitics is becoming unmoored from its traditional post-1945 anchors, and international cooperation – and the very idea of peaceful co-existence – is struggling to survive. Those yearning for more cross-border engagement will find that today the very idea of the 'global citizen' is, like talk of 'the international community', raised positively in conversations only by elites at international conferences – or, more likely, expressed in negative terms by an emerging global coalition of anti-globalists led by Make America Great Again populists.

The return of nationalism is the death knell for the widely held belief that we were already in a post-nationalist age. Writing in 1990, as the Berlin Wall fell, historians such as Eric Hobsbawm predicted that nationalism would be in headlong retreat by now, disappearing in a more mobile, globally integrated world, relegated to history as no more than a force in the transition from medieval to modern societies. Hobsbawm expected nationalism to be 'no longer a global political programme'.[4] Nations would, he said, be absorbed by the supranational restructuring of the globe.

And yet here we are. But it must be recognised that the new nationalism is far removed from an older idea of the nation. Until four centuries ago, we thought little of nation-states and would instead have recognised tribes, empires, kingdoms, theocracies and dynasties. The nations that replaced that messy patchwork of medieval communities emerged from the dramatic changes in the way we communicate, from the printing press to the railway.[5] The map of the modern world arose in response to the decline of the Holy Roman Empire, the Hapsburg monarchy, the Ottoman and the Austro-Hungarian empires and later the British, German and French empires. In its earlier, more progressive form, nationalism played a vital role in the anti-imperial struggles of the nineteenth and twentieth centuries: it represented a popular mobilisation against cultural discrimination, economic exploitation and political exclusion. Without such anti-colonial nationalism, the world would not have progressed from 45 states in 1945 to the 195 states formally recognised by the United Nations today.

It could be argued that earlier nationalism had more in common with what we today call patriotism – and although the two concepts are often confused or even conflated, there are important distinctions. George Orwell refused to hand over the idea of patriotism to right-wing populist nationalists and permit a patriot to be defined as a xenophobic, anti-immigrant, prejudiced zealot. In a famous essay of 1945, Orwell drew the distinction between patriotism – which is the positive love of your country – and an exclusionary nationalism – which is to see the world in terms of a permanent struggle between irreconcilable adversaries.[6] That first sentiment, love of your country, reflects something fundamental to all of us: our need for an identity which defines us and reflects our desire to belong to a community bigger than ourselves. But the positive patriots can themselves descend into being an exclusionary nationalists if they feel the need to affirm, or see advantage in asserting, their status by defining themself in opposition to others. It is no accident that the Greek word *thymos*, originally defined as the very human desire for recognition, has also become, over time, the word for 'anger', illustrating the populist nationalists' view that your status and even your identity are found in your hostility towards and demonising of 'the other'.[7]

And so, instead of the end of history, the talk now is of the 'return of history'. Old conflicts and ancient tribalist nationalisms rear their ugly heads. And as continents divide and trade blocs resurface, there is talk also of 'the revenge of geography'.[8] Few now talk of a peaceful future as a given; instead, the conversation is once more about being 'ready for war' between nations, with some serious commentators arguing the Third World War has already begun. Or perhaps, as Germany's Chancellor Friedrich Merz put it, 'we are not at war but we are not at peace either'.[9]

The new character of twenty-first-century nationalism

What, then, is 'new' about this twenty-first-century nationalism?

Well, the brazen, unapologetic and aggressive pursuit of self-interest by populist nationalist governments and parties, which can be seen in the prosecution of neo-mercantilist trade policies dedicated to achieving an absolute advantage over rivals as well as in the adoption of industrial policies designed to achieve national self-sufficiency. Whenever you hear the words 'America First', 'China First', 'India First' or 'Russia First', or 'Buy America', 'Made in Europe' or 'China 2025'; when you read about 'onshoring', 'reshoring', 'decoupling' or even 'de-risking', or hear talk of countries as 'swing states', 'fence-sitters' or 'hedgers'; you are being bombarded with language that reflects a new reality: not just an aggressively protectionist world but a more xenophobic one too.

The crudest and most visual form of this xenophobia is the rapid proliferation of physical walls, fences and barriers dividing nation from nation. In 1990 when the Berlin Wall fell the number of border walls dropped to fifteen. Today, after a surge in construction especially from 2015 onward, there are at least seventy.

We see rising numbers of border disputes across the world: when citizens of different nationalities were asked in 2020 if there were parts of neighbouring countries that really belonged to their country, 60 per cent of Greeks, 58 per cent of Turks, 48 per cent of Poles, 46 per cent of Slovakians and 58 per cent of Bulgarians agreed.[10] Even in Germany, 30 per cent of citizens still say that there are parts of neighbouring countries that really belong to them. This suggests that in many parts of the world, peace is held together by a veneer of stability which can disappear at almost any time.

In common with the exclusionary nationalism of the 1920s and 1930s, modern nationalism is marked out by the 'othering' of people considered outside the nation, as discussed above. This is obvious in the anti-immigrant message that came to the fore in campaigns from the mid-2010s onward. In Britain's case, this was heralded by a poster of hordes of bearded men queuing up to enter the UK under the words 'BREAKING POINT', a poster that was later deployed in Hungary with the headline 'STOP'. Such images were then repeated across the world over the next decade, in an attempt to unwind pluralist societies in favour of race-based ideologies.

But as well as being exclusionary, modern nationalism is also marked out by its populism. It offers easy solutions – rejecting and removing the 'other' – and pairs an attack on national outsiders with an attack on established elites within the nation – creating an 'enemy within'. The 2010s saw a rejection of out-of-touch business and political elites as well as a rejection of immigrants. From the Philippines to Poland, from Italy to India, from Brazil to Turkey, the rhetoric has similar features: leaders claiming to speak for 'the real people' label democratic institutions as obstacles to be bypassed or instruments to be captured.

In Russia, but also, intermittently, in eastern European countries, the anti-immigrant, xenophobic nationalism which has been actively cultivated has brought, since the early 2010s, systematic assaults on courts, media pluralism and minority rights. In India, an anti-Muslim Hindu nationalism has been given full expression by Prime Minister Modi and his party and has been accompanied by the centralisation of authority, politicisation of the bureaucracy and widespread discrimination against minorities, which seeks to reshape the political life of a once-secular state along religious and ethnic lines. In the Philippines, Rodrigo Duterte justified extrajudicial killings and attacks on institutions and did so in the name of national restoration. In Brazil, Jair Bolsonaro – now under house arrest for organising a post-election coup – challenged health officials, environmental regulators and the electoral system itself. In Turkey, the aftermath of the 2016 coup attempt allowed President Erdoğan to purge thousands of judges, detain journalists and academics, and turn the media landscape almost entirely pro-government – all in the name of a religious nationalism that appealed mostly to the rural communities. And as we have seen in the United States, Trump's two presidencies have marked a profound break with democratic norms, threatening the independence of the media, the courts and the legislature and in his second presidency headlining his 'Make America Great Again', 'America First' message. What began as a crisis of globalisation has become, to repeat the argument above, a crisis of democracy itself.

Today nationalism and illiberalism go hand in hand. And as the liberal elements of what constituted the global order – 'open trade, open borders, individual rights, democratic institutions and the rule of law' – have increasingly been decoupled from one another, populist nationalists have been able to pick and choose from what Yuval Noah Harari calls 'the liberal buffet'.[11] Many right wing populist leaders have retained only those neoliberal elements of the world order that suit them – promises of low taxes, deregulation and privatisation – and have dispensed with those that relate to pluralism, multiculturalism, civil liberties, open trade and cooperation across borders.

In combining hostility to insiders and outsiders alike, populist nationalism is now almost as self-consciously reactionary as its predecessors in the first half of the twentieth century. It has come to dominate as an ideology because it offers an easy solution to the problems of managing a complex planet: if the world as you see it feels threatening, cordon it off with a form of protectionism that appears to shelter you; if institutions feel unresponsive, delegitimise them by supporting a populist response; if pluralism feels overwhelming, suppress it by taking out the institutions that provide checks and balances; and if globalisation feels like a loss of control, reverse it by retreating into a nativist shell, giving you the illusion of control by narrowing your circle of concern.

After the populists: where is modern nationalism heading?

The blend of illiberal, nationalist and populist positions that have defined the past decade is not set in stone. We are witnessing an ongoing evolution in the thinking of right-wing populists, which may lead to them shedding 'populism' as a new ideological elite develops.

Nationalism has to contend with the fact that nations are not as monolithic as ethnic nationalists imagine them to be. Only a few are as homogeneous as Japan, where approximately 98 per cent of the population share the same ethnic background – although this figure is contested, since Japan's government records nationality rather than ethnicity, and the country has significant indigenous minorities, including the Ainu and Ryukyuan peoples, whose distinct identities are increasingly recognised.

History tells us that national identity shifts with changing borders, the rise and fall of empires, the movement of people – the Germany of 2026 is not the same as that of 1918 when the Treaty of Versailles redrew the map of the world, or 1945 when a new settlement was imposed, and certainly not the same as at the Peace of Westphalia of 1648, the first treaty to recognise the sovereignty of nation-states. To continue with Germany as an example, it was once a loose organisation of separate states within a wider empire – the Holy Roman Empire comprised several hundred near-sovereign territories, including prince-bishoprics, secular principalities, counties and self-governing imperial cities, each with its very different economic specialisations and legal arrangements. Or there is Italy, which only became a unified state in 1861, at which point its people were so divided that one of its leading statesmen, Massimo d'Azeglio, observed: 'We have made Italy; now we must make Italians.'[12]

What we are seeing is concerted attempts by leading American nationalists to build and popularise around the world, especially in Europe, an anti-internationalist ideology around culture, history and bloodlines that attacks what they consider to be a dying liberal world order and tries to create a new, purer idea of nation. At the Munich conferences of 2025 and 2026 the American vice president, JD Vance, and secretary of state, Marco Rubio, argued the case for an ethno-nationalist West and against what they termed 'civilisational decadence' and 'erasure'.

Vance presents his country to the world as a homeland built around family and heritage.[13] But with his claim of America as 'a particular place with a particular people and a particular set of beliefs and way of life',[14] he deliberately overlooks the true uniqueness of America: an inclusive nation comprised of people from everywhere who have made America their home because they expect to be treated equally and enjoy the liberty to choose their way of life in a tolerant society, and whose commitment is to a common set of foundational values rather than to a narrow exclusionary nationalism. And by appearing to support ethno-centric nationalism, he has encouraged what is now called the 'heritage American' movement, which suggests that citizenship or even birth or naturalisation is not enough to be a 'true' American. Vance frames his philosophy through the Catholic theological concept of *ordo amoris* (the order of love), which he says prioritises loyalties in a hierarchy: family above community, and nation above foreigners. Vance invokes this to justify 'America First' policies, arguing that loving one's own – family, fellow citizens – more intensely fulfils both a moral and spiritual duty, as in 1 Timothy 5:8's call to provide for household first. Critics, however – most notable among them the late Pope Francis – have pointed to our obligations to both neighbours and strangers. But Vance appears to view exclusion as natural, at the expense of any obligation to intervene on matters of global concern. In this way he appears to champion a blood-and-soil, us-versus-them nationalism that is qualitatively different from a purely civic patriotism.

For Rubio the unity of the West is not grounded in our shared commitment to democratic accountable government. For him it certainly does not rest on our support for multilateral institutions which the West created but which his Munich speech disparaged. Instead he sees the West defined both by a shared Christian faith and by what at various times he refers to as 'heritage, language and ancestry', but these for him are not rooted in the rational and tolerant values associated with the Enlightenment and the equal dignity of all human beings. Instead he claims that unchecked immigration into Europe is causing the 'erasure' of 'thousands of years of western civilization' and represents 'an urgent threat to the fabric of our societies and the survival of our civilization itself'.[15] By defining the West in this way, Rubio is, like Vance, championing an ethnic nationalism, and he is, as critics have written, 'building a wall around Christian Europe and its diaspora' that leaves on the outside people of other religions and ethnicities, whether they be Muslims, Hindus or Sikhs.[16] His championing of a form of ethnic nationalism takes him far beyond the natural pride of a patriot and towards a suspicion of groups that do not share the genealogy he describes. This stance, as many have argued, is a repudiation of 200 years of American civic patriotism founded on Enlightenment values. 'The liberal notions that underpinned the geopolitical West were fundamentally universal,' Stewart Patrick, a leading US diplomat under George W. Bush, concluded. 'The nationalist ones that raise up the civilizational West are instead fixated on the defense of borders and fear of others.'[17]

This more extreme programme of Western nationalists

undermines post-war claims of a world brought together by universal values. At the same time, we have heard in Russia, China and India – to name but three powers – increasingly vociferous claims to be civilisations in their own right, ascribing to themselves separate and unique cultures, traditions and histories that are at odds with any liberal world order or any idea of 'universal values'. These self-described 'civilisational states'[18] are now asserting their own spheres of influence and pursuing expansionist neo-mercantilist policies. Together, those who had until recently been insurgents in their own country, set against the old world order, are consolidating themselves as the new masters: championing and reasserting religious and cultural ideologies to secure their position as a new elite.

What has been the liberal response to this new, more assertive and more ideological nationalism? From Cicero onwards through to the Enlightenment, liberalism was seen as an ideology inspired by the idea of liberality, which meant generosity of spirit, and was identified with the pursuit of the public good. As Helena Rosenblatt writes of its adherents in her book *The Lost History of Liberalism*, 'Their liberalism had nothing to do with the atomistic individualism we hear of today. They never spoke about rights without stressing duties . . . Most liberals believed that people had rights because they had duties, and most were deeply interested in questions of social justice . . . ad infinitum they warned of the dangers of selfishness. Liberals ceaselessly advocated generosity, moral probity, and civic values.'[19]

But modern secular liberalism – our current alternative to the revivalist nationalism – has struggled to find a deep emotional pull capable of competing with nationalism's tribal, visceral appeal. This is especially true if we present it, as it is so often described today, as little more than a procedure to manage disagreements and conflict, and distinct from the pursuit of any ideal. Ronald Dworkin terms this 'procedural liberalism' and contrasts it with 'substantive liberalism', which would set out what constitutes the good life.[20] Procedural liberalism says that a society need not have an agreed collective goal, but that we should treat each other fairly and with respect. But it could be argued that the reason for liberalism's success in the second half of the twentieth century was, as the writer Timothy Garton Ash has argued, that it counterposed a social-democratic market economy against fascism and communism. In other words, for liberalism to flourish, there can never only be liberalism.[21]

And we have to recognise that the new nationalists have stumbled upon a lesson liberals must quickly learn themselves: a politics viewed as no more than the art of the possible will tend to fail, unable to channel the power and depth of gut emotions that can be brought to the surface by nationalist demagoguery. It suggests that politics must show it can make the desirable possible. It must appeal to the heart as well as the head.

Populist nationalists, who initially defined themselves 'against' foreigners and elites, claim they will achieve a form of cultural restoration. Of course, the real benefits of today's liberalism – inalienable rights to freedom of speech, assembly and worship, and the idea of limited government – should never be understated. Few may live for liberalism, but many live off it and because of it, as Adrian Wooldridge reminds us in his defence of liberalism, *Centrists of the World, Unite!*[22] The core belief of modern liberalism is, as Wooldridge recounts, that the individual must be cherished but that an excessive 'do your own thing' individualism will dissolve society into a collection of selfish atoms. But while some say we need more *from* liberalism, others write that we need more *than* liberalism. If there was a substantive and not just procedural liberalism that became a sufficiently powerful alternative to populist nationalism, it would need, as he says, to place individuals in their broader social context, not to enhance the power of the state nor to weaken individual autonomy, but so that individuals can fulfil themselves by having more control over their lives.

Restoring patriotism against nationalism

I have attributed the success of modern populist nationalists to their ability to create or harness widespread feelings of economic insecurity, cultural pessimism and political exclusion, and to provide a home for those who feel that they have been left out from globalisation's benefits and that their very identities are under assault as traditional sources of pride and dignity have eroded in the wake of deindustrialisation. But there is no reason why modern nationalists should have a monopoly on appealing to people who feel their identities are under threat. The resurgence of exclusionary nationalism is not destiny but choice.

Crucially it is exclusion, not diversity per se, that breeds conflict. Almost 40 per cent of independent countries today have experienced at least one ethno-political rebellion since the Second World War where a minority are being excluded from formal power structures, and research has suggested that an increase in the size of the excluded population by 30 per cent increases the chances of civil war by 25 per cent.[23] To help us understand how this new authoritarian populist nationalism can be defeated, it makes sense to look at those countries which are home to ethnic and religious minorities but which have avoided this fate by ensuring that power is broadly shared, as the basis for a more inclusionary sense of national identity and a civic patriotism. The question is how we can prevent a healthy patriotism tipping into an aggressive political nationalism? The key appears to lie in answering people's anxieties about economic decline – as we have examined in the previous chapter – but also in building a cohesive civic society that is strong enough to transcend ethnic, religious and ideological divides.

Switzerland, for example, is not one ethnic community, nor one religious or linguistic community. Instead, it is made up of many ethnic communities, comprising four national languages and two main religions. Switzerland is approximately

63 per cent German-speaking, and the remaining 37 per cent is divided primarily between people of French and Italian connection. But cross-cultural networks that emerged prior to the establishment of the modern federal Swiss state in 1848 linked each region's religious, linguistic and ethnic communities with one another, and created diverse but inclusive networks composed of men and women in clubs and associations dedicated mostly to business, the arts, culture and science. A national consciousness, a pan-ethnic Swiss identity, emerged out of the interaction of these associational networks and voluntary professional organisations.

These civil society organisations – as diverse as choral societies, reading circles and shooting clubs – developed during the late eighteenth and first half of the nineteenth century. For a time, a strict bifurcation was enforced, with Catholicism illegal in Protestant areas and vice versa. But when the transition to a nation-state occurred after a brief civil war in the late 1840s, these inter-regional, multi-ethnic networks of civil society – whose growth coincided with the rise of literacy and the relatively even spread of industrialisation across each region – underpinned the new constitutional settlement, which guaranteed political representation to every main language grouping. Today, Swiss unity is under pressure too from a populist nationalist bloc but the country's long-run stability has been maintained by ensuring greater autonomy to the cantons, by national referendums to resolve important issues and by cross-cultural representation in the Swiss executive.

Neither industrialisation itself nor even the spread of literacy were decisive, according to the political scientist and historian Andreas Wimmer, whose persuasive account I have relied on, in the creation of the multinational, multicultural state that Switzerland has become.[24] Instead, as he finds, the key to successful integration lies within civic, political, cultural and commercial networks and associations. Of course, this can only happen where there is no discrimination against any ethnic group, large or small, and has only been workable because of a determination to eliminate all forms of discrimination, exclusion and exploitation. But for almost two centuries ethnonationalism never got off the ground because each ethnic group and linguistic community was, from the outset, integrated into the Swiss polity.

'Nothing,' Wimmer writes, 'substitutes for the sense of belonging that emerges when there are people in the seats of government.' He adds, 'Identification with the nation follows from political representation.' And so if we are to follow Wimmer's line of argument, a focus on building support for the symbols of national unity – anthems, flags, pageantry, national days – changes little unless accompanied by cross-cultural civic interaction, extending all the way to the top of politics.

The importance to be attached to broad-based civic and political engagement and representation is emphasised when we draw a contrast between countries that, on the face of it, are not too dissimilar in size and economic structure. In Belgium, there exists no strong unified civic society, with the result that there is nationalist conflict between the Flemish and Walloon populations. As late as the 1990s, only 20 per cent of Belgian citizens stated that they identified as Belgian above their identity as Walloon or Flemish. Belgium is so divided today that it has two types of federated entities: 'communities', focused on cultural policy at the request of the Flemish, and 'regions', focused on economics – each with distinctive arrangements to accommodate their needs.[25]

An examination of the history of Quebec nationalism also confirms the two major themes we have explored here: first, that an us-versus-them nationalism flourishes most when there is substance to claims of economic exploitation or cultural and political exclusion; and second, that an effective set of policies that devolve power to specific cultural regions – in Quebec's case responsibility over taxation and immigration – and the recognition of language and cultural rights at all levels of government can defuse the nationalist timebomb, even if those who seek a wholly autonomous existence will never be fully accommodated. The recommendation most recently posited by Canada's renowned philosopher Charles Taylor, who has proposed various versions of 'interculturalism' to bring the country together, is that we recognise what he calls 'deep diversity' by granting people of different cultures different ways of belonging to the state,[26] which will lead the country to be united not on every front, but on the goals that matter.

Jürgen Habermas argued that different ethnic groups can come together not necessarily, as in the Swiss case, through a history of networking, but rather by an agreement on the shared values that underpin the state, adherence to which can transcend ethnic, religious or other regional or cultural differences.[27] In studying countries where nationalism has failed to take hold, even when there are ethnic, religious and ideological differences, it becomes clear that policies that prevent cultural discrimination, political exclusion and economic exploitation are essential – and that building cross-cultural civic and political connections really does matter. This also gives us a clear insight into the substantive and positive agenda that patriots need to mobilise against the modern nationalists: not serving as apologists for a broken status quo, but offering a bolder agenda for inclusion and devolving power. The fact that this system is now under strain does not negate its past achievements; it simply reminds us that under certain conditions progress is reversible. We should bear in mind that institutions are only as strong as the political will that sustains them. And we should be wary of political decisions made in moments of insecurity, of leaders willing to weaponise grievances for their own partisan ends, of societies unsure how to reconcile openness with cohesion, and of an unwieldy international system that is struggling to adapt to new realities.

The option of cooperation

We should be under no illusions about the real damage nationalism continues to cause the world. According to the UCDP/PRIO Armed Conflict Dataset, which records all 'state based armed conflicts' and includes a measure for secessionist or autonomy wars, such conflicts numbered seventeen in the immediate aftermath of the Second World War, fifteen by 1960, and between thirty-one and thirty-nine from 2000 to 2013. But they have surged in the last decade to a post-Cold War high of sixty-one in 2024.[28]

For all the turbulence of recent years, there was – and still is – nothing inevitable about the rise of authoritarian nationalism. Authoritarian nationalism rose because it was permitted to rise – because democratic forces were weak and often divided on the small issues, while forgetting the importance of the larger issues. It rose because economic grievances about who benefited from globalisation went unaddressed, and it rose because the champions of internationalism assumed their gains were irreversible and thus permanent when they were, in truth, fragile and always at risk. That has left the gate open for wreckers.

Some say that the lesson of history is that there are no lessons from history, but if there is one that might be considered when facing recent events, the democratic breakthroughs and democratic breakdowns of the past decade, it is that the future remains open. There is no iron law that says nationalist strongmen must prevail or that democracies must fall apart. There is no fixed trajectory or immutable law that demands a fractured international system.

History is not something done to people. It is what people do that makes history. But each generation does what they do in conditions they inherit from those who have come before. And so history turns on how people interpret their inheritance and mobilise to shape it, requiring civic engagement and courage, national leadership and vision, international statesmanship and a belief in the power of cooperation. It depends therefore on the choices people make when they are asked about what kind of world they want to live in and pass on to their children. It is clear that we have a fight on our hands against a populist, adversarial and increasingly authoritarian nationalism. To defeat it, we need to draw on moral as well as procedural liberal values, and on the original idea of a liberal society where freedom for each of us is matched by generosity to others as we construct a new world order around a shared mission – of justice, dignity, equality and democracy.

But I have also argued throughout this chapter that central to the demand for change has been a concern – and indeed a rising anger – about social exclusion and economic insecurity. Any response to what is happening now, and to what may happen in the future, must first take into account the anxieties that have arisen from the speed of economic and social change. One conclusion is that we need to cultivate a more inclusive patriotism that avoids the adversarial character of today's populist nationalism.

But if we are to understand how to quell, for good, the relentless rise of identity-based politics that is driving so much of what is going wrong, we need to delve deeper – to better understand both the fears and the aspirations of people across the world. It is to the link between the surface manifestations of nationalism, and the deeper causes that lie beneath them, that we now turn.

6

WHAT THE PUBLIC SAY (1): UNDERSTANDING THE ROOTS OF POPULIST NATIONALISM

I can recall the exact moment I first realised that the self-styled democratic, pro-European Turkish prime minister Recep Tayyip Erdoğan was actually well down the road to becoming an authoritarian populist nationalist. When his Justice and Development Party (AKP) had won the 2002 Turkish elections, he was a democratic reformer seeking European Union membership, supportive of human rights, and a known opponent of radical Islamism. Now, it was September 2008, and first Germany and then France had just rebuffed his approaches for Turkey to become a member of the EU.

That day in 2008 I phoned him to say that in face of what I considered to be wrongheaded French and German opposition, Britain would still be steadfast in supporting his application for European membership, and I would do what I could to help. He asked me to give a supportive interview to a Turkish media outlet, to which I agreed. And within twenty-four hours the editor of the best-selling Turkish newspaper duly arrived at my office. The swiftness of this move made me uneasy; I sensed then that if an editor could be pushed around in this way, Turkey would soon be without a free press.

And that is exactly what happened. Erdoğan's shift from pro-European democrat to populist nationalist proceeded at pace. While claiming to be 'the voice of the real people', he tightened his control over the media and the political system, arresting journalists and opponents alike. In July 2016, when a faction within the military was alleged to be attempting to overthrow his government, he declared a state of emergency under which thousands of soldiers, judges, teachers and civil servants were dismissed. He had already moved from prime minister to the more grandiose office of president, and as I write is seeking to end any term limits on his hold on the presidency.

But what starts a country on the path to a populist nationalist takeover? Over the last decade, millions of words have been committed to ink to explain and define populism, especially in its right-wing nationalist and authoritarian variant. One approach is to focus on the character of its leaders – the likes of Trump, Putin, Modi, Orbán and Xi, as well as Erdoğan. The 'great man' theory of history is the method so often favoured by journalists, and some historians and psychologists. But to overfocus on leaders would be misplaced: we might think of the Trump presidency, for instance, as a cause of our current predicaments when he may just be a symptom, and we may need to dig deeper to find a common thread that explains the appeal of strongman authoritarian politics.

A second approach, drawing on the disciplines of economics, sociology and international relations, focuses on what has gone wrong with the institutions and the policies that may have contributed to the rise of populist nationalist politics. Here, we can point to the failures of economic, migration and other programmes and the subsequent loss of trust in governments, justice systems and media. But such an approach may do too little to take into account all the reasons why people feel their political system does not represent them. And that leads to a third approach: a focus on the influence that ideologies like nationalism have and what may lead people to demand new institutions and organisations in place of the old.

I would argue that all three approaches need to be underpinned by something more basic: how people, in their everyday lives, perceive and experience the world. In the previous two chapters, as we examined first what has been happening to our economies and then why a populist nationalism has come to prominence, we have seen the fundamental importance of what is happening to both economic and civic life. And so in this chapter, I set out what might be an alternative explanation of the rise of populist nationalism, starting with public attitudes and what the general public, and not just their leaders, are saying.

Grounding my argument in public opinion is, in my view, important because we will need not only public support but the active engagement of members of the public if we are to effect change. The question I ask is whether the future of not only civic society, but also democracy and a stable world order, depends far more than we have ever considered on recognising the importance of active citizenship and not just public vigilance but public participation. And so, if this is the case, a focus on where the public stands now and what their hopes are for the future is an essential foundation not just for any civic renewal but also for prosperity generally.

In original polling undertaken for this book, of over 32,000 people in twenty mainly OECD countries,* including South

---

* The polling and analysis was conducted by Focaldata in July and August 2025, using nationally representative samples in the following twenty countries: Argentina, Australia, Austria, Belgium, Brazil, Canada, France, Germany, Italy, Japan, the Netherlands, New Zealand, Poland, Portugal, South Africa, South Korea, Spain, Sweden, the United Kingdom and the United States. Funding was kindly provided by the Schaeffer Institute of Public Policy and the University of Southern California, where I serve as the Ronald L. Steel chair in foreign policy and international affairs. The data was used to empirically test a theory of right-wing populism as an emergent property of everyday interactions rather than a fixed identity. In the survey of respondents, Focaldata created a structural equation model (SEM) to trace how everyday social experiences – including neighbour trust, social diversity in interaction, support networks and financial disappointment – aggregate into broader political worldviews including cultural backlash, institutional trust, inclusivity and economic optimism. These macropolitical constructs were found, in turn, to predict intention to vote for right-wing populist parties. The findings of this study offer a novel theoretical lens and provide clear and actionable points for policymakers to address the root causes of populist nationalism. A detailed technical and public-facing version of this study is expected to be published in 2026.

Africa, Brazil and Argentina, we find a striking similarity in the way that right-wing populism has emerged in nation after nation. In our attempt to measure the relative impact of perceived economic, social and cultural pressures on people's political aptitudes, we have created a statistical model that allows us to test these pressures and the relationships between them.

In the next chapter, I will share the findings of a second set of polls, which covered thirty-four countries and over 36,000 people across the Global North and South, charting public attitudes towards cooperation, multilateralism and the global order. And here we will find evidence that challenges the assumptions that the majority of people are either isolationist or cosmopolitan. In fact, the majority of citizens are open to cooperation between countries, but their support for it must be earned.

This twin focus on the local and the global is critical, as it allows us to tell a single story of a changing world in a narrative that takes us from the local, through the national, to the global. As I asserted in the preface, the view we take of what's happening in the wider world begins at home, and it is our everyday experiences that create the lens through which we interpret both national and global issues. But perhaps surprisingly, our results, which were remarkably consistent across countries, give ground for optimism about the possibilities of a world in which people of different ethnicities, religions and ideologies are prepared to work together to meet objectives they have in common.

It may be that by starting our search for answers and explanations with the sentiments of the mass of people rather than with the policies or the rhetoric of politicians or ideologues, we are able to unlock a far deeper understanding of our world.

Who are the populist nationalist voters?

If a person or a community experiences repeated shocks and setbacks and has no faith that things will improve, their entire worldview shifts – not just their preferences across political parties. When resources are scarce, they move from a worldview where their attitudes are shaped by problems considered to be temporary to a fixed psychological state. They move away from optimistic, long-term, win–win thinking, and towards zero-sum, 'if they win, I lose' attitudes that dominate their daily life and – when asked – who they say they will vote for.

But zero-sum thinking is, paradoxically, not an all-or-nothing game. We asked those we polled a series of questions to test their zero-sum thinking across five different dimensions: trade, income inequality, immigration, multiculturalism and technological change. We found that some people can hold zero-sum views about one dimension of policy – say, immigration – but not another. Only a minority – 24 per cent in Italy, 25 per cent in the UK and Canada, 26 per cent in Germany, and 34 per cent in the US and France – had a consistently zero-sum worldview across all five dimensions, which is the basis of an insular, even isolationist voter bloc and is the natural constituency for far-right populist parties.

On the other end of the spectrum we had those we term the 'civic core' – people who are well connected to a diverse community, doing relatively well economically, and are committed to long-term, win–win policies. If a party could group these voters together, they would form the political base for policies that could trigger the 'virtuous cycle' I set out below of extensive social interaction and economic prosperity reinforcing each other, which may turn the right-wing populist tide. But the civic core is also a minority, and while they outnumber their isolationist counterparts in the UK with 28 per cent of the vote and Germany with 30 per cent, in France (25 per cent) and the US (26 per cent) they do not constitute a majority. Sweden, predictably, comes out top of the league table with 32 per cent in its civic core against 24 per cent of isolationist voters.

This means that the biggest group of voters are those in the middle, but who are open to persuasion and could, under certain circumstances, be brought together with the civic core to form a civic majority for progressive change. Some occupying this ground are left-leaning voters (12 per cent in the UK) who are already happy to engage with those of different cultural backgrounds and immigrants, and feel the country is richer for the diversity that this implies, but they have become left-populist due to economic disappointment. They are natural allies of the civic core, both groups being hostile to the exclusionary politics of the populist right. But building a majority civic coalition in the UK will require also convincing the uncommitted (21 per cent) or those on the traditional centre-right (14 per cent) to lend their support – and stopping those voters tipping into isolationism and nativism.

But how do we build that coalition? To answer that question, we must distinguish between the symptoms, the surface manifestations of popular discontent – the anxieties, the anger and alienation we can identify today – and the underlying causes, and we must find ways to show people that their hopes and ambitions for the future are more resonant than their fears and anxieties about the present.

Surface manifestations

When we looked at members of the public who have been shifting to the right and who are doing so because they feel ignored and forgotten, we found three recurring attitudes in our polling: distrust in institutions, a sense of cultural dislocation, and an increasing intolerance in their view of the world. So, on the surface, the evidence supports the everyday anecdotes we read in the papers or hear on the news. The first of the three sentiments, felt most strongly and voiced most frequently by populist nationalist voters, is that 'you can't trust any politicians' and 'nothing ever really changes', reflecting not only a distrust in the government of the day but a wider loss of confidence in all institutional authority. The second is a strong sense, widely felt by people, that their country is suffering from a form of cultural malaise or decline – that 'things used to be better before', and 'the country isn't what it used to be', 'we're going backwards' or 'we've lost sight of the values that made us great'. And the third common view, held by the most extreme, reflects a rising frustration and loss of patience with the entire political system – particularly the compromises, the inertia and the lack of authenticity that, in their view, define it – manifesting in a loss of tolerance for democratic values and a shift towards the far right. You might hear people in this camp say that 'they [politicians] are all the same' and 'the whole system is broken'.

But the question we need to ask is whether these attitudes reflect more profound underlying causes of dissatisfaction. These sentiments may explain how right-wing populism expresses itself, but not its origins and why it gains support.

Take, first, trust in government. We asked people whether or not they trust a number of institutions – the government of the day, the courts, the media and experts. In the UK we found that just 23 per cent of people trust the government; but even in the most trusting country, Sweden, that figure was only 42 per cent. Alarmingly, then, the majority of people in every country we surveyed do not trust their own governments. Note, however, that while the sentiment cuts right across the voting public, the supporters of populist nationalist parties and policies are far more sceptical than other voters. In the UK, just 10 per cent of this group have trust in the government, only 9 per cent in Germany and 12 per cent in France. Typical views we heard in focus groups were that 'those in power sit in their ivory tower . . . they do not work for the people', 'I feel that politicians are corrupt and there are rules for them and rules for us', or that 'we are ruled by people so out of touch with the common British person, it's actually laughable'.

We found similar results when we asked about trust in the media. One person we spoke to told us, 'I do not trust a word that comes out of their mouths . . . I think we are being gaslit about how bad the situation is', and another that 'the media is biased, big business can influence politicians, the courts are biased'. Only a quarter (26 per cent) of UK adults and less than a third (30 per cent) of US adults trust the news and media.

But this is not to say that there is an across-the-board and uniform lack of trust generally: in every country polled, a majority report trust in 'scientists and experts', reaching highs of 82 per cent and 81 per cent in Portugal and Spain respectively. In the UK, even populist nationalist voters continue to trust scientists and experts at 58 per cent. And for the UK public as a whole, that figure rises to 68 per cent.

But the recent decline in trust may not be because leaders are corrupt, behave badly, have failed to deliver, seem out of touch or ignore the will of the people – these are criticisms levelled against authority from time immemorial – but rather, as Chris Clarke has argued,[1] because we are now less deferential, more knowledgeable of what is going wrong, and society is more polarised. But as important, he suggests, is that in an era of globalisation where national governments have far less control over events, leaders keep making promises they cannot honour. That could explain why popular protest has moved from being anti-incumbent to anti-system, and we can, as a result of the model we are developing, start to quantify just how much this cynicism matters.

Trust in our shared institutions has the potential to be a powerful protective shield against the rise of populism. If we think of voters moving up a 'ladder of trust' – from absolute to partial distrust, to neutrality, to partial and then absolute trust – then for every 'step' a voter moves up this ladder of trust, our initial analysis suggests that their likelihood of voting for a populist nationalist party could fall by around 2–2.5 percentage points. If we move from absolute trust to absolute distrust, then the chances of voting for a populist party could rise significantly, to be 10 points higher, from, say, 20 per cent to 30 per cent. While these kinds of percentages seem relatively small, there have been countless elections over the last decade where it would have made the difference between parties winning and losing. If we could move a voter who is currently identified as deeply distrustful to even minimal or basic confidence in the state, their probability of supporting a populist nationalist party would fall on average by 5 percentage points. The impact would be the largest in Austria, Brazil, France, Germany, Spain, the UK and other countries where right-wing populist parties are currently on the rise.

Moving to the second characteristic attitude of the populist nationalist voter, what Pippa Norris and Ronald Inglehart have described as a 'cultural backlash' against a changing world (also dubbed 'status anxiety' or cultural nostalgia), this is deeply felt in all countries we polled.[2] Expressions of it range, as mentioned above, from 'we've lost sight of the values that made our country great' to 'things were better in the past', and accompany a feeling that, with a restoration of traditional values, the country could be great again.

Such is the anti-government mood across all countries that these views are widely held among non-populist as well as populist voters. In the UK and US, more than 70 per cent agreed with the statement that 'we've lost touch with the values that built this nation' (though it may mean different things to those on the political left and right). Similarly, 70 per cent of all respondents in the UK and 66 per cent in the US agreed that 'our society's traditional moral values are being ignored', a high overall majority, but there is still a big divide between populist nationalist and non-populist voters: the overwhelming majority (88 per cent) of UK populist nationalist voters strongly or somewhat agree on the erosion of traditional moral values, against 65 per cent of non-populists.

In every country we polled, a solid majority of populist

nationalist voters believe that traditional values are being ignored. But there is a discernible distinction between the populist right and their more mainstream counterparts, and that is the role played by immigration, and in particular how it relates to 'traditional values'. In our more detailed interviews, immigration came up repeatedly in the responses we heard. On the one hand it is seen as contributing to the loss of these values: 'The country I know is falling . . . we are being replaced', 'Nobody wants to feel like they are in a foreign country in the place they grew up in'. But by contrast, some more centrist members of the public talk about inclusion as being one of the traditional values they support: 'I hate how much anti-immigrant sentiment is around at the moment. This used to feel like a welcoming country . . . I feel like this country is going backwards', 'I'm quite ashamed . . . I feel like we're being drowned out by . . . racist idiots'. There is a risk that the rise of 'culture wars' leads to sectarian voting, including by religious or ethnic minorities seeking to protect or advance their interests. As the UK's political history shows, efforts from whatever side to inflame racial and inter-religious tensions can easily become the defining divide in politics, with the potential to spark violence.

This cultural backlash, which may sometimes look like a moral contagion, is the driver of a more generalised political discontent, with over 70 per cent in the UK believing 'the political system is broken'. Again, we can use our polling to put a number on how much these feelings contribute to the appeal of right-wing and authoritarian populism. An increasing trust in our institutions protects democracy, and it will come as no surprise that stoking cultural resentment strikes directly at it.

In western Europe, in particular, the backlash is especially intense. If we again think in terms of a five-step ladder from low to high cultural grievance, our early analysis finds that moving two rungs upward – from feeling highly disenfranchised to feeling even minimally included in one's community and represented in one's society – could reduce the probability of support for populist nationalist parties by up to 6 percentage points. This could shift a party from, say, a third (33 per cent) of the vote to only 27 per cent. In other words, the more included people feel in a modern, diverse community, the more likely they are to reject right-wing populist parties.

The third set of attitudes, which marks someone out as a populist nationalist rather than merely a sceptical conservative, is a lack of tolerance. This happens when frustration with traditional institutions – such as government and mainstream media – tips over into rejection of the open and inclusive norms and values that for decades have underpinned our representative democracies. What people say is 'Why can't they just get a grip, instead of always just talking about the problem?' and 'We need someone who can cut through the noise in Washington or Westminster' and 'We need someone from the outside who doesn't mind shaking things up', opening the door for the populist authoritarian leader.

Toleration of different backgrounds, cultures and views is a belief that runs deep in Western democracies, not least because of the hard-fought victories of past centuries. But while there is near-universal support (81 per cent) for the broad principle that 'good solutions come from hearing many different viewpoints', and while there are large majorities who say they value diversity of opinion, enthusiasm for pluralism is far weaker among populist nationalist voters. This is particularly the case when we ask people about their everyday experiences, and specifically about how they interact, whether positively or negatively, with people of different ethnicities or religions in their own neighbourhood. Only 22 per cent of UK populist nationalist voters agree that their neighbourhood is better when people from different backgrounds live there, with double that (45 per cent) disagreeing (in contrast, only 11 per cent of non-populist party supporters disagree). This pattern tends to be repeated across all countries we surveyed: a majority support the principle of being open to different views, but fewer embrace it in their own communities.

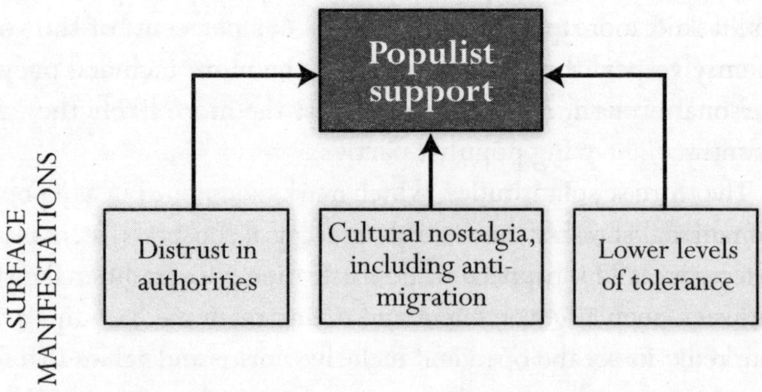

We posed these questions, designed to reflect on trust, culture and tolerance, to allow us to identify the general character of authoritarian populism, as set out in the diagram above. Distrust in authorities is common to populists, but on its own tells us nothing about whether a disaffected citizen will embrace left-wing or right-wing populism. It is cultural nostalgia that gives contemporary populism its right-wing stamp, but populist nationalists are also marked out from traditional centre-right voters by their distrust of the system and their intolerance of others. When all three sentiments – nostalgia, distrust and intolerance – are present, we can clearly identify where a surge in authoritarian populism is most likely to occur.

From surface manifestations to root causes

It is important to understand how the political attitudes we have just outlined emerge from, and can be traced back to, more fundamental changes that have been taking place in the everyday life of individuals and their communities. It is only by getting to the root causes of dissatisfaction that we can move from a *description* of what populist nationalists think to understanding *why* they do so and what can be done about it. So in addition to the questions we asked above about attitudes towards politics and society, we also asked more personal questions about how individuals see themselves and their neighbourhoods, and how they assess their personal economic wellbeing and that of their community and country.

Two forces stand out as driving the upsurge of populist nationalism. The first and most familiar is economic: financial insecurity, and in particular financial disappointment at the gap between people's expectations and their experience, found most markedly in areas of industrial decline. The second was one of our most surprising finds, especially surprising as it is far less recognised but yet all around us: the crumbling, and in some places the collapse, of the clubs, connections and community spirit that comprise civic life. The weakening of these civic bonds leads those affected to believe that there is no one on their side, no one to whom they can turn if things go wrong or who can speak up for them.

Both these economic and social forces shape a person's views in profound and lasting ways, and can account for the form and tone of the populist nationalism we see around us. And we can detect what appears to be a causal chain between these two forces and the surface manifestations already identified. Economic pessimism fuels distrust of government; financial insecurity in a close-knit, closed-off community leads to a cultural backlash; and where there is little contact or interaction between people of different backgrounds, there is less tolerance. In the figure below, I set out a version of the relationships.

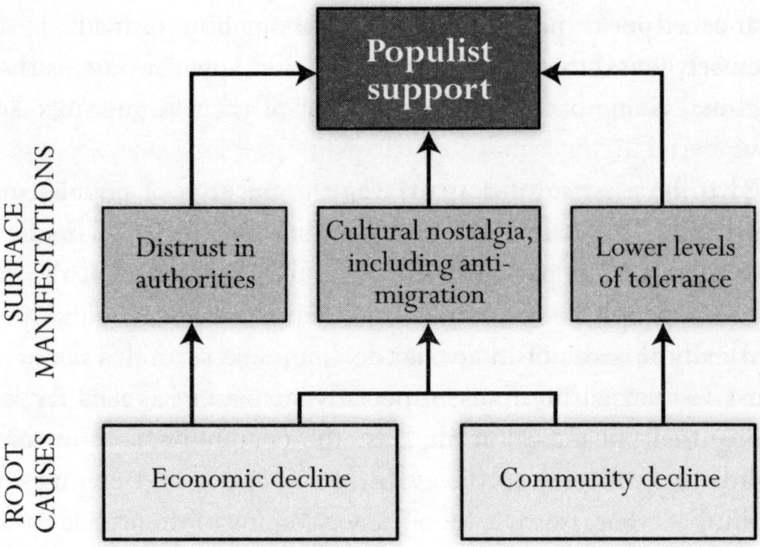

Taking first the underlying economic causes of populist nationalism, this takes two forms: personal financial disappointment and pessimism about the wider state of the economy and jobs market. Starting with the former, we already know that financial strain shapes political views, but so does the frustration of feeling worse off than expected. Half of people in both the UK and the US say that they are financially worse off now than they predicted they would be five years ago. These numbers reflect a global pattern, seen for example in France (52 per cent), Germany (47 per cent), Italy (48 per cent) and South Korea (53 per cent). In a similar vein, majorities in France (44 per cent), Germany (50 per cent), Italy (51 per cent), South Korea (62 per cent), the UK (55 per cent) and the US (61 per cent) feel they are not where they thought they would be at this stage of their lives, with only 21 per cent in the UK and 18 per cent in the US disagreeing. This is not to say that the majority think they are struggling, but that their experience, often irrespective of income, has fallen short of their expectations. Tellingly, it is populist nationalist voters who say they feel they are the most left behind: in the UK and France 60 per cent of them, and 63 per cent in Germany, agree they are not where they expected to be financially. One person told us: 'Going back decades – we expected each generation to have better living conditions than the previous one . . . There used to be a sense of despair when those at the bottom were just left . . . I think we should be ashamed that it got so bad but hopefully we can haul ourselves back to being proud of the way we treat people.'

A critical finding is that it is this gap in expectations that does most to fuel cultural resentment. When people feel they are losing their financial footing, they understandably cling more tightly to the most deeply felt identities and become more inward-looking – what, in the case of national or racial identities, some call a nativism. This, in turn, makes people more open to populist rhetoric, especially that which points the finger of blame at others, thus absolving the individual of any perceived failure on their own part.

It is because financial disappointment looms large that the recent rise in right-wing populism has been concentrated in the so-called 'left-behind' places, where livelihoods have become more precarious and where economic and social status has been eroded – and this is true even if the community has not experienced high levels of immigration. 'Status decline' is not, however, the same as actual economic decline, so loss of status is felt not only by the impoverished but all the way up the income scale in cases where expectations have not been matched by experience.

As we heard in our focus groups, and as is confirmed by our deep dive into the causes of unrest, this loss of status combined with financial disappointment feeds into the anti-immigrant backlash. As one person told us, 'I should be living a comfortable life with the wages my family bring in but instead we are taxed on everything, my food shop has gone up by £200 per month and then every day I drive past an immigrant hotel and see them getting bed and board for free, our health service for free, in new trainers and clothing! It's a kick in the teeth! I've had enough.' Another said, 'I don't feel respected for the hard work I do. I worry about money every day, I'm feeling stressed but the government doesn't have the time to see me, which causes frustration again as the illegal immigrants are getting their appointments, and free at that.' By contrast, another person we spoke to made clear how foundational financial security was to a sense of fairness in society: 'A fair society is one where people don't need to scrape by . . . they can live comfortably on a single salary. I'm not talking about living extravagantly, I just mean an ordinary life . . . Something has gone wrong, I feel. There seems to be a much bigger divide between the rich and poor these days.'

The second of the two economic drivers is a more widespread gloom about the country's general economic direction. We measured the disappointment felt by people at an entire economic system that they feel no longer delivers for them by asking a series of questions that reveal whether people see the country as moving in a positive or negative direction. When UK respondents were asked about 'the condition of the country as a whole', just 23 per cent expressed optimism, with a very clear majority – 56 per cent – expecting things to get worse. A clear majority of people feel the country is moving in the wrong direction, but it is significant that only 10 per cent of populist nationalists feel the country is moving in the right direction compared with 29 per cent of non-populists. Australia, Austria, Brazil, Canada, Germany, Portugal, South Korea and Spain offer similar results.

We asked voters whether more specifically their economy was moving in the right direction, and what they thought were the prospects for employment. In every country we investigated, pessimism about economic prospects over the next five years outweighed optimism. In the UK, more than half the population are pessimistic about the national economy, with over 20 per cent 'very pessimistic'. As you would expect, right-wing populist voters in the UK are even more pessimistic than the rest: only 14 per cent have any economic optimism in the UK, compared to 23 per cent for the wider population. In France and Germany, by comparison, only 16 per cent and 11 per cent respectively of populist nationalist voters have any optimism at all about the national economy in the coming years. Those planning on voting for right-wing populists repeatedly described a crisis in the economy, with several references to a 'state of collapse':

> The country is currently in a state of collapse, we the people are suffering more than ever with higher taxes, inflation, a lack of employment – not to mention a critical immigration emergency.

> I think we are in an era of stagnation, where nothing ever gets better or much worse, it just feels endless with no hope of things improving . . . There is never really anything positive, everything just seems to stay the same, like wages never seem to increase and policies never seem to have any noticeable change.

> Everything is too expensive . . . the social contract feels broken . . . I don't blame younger people if they feel a detachment because they can't get ahead.

When we asked about employment opportunities, we found a similar result: only 24 per cent in the UK are generally optimistic, whereas 40 per cent are pessimistic. For populist nationalist voters, 15 per cent are optimistic compared with 32 per cent of non-populists. This pattern is repeated in Australia, Austria, Brazil, Canada, France, Germany and Spain.

People can, of course, feel a strong sense of personal financial disappointment without feeling that their nation is in decline. Equally, they can have a strong sense of a nation in decline without personally feeling there is a gap between their expectations and experience. Some 59 per cent of the UK public, 64 per cent in the US, 60 per cent in France and 54 per cent in Germany say they worry more about money with each year that passes. In addition, nearly a quarter (23 per cent) of UK respondents and a fifth (18 per cent) in the US are worried about the condition of the country as a whole even though they do not feel financially worse off than they expected to be. This is even more true of the retired. Over a third (37 per cent) of UK and a fifth (21 per cent) of US retirees express worries about national economic decline, while younger people tend to be more optimistic about the future even when more subdued about their own straitened personal finances. In France, we find that as many as 37 per cent of retirees are where they expected to be financially, but they despair about the broader condition of the country.

A total of three quarters of the UK population are therefore either anxious about their own financial position or worried about the economic position of their country, or both, a not inconsiderable majority whose concerns provide fertile ground for populist nationalists. This fear of the future is creating what is becoming a doom loop, whereby economic anxiety about the here and now and economic uncertainty about the next few years translates into even more cultural resentment and the apportioning of blame.

If the first driver of populist nationalism can be identified as economic decline, the second is civic decline. People talk of a 'broken society' as well as a 'broken economy'. As Robert Putnam first warned in the late 1990s, Americans were 'joining less';[3] and a generation on, our evidence suggests this trend has not only accelerated but gone global. Across the twenty countries we polled, around half (45 per cent) of adults report they do not belong to any club, association, religious group or other civic organisation at all, whether that be trade unions, social clubs, professional organisations, political parties or even sports clubs. In Europe, France stands out with 54 per cent reporting they do not participate, while Germany, Italy, Poland and Portugal all sit above 50 per cent non-participation, with the UK at just under half (48 per cent). Japan is an outlier with 68 per cent of respondents not part of a single civic group. Breaking this down, religious participation has fallen to 20 per cent in the US, to 12 per cent in the UK, 11 per cent in Canada and just 5 per cent in France. And just 13 per cent of people report being members of a social club in the UK, 6 per cent a parenting or family group and 4 per cent a civic group.

Even those who do participate do so far less frequently. Today we find only a quarter (24 per cent) of people globally report being involved in a weekly group activity – unlike the church-going communities of the past – while another 16 per cent participate monthly. Put another way, across the world, 60 per cent of the adult population are not participating in any type of social or civic activity on a regular basis. In Japan, this measure of civic decline stands at 80 per cent, while Germany and Italy sit at 67 per cent non-participation, France 65 per cent, the UK 59 per cent and the Netherlands 54 per cent. Outside South Africa, which has a 40 per cent non-participation rate, no country we sampled had a majority of citizens taking part in a civic activity at least once per month.

These structural and civic shifts are also reflected in the way we live our personal lives. Across the developed world, informal social life – the day-to-day contacts we have with friends and family – is in as much decline as formal community activity. To gain the best understanding of how connected people feel, our poll asked respondents how many close friends they have. In the UK, 65 per cent of adults report having three close friends or fewer, and 12 per cent – nearly 8 million adults – say they have no close friends at all. That is a number of people with no friends at all that is equivalent to the entire populations of Scotland and Wales combined. And the UK is not an outlier, but about average in this league table. In Japan, as many as 28 per cent report having no close friends, in Italy 16 per cent, and in the USA and

Germany 14 per cent. The countries which fare best here are the two Latin American countries in our sample: Brazil at 7 per cent and Argentina at 6 per cent. Sweden and New Zealand also perform better than the average – but even there 10 per cent report having no close friends.

Taking both results together, our evidence confirms what seems intuitive: active participation in civic association is the most common way of forming meaningful connections. Across the twenty countries we polled, two thirds (67 per cent) of those with no close friends do not participate in any groups, with only a third (33 per cent) joining something. But of those who report having five friends or more, the pattern is completely reversed: as many as 64 per cent participate compared with the 36 per cent who do not participate.

When British respondents were asked if they feel part of their local community, only 12 per cent said this is 'very true' for them, the same proportion who said it's 'not true at all'; just over a third (37 per cent) of adults feel reasonably strongly that they belong, with a quarter (27 per cent) feeling they don't. The most common answer – 'a little true' – points to connections that, as the low active memberships reveal, are thin and partial. A similar pattern of feeling like an outsider can be detected across most of the countries we polled. Again, the main outlier is Japan, where very close to half of respondents feel they are not in any way part of the community in which they live.

As is to be expected, a clear relationship exists between the extent of civic participation and feelings of belonging. Those who do not participate in groups at all are three times as likely to feel like they don't belong, Participation is, unsurprisingly, heavily correlated with feeling able to turn to people beyond close family in times of need.

The type of participation is also relevant. Contact with people who are different to us is an important determinant of tolerance, and a breakdown in contact between people of different backgrounds is one of the drivers of the right-wing populist surge of the last decade. We found that those who take part in at least one civic group are significantly more likely to have daily or weekly contact with people of different ethnicities (in the UK, 71 per cent versus 53 per cent for non-participants), with people of different religions (70 per cent versus 48 per cent), and with people from different social classes (70 per cent versus 46 per cent), suggesting that the more we actively participate in civic life, the more we interact with people of different backgrounds, ethnicities and religions, and the more tolerant we are towards others across lines of difference. And this held true in all of the countries we surveyed, with the exception of Portugal, which stands out for higher levels of tolerance even among those who are not active in their communities.

Workplaces are of course important arenas for inter-group contact. Those in work in the UK are far more likely to meet daily or weekly with other ethnicities (72 per cent compared to 47 per cent of those not in work) and with people of different religions (69 per cent versus 45 per cent), as well as people from different social classes (67 per cent versus 47 per cent). In France, only 36 per cent of those not in work interact daily or weekly with other ethnicities, while 62 per cent of those in work do; in Germany this stands at 41 per cent for those not in work and 69 per cent for those in work. This suggests that when the decline of civil life is aggravated by the decline of offices, factories or other workplaces where people congregate, the tolerance levels in a community fall to the point at which cohesion can break down, and hostilities arise and rioting breaks out.

Increasing people's level of diversity in their social contacts, from never interacting with others from different ethnicities, religions or classes to doing so even weekly, can reduce populist nationalist voting by up to 3 percentage points. More frequent interaction has an even stronger effect. Where such contact is sporadic, communities can become breeding grounds for distrust and fear. The testimonies we collected illustrate this vividly. One respondent described the loss of 'unconditional support' that once made the community feel like an 'extended family'. For him and others proximity has led not to positive interaction but to mutual suspicion: 'They live in their own little bubbles . . . what I see as community and what they see are two very different things.' As one respondent summed up, 'Community belonging went years ago . . . I can walk down a street where I knew everyone and now I know maybe ten of them. The lack of community is a lonely place to be.'

But people also stressed that their community has the potential to be once again a source of strength, and this is true even of those respondents who are frustrated with the state of the economy and feel let down by the government:

> Yes [I feel I belong] . . . My daughters go to local schools and we are members of local groups and sports clubs . . .[I feel included because] I have lived here most of my life and know lots of people. I help out with [the] Scout group I attended as a boy. I am a member of the local GAA club and the gym.

> I am part of a local nature group and involved in volunteering and bump into people in the village for chats all the time! [. . .] It makes me feel like I am really part of something worthwhile and that my life has meaning . . . Working with people who care makes me feel hopeful still, as does working in the community.

> We are members of local groups and sports clubs . . . It gives my life a purpose.

The secret to building a civic coalition may be appealing to people's existing intuition about the value of belonging, while addressing their legitimate anxieties about a precarious existence and the threats to their economic dignity.

What can we conclude and what have we to emphasise? Francis Fukuyama, who, in an impressive overview, looks at the rise of right-wing populist nationalism (mainly in America), suggests that most explanations do nothing to explain both its unique form and why it has become so prominent now in the 2020s. 'Economic inequality brought on by globalization has been persistent even in periods where populism has been receding,' he tells us. The failings of traditional parties are an accepted fact over a long period of time. He does not deny that 'immigration and the dilution of the power of countries' dominant ethnic groups' can be 'a powerful motivator of populist support', but notes that President Trump was able to assemble a multiracial working-class coalition. 'The problem with seeing cultural issues as central to the rise of populism,' he suggests, 'is that they have been around for quite a while,' even while the records show that 'human behavior has been getting less violent over time'.

Fukuyama also rejects what he sees as surface manifestations and not causes. The 'special talents' of Trump and populists like him will always be a symptom. What we need to explain is our 'susceptibility' to populist demagogues. Education, suburbanisation and what he calls 'sorting' have created new and big social divides but 'this is more likely to be an effect of a deeper sociological change rather than a factor driving that change'. And so Fukuyama focuses on the most contemporary manifestation of populism's success – its ability to exploit the new social media.

But perhaps because of the way he has framed his questions, Fukuyama does not quite capture the cumulative impact by the 2020s of both economic and civic decline and how this underlying belief that we have come to live in a 'broken economy' and 'broken society' is reflected in the surface manifestations we have described, a heightened loss of trust, a growing sense that the country is going backwards, a willingness to blame others for what is going wrong and, perhaps most of all, a strong sense among people that no one is on their side, no one speaks up for them and they have no one to whom they can turn when things go wrong.[4]

Our findings suggest that if people are experiencing economic decline but live in strong communities, then only one of the three 'surface manifestations' – distrust, nostalgia and a lack of tolerance – is likely to be potent: distrust in authority. Similarly, people living in communities that are not strong but nevertheless doing well economically may distrust the government without adopting an exclusionary politics. But a community that is both strong and inclusive is less likely to give in to intolerance and instead may be a bulwark against the fallout from financial disappointments and even national economic decline.

Our results suggest that there is a way to turn a vicious cycle into a virtuous one. The vicious cycle I have described is one where financial insecurity grows among those who feel most exposed, and where communities become less inclusive. As a result people feel less confident about interacting with each other. Trust erodes both locally and nationally, which in turn exacerbates feelings of insecurity and exclusion, reinforcing the negative loop.

But we can convert the vicious cycle into a virtuous one by tackling the financial insecurity of those who feel most exposed through building a more inclusive economy and, at the same time, by creating more inclusive communities where people feel more confident about interacting with each other. By doing both, we can build trust both locally and nationally.

Our research allows us to quantify the threat of right-wing populist nationalism if we do the wrong things, but also the benefits if we do the right things. I have already suggested that, according to our initial results, raising community trust or interaction with people from different backgrounds could cut demand for populist nationalist parties by 3 percentage points. Similarly, when we look at people's financial situation, moving them from the bottom rung to the top rung of financial security on a five-rung ladder could reduce right-populist support by 4 to 5 points. And turning economic pessimism around into economic optimism appears to have the greatest effect of all – by rebuilding trust in the system – with a shift from moderate pessimism to cautious optimism reducing the right-populist vote share by 6 percentage points. If we could return the economy to good growth, tackle financial insecurity, improve intercultural interaction, improve neighbourhoods and increase trust in our institutions, our early results suggest that we could see support for right-wing populists fall by 16 to 20 points.

These changes, while a tall order, would, in my view, bring about a step change in electoral outcomes and by marginalising even if not eliminating support for populist nationalist extremists, would offer the potential to transform our politics. This would, for instance, wipe out a decade of gains made in the UK by the Reform party and its antecedents and at the same time make a decisive difference to the results of forthcoming elections in, for example, France and right across the West, preventing the far right from attaining power. Populist nationalism is thriving in the areas experiencing economic knocks, where people feel left behind and their civic institutions become insular or disappear altogether.

Growth cannot be delivered overnight, but community renewal can come sooner. And with stronger communities, people may stop feeling that economic change is something 'done to' them, which they at best must tolerate. Without strong civic leadership and without building a civic consensus, even the most sophisticated of economic policies may not curb populist appeal. So to summarise our emerging conclusion: if we could bring about economic and civic renewal across the West, then this would not only reverse almost in its entirety the populist nationalist wave of the last decade, and make it difficult if not impossible for such parties to form governments, but offer a new kind of politics full of hope.

I started writing this book to get a better sense of the populist nationalist challenge. What we have discovered through our polling and statistical modelling is that both a strong economy and a strong society are necessary if we want to defeat right-wing populist nationalism, on a national and international stage. Our analysis shows that mainstream politicians would be justified in appealing to populist sentiments that demand action to address broken-down communities and unfair economies, and to mobilise support for policies that can fix the underlying malaise.

But merely tackling the surface symptoms – adopting policies directly aimed at reasserting older cultural values, or simply attacking migrants and posturing as a strongman authoritarian – will not be the right approach and may indeed be counterproductive. Policies focused on restoring trust in government through formal mechanisms like anti-corruption drives and greater transparency in decision-making are necessary but not sufficient. Mainstream politicians will not succeed in turning the populist nationalist tide without tackling the underlying issues of community breakdown and economic stagnation and precarity. But even then, there is only so much that politicians can do on their own. Rebuilding civil society – and creating a participatory democracy – cannot be a top-down exercise. Rather, it relies on each of us to change not just our views on individual policies but our broader ethical and ideological attitudes: not succumbing to zero-sum, conflictual, adversarial ways of understanding the world, but rather promoting a more universal and positive outlook that sees the virtues of a positive-sum, cooperative worldview.

This is not a purely intellectual exercise. It is not simply a case of us building confidence in our institutions, our communities and our economy. We need to become active participants in improving each of these dimensions of our lives. We cannot leave it to others, but each take some responsibility ourselves.

7

WHAT THE PUBLIC SAY (2): LINKING THE LOCAL TO THE GLOBAL

Nearly two hundred and fifty years ago, on 6 September 1789, Thomas Jefferson, the author of the first draft of the American Declaration of Independence, wrote to his fellow founder James Madison, cautioning against clinging to the old when it was time for the new to take its place. He warned against holding fast to the ideas of past leaders when new leaders had more to say. 'The principle that the earth belongs to the living, and not to the dead', Jefferson argued, should mean that 'every constitution, every law' ought to be reconsidered by each generation afresh.[1]

Jefferson believed that orders and constitutions were not set in stone, nor God-given. Yet when a change was made to his original wording of the Declaration of Independence – from 'these truths are sacred and undeniable' to 'these truths are self-evident' – thanks largely to founders John Adams and Benjamin Franklin, themselves influenced by Scottish Enlightenment philosophers, Jefferson privately lamented it as a 'mutilation'.

Nevertheless, the founding fathers were all agreed on something we appear to have forgotten: that constitutions must be rooted in values, and not just interests. Hence the commitment, written by Jefferson and agreed to by all signatories, that the new country had to stand for the rights of all – even if at that time this meant only white, propertied men – to 'life, liberty and the pursuit of happiness', where that last word was understood to mean wellbeing rather than anything approaching hedonism.

Jefferson's values are as relevant today as they were then. As the world changes and one generation gives way to the next, we must reinterpret these enduring values for new times, and in turn reform and revitalise the institutions we have created to govern ourselves. Nowhere is this more important than in the global cooperation that is required to meet shared challenges. In the previous chapter I showed that there has been a retreat in civic engagement at home. This has been accompanied by a retreat from global cooperation and engagement abroad. Nationalism at home is being matched by a lack of internationalism abroad. Division within countries goes hand in hand with division between countries.

It is easy to despair. But the second poll we undertook – drawing on global public opinion in both North and South* – shows that while there has been a significant increase in support for populist nationalist parties, their leaders are not necessarily representative of a wider public opinion, which is far more open to cooperation across borders – much as they would like us to believe this is not the case. Indeed, as this set of surveys reveals, there is a gulf between public opinion across the world and the actions of some of our leaders.

People are not, in the main, so introspective or insular that they cannot see beyond their own neighbourhood. Clear

---

* Based on research commissioned by the Rockefeller Foundation. Focaldata surveyed a nationally representative sample of 36,405 adults across thirty-four countries between 8 August and 10 September 2025. The countries comprised Argentina, Australia, Brazil, Canada, Chile, China, Colombia, France, Germany, Ghana, Hungary, India, Indonesia, Italy, Japan, Kenya, Mexico, Morocco, Nigeria, New Zealand, Norway, the Philippines, Poland, Romania, Saudi Arabia, Singapore, South Africa, South Korea, Spain, Sweden, Turkey, the United Kingdom, the United States and Uruguay. The survey considered how connected individuals felt to world events and aimed to establish baseline attitudes towards international cooperation, i.e., cooperation between countries. The findings of this research can be found at https://www.rockefellerfoundation.org/reports/demanding-results-global-views-on-international-cooperation/

majorities of global opinion say they have been affected by global events: 71 per cent by the pandemic, 58 per cent by climate change (rising to 61 per cent among younger respondents) and 55 per cent by disruptions to food supplies. Given the intensity of coverage of the tariff wars, it is not surprising that 65 per cent – nearly two out of every three people – recognise that they are directly affected by what happens to global trade. More than half the adult population say they are affected by what happens in countries other than their own, and as a result they want cooperation. Fully 93 per cent of respondents worldwide say international cooperation is important for food and water security, 92 per cent for protecting human rights, 92 per cent for conflict prevention and peacekeeping, 91 per cent for global health and 90 per cent for poverty reduction. Only a small rump – around 6 per cent of the global population, and no more than 7 per cent in any region – believe international cooperation is 'generally a waste of time and resources'.

There is overwhelming agreement that no single country can tackle the greatest challenges of our age on its own – whether climate change, pandemics, financial instability or food insecurity. People are not only aware of what is happening outside their own country but, by overwhelming majorities, they want nations to work together and indeed demand that they do so. This broad consensus gives leaders a mandate for collective action, if they are willing to seize it.

What type of global cooperation do people want to see?

When asked to choose which five global issues are most important, people are most in favour of cooperation that will deliver on their most fundamental needs, at the top of which are those ensuring mutual prosperity, peace and stability: security in the provision of food and water (chosen by 40 per cent) and relief from poverty and inequality (chosen by 37 per cent), with these areas commanding majority support in sub-Saharan Africa. A significant minority also favour cooperation to ensure the protection of human rights (36 per cent) and to deliver jobs and employment (36 per cent). Support for cooperation on public health and climate is higher in Asia, and support for human rights is especially strong in eastern Europe, Asia and sub-Saharan Africa, where such rights are under threat or only recently won.

At a time when populist nationalism is so prominent, what is perhaps surprising is that cooperation to meet pressing global challenges enjoys majority support, even if it means compromising on national interests. Fifty-five per cent of people across the 34 countries surveyed agree with this proposition. If forced to choose, 46 per cent say their country should follow its own interests and entirely disregard those of other countries, with an almost identical number (44 per cent) saying their country should account for other countries' interests and be willing to compromise when it comes to cooperating (10 per cent say they don't know). And these figures would be even larger if there were not such large majorities favouring national self-interest in war-torn regions: 56 per cent in the Middle East and north Africa, and 54 per cent in sub-Saharan Africa, say countries must look out for their own national interest only. Despite what the news may tell us, only 34 per cent of US adults promote a purely self-interested view of international cooperation.

In North America and western and northern Europe, most people lean more clearly towards multilateralism even when it means some compromise of national interests. This is a direct refutation of the slogans of 'America First', 'China First', 'India First', 'Britain First' or 'Russia First'.

The zero-sum worldview that nations are in a permanent tug of war with each other, from which there can be only one winner, is held by hardline nationalist lobbies. And they are a clear minority. Globally, just 21 per cent think other countries' growth makes their own country poorer. While in the Middle East and north Africa the zero-sum cohort rises to around 30 per cent, in sub-Saharan Africa – where, although inequality remains high, living standards have nonetheless been improving – just one in five (19 per cent) endorse zero-sum thinking. And in east and south Asia, this shrinks to only one in ten (11 per cent).

This is a hopeful sign: if most citizens believe in sharing, they are more open to multilateral solutions and to working with global institutions. But if people tend to the view that a rising tide can lift all boats, they will want a fairer distribution of the benefits. Cooperation that serves the interests of elites is of little interest to the general public. Leaders must demonstrate that global cooperation delivers for ordinary people – jobs, stability, health, food security. People are 14 percentage points more likely to back efforts to improve the effectiveness of foreign aid than efforts simply to minimise its cost, reinforcing the emphasis on delivery over symbolism.

People want quick, concrete progress – stabilising food prices, accelerating climate action, preventing conflicts and humanitarian crises. Citizens will back global efforts only if they see tangible improvements – in their communities as well as abroad. Without visible 'wins' that make everyday life safer or more prosperous, today's cautious support for multilateralism could collapse with alarming speed into disillusionment.

A coalition for global cooperation

There is hope. Our findings from the international cooperation poll suggest it is possible to build a global majority for cooperation abroad. Our analysis identifies five distinct groups of public opinion that are roughly equal in size.

The smallest of the five, representing around 16 per cent of the global population, is the group of hardened anti-internationalists who might side with President Trump and certainly with

President Putin. They have the zero-sum mindset: if they or their country do well, it has to be at the expense of others doing badly, and at their most extreme they feel that coexistence between ethnic and religious groups is impossible.

But there is another sizeable minority at the opposite pole: the 21 per cent whom we might call committed internationalists, who see cooperation across borders through open trade as a positive-sum, win–win proposition, or who are what the philosopher and writer Kwame Anthony Appiah calls 'rooted cosmopolitans' – people who feel moral obligations to others without becoming detached from their local communities.[2]

The vast majority of the global public are somewhere in between: neither narrow, inward-looking nationalists nor all-in cosmopolitans. They are patriotic but do not necessarily see the world as locked in a struggle between 'us' and 'them'. They are prepared to accept obligations beyond their garden gate or city wall, but only under certain conditions, three variants of which we can identify.

Twenty-one per cent will back humanitarian action to relieve suffering and are prepared to act out of altruism, supporting emergency help for disaster zones. We might call them 'good-cause multilateralists', who feel the pain of others and believe in something bigger than themselves. A second group, comprising 22 per cent, whom we might term 'pragmatic multilateralists', want to know that any taxes paid out for international development are spent well – in other words, their support depends upon the cost-effective delivery of results. And there is a third group, 21 per cent, 'self-interested multilateralists', who will endorse cooperation if they can see that it benefits them and their communities, whether through guaranteeing supplies as basic as food on the table or as fundamental as peace and security at home.

So what will it take to establish a decisive majority in favour of sustained international cooperation? One that could command the support of both those motivated by self-interest and those guided by altruism? To build majority support for international aid, you would have to persuade pragmatic multilateralists to join good-cause multilateralists and rooted cosmopolitans by demonstrating value for money. If you wanted to build an active coalition that promotes collective security, you would need to persuade self-interested multilateralists to join rooted cosmopolitans and good-cause multilateralists on the grounds that a threat to one is a threat to all, and that burden-sharing guarantees their safety. For example, statistically you could build 80 per cent support for pandemic prevention by showing all groups except zero-sum nationalists that when infectious diseases threaten, no one is safe until everyone is safe – and in particular, for self-interested multilateralists, that there is no point in opposing pragmatism if it means losing your life.

The question is not whether people support cooperation in principle – we have shown that majorities for it can be built – but how it can be advanced and whether the global institutions that would have to be mobilised are fit for purpose. The public have a clear view on how this can be achieved: they want leaders to put forward and deliver a vision of the world that can be shared. We commissioned a parallel survey focused on G20 countries, where we asked people what was most essential to maximising effective cooperation; their response was for world leaders to agree a 'long-term vision for peace and progress'. Effective leadership is seen as the most significant determinant of successful global cooperation. Of second but equal importance is that countries keep their commitments and are held accountable, and that fair and balanced international rules are followed. Far from demanding that their leaders retreat behind national borders, people appear to be crying out for an ambitious and coordinated leadership capable of making cooperation work.

There are also grounds for believing that a new set of initiatives to speed up and expand international cooperation could enjoy popular support. It is true that trust in the global financial institutions is lower than in other multilateral bodies: only 44 per cent trust the IMF and only 46 per cent have faith in the World Bank, their lower ratings likely reflecting the wounds left by the global financial crisis and by the rise of populist nationalism in the United Kingdom, the rest of Europe and the United States. But, contrary to the most cynical critics of multilateralism and despite propaganda campaigns against them, trust in the World Health Organization stands at 60 per cent globally (rising to over 80 per cent in sub-Saharan Africa and over 70 per cent in east, south and south-east Asia), and trust in the United Nations at 58 per cent – figures that are higher than for many national governments. And this is for unreformed institutions yet to be brought up to date. When we look across public opinion as a whole, we can see how support for international cooperation, and for the global institutions that further it, already exists and can be built upon.

Connecting the local and the global

What, then, do the surveys of public opinion on both domestic and global concerns, when taken together, tell us? People judge political projects – nationally or globally – by whether or not they deliver the goods. And moreover, we can see what those 'goods' are: a decent job, secure living standards, fundamental rights, a cohesive community and progress to cut poverty and raise opportunity. A fragile global consensus is telling leaders: act now, deliver now.

This openness to cooperate across borders shows how we can turn back the xenophobic tide both at home and abroad. We should not be misled by the rhetoric of populist nationalists into thinking that reducing immigration and ignoring the underlying frustrations will itself renew centrist politics. Today's negative, inward-looking, and often aggressive and authoritarian nationalism that demonises immigrants, foreigners and 'others' can be defeated by championing a positive, outward-looking and inclusive patriotism that responds to people's desire to belong and resonates with their more profound concerns. To confront the latter, we must address head-on the breakdown of community and the economic insecurity that millions experience.

Our findings suggest that we are caught in a vicious cycle. Economic stagnation and the legacy of neoliberalism in our communities have forced at least a growing minority of people into zero-sum thinking. As political parties have risen up over the last decade and a new generation of authoritarian populists has emerged to speak on their behalf, they have found their interests best served by stoking resentment, identifying and exploiting new divisions, and doing nothing to help the economic lot of the ordinary voter – provided they can continue to find other 'elites' to attack. Before long, they bring down the international bodies that have historically helped reduce tensions between nations, raise economic growth and provide the global public goods we all depend on. And then the failure of those international institutions to deliver better prospects for peace and global growth – and the higher living standards that flow from them – adds to the insecurities that people experience.

So in recent years, populist nationalists have upended and then rewritten the script of international politics. Developments in domestic politics have 'infected' geopolitics and vice versa. Instability at home has led to instability abroad and instability abroad has then intensified insecurity at home.

How do we break out of this cycle? As the last two chapters have shown us, the route out of this impasse starts in local communities. Citizens learn habits of cooperation through their daily experiences – meeting people of different ethnicities, respecting cultural differences, negotiating common spaces and balancing their individual interests with the collective good. These local everyday practices shape how people imagine relations beyond their borders, and if that is the case we are more likely to view international engagement not as a loss of sovereignty but as an extension of the way we interact at home. At its core, cooperation between nations is an extension of cooperation between people.

Yet the danger we face now is 'throwing out the baby with the bathwater' – blaming our present state of affairs not on the global elites who have failed us but on the very idea of cooperation itself. So we need a plan for a reset – for a breakthrough in global cooperation. And we need a programme for breaking through into a virtuous circle, at home and abroad. How we might achieve this forms the second section of this book.

PART TWO

Breakthrough: Values-led pragmatism and global order

8

INTERDEPENDENCE: UNDERSTANDING OUR CONNECTED WORLD

In a striking piece of imagery that captivated the Expo 92 trade exhibition in Seville, Hungary portrayed itself as a tree. Having recently broken free from communism and seeking to join the European Union, its intention was to present itself not as a new nation but a very old, well-established one. It sought to reassert itself not at the periphery of Europe but at its very centre, in a position to influence all around it. The tree in the Hungarian national pavilion stood on a glass floor, its roots visible and extending outward to the east and to the west, to the north and the south, as if right in the middle of the European continent.

Perhaps today's Hungary, which from 2010 until 2026 was all but isolated within the European Union under Prime Minister Orbán's leadership, but which in April 2026 elected a new anti-Orbán government, is now recalling that image of itself. A tree that stands apart in an open field is vulnerable to every storm. Roots left unnourished wither: 'As long as the roots are not severed, all is well,' the character of Chauncey Gardiner observes in *Being There*, 'and all will be well in the garden.'[1] Severed connections can undermine and eventually destroy the whole tree. Connection sustains life, and it is important, as our last chapter showed, to remember that people do appreciate that interdependence is a necessary and vital element of the modern world.

In an age where personal autonomy has often been valued above and at the expense of social obligation, it is too easy to forget that the interdependence illustrated in the Hungarian exhibition is a basic condition of human existence. As James Stockinger put it:

> It is the hands of others
> Who grow the food we eat, sew the clothes we wear and build the houses we inhabit.
> It is the hands of others who care for us when we are sick and lift us up when we fall.
> It is the hands of others who bring us into this world and who lower us into the grave.[2]

So while we are right to prize our personal independence, each of us has to balance this with our interdependence and our dependence on others. This is now as true for relations between societies as those within them. We only need to name the major incidents and trends of recent years to recognise the impact of the global on our everyday lives: Covid, the climate crisis, the global financial crisis, mass migration, repeated energy shocks and the permanent threat from nuclear weapons.

Interdependence is a fact of our social and cultural existence, especially now that global communications connect people instantaneously across borders. Even more fundamentally, for just about everything from food supplies to security, we rely on others. Protectionism is on the rise, but we may not have yet reached the limits of economic integration. Digital trade continues to expand, creating new forms of interdependence, and anyone reckoning with the breakup of the world order cannot afford to ignore the benefits that flow from increased trade.[3]* The fact is

---

* Countries that remain open to trade still have a lot to gain. Most economies trade between 20 per cent and 70 per cent of their GDP, and imagine the latter to be a limit. Compare this to Singapore, which trades between 300 per cent and 400 per cent of its GDP, and has leveraged this to create a profound economic transformation.

that this interdependence is a global given – but it can be both a global good and a global bad.

The myth of the 'island' nation

In 1945, when leaders sat down to devise the post-war world order and shape the international institutions that would define it, most still thought of the global economy as a diffuse collection of relatively self-contained nation-states, like islands which managed their internal affairs without ever needing to admit how much they relied on others. That is why the main focus of the then newly created International Monetary Fund was not to manage the risks that come from global economic integration, but to bail out individual countries that had borrowed too much and couldn't balance their books.

Of course even then, the image of nations as economic islands – or, in a more extreme form, fortresses – was more myth than reality. But today such an image is as obsolete as horse-drawn travel. This changed reality is a reflection of not only how much trade between countries has grown (fivefold since 1945[4]), but also how much we depend on global flows of finance (up tenfold since 1970[5]), transnational companies and global financial institutions – as well as our capacity to communicate instantly and globally with each other. Modern economies don't operate in isolation. They are like nodes in a dense web of global networks, linked by the flow of people, capital, goods, services, data and communications.

Even island states such as the UK, or those with dominant economies, like America and China, can never isolate themselves from the fallout from infectious diseases, financial contagion, international migration, pollution and nuclear risk. Indeed, in the event of a pandemic, no one is truly safe until everyone is safe, as the avoidable loss of life in recent years has made painfully clear. Failure to prevent the spread of Covid was compounded by an inability to extend vaccination at scale to the poorest countries, constituting a moral failure that was also a strategic one in which the weakest health system became a threat to the strongest. What have come to be known as 'global public goods' – a concept almost unknown in 1945, but now including a pandemic-resilient world, a stable climate, open sea lanes and financial stability – have become not just marginal but central determinants of security and survival.

In recent years, the world has moved from being merely interlinked and interconnected to being interdependent, and from being 'flat' – the insight of the writer Thomas Friedman – to, as Dov Seidman has suggested, being 'fused'. As recent events have demonstrated, no country acting alone, or even bilaterally, can guarantee its own stability in the domains outlined above, no matter how wealthy or militarily dominant. The thesis of this chapter is that we are so inextricably linked together that we can no longer promise our citizens the security they desire, let alone the prosperity we should aspire to, unless we find new ways to co-exist and cooperate. This 'fused' world could, of course, attempt to live by interdependence without cooperation. However, cooperation is so essential to our modern world that what Professor Danny Quah refers to as 'inadvertent cooperation' has become a feature of the system, a form of cross-border collaboration that happens without countries consciously planning or even intending to cooperate.[6] While international cooperation is commonly understood to be a deliberate decision, expressed in treaties, alliances and contracts, and delivered through shared institutions, Quah argues that even when individuals act in their own self-interest, the gains from interaction automatically make everyone better off. Globalisation has led to a twenty-first century version of Adam Smith's 'invisible hand'. States benefit from working together even when they do so unintentionally or for selfish reasons. When countries act to secure their own domestic prosperity, the resulting growth and stability spreads globally. States act independently, yet collective outcomes result. Quah also argues that despite the growth of geopolitical divides, functional cooperation continues. This inadvertent cooperation challenges the idea that every state, whether a monarchy, democracy or autocracy, must have total undiluted sovereignty that is never pooled or shared but is, in the words of Don Herzog, in his book *Sovereignty RIP*, 'unlimited, undivided and unaccountable to any external authority'.[7]

Even when subject to the realities of economic integration such as a reliance on externally owned technologies and vulnerability to the weaponisation of that interdependence, the leaders of most states continue to talk as if you either have sovereignty or you do not. As if it can never be shared or diluted by treaties as happens with, for example, membership of NATO. This leads to a resistance to compromise which is perhaps most acute in the rejection of the many commonsense proposals for shared defence. Even if we can solve the problems of who does what – for example, who pulls the trigger, and who arbitrates if disputes emerge – we run up against the idea that a nation cannot be sovereign unless it acts on its own. And yet the logic of cooperation in an interconnected world makes it increasingly difficult to exercise sovereignty wholly independently of others.

The weaponisation of interdependence

While interdependence can lead to cooperation, it can also be weaponised in uncooperative ways, leading ultimately to economic warfare. Global interdependence is, as Finland's president, Alexander Stubb, puts it, 'a double-edged sword'.[8] Economic integration not only brings prosperity, it can also dramatically increase vulnerability at the hands of those who wish to deliberately exploit our dense interconnectedness – and their control over vital supplies of goods and services.

Canadian prime minister Mark Carney highlighted this issue at Davos 2026. Not only have recent crises laid bare how global integration is itself a source of risk, he argued, 'but more recently, great powers have begun using economic integration as weapons, tariffs as leverage, financial infrastructure as coercion, supply chains as vulnerabilities to be exploited'.[9] Indeed, a few powerful countries can devise binding and one-sided defence agreements – on maintenance, repairs, replacement parts and even the training of operatives – that make their foreign purchasers continuously reliant on the seller. Sovereignty amounts to little if someone can effectively veto your defence policies by threatening to stop resupplying your armies. When, as Venezuela and Iran discovered in early 2026, states are faced with stronger adversaries, all the legal powers in the world are mere scraps of paper. And with nine nuclear weapon states, and just two – soon to be three – nuclear superpowers, the rest of the world will always be vulnerable to nuclear blackmail.

But if nuclear power is limited when the aggressor knows that a major nuclear weapons attack risks its own total annihilation, there are fewer limits to a country's ability to exploit others using economic power, through sanctions – a leading Russian university has just introduced a degree in sanctions evasion – export controls, investment screening and technological decoupling. This is made easier when around two-thirds of global trade in manufactured goods is not in finished goods but in intermediate components, many of which are manufactured by just one supplier, which creates elevated risks if there is a disruption of supply chains.

Indeed, the world is becoming increasingly vulnerable to this kind of disruption as tariffs, import and export bans and sanctions multiply, often driven by the richest economies.[10] In this way, economic policy is becoming a political lever which changes the character of power itself.

For decades, as the only superpower, the United States held this leverage over others. But it was an age when, in the richest countries, economics dominated political decision-making and not the other way round. And so, with what Professor Ikenberry called 'strategic restraint'[11] and through the global economic institutions it created – which bound both itself and others into a web of rules and obligations – the most powerful of all states kept the flow of trade and finance open, largely resisting the temptation to do otherwise. It was a policy choice. America could be seen, most of the time, as the benign hegemon pursuing, in the words of the theorist Arnold Wolfers, 'milieu goals' in order to shape the international environment through a more subtle and less coercive exercise of power.[12] While, as the international relations scholar Stephen Walt notes, the United States was not averse to using the power at its disposal to compel, co-opt or even overthrow other governments, its actions were directed at acknowledged adversaries and not towards its partners with whom it normally traded freely.[13]

Now, however, in an era where there are multiple sources of decision-making power, the weaponisation of trade and financial advantage is becoming an increasingly acceptable tool. Any large state with a near-monopoly in one area can exercise power over adversaries and allies alike – not just to protect its own economy but, often, to hurt others. It might seek to bring competitors into line, whether by severing critical supply lines, restricting access to key international markets, denying liquidity or refusing access to globally coordinated payment systems. Many of these points of leverage are now in daily use: from the banning of exports of semiconductor equipment and critical software (as now practised by the US, Japan and the Netherlands against China, and by China in response); to the tightening of rules on cross-border data flows (with America and China both suspending transfers).[14]*

Competing powers can now seek to assert and impose their own technologies, financial systems and even their own rules

* Other examples include the boycotting of another country's imports (as China did to South Korea after it deployed a US-backed missile defence system, and as is now happening regularly between China and the West); the restriction or interruption of the open supply of minerals to adversaries (as with Iran and Russia); the severing of vital gas and oil supplies (as Russia did over Ukraine); the sudden closure of crucial borders or land routes (little reported is the suspension of the Attari–Wagah land crossing between India and Pakistan); and the manipulation of access to critical metallic resources (as with Chinese rare earths to the West).

and values. In a June 2026 speech, US Treasury Secretary Scott Bessent elevated weaponisation into a new form of what he called American 'economic statecraft' – 'the disciplined use of power to safeguard our national interests' – which breaks with past US commitments to free trade and laissez-faire. He would entrench American leadership by building 'national capacity to master all supplies' through US-imposed protocols and, where necessary, sanctions.[15]

One of the consequences of the transition to renewable energies, and the shift from dependence on minerals to a new dependence on metals, is that metal producers now also have the power to cut off supply for strategic advantage. By 2050, lithium demand could increase fivefold, graphite and nickel demand may double, cobalt and rare-earth demand could climb by more than 50 per cent, and copper demand could grow by nearly a third. China is dominant in this field, with an average market share of 70 per cent in nineteen of the twenty minerals the International Energy Agency deems to be strategic. But other countries have leverage too: Indonesia produces nearly 60 per cent of the world's nickel and the Democratic Republic of Congo – or those who control it – produces about 70 per cent of the world's cobalt.[16]

There are also non-physical barriers – what are sometimes called 'paper choke points' – such as the withdrawal of insurance cover and sanctions that will disrupt trade. And, as Jonathan Haskel and Stian Westlake have argued, behind the intangible AI systems often lie tangible materials.[17] Geopolitical disputes can quickly escalate, making normally efficient and cost-effective routes impassable or prohibitively expensive, and in spring 2026, the world saw how once-reliable trade routes can be deliberately cut off. And while 6 per cent of maritime trade is affected, at the time of writing, by the closure of what is currently the best-known choke point, the Strait of Hormuz, the closure of the Taiwan Strait would affect 13 per cent, the Suez Canal 16 per cent and the South China Sea 24 per cent – and within a very worst-case scenario according to *The Economist*, if straits from Malacca (it carries 80 per cent of China's energy imports) to Australia were all closed, 26 per cent of maritime traffic would be affected.[18] So ports, major waterways and key logistics hubs have become such critical bottlenecks through which enormous volumes of goods, energy and food move daily that disruption in just one can have global repercussions.

This form of economic warfare is becoming more common. The 2021 Suez Canal blockage cost nearly $10 billion per day in trade losses and led to immediate supply shortages around the world.[19] This was compounded by a further disruption in 2024 when conflict saw shipping fall by 70 per cent.[20] No country is immune to the potential disruption caused by these choke points, not least because for decades countries and companies have been more concerned to achieve the lowest price than to guarantee the most secure supply routes. More than four fifths of Iran's exports went eastward to China in 2025, constituting around 13 per cent of its oil imports. As the world's largest oil and liquefied natural gas (LNG) importer, with around half of its crude imports and a third of its LNG imports transiting through the Strait of Hormuz,[21] China is therefore particularly vulnerable. While new pipelines and new seaborne routes are being planned to escape the stranglehold of dominant supply routes, the most durable hedge against oil shocks is to consume less oil, and with 30 per cent of China's final energy consumption now from clean sources – compared with just over 20 per cent globally – and peak oil demand expected in 2027, China's best protection against disruption is to seek to become an 'electrostate'.[22] And so clean-energy industries – solar, batteries and EVs – accounted for more than 11 per cent of China's GDP by 2025 and over a third of its growth.

European union countries, too, aspire to become electrostates for security reasons and to deal with climate change. As a major trading power, Europe has always depended on others – especially for its energy – but it is now aware that it depends on too many suppliers who have increasingly become willing to use their stranglehold. For this reason, as Tatiana Mitrova and Anne-Sophie Corbeau have explained, European leaders are hesitant to exchange reliance on imported oil for dependence on Chinese clean-tech energy supply chains.[23]

One recent analysis identifies 'sixty-seven critical choke points where America depends on the European Union for more than 80% of its imports', and Europe has forty-one equivalent points of leverage over China – giving the continent the capacity to punish or compel political concessions from these rival powers.[24]

At first sight, thanks to its near-monopoly in certain highly sophisticated technologies, Europe looks sufficiently well placed to weaponise its own assets if deemed necessary. These include the Dutch semiconductor lithography giant ASML, the German software firm SAP, the Swedish 5G provider Ericsson, the turbine maker Siemens and Euroclear, which runs the infrastructure for cross-border financial settlements. But in recent times Europe has appeared less able than China or America to weaponise its technological assets. While millions rely for their cross-border financial transfers on the European-led SWIFT system, under post-9/11 agreements, US authorities have had access to all of its transaction data. And while SWIFT seemed to give the West a near-monopoly of payment systems, we have seen how it can be challenged in the wake of the expulsion of Russia, Iran and other countries. In 2015, China launched an alternative to SWIFT called Cross-Border Interbank Payment System (CIPS) which today has a presence in over 120 countries.[25] We can be sure that every time one country weaponises a geographical or other choke point competitors will not only find new ways to insulate themselves from it but also develop their own weapons of economic warfare.

There is another, less visible, dimension to this weaponisation of interdependence, one that is growing fast: globally significant technologies. Undersea cables and satellites in space both carry, and amplify, an additional threat to the continuity of supply. Attacks on these undermine our ability to navigate sea, air and space, and to communicate and trade globally. The production and management of these technologies has become highly concentrated and centralised around a small number of key firms and agencies, giving them a status previously enjoyed only by monopolies. Undersea cables carry 95 per cent of global data,[26] and are owned by just a few telecom giants and Big Tech companies – Google, Meta and Microsoft. The expanding satellite networks are in the hands not of governments but of a few private operators – including the Elon Musk-owned SpaceX, which now controls two-thirds of all global low-earth-orbit satellites, and whose Starlink performs the majority of the world's annual orbital launches.[27] Together, the big US technology companies Amazon, Microsoft, Google and Oracle represent over 70 per cent of global cloud services, leading Europeans to fear they could be weaponised.[28] Together these systems form the backbone of global digital connectivity and dominate communications not just for civilian but for military purposes – and they are at permanent risk of manipulation or sabotage, through jamming, hacking or attack with anti-satellite weaponry.

Today, we live in a world being shaped by these choke points. This manipulation of market forces has become a defining feature of contemporary geopolitics. It has proved to be an unforeseen but dangerous by-product of globalisation. What was expected to push us together is once again pulling us apart.

The result: a world of fortresses?

In a tightly interwoven, networked world, these kinds of disruptions have global impact, which in turn can destroy public support for globalisation and appear to justify trade barriers or isolationism. 'A country that can't feed itself, fuel itself or defend itself has few options,' said Mark Carney in Davos. 'When the rules no longer protect you, you must protect yourself. But let's be clear-eyed about where this leads. A world of fortresses will be poorer, more fragile and less sustainable.'[29] And the cost of states protecting themselves, whether through redirecting trade, increasing self-sufficiency and putting guaranteed supply before the cheapest option is also very high. Managing risk comes at a price.

Countries, Carney says, conclude that they have no alternative but to pull up the drawbridge: to speed up a push for their independence so that their decisions are no longer dictated by the world around them. And so Canada, for example, is planning greater self-sufficiency in its agriculture and in energy, spending more on defence, and working to reduce its reliance on trade with the US by seeking new trading arrangements across all continents.[30] 'We are calibrating our relationships, so their depth reflects our values,' Carney puts it, 'and we're prioritising broad engagement to maximise our influence, given the fluidity of the world at the moment, the risks that this poses and the stakes for what comes next. And we are no longer just relying on the strength of our values, but also the value of our strength.'[31]

But if that were all that was proposed, it would be defeatist: to a resignation to a protectionist future. This is not too dissimilar to the policy of 'strategic autonomy' that President Macron has sketched out as Europe's best future, which aims at the ability to operate in all major fields without reliance on the US and China. This approach offers a protective shield for some countries threatened by others but could end up with the creation of new choke points. Of course, critical dependencies must be minimised, but the search for self-sufficiency and even resilience is impossible to achieve when the distribution of the world's essential resources is so unequal. Going it alone may increase vulnerabilities, not reduce them. If countries and even continents conclude that the most effective defence mechanism against those who practise economic warfare is to retaliate, we enter into a zero-sum game from which no one really wins. In the end, this form of unilateralism weakens us all.

Of course, some of the connections that created this interdependent world can be severed and ties unwound without massive damage, and the political pressure to pursue this protectionist course is real. When trade is free but not fair, isolationism will enjoy popular support. Undoubtedly, the politically influential downsides of globalisation will put pressure on governments to respond. But there are many connections and cross-border links whose severing would bring an unbearably heavy cost.

There is a better way: partnerships with reliable allies, and, where possible, broader multilateral cooperation. Without it we will all be vulnerable to disruption and economic warfare. And if interdependence remains a fact of global life, weaponised or not, then the real choice before us is not between dependence and independence, but between an interdependence managed well and one managed badly.

The global commons in an interconnected world

The reality is that we need each other. If interdependence has created existential threats outside the control of any single nation, such threats will only increase in years to come, when America is no longer the only player, non-state terrorism is a constant threat and the nation-state is no longer the only game in town. Further, the deliberate weaponisation of strategic assets is not the only blockage that can disrupt supplies. The impact of climate change cannot be addressed by go-it-alone policies. The Panama Canal can be closed by aggressive actions from a great power but it can also be stricken by low water levels, leading to extended waiting times, damaged delivery schedules, increased shipping costs and thus more limited movements of goods. No single national carbon budget is going to address this adequately, unless it is embedded in a shared global framework.

The same logic applies to the world of cybersecurity, which operates in a modern 'no man's land'. Legal ownership of digital infrastructure matters little if you cannot actually control it. We know that AI concentrates private power in the hands of tech companies in the West and what are becoming surveillance states in the East. But AI-enabled disinformation campaigns and cyberattacks are notoriously hard to trace to their source; attacks launched in one part of the world can shut down everything from hospitals to pipelines and power grids in another. Such attacks can be mounted not just by criminals but by governments, companies and non-state terrorists. AI will raise new kinds of cross-border threats that cannot be contained by national laws alone, but such is our new found vulnerability that cyberattacks can, as can drones, strike virtually anyone anywhere at any time in what are now 'grey zones', making geography, and the very idea of protected borders and unassailable frontiers, less relevant and no guarantee of our security.

Global communications have turned information itself into a weapon. Once a unifying force, it can be weaponised as propaganda on a scale and level of sophistication never seen before, to exploit and exacerbate already existing divisions within societies. 'Falsehood spreads faster than fact, dividing communities and distorting reality,' said UK MI6 Head, Blaise Metreweli,[32] referring to what US Vice-President Nelson Rockefeller termed 'a new geography of defense',[33] whose focus is not controlling physical territory but peoples' hearts and minds. AI's algorithms 'flatter our biases and fracture our public squares, and as trust collapses, so does our shared sense of truth' – one of the greatest losses a society can suffer. 'Those hyper-personalised tools,' she explained, 'could become a new vector for conflict and control.'

And so we already face, she argues, a constant barrage of cyber-attacks and state-sponsored sabotage – the 'grey war' tactics are a form of ideological warfare which fall short of outright armed conflict. Yet control over new technologies is shifting from states to corporations, and sometimes to individuals, without, Metreweli says, any supervisory system of a global nature that can ensure some accountability.

Cooperate or perish

Taking external challenges from cyberwarfare to climate change into account, a clear picture begins to emerge: in a multipolar world, no nation on earth can opt out of the consequences and costs of there being multiple centres of decision-making power and leverage. Retreating into isolationism will not protect us, nor will the predatory exercise of hegemonic power, what Stephen Walt calls weaponising bilateral relations as inherently zero-sum and seeking to extract the greatest possible benefits from each one. This American answer, says Walt, 'is not a coherent, well-thought-out response to the return of multipolarity; in fact, it is exactly the wrong way to act in a world of several great powers'.[34] Quite simply, as he says, it cannot work: there are few who would today justify a reassertion of hegemony even on the basis that one power's rules are easier to navigate than another's, or that a world in which power is diffused widely is less 'globalised' than a hegemonic one. Using the promise of American protection to extract what Walt has called 'a never-ending series of concessions' is 'not a sustainable strategy'. It is, as he concludes, 'doomed to fail'.[35]

Multipolarity implies a world where not only do other great states have coercive power of their own, but they can find many allies. It is not therefore surprising that in quick succession over the last year we have seen India lining up with Russia and describing their unity as 'like the North Star'; China, Japan and South Korea agreeing to 'deepen economic cooperation'; Vietnam expanding its military ties with Russia; and the European Union signing trade deals with Indonesia, Mexico, India and South America. While ad hoc alliances may suggest hedging against the big powers works, some have argued that we may be replacing the old world of mutually assured destruction with a new world of mutually assured disruption.[36]

But the higher levels of cooperation we seek can also nudge a dangerous world of multiple poles towards a safer and more stable world of multilateral cooperation. It can turn us away from an interdependence weaponised by disruptors towards one that, managed well, can become a source of shared security and shared prosperity.

This is not some idealistic exercise, so divorced from everyday life that it is meaningless to the ordinary citizen. International cooperation is comparable to international law, which, as one writer has noted, is 'essentially a set of reciprocal expectations that only works if states believe others will follow the rules too – anything that departs from these expectations weakens the system'.[37] This suggests a new settlement, brought about by recognising the realities of our interdependent world and how it affects ordinary people, binding together the global and the domestic. And the question we have to answer is no longer whether we need new forms of cooperation, but whether we can construct them before disruptive events force them upon us.

We can no longer rely on institutions that were not designed for today's challenges. The lesson of recent events is that we cannot continue to approach twenty-first-century problems with twentieth-century mindsets. We must reject the old logic of force in favour of a new logic of extended and enhanced cooperation. Of course, countries must work to reduce their critical dependencies on others. And in Europe's case, this means establishing clearly defined diversification targets, promoting a European circular economy and embracing joint European procurement – for no one can be an utter monopolist in the realm of geopolitics.

So even if countries can make bilateral deals, there are steps they cannot take on their own without multilateral coordination – controlling climate change, preventing pandemics, protecting against financial contagion, safeguarding against terrorism. And without cooperation most countries cannot, as Mark Carney told the Australian parliament, guarantee reliable access at a reasonable price to space-based communications and storage, payment systems and capital, and even vaccines. Semiconductors can only be secured at an unacceptable price without cooperating with other countries, and America, and to a lesser extent China, still control systems covering finance, technology, minerals, energy, shipping and data that the rest of us depend on.[38] The truth is there is only one way to minimise the damage to ourselves if the big powers decide to weaponise these assests. We are compelled to cooperate.

Seeking our own form of strategic autonomy, or mimicking the 'economic statecraft' proposed by the US Treasury Secretary, can only result in more widespread blackmail from weaponised interdependence. The most effective system for delivering global public goods and global prosperity will be a new multilateralism that is best founded not on the shifting sands of expediency, but anchored in shared interests and shared values, and driven forward by dialogue, diplomacy and democratic accountability. While I do not doubt that cooperation can only be sustained if it rests on clearly defined interests, I would stress the importance of values in underpinning the global system, on the grounds that legitimacy over the long term is found in honouring the public desire for justice and respect for human dignity. I would also emphasise the importance of accountability. For a new multilateralism to be successful, it cannot be founded on backstage deals between elites to balance their power, but must rest on support from a global public which remains open to working with other countries.

I have argued that in a multipolar world where interdependence can be weaponised, the response of the populist nationalists – to reject international cooperation in its entirety – leaves us more vulnerable than ever. The economist Eswar Prasad has given this dynamic a name: the doom loop. In his recent book, Prasad argues that we are caught in a destructive feedback cycle linking economics, domestic politics and geopolitics.[39] Economic problems – slow growth, inequality, financial shocks – fuel domestic political anger and populism. That in turn leads governments to look inward and put up barriers, which in turn weakens international cooperation. The resulting geopolitical tension and fragmentation further damages the global economy, which then worsens the original grievances, and the cycle repeats.

It is the weaponisation of interdependence that creates the doom loop, when sources of shared benefit become sources of mutual threat. But this is also the point at which the loop can be broken and then reversed, by making cooperation work for those millions of people who reject it because they feel globalisation has not been fair to them. Without a stable and prosperity-enhancing international order, which can only be delivered through sustained cooperation, there will be chaos, and in these circumstances no domestic social contract can remain secure for long.

It is interesting that the word 'competition' comes from 'compete', which itself derives from the Latin *competere*: *com* ('with' or 'together') and *petere* ('to strive'). Originally, then, it meant 'to strive together'. In the second half of the twenty-first century, it is by striving together that we will succeed. And there are glimmers of hope. Every day, encircling the world above our heads, is the International Space Station, jointly manned by Russian and American astronauts, with, in all, the nationals of fifteen countries joining on a regular basis. The Station will not last for ever – but it is a sign that cooperation can work. Even as US–Russian relations have again deteriorated, collaboration in space has still been possible. In this area at least, adversaries have found common purpose, 'striving together'.

9

POWER: THE MAKING OF A MULTIPOLAR WORLD

In April 2026, the US astronauts on board *Artemis II* journeyed further from earth than ever before. When they sent pictures of the world as seen from deep space, they reminded us of how infinitesimally small and fragile our planet appears when set against the immensity of our solar system. Fifty years after the Apollo missions, *Artemis II* is one of more than 400 planned missions to the moon over the next twenty years by not just America, but China, India, Russia, Japan, Canada and Europe.

In a picture captioned 'Hello, World', sent from over 100,000 miles away, you could see the dimly lit edges of the Sahara. But when in 1972 the *Apollo 17* astronauts sent back images of our world, they showed Africa in full prominence, reminding us of the sheer scale of the continent. And this view we have had from above is now challenging what has for 400 years been a Western bias in the way we have viewed the world, with the size of the West and particularly Europe enhanced at the expense of the continents of Africa and Asia.

More than four centuries ago in 1569, the Flemish cartographer Gerardus Mercator created the projection that bears his name. By placing Europe at the centre, it expands the size of the Global North while shrinking the land masses of the Global South. It suggests Europe is of a similar size to Africa even though the latter is three times larger. It also shows Greenland as equivalent to the entire African continent even though it is one-fourteenth of Africa's size. Yet this map became the standard used for navigation and, rightly, Africans and Asians have argued that it cements a colonial bias, a Eurocentric view which is not justified by the physical size of each of the world's land masses.

Such a mapping of the world was challenged as early as 1602 by a European who had emigrated to China. In 1602 Matteo Ricci published what is called the Kunyu Wanguo Quantu map. It positioned Asia at the world's centre with the Middle Kingdom of China the focal point. A more realistic recent map, the Hobo-Dyer projection, places Africa and the equator prominently at the centre and in doing so ends the centuries-long miniaturisation of Africa in a world that is no longer Euro-centric.

The debate about the maps shows just how much the global balance of power is shifting. The question is what kind of world order is it going to produce. The landscape has not yet settled in a decade when tectonic plates have shifted. Marco Rubio, Thomas Jefferson's most recent successor as US secretary of state, recently argued that the world is again experiencing a fundamental shift in power. He rejected liberal internationalism, what he called the 'dangerous delusion' and 'the foolish idea that ignored both human nature and the lessons of over 5,000 years of recorded human history'. And he asserted that the international system is 'going to reach back to a point where you had a multipolar world, multi great powers in different parts of the planet'.[1]

While we might yet see great powers at war with each other and a return to hegemony, what is more likely is a return to spheres of influence, which as defined by Zaki Laïdi represent 'the exercise of authority over subordinate actors within a defined area through suzerainty, protectorate arrangements, or outright domination'.[2] This is reminiscent of the late nineteenth-century world of a number of competing nationalisms, or even, as Chinese and Russian thinkers increasingly suggest, and statements from Rubio and JD Vance imply, a struggle between 'civilisational states'. This implies a battle between countries that do not just claim to represent a settled and secure territory with their own language or ethnic group, but a separate culture and a distinctive way of life. But spheres of influence can be defined today not only by military and geographic dominance, as they were in the nineteenth and twentieth centuries, but also by the control of critical technologies or infrastructure and the capacity this allows to ward off any challenges – not least through AI-led disinformation and cyber-led interference. This would usher in not just an unbalanced but an unstable multipolarity: a world not at war, perhaps, yet a world never at peace, what Mark Leonard has called an 'unpeace'. Ray Dalio goes further to suggest we are 'in the early stages of a war that is not going to end any time soon', citing the likelihood of a continuing Iran–America conflict but also suggesting a 30–40 per cent chance of war between China and America over Taiwan by 2028, a similar probability of wars between the Philippines and China, and a broadening out of the Ukraine–Russia conflict. Dalio also believes there is an even higher chance – 40 to 50 per cent – of war with North Korea.[3] His remarks do not seem far out of line with the forecast attributed to President Truman in 1945 that he hoped the new United Nations organisation, which he saw as mankind's last hope, would survive ninety years, after which would come World War Three.

We might, however, drift towards an equally unstable bipolar 'one world, two systems' future, with China and the United States, supported by their satellites, facing off across a divided globe. Or we might see, as described by Finnish president Alexander Stubb in his recent book, a more rebalanced tripolar world consisting of the Global West (which, for him, includes the United States, Europe, Japan, South Korea, Australia and New Zealand), the Global East (led by China and Russia) and the Global South – with the South being 'kingmaker' or arbiter, determining whether, as the US and China compete for its allegiance, the world 'tilts' towards multilateral cooperation or multipolar fragmentation.[4]

At various times, President Trump has appeared to embrace each of these visions of world order. On some occasions he speaks as if power is simply divided between China and America. But at others he speaks of a multipolar world of spheres of influence, the scenario outlined in the 2025 National Security Strategy, whose aims include to 'enlist and expand Western Hemisphere influence' and to 'reassert and enforce' the Monroe doctrine of American pre-eminence in the Americas.[5] 'American dominance in the Western Hemisphere,' the president has said, 'will never be questioned again.'[6] Greenland, he says, America 'needs'.[7] It is not just control of Venezuela and the Panama Canal that is in Trump's sights but also of Cuba: 'I think I can do anything I want with it,' he is reported as saying.[8] The longer, unpublished version of the National Security Strategy takes the idea of spheres of influence furthest of all, proposing to replace the G7 with a new 'Core 5': a grouping of the United States, China, Russia, India and Japan – what one writer has called an 'oligopolar world' – whereby the great powers would regularly meet to carve up the management of the globe between them – with, in this instance, Europe conspicuously excluded.[9] This would replace hegemony, which was, it says, 'the wrong thing to want and it wasn't achievable' and was 'a failure'.[10]

As Stephen Walt writes, Trump 'has been called a realist, a nationalist, an old-fashioned mercantilist, an imperialist, and an isolationist', before, counterposing it to America's previous status as a 'benevolent hegemon', he settles on the words 'predatory hegemon'.[11] It is a term never used by Trump himself, but Walt believes it captures the essence of his worldview. Stephen Holmes is also right to talk of the Trump postliberal order as 'hierarchy without order' or in the words of Daron Acemoglu, 'an agenda that seeks to remove all constraints on future behaviour'.[12] And the president's presentation of America as a fortress that appears untouchable and free to play outside any normal rules has been a feature of the first months of 2026. One observer characterised Trump's predatory approach as 'you can just do things', in a manner, he said, reminiscent of a Bush official's pre-Iraq assertion that 'when we act, we create our own reality'.[13]

What might a new world order look like?

At its peak of recent influence, in the first Gulf War and then after 9/11 when it invaded Afghanistan, the United States had the support of the vast majority of the world's 190-plus countries. The Afghan coalition comprised 130,000 troops from fifty countries but the supporters of US action in Iraq numbered only forty countries, and the same number were prepared to follow America's lead in imposing sanctions on Russia after its invasion of Ukraine. However, when it comes to Iran – with Europe standing apart – no more than twenty countries have supported the American intervention. So with American hegemony under fire, what kind of leadership is possible in a multipolar world?

China can lay claim to being a superpower because of its industrial strength (30 per cent of total global output rising to 40 per cent in the coming decade), its dominance and technological leadership in electric cars, batteries and solar power, and its rising military power at sea, on land and in the air. Each manufacturing plant is seen in Western countries as akin to a gun pointed at their own domestic industries. And as long as it does not blockade or invade Taiwan, it can argue that, unlike America, it has not been distracted by 'forever wars'. But China has other challenges to meet and master. Barry Posen asserts that the first rule of a bipolar order is that 'peripheries disappear', which is clearly not what is going to happen in Asia.[14] On its own doorstep, China has to deal with the concerns and ambitions of significant neighbours including Japan, South Korea, India and the Philippines if it is to be the regional hegemon. Then of course there is the China–America relationship, which is very different from the USSR–USA Cold War standoff. The defining phrase of the Cold War, 'iron curtain', testified to minimal trade, exchanges and contact between the two superpowers – the opposite of the mutual trade and regular interaction that has until recently been the distinguishing feature of the China–America relationship. Washington and Beijing are not, as Michael Beckley says, 'building rival worlds separated by an iron curtain, they are fighting for dominance within one global economy'.[15] But with, as Zheng Wang says, 'limits on each side's ability to brandish its economic weapons' and to use its leverage to fully isolate the other side from influence on the global stage, they are thus 'structurally bound by competitive coexistence – a relationship in which neither side can triumph on its own terms nor afford to be drawn into sustained conflict'.[16]

Wang talks of G2 summitry, China and America carving up the world between them, while another writer Da Wei talks of a less threatening 'dual core multipolar order' which, by allowing space for other countries, could avoid Cold War-style blocs.[17] But whatever short-term deals have recently been agreed – on soya beans, rare earths, fentanyl and the creation of joint trade and investment councils – there are at least ten unresolved issues: five mainly economic (currency, industrial subsidies, AI controls, cyber and climate) and five mainly non-economic (nuclear weapon proliferation, Taiwan, the South China Sea, Hong Kong and the treatment of religious minorities). These issues mean that at the least, as Wang says, any G2 could never be 'comfortable', nor 'be built on friendship, shared values, or deep trust', but would be 'marked by competition, suspicion, bargaining, and periodic crises'. But set against China's main economic assets – its superior industrial capacity, manufacturing pre-eminence, trade surpluses, lead in renewables, dominance in rare earth refining, and build-up of dependent countries – America retains much greater advantages. Its leverage over the global financial system, energy independence, stronger and deeper alliances, superior strength in military bases, nuclear weapons and advanced weaponry, as well as its greater soft power. Both have similar weapons at their disposal: their ability to weaponise their key assets, identify their adversaries' vulnerabilities and restrict access to key technologies and both can neutralise many of the advantages each has. America and China may be derisking rather than decoupling but as I write a 'one world, two systems' future is the more likely outcome. And while both countries should share a common desire for stable trading and financial arrangements and even for mutually beneficial action on climate and the supervision of AI and cyber, anything other than short-term deals, probably only on single issues between a Trump who can be impulsive and a Xi who can be inflexible, seems unlikely.

What's more, even when it is cultivating allies, China's often intransigent approach makes it a difficult and uneasy partner. China froze diplomatic relations for months in 2021 with Lithuania just because it allowed Taiwan to open an office in its capital, and later with Australia alongside issuing tariffs and informal bans on barley, wine, beef, coal, cotton and lobsters after the Australian government called for an inquiry into the origins of Covid. A similar freeze occurred when I met the Dalai Lama not in Downing Street but at the Archbishop of Canterbury's official residence, thus recognising him as a religious leader, and again when Petr Pavel, the Czech president, did no more than offer the Dalai Lama a 'happy birthday' message.

China is also having to work a third front: its relationship with its own people. China needs political stability if it is to deliver on its principal economic objective – to be a high-income country by 2035. And so China has to balance its desire to integrate Taiwan against the economic chaos that would result from the inevitable sanctions that would follow any attempt.

Russia may eventually have to settle for operating within China's orbit. Russia may look stronger than China militarily, but it is far weaker economically. It is dependent on one resource – fossil fuels – and even then its economy is no bigger than Portugal's. But its leader, whose 2021 manifesto, 'On the Historical Unity of Russians and Ukrainians', shows him obsessed with historical claims to a Greater Russia, continues to pursue a strategy of aggression, irrespective of the strength of his position.[18] But while Russia claims ownership of half the Arctic and intends to benefit from its melting ice by creating a potentially powerful sea route there, it remains diplomatically isolated, with a still uncertain hold on power even within its own region. When it comes to the configuration of global order, Russia is at best a spoiler, not a hegemon.

India has the world's largest population (by 2050 it will have reached 1.7 billion in contrast to China's 1.3 billion, and only 20 per cent will be over sixty, as against 40 per cent in China), a nuclear arsenal and a rapidly growing economy.* It has recently made clear its strategic calculus: that it can achieve great-power status through both economic and military strength. It has been said that if you are not a sphere of influence, you are in one, and India hopes to be the exception. It seeks to play the great powers off against each other by making defence and energy deals with Russia, economic and security deals with the United States, and commerce agreements with the United Kingdom and the European Union, including what European Commission president Ursula von der Leyen described as the 'mother of all deals', with an estimated €30 billion in export gains for both sides. Meanwhile, India balances making common cause with regional neighbours against China with occasional cooperation, including in the BRICS group. To maintain its tariff regime, India has refused to apply to join the Comprehensive and Progressive Agreement for Trans-Pacific Partnership (CPTPP), whose twelve members account for about 15 per cent of the world economy and membership of which would integrate India more tightly into Asian supply chains.

India remains a candidate for superpower status in, say, fifty years, but is today unable to wield the economic, military and

---

* Although it currently accounts for just 4 per cent of world trade and its national income per head is also around 4 per cent of that of the US, India will be the fourth or even the third largest economy in the world by 2030.

soft power required.[19] Devesh Kapur and Arvind Subramanian describe the Indian economy as historically characterised by 'prolonged ruralization, stunted industrialization, and precocious servicification',[20] and the country is currently plagued by uneven development, demographic pressures, unstable state governments, ethnic divisions, populist voting and persistently high levels of poverty, as well as an apparent inability to create jobs for unemployed young people.* And while India has more billionaires (205 in 2025) than any country apart from the United States and China, it seems powerless to escape the middle-income trap that has held back so many of its Asian and Latin American neighbours. It is caught between non-alignment, by which it means operating outside the orbit of China and America, and what it itself calls 'multi-alignment', playing all sides off against one another. Illustrating this ambiguity, India's foreign minister, S. Jaishankar, said in April 2026: 'Everything today is being leveraged, if not actually weaponised . . . This has necessitated the need to hedge, de-risk and diversify . . . building national capabilities to secure resources, technologies and essential goods. It looks after Indians . . . and it promotes Brand India.'[21] Or as he put it in his 2020 book *The India Way*, 'This is a time for us to engage America, manage China, cultivate Europe, reassure Russia, bring Japan into play, draw neighbours in, extend the neighbourhood . . .'[22]

An alternative to one-nation leadership could be a bloc – BRICS, made up initially of China, India, Russia, South Africa and Brazil, is now eleven-strong, with applications from many other countries. Together its members make up two fifths of the world's population, roughly a quarter of economic activity and just under a fifth of trade in goods. But while it has ambitions to create a separate global currency and has sponsored global institutions like the New Development Bank, this now motley

* In December 2025, in just one small part of India, 8,000 people competed for 187 posts in the police service.

collection of democracies and autocracies, monarchies and republics, is united more by what it is against – American hegemony – than by what it is for. For the same reasons we can discount the importance of the eleven-nation ASEAN grouping, which requires unanimity to act but whose members are not agreed on the threats they face. Recently, OPEC has suffered from losing two of its original members and its remaining members are not a unified bloc but a one-issue cartel based on oil and gas interests, which can often diverge.

The European Union can be considered a genuine superpower in many more of the key dimensions: it represents 18 per cent of the world economy in nominal terms (and just 14 per cent on a PPP basis) and is the world's leading trading bloc, with almost 80 agreements covering nearly 150 countries. But it is energy dependent on outsiders for 80 per cent of its oil and gas, and security dependent on America for its air defences, long-range strike capabilities as well as logistics and munitions. Europe looks less like the successor of American hegemony than its dependent offspring. And it is losing economically to both America and China. While between 2008 and 2023 GDP rose by 87 per cent in the US, it grew by just 13.5 per cent in the EU. At market exchange rates, the EU's GDP per capita fell from being nearly identical to that of the US in 2007 to 68 per cent of it in 2023,[23] low enough that Mississippi, the poorest US state, now earns more per head than France or Italy. While roughly half of the world's fifty largest technology firms are American, only four are European.[24] One report estimates that 80 per cent of digital products and services in the EU are provided by non-EU companies.[25] In 2024, the EU accounted for only 12 per cent of global AI venture capital issued in the West, compared with America's 74 per cent. And Chinese demand for European goods – especially German machinery – is falling as China develops its own indigenous industries. This has created a record bilateral trade deficit – €89 billion in 2025 – causing a protectionist response in European capitals.

When, in the 1960s, an as yet little-known Henry Kissinger penned a book, *The Troubled Partnership*, at least one bookshop displayed it under the heading Relationships and Self-Help. But the partnership he was referring to was of a Europe seeking to become more independent of America, despite its unwillingness to pay to reduce its dependence upon America for its own security. At a minimum, as Dan Baer and Erik Brown state, Trump's America has traded reassurance for what they call 'unstrategic ambiguity', a posture that might be relevant to making China unsure how America will react to a blockade of Taiwan, but not helpful when dealing with a trusted partner with whom coordination and alignment are required to meet shared challenges. It is not, they say, 'tough love' (the president has declared Europe 'nastier than China' on trade) but it is making for an unreliable partnership that at times demands American contracts for European equipment which would maintain European dependence on America.[26]

But France's President Macron has made the positive case for 'strategic autonomy', calling on Europe to act independently of both Washington and Beijing, and in his Sorbonne speeches for Europe to agree defence integration, assert technological sovereignty and champion a new European-inspired multilateralism.[27] However, recent studies suggest that Europe doubts its own power. A European Council on Foreign Relations study concluded that 'in some parts of the world, people see great potential in Europe', but 'much remains for Europeans to embrace their own power, and they are starting from a gloomy place. Most Europeans do not believe the EU is a power able to deal on equal terms with the US or China – and these doubts have grown over the past 12 months.'[28] Europe remains far too security-dependent on America, trade-dependent on China, and energy-dependent on outside sources – whether Russian oil and gas, or LNG from the Middle East or America. 'Europe can no longer be a custodian for the old-world order, for a world that has gone and will not return,' concludes Ursula von der Leyen, as if the continent should now focus on a limited and negative goal, protecting itself in a purely transactional world where might has triumphed over right.[29] Former French premier Gabriel Attal has gone so far as to label Europeans as 'powerless spectators of the unravelling of global rules' in a world 'governed by force', even suggesting that those who lament the loss of an international order 'no longer have the means for such indignation'.[30]

At the heart of this lies the dilemma that the EU has yet to resolve: is it an association of many nations or a power in its own right? Europe is home to nearly 750 million people across 44 countries. The European Union comprises around 450 million people in 27 countries, while the euro area includes approximately 350 million people across 21 states. It is made up, one former Belgian prime minister said, of two kinds of countries – those that are small and those that do not know they are small.[31] And even though EU membership is underpinned by common goals,* the bloc remains divided. Foreign-policy decisions still require unanimity, economic integration is incomplete, and domestic electoral pressures push member states apart on policy. 'We all know what to do,' former European Commission president Jean-Claude Juncker said, 'but we don't know how to get re-elected once we have done it.'[32]

Can Europe ever truly rival the two superpowers? Increasingly it is taking more responsibility for its collective defence, but only because America is doing less. As Christopher Chivvis has argued, 'the shift to a NATO led by Europe should be driven by deliberate transatlantic strategy, not neglect or coercion'.[33] The reality is that with no military capacity of its own, and without greater political coherence, the European Union's geopolitical influence may be limited geographically, and restricted to areas such as setting the rules of trade and offering humanitarian aid.

---

* Including the rule of law, democracy, and human rights, social and economic as well as civil and political.

Alexander Stubb implies that Europe can only lead as part of a Global West. Instead, he argues for the pivotal influence of the Global South. This notional grouping is home to roughly 60 per cent of the world's population and already accounts for nearly 30 per cent of global economic activity, even if it only represents just over 17 per cent of global trade. Stubb points to the independence shown by many of its constituent states, reminding us that the majority refused to support sanctions against Russia after its invasion of Ukraine. He situates this stance in a longer tradition of resistance to perceived colonial attitudes, stretching back to the Non-Aligned Movement over half a century ago.

However, this 'group' of around 125 of the world's 195 states is far from cohesive. It encompasses countries with vast differences in population, income and resources. It ranges from small island nations with few natural resources to large, landlocked countries and resource-rich economies with significant fossil fuel and rare earth deposits. It includes forty-six of the least developed countries whose interests do not necessarily align with the eighty lower-middle- and middle-income economies. And it spans democracies, autocracies, monarchies and religious states. As a result, a wide and often competing set of interests is in play. For the Global South to become a genuine third power, it would need unity, stability, a shared agenda and economic and military strength to rival, if not match, the other two blocs. At present, it cannot meet these conditions and, as Stubb has to concede, is somewhat agnostic about the future order.

Middle powers?

So perhaps it is time to take Jefferson's advice: a new world calls for a new world order. It is time to think differently and to consider power in less traditional forms – not just its military and economic dimensions but also soft power: the influence states gain when others admire them and look to them for leadership. But consideration should also be given to what Peter Katzenstein and Lucia Seybert call 'protean power' – the capacity that emerges from a country's ability to adapt, improvise and innovate in the face of uncertainty – and its counterpart, 'control power', which derives from the ability to plan ahead in a predictable and consistent way.[34] We know from the work of Daron Acemoglu and James Robinson that the power of the central state combines with the influence of civil society to 'create a narrow corridor in which liberty flourishes'.[35] So while economic and military power can be decisive, those countries whose institutions are stable and well organised, and whose behaviour is predictable, consistent and appealing to others can exercise more influence.

What, then, could a new kind of multipolar world look like and what is the likely balance of power? First, let us consider the perspectives of those who live outside the traditional West. According to the European Council of Foreign Relations, many of the more important middle countries – Brazil, South Africa, South Korea and India – expect to enjoy greater opportunities to grow and thrive in a multipolar world. They not only resist the claim that China and America are in what the Council calls 'a bipolar, ideological struggle for primacy',[36] but they think of a world made up of many powers, big and small, which are free to move between poles as they choose. This sentiment, far removed from the considered view of international-relations scholars, suggests that public perceptions are at odds with geopolitical realities. And we have to ask whether, if enough countries acted as though the world were truly multipolar, a successful multilateral order could follow.

Multipolarity is regarded by some American scholars as an anti-American political project 'aimed at curtailing American power, eroding Western-led institutions, and constructing alternative models of governance, development, and security in which the United States is not the country in charge'.[37] In this telling, a 'pole' is defined by its ability not only to project military and economic strength, but to bind allies to their will and shape their behaviour. By such a definition, the US might be considered to be the only current 'pole'. But 'multipolarity', for me, does not imply the existence of three, four or five states of equal power and status relative to the United States, but at its simplest, the existence of multiple centres of decision-making power. And multipolarity is very different from multilateralism. A multilateral world is characterised by global cooperation, usually through shared rules and common institutions, and is therefore relatively orderly. By contrast, a multipolar world may be no more than a shifting set of temporary and transactional alliances always at risk of descending into violent conflict. The challenge is to convert this multipolar but disorderly world into a multilateral one that is stable and fair.

It may be more accurate to describe today's multipolarity as unbalanced or what Stephen Walt calls 'lopsided'. In this telling, the shift away from unipolarity is not an event, but a process: the inelegant term 'multipolarisation'[38] describes something that may be inevitable but is, as yet, still in transition, with power moving away from one hegemon and diversifying to a number of countries with differing capacities to influence global issues. It is a multipolarising world in the sense, too, that each country has different strengths – economic, military, or soft and smart power – reflecting different ideologies and agendas.

What will emerge from this transition is not yet clear. But I would draw special attention to the role that the countries outside of the great and revisionist powers – Russia, China and increasingly the US – might play. And, in particular, we should look at the leadership that so-called 'middle powers' might play in helping this coalition-of-the-rest overcome its own collective action problems in the face of pressure from global heavyweights.

We might define middle powers as ones which gain their status through possessing one or more of several attributes: strength within their own region; or a recognised global status derived from control of resources, as the petrostates enjoy; or a leadership in technology; or from a strategic geographic position that gives them some capacity to influence others. No one can push them around on every issue and all of the time. The middle powers form part of a larger group of nations – indeed, the overwhelming majority of nation states that make up the world economy and together could set the agenda of multilateral institutions. The other nations of the world account for 75 per cent of the world's population, 75 per cent of world trade, and 75 per cent of the votes at the major international organisations – 76 per cent of the quotas at the IMF and World Bank, and 70 per cent of the UN Security Council, including two of the five permanent vetoes.

On their own, these countries can be little more than subordinate to the superpowers. Today they still depend on America and China for too much of their finance, technology and data. Even if the Dutch lead on lithography, the Koreans on memory chips, the Taiwanese on semiconductors, the Indonesians on nickel (though China refines much of it), and Iran and Oman control access to the Persian Gulf, they do not, in the end, as Michael Beckley argues, have the all-round structural power – the combination of finance, energy, software, cloud services and military ascendancy – required to control rather than merely disrupt the global system.[39] And as long as they remain isolated, they will always, he argues, have to fall in behind a bigger power.

Beckley argues that even when taken together, the economic output of the thirteen regional powers designated by the Harvard Belfer Center – Brazil, Egypt, India, Indonesia, Kazakhstan, Nigeria, Pakistan, Saudi Arabia, Singapore, South Africa, Turkey, the UAE and Vietnam – amounts to only half of US GDP and only one quarter of its defence spend, and that they therefore have too little firepower to rival America or even China. But if we add in Europe, the UK, Canada and Australia, the question becomes whether middle and small countries acting together as a bloc could become such a force for change that even America and China might come to view it as in their interests to join them. As Beckley himself concedes, 'middle powers' assets – ports, bases, chip-making tools, mineral deposits, drone industries, shipyards – can become bargaining chips for a superpower's protection, intelligence, technology, capital, market access and influence over their strategy.'[40]

The question remains whether, by banding together, the 75 per cent of the world outside America and China (together with Russia) could break that dependent relationship with geopolitical superpowers altogether. Could the assets which are currently tributes to be offered up be converted into the basis of a new, independent, balance and autonomous coalition? And could that coalition be built without antagonising the Americans or the Chinese – by, for instance, offering to take on or share the burden of providing global public goods? Dependence could be replaced by reciprocity, and hierarchy by fair burden sharing – exactly the deal President Trump says he is seeking in America's interests. Small and middle powers will have distinct roles in this alternative world order.

The case for small states being more agile and adaptive is made by Armen Sarkissian, former president of Armenia, emphasising their ability to gain influence because they are oases of stability, and centres of scientific and cultural innovation – giving them outsized power in world affairs.[41]

But smaller powers alone will be vulnerable without a global order that makes sovereign equality a reality rather than an empty soundbite. To achieve that shift, the world will require the leadership of a vanguard of middle powers, together strong enough to resist pressure from the great powers, legitimate enough to command the support of smaller nations, and resilient enough at home to maintain domestic political support for global action.

Recognising the potentially influential position of middle powers is not to say – and this must be emphasised – that any of them has sufficient economic and military power on their own to tilt the global order decisively. There is little doubt that, under sustained pressure, most middle powers, if acting alone and unable to combine as a unit, would be forced to choose between China and the US. Even if their preference were to remain unaligned, it would become increasingly difficult to remain forever as 'hedgers', 'fence-sitters' or 'swing states', purporting to be 'command centres' in their own right.

Even if most of the 195 states registered at the UN cannot be considered anything other than small powers by this definition, would-be middle powers include three of the five permanent Security Council members who are not superpowers – Russia, the UK and France – and the so-called G4 coalition comprising Brazil, Germany, India and Japan, who believe they deserve a permanent place on the Security Council.

Each has its own arguments for special status. And yet they all face important rivals within their own region: Argentina, Mexico and Canada in the Americas; Italy and Poland in Europe as well as others from eastern Europe like Kazakhstan; Pakistan, Indonesia, South Korea, Vietnam and Singapore in Asia; South Africa, Egypt and Nigeria in Africa; and Iran, Turkey and the petrostates of Saudi Arabia, the UAE and Qatar in the Middle East. None of the major middle powers – Germany, Japan, France, the UK and India – comes close to superpower status in military or economic terms. They continue to rely on others for their security, and given the dollar's dominance, they have less leverage over the global financial system than their economic scale would suggest. Outside the UK and France, no middle power has had a seat on the UN Security Council on more than one occasion every ten years, translating to no more than two terms of two years versus the permanent members' eighty years. Even some of the more powerful economies have no more than 6 per cent of the voting power at the IMF and 6.8 per cent at the World Bank each.

But focusing on potential division and individual weakness is to underestimate the ability of states to be effective if they work together in a new era of middle-power leadership and small-power collaboration. The question is this: can a constellation of middle powers, acting together, combine to create a multilateral order in which they can play a significant role?

Firstly, the drawbacks critics identify include a divergent set of interests and even values –including disagreement about what kind of multilateral order they would want to create, with perhaps the only thing they share being a common adversary. But set against that is a possibility that a group of powers with some military capacity as well as shared ambitions could, by joining together, be a force to be reckoned with. Middle powers and their potential supporters between them currently hold twelve out of the fifteen votes at the UN Security Council, and were Britain and France to be on board, they have the power of veto. At the IMF and World Bank, the middle powers and smaller countries together could wield more than 75 per cent of board votes. But only if they could become a group of powers with similar values and shared long-term interests could they wield effective influence.

And because a declining proportion of the world's trade – from today 17 per cent to a predicted 10 per cent in ten years – goes through America, a trade partnership between the EU and the CPTPP – which Canada's prime minister, Mark Carney, is seeking to orchestrate – would cover 37 per cent of world trade and 30 per cent of the world's economic activity, and would represent 1.5 billion people. By including India it would be bigger still – 2.5 billion people – a genuine counterweight to China and America with the leverage to determine the rules not just on trade but on health and humanitarian aid, even if areas like AI and cyber remain superpower-dominated.

There is ample precedent for like-minded states to cooperate without a hegemon and outside a formal hierarchy. From the 1955 Bandung Conference – when twenty-nine Asian and African countries united around decolonisation and non-alignment – to the Helsinki process of 1975 in which European states led by Finland brought the US and the USSR to the table and secured the creation of the Organisation for Security and Cooperation in Europe, middle-power states have repeatedly come together around shared objectives, without great-power leadership. The Ottawa Treaty of 1997 showed how middle powers and NGOs, led in this case by Canada, could act collectively to ban anti-personnel landmines, despite initial opposition from major military powers.[42] The Rome Statute of 1998 established the International Criminal Court through a coalition of willing states, demonstrating that 'legal institutions can function without universal membership'.[43] More recently, the International Solar Alliance, launched by India and France and now comprising over 120 countries, is illustrating how middle powers can build practical joint ventures in renewable energy.[44] The V20 group already provides a standing platform for climate adaptation among the most vulnerable states. The WHO Pandemic Agreement, adopted in May 2025 after three years of negotiations, was driven in large part by middle-power governments determined to fill the gap left by American disengagement. The recent attempt to agree a Covenant to outlaw crimes against humanity has the support of more than 100 governments and is led by middle countries. Another example of middle-power multilateralism that may be the shape of things to come is the Multi-Party Interim Appeal Arbitration Arrangement (MPIA), launched in 2020 by sixteen members of the World Trade Organization to provide arbitration in trade disputes, as a substitute for its stalled appeal system. It now has sixty members.[45]

Middle powers are, in many respects, better placed now to operate as leaders in such coalitions than at any previous point. According to the World Economic Forum's Global Cooperation Barometer 2026, fully multilateral forms of cooperation have declined; yet smaller and more agile coalitions of countries have grown in number and importance, extending well beyond trade into technology, climate and global health, proving instrumental in ensuring that cooperation is evolving rather than being in complete retreat.

The case for middle powers acting collectively and coalescing smaller states alongside them is often made alongside the broader argument that we now inhabit a 'multiplex' world, where NGOs, companies and public opinion can combine to exert independent influence. After all, more than 50,000 NGOs and forums with a focus on international cooperation already exist.[46] Anne-Marie Slaughter has written of the power that flows through networks of states, firms and citizens, arguing in *The Chessboard and the Web* that in a networked world, influence belongs less to those who dominate geopolitics and more to those who can shape the space around it.[47]

Yet, despite a willingness to collaborate, no stable middle-power-led grouping has formed that comes close to matching NATO in coherence or collective power. Most initiatives that are working well can be thought of as relatively fluid arrangements. They are often ad hoc and transient partnerships organised around a single issue or a strictly defined set of interests. Their very flexibility implies that such alliances are not mutually exclusive; they are transactional and pragmatic rather than principled and more often than not time-limited rather than likely to endure.

Are we then to conclude that middle powers can lead only on selected issues, and even then only if they are nimble and focused on limited objectives when they work together? Mark Carney has called this 'an era of variable geometry' characterised by diffuse, issue-by-issue deals and flexible alliances that often settle for the lowest common denominator and looser agreement around shared values in order to reach consensus.[48] And if we are, as Australian foreign minister Penny Wong said, moving into a new era of 'amplified middle power diplomacy', will this be more about what we can prevent than what we can pioneer?[49] Wong speaks of 'purpose-built coalitions', but will this high-sounding rhetoric lead to another iteration of self-interested manoeuvring, with groups of middle powers opting in and out of arrangements as it suits them, always mindful of falling foul of America and China?

The question remains how much of the 75 per cent of the world that I have described can come together to pursue anything other than limited objectives and whether if this happened such alliances can ever effectively alter the trajectory of global decision-making, by qualifying or at least moderating the influence of the major powers. Can they make progress in tackling major global problems like climate change, pandemics and financial instability, in the face of superpower indifference or even hostility? And does this add up to anything more than middle-power minilateralism[50] – building diffuse but floating deals that may fill a gap here or there – or can they become building blocks for a genuinely new multilateralism?

Who could lead the middle powers?

There is, in my view, a way forward. For the first time, we are moving beyond a past in which power in international affairs was wielded solely by elites, who made decisions in summits and conference halls far removed from the public square, with their treaties invariably rubber-stamped rather than rejected by parliaments. In the second quarter of the twenty-first century, foreign policy decisions can be influenced and even determined by engaging the general public.

In his Fourteen Points of 1918 Woodrow Wilson called for an end to secret diplomacy and for an open way of making decisions that could engage the public. But ours is the decade when for the first time, public opinion can become a decisive force. An active citizenship can give leaders the mandates they need to lead these middle powers and forge a route that could over time unite 75 per cent of the world and then engage the US and China, however unlikely it might seem now. But to get there, we need to consider both the moral and the self-interested arguments supporting international cooperation.

The good news is that, as we saw in Chapter 7, there is wider public support for sustained cooperation than we might expect. Indeed, in further polling funded by the Rockefeller Foundation in 2025, we asked people what a new world order should look like. Among electorates in the G20, the most popular view of what would make international cooperation effective was positive: 'world leaders agreeing on a clear long-term vision for peace and progress' (38 per cent of respondents across eighteen countries polled chose this). That was followed by 'countries keeping their commitments and being held accountable' (34 per cent), ensuring 'fair and balanced international rules that are followed' (34 per cent) and 'protecting the interests of future generations' (30 per cent). In other words, the public of those middle-power countries appear to favour a values-based, rules-based, long-term international system.

When we asked about the right focus of international cooperation, the lead response was unsurprisingly to 'prevent wars and conflict' (48 per cent). Securing peace was seen as the joint responsibility of nation-states and international bodies. But there was also broad agreement on the need for cooperation between nations on an important range of issues where it seems the public understand the need for global solutions to global problems. These middle-power voters wanted cross-border cooperation to tackle global climate change and protect the planet (30 per cent), to build a fair global economy and trade system (28 per cent), and to ensure everyone has enough food and clean water (25 per cent). And while building a fair economy was mainly seen as a task for national governments, despite the events of recent years, there has been a shift in public opinion whereby realising basic economic rights – such as access to food and clean water – is increasingly seen as an area where international organisations ought to lead.

What surprised me was that even among what we might call 'my country first' voters, many still believe cooperation can deliver political dividends. Of those who said that their country 'should prioritise its own people first' over global impacts, more than two out of three of them (69 per cent) nonetheless agreed on the importance of at least one of these propositions: the equal treatment of nations, a fair system of global decision-making, protecting future generations, or helping vulnerable people wherever they live.

Public opinion also bore out the desire for a new form of multilateralism, which is encouraging though perhaps surprising in an age where America First-style ideologues dominate the airwaves and the internet silos. We asked people to choose between two options: whether they think the world works best when countries make direct deals with each other one-on-one, or whether it works best when countries work together in groups or organisations to solve shared problems. Across the G20 as a whole, 70 per cent of people preferred multilateralism. In each of the middle countries, three quarters or more back multilateralism over bilateral deal-making. Indeed, across the G20 countries we polled, nearly three quarters (72 per cent) said they have confidence in groups of like-minded countries – such as the G20 – working together to solve global issues. It's notable that this confidence is higher than that in international organisations taken together (such as the UN, WHO, IMF or World Bank; 66 per cent), international NGOs (67 per cent) and regional organisations like the African Union, European Union or ASEAN (59 per cent).

But did the public think that countries other than China and the US could take the lead in shaping the world of the future? We attempted to identify which states, if any, outside the two superpowers have the legitimacy to lead broad global coalitions, so we asked people in each country what they thought of other nations. The highest net favourability ratings from the populations of other countries are Canada (57 per cent), Australia (56 per cent), Italy (55 per cent) and Japan (also 55 per cent). They are followed by Germany (51 per cent), the UK (48 per cent) and France (45 per cent). Russia is the only G20 country with a negative net favourability rating, while India sits at 5 per cent, Saudi Arabia 9 per cent, China at 10 per cent and the US at 22 per cent.

So by bringing these two results together, we can indeed identify a number of countries that meet both criteria: first, that command the global support to lead a coalition of middle powers and, second, that have, in their own land, a general public who would stand behind politicians for doing so. The countries that by this metric stand the best chance of being middle-power leaders are Canada, Australia, Japan, the UK, South Korea and Brazil. Some, like South Africa, have citizens who want to take on a leadership role but lack favourability ratings abroad – something which could change – while European states like Germany and France have the global backing but seem to find it difficult to bring their home voters along behind any leaders' efforts for reform, although, over time, they could do so.

It is perhaps unsurprising that the countries that came out as frontrunners did so – they already have a reputation for leadership across global issues including climate, nuclear non-proliferation, the oceans and biodiversity. European countries may have lost some confidence in themselves but the world still looks to them – and countries like Brazil or Japan – for leadership. But this is not to say that they should go out on their own and form blocs that are exclusive rather than inclusive. Some leaders of smaller countries are outstanding for their vision, sense of direction and ability to build alliances. The point is simply this: there are countries and leaders who are able to bring together the 75 per cent of the world we have identified as open to cooperation on equal terms. The leaders of these middle countries can enjoy public support when they champion the rule of law, human rights and cooperation on matters as important as climate and humanitarian aid. As the table below shows, those territories to which other countries look for leadership and which are already strong supporters of international cooperation can come together to create a global majority. Once we bring in Europe, Africa and India and Indonesia in Asia, a middle country bloc could represent 51 per cent of the world's population – and if we are wholly successful, three quarters of the world's population can be brought on board. Alongside this is the need to revitalise global institutions that are no longer fit for purpose in this new era, and should be remodelled for the challenges ahead.

Country	Population % of world	GDP % of world	Focaldata polling (Oct-Nov 2025)	
	2025 (IME WEO)	2025 (IME WEO)	% Local support for mulilateralism (over bilateralism)	Global net favourability towards these countries
Middle countries: Canada, Japan, Australia, UK, South Korea, Brazil, Mexico, South Africa	9%	16%	75%	**+39**
Middle countries + EU	15%	34%	73%	**+40**
Middle countries + EU + India and Indonesia	37%	39%	72%	**+35**
Middle countries + EU +India and Indonesia + Sub-Saharan Africa	51%	40%	72%	**+39**
US	4.3%	26%	71%	**+22**
China	17.5%	16.6%	59%	**+10**

Sources: Population (2025) and GDP (2025, current USD) – IMF World Economic Outlook April 2026 (WEO 9.0.0). World GDP = $118,175.5bn; World population = 8009M (sum of all IMF WEO member country LP values; excludes Cuba, North Korea, Syria and a small number of territories not in the WEO). Population % and GDP % for all country and regional rows computed from this file only. Multilateralism & net favourability – Focaldata, n=20,000, Oct-Nov 2025.

It matters that this constellation of leaders contains countries from both the Global North and South, and are from diverse ethnic groups and different religious traditions. If they could lead together – whether on single issues like the climate or financial stability, or by combining to reshape how international organisations make decisions – a new, broader and more balanced network would emerge. But they would have to be prepared to share the burdens as well as the benefits of global leadership – something yet to be put to the test.

The countries I have identified qualify because their public opinion favours multilateralism and would back political leaders in delivering global public goods. In this new age, therefore, the focus must be on an active citizenry. The previously understated and under-mobilised force of public opinion can now drive global change and, in particular, help advance global cooperation. There is a further reason why we should act now. Xenophobic anti-internationalist leaders, countries and coalitions are now pursuing a world order characterised by ideological opposition to what they call 'civilisational erasure'. If responsible coalitions do not lead, the irresponsible ones will take over. Our polling shows that most people in middle-power countries are sufficiently aware of the need to cooperate and actively want their countries to lead. We should not, however, underestimate the potential for the return of America, and for a new multilateralism advocated by its future leaders – one in which the costs and benefits of cooperation are more broadly shared, but which is built on persuasion, not dictation. No one should write off an America that for most of the last eighty years provided global leadership, and that, when under pressure, has a proven ability to adapt to change.

But, first, we need to discover the basis on which cooperation can be agreed and can endure.

10

COOPERATION: PRINCIPLES TO UNDERPIN A NEW WORLD ORDER

At one of the darkest moments of the twentieth century, when the forces of Nazism and fascism appeared unstoppable, and most of Europe had already fallen to Hitler's armies, American president Franklin Roosevelt and British prime minister Winston Churchill met at sea.

It was August 1941. Aboard the *Prince of Wales* near Newfoundland, Churchill had only one aim – to persuade America to join the war. Roosevelt, however, delayed the decision, insisting instead on an initiative that seemed to reflect concerns far from the immediate task of defeating Hitler and holding back the advancing German forces. He proposed a public statement – what came to be known as the Atlantic Charter – to set out the principles of the new world order that he hoped would emerge from the conflict: something better and fairer, and founded on humanitarian values.

The Atlantic Charter, though short in length, was both grand in scale and audacious in its ambition. Roosevelt and Churchill had come to recognise that Nazism was an attack on the very values that underpinned civilised societies. The Charter guaranteed support for national self-determination, set out how the rule of law would be enforced, democracy upheld and human rights championed, as well as insisting that fairness, equality and justice be embedded in domestic laws and practice. It was also the first political charter to focus on trade and commerce, based on the belief that protectionism had destabilised nations between the wars, and that the incomes of ordinary people would benefit from participating in a global system of trade in which the freedom of the high seas was guaranteed.

The Charter's principles were designed to appeal to many countries rather than just its initial signatories, and to appeal to their inhabitants because its objectives extended beyond the peaceful resolution of disputes to fair treatment for all nations and their citizens. It set out the principles that should govern domestic settlements in every country – social contracts that would be strong enough to bind national citizens together after the horrors of depression and mass unemployment that had characterised the 1930s. And so, for the first time, a global charter called for 'the fullest collaboration between all nations in the economic field with the object of securing, for all, improved labour standards, economic advancement, and social security'.[1] At what seemed the twilight of Western democracies, Roosevelt recognised that people needed something to fight for: a vision of a fairer future. He saw the connection between the local and the global. He could not win support for military action abroad if he did not offer a better future at home.

The document emerged only after vigorous argument. Determined to preserve the British Empire, Churchill objected to an America-inspired section proclaiming opposition to continued colonial rule, but Roosevelt made his bottom line clear: victory in war had to mean the end of empires. Initially, Churchill was also reluctant to incorporate a domestic section into the Charter that championed a commitment to social security and workers' rights. Eventually – but only after Churchill's deputy, Clement Attlee, and other Cabinet members intervened with a late-night ultimatum – the section of the Charter on social security was agreed.

It was not just a UK–USA agreement. By September 1941, it

encompassed twelve countries including the Soviet Union, rising to twenty-six countries in 1942, and thirty-five in 1944 including India, South Africa and Yugoslavia. By 1945, the Atlantic Charter had become the foundation stone for the United Nations Charter of 1945, signed by the fifty nations present at the San Francisco Conference. The historical significance of this should be emphasised: even at the height of the most violent armed conflict our planet had yet seen, the world needed more than announcements about military mobilisations. The global public needed a values-led statement that pointed to a future that the peoples of most countries could embrace.

The evidence I have presented for the breakup of the world order and the breakdown of community might suggest a counsel of despair. But the example of the Atlantic Charter, emerging as it did from a world in turmoil, offers hope – and a positive way forward. Today, at another critical turning point in world history, should we not consider our own charter, one for our times and for a generation facing new and quite different challenges?

The burning question is whether it is possible for enough of the international community today to agree on a mutually acceptable set of foundational values and basic rules. Our many differences preclude a rigid or doctrinaire set of treaty requirements, but could there be space for a statement of intent, developed through consultation, committing states to working within a new multilateral framework? Could that framework include not just procedures for dispute resolution, as was the stated intention of the Concert of Europe in 1815, but also principles of cooperation inspired by the Atlantic Charter of 1941 and the UN Charter of 1945? And could there be, arising from the principles, a programme of action that addresses the challenges of 2026 and beyond? Such an agreement, taking into account – while also transcending – our cultural diversity, could provide the means by which we both avoid continued conflict over fundamental issues vital to the future of humankind and advance our collective wellbeing.

Values-led pragmatism – from power to persuasion

But how do we come to an accord on the central values of such a charter? In a unipolar world, the hegemonic power could impose its preferred system of values on others; cooperation could be achieved by the threat of compulsion or compulsion itself. Iraq stands as the starkest illustration of that logic in practice. But as in that instance, even before the political costs became visible, the moral costs were already clear. In a multipolar world – even a lopsided one – dictation cannot work. Values, not least support for democracy, cannot be imposed from the outside. We must rely on the attraction of our ideas, beginning with appeals to self-interest but building towards a shared understanding of the common good, what we might call values-led pragmatism. By this I mean a world order that creates a global rule of law, promotes activities which benefit others, provides global public goods, and, in general, brings about international cooperation sharing its burdens and benefits of globalisation equitably, while avoiding undue infringement of national sovereignty.

Values-led pragmatism recognises that, while order was once achievable by elites balancing their own power, the world order of the future – and the cooperation it requires – will only hold if it is perceived as legitimate by the peoples of the world. And it accepts that legitimacy cannot be manufactured by process alone. International initiatives must be built on values shared by the majority of nations, even if – for now – global consensus seems out of reach. Countries that do not align with those values would have to be persuaded by the majority, or remain a minority excluded from benefits of the charter. For dialogue and negotiation, not dictation or coercion, must now become the way the next world order is built. It may be that both China – which still shows little intention of liberalising politically – and America – which has retreated in recent years from the rules-based order it once championed – would initially stand outside such a compact, although the invitation must be open to all. But both countries must surely understand one central idea underlying such an approach – reciprocity. After all, it is central to what President Trump says is the basis of both his trade policy and his approach to mutual defence through NATO. And it is, on paper, at the heart of China's Global Development, Civilization, Governance and Security initiatives.

Shared goals: civil, political, social and economic rights

Throughout history, individual civil and political rights have been indispensable tools for the powerless. The Canadian politician Michael Ignatieff has conducted research into human rights on every continent, and found that even in the poorest corners of the world, long-oppressed groups such as women and ethnic minorities have a strong sense of their own rights.[2] He also found this to be true in patriarchal or authoritarian societies. Less common is the recognition that those rights depend upon the rights of others. Ignatieff describes this as a form of moral individualism: the belief that human rights exist primarily to protect one's own autonomy against institutions such as the state, the family or the church. Yet the citizen can enjoy freedom of expression or the right to political participation only if others enjoy the same protections. Rights are reciprocal and their legitimacy rests on mutual recognition and restraint.

The modern doctrine of the indivisibility and interdependence of rights reflects this. Civil and political rights, and social and economic rights, need not be seen as competing categories: they are mutually reinforcing. It is self-evident that political freedoms remain hollow as long as people are illiterate, underfed, homeless or unable to access basic healthcare. Civil liberties without social rights leave individuals permanently vulnerable to domination and abuse.[3] Equally, having strong social provision is inadequate in itself if people are not allowed to think, debate or share opinions and ideas.

The deeper challenge is to restore public trust and engagement. The law can often appear remote and technocratic, a matter for judges and lawyers but far beyond the lives of ordinary people. If the defence of human rights is framed in purely legalistic terms, it will fail. One problem arises when rights are seen as absolute claims detached from social responsibility. In a democratic society, rights are limited where necessary to protect the rights and freedoms of others. For example, the right to free speech is qualified by prohibitions on expressing or inciting hatred according to race, gender, disability or sexual orientation. This emphasises that rights protect autonomy, but they only function when part of a reciprocal social contract. Courts will routinely balance rights against public interest, security and proportionality. And so, as many have argued, human rights are not a licence for selfishness but a framework for coexistence.

Rights endure when they are understood as expressions of shared values, not as gifts bestowed from on high. This means that resources spent on specific projects, such as building capacity in a country's legal system through training judges or equipping police, may be better used engaging with the public on why rights are important to begin with, how they relate to everyday challenges, and why the rule of law is essential for protecting the powerless against the powerful. The task, as Harold Koh has persuasively argued, is to engage, translate and leverage popular support for just laws. This means civic education programmes which start in schools and extend into workplaces and the broader community by incentivising and supporting the emergence of civic leaders. Swedish law already mandates student councils that have statutory rights to enact changes in their schools. We will return to this theme in detail in Chapter 14. But to be truly secure, rights must be embedded in the culture of a society through a combination of laws, education, citizen action and a recognition of reciprocity.

In turn, we must ensure rights are delivered in a meaningful and tangible way. Rights are not only protections against the state; they are claims on the state to secure conditions of dignity. Human rights must include the right to decent employment, social protection and good public services. When poverty and inequality deepen, talk of rights loses credibility – and authoritarian alternatives gain ground. South Africa's constitution includes a comprehensive set of social and economic rights, explicitly guaranteeing rights to housing, healthcare, food, water and social security, with particular attention to the rights of children.

This broader understanding of rights is more urgent than ever in a world where private power is growing, inequalities are widening and the vulnerable continue to be exploited. Insecurity has become a permanent feature of many lives – lowering living standards and diminishing the sense of agency that democracy requires. Technological change in the form of uncontrolled expansion of AI and algorithmic manipulation will only exacerbate this situation, creating new threats to privacy, autonomy and job security which existing rights frameworks were not built to manage.

However, there continues to be a mismatch between our aspirations and what we can tangibly achieve, even where the necessary legal and regulatory frameworks exist. Rights to welfare and social protection are encoded in many European constitutions (Germany's Basic Law is one example), but legal enforcement is another matter. As a result they are more guiding principles than binding guarantees. South Africa's example is instructive again. Its constitutional provision of social and economic rights has led to real progress, including in the Treatment Action Campaign case, where a Constitutional Court ruling required the government to deliver a comprehensive programme to limit mother-to-child transmission of HIV. The Grootboom case also demonstrates the promise and limitations of constitutionally protected rights. The court prevented the removal of an informally housed community and strengthened protections against arbitrary eviction. Yet enforcement has been uneven, and implementation of court orders has often been poor due to resource constraints and because rights are subject to progressive realisation (gradual implementation over time). Despite its strong constitution, South Africa continues to struggle with dramatic levels of inequality: in 2024 around 63 per cent of people were living in poverty. However, this is not to say that reflecting social rights in law is futile, but simply that it is not enough on its own. Courts can use their enforcement powers, but sustained delivery requires political will, administrative capacity and public pressure.

Several Latin American constitutions go further in making social rights formally enforceable. The constitutional frameworks of Brazil, Colombia and Ecuador all provide for rights to education, health, housing, work and social security.* But they struggle with enforcement: courts find it hard to articulate what these rights actually require, and to identify who is responsible for ensuring them. In Brazil, judges frequently opt for financial compensation over demanding that services be provided, raising questions about fairness and long-term delivery. Even where rights exist in law, they must reckon with uneven access and structural inequality. Chile's failed constitutional reforms of 2022 and 2023 illustrate the political sensitivity of this terrain. They sought to establish the country as a social and democratic state governed by the rule of law, and enshrine rights to health, education, housing and water. Both proposals were rejected, reflecting public concern over cost, feasibility and institutional trust.

The first lesson we learn is that constitutions must be explicit, not only about the existence of rights but about who is responsible for delivering them. Ambiguity undermines enforcement and public confidence. Second, judicial enforcement, while essential,

---

* Brazil's 1988 constitution lists education, health, housing, work, social security and protection of motherhood and childhood as fundamental rights (Article 6), with labour protections detailed in Articles 7–11. Colombia and Ecuador have similarly robust frameworks.

cannot carry the burden alone. As scholars such as Jeff King have argued, social rights must be developed incrementally through democratic processes involving legislatures and citizens, not simply left to courts.[4] Third, rights are strongest when upheld by social movements and explained and defended by civic leaders and organisations. Brazil's Movimento dos Trabalhadores Rurais Sem Terra (MST) has mobilised millions of rural workers to secure land reform and social rights, demonstrating how economic justice movements can act as bulwarks against authoritarianism. In the Democratic Republic of Congo, the youth-led Lucha movement has linked demands for water, infrastructure and democracy through sustained civic activism, even amid conflict. Such mobilisation is reinforced where there is a legal duty to report abuse, protection for whistleblowers, an obligation on public authorities to act, and systematic monitoring.

These cases show that rights are an essential element of a shared social contract, fought for and renewed across generations. They provide the structure within which we all define our shared values and heritage. My contention is that values-led pragmatism on the world stage ought to rest on the same three legs as effective domestic rights: shared values, the support of civil society and active citizens, and the rule of law. I believe that all three already exist; we must now bring them together.

What are our shared global values?

Have our ideological differences grown so deep – within and between nations – that we can no longer agree on even the most basic rules? If so, the risk of disorder, instability and conflict will only grow. Order depends on people finding common ground. Even a transactional foreign policy must rest on some fundamental commitments: for example, prohibition of the use of force, protection of human rights and fundamental freedoms, and respect for the sovereignty and territorial integrity of states. These are not abstract ideals opposed to national interests. On the contrary, countries enjoy a clear and enduring benefit from upholding them, and from ensuring that violations carry real consequences.

Rules without values lack legitimacy, and legitimacy – the widespread belief that arrangements are fair – is the foundation of any sustainable order. Without it, institutions become empty shells, obeyed selectively by the powerful and ignored when inconvenient. That is why no durable world order can be built on formal rules alone, nor imposed by any state or coalition of states, however powerful. It must be grounded in values broadly shared by the majority of people.

The philosopher Jürgen Habermas argued that democracy and civilised society depend on what he called a 'background consensus': an underlying set of shared moral assumptions about right and wrong, fairness and solidarity. For much of the post-war era, that consensus in the West drew on the traditions of Judaeo-Christian morality and Enlightenment rationality, and it was rarely questioned because Western dominance made such claims appear universal. At its height in the years after 1945, the West accounted for around nine tenths of global trade, two thirds of the world's economic output, and, for a long time, an even larger share of wealth and consumer spending, as well as unassailable military power.

That world is no more. Western nations now account for only around a quarter of world trade, and within a decade close to half of global economic activity will be centred in Asia. The American-led order is likely to be remembered as the last of the Western-dominated world orders. Western conceptions of rights, law and political economy can no longer claim to be the unquestioned basis for agreement for a genuinely global system.

This demands humility from those of us in the West. In the 1980s, Alasdair MacIntyre warned that Western societies were entering a condition he called 'emotivism', in which moral claims come to be seen as little more than expressions of individual preference. Asked to name a society which remained unaffected, he mischievously replied that he could point only to one, the caste-bound traditional society of Rajasthan.[5] But his warning was apt: the Western moral inheritance had worn so thin that no Western society could convincingly act as a model for others.

And yet across the world's major religious and moral traditions, there exists a shared ethical core. Central to Islam, Hinduism, Sikhism, Judaism and many other non-Western traditions is not only reciprocity, but the defence of the powerless against the powerful. It can be summed up in the Golden Rule: the injunction to treat others, including strangers, with respect and restraint.

Once again, putting these values into practice requires active citizens. In Chapter 7, I set out our findings for broad, international support for a rights-based programme of global cooperation. Others have found the same: a recent nine-country study on international law found that between 80 and 95 per cent of respondents – from Indonesia to the United States – object to torture, attacks on hospitals and the deliberate creation of famines, and reject the idea that might makes right, even when justification for it is framed in terms of national security.[6] This suggests that such ideas are not parochial Western values, but universal ethical standards that are a viable moral foundation for a renewed world order.

The same study found that 71 per cent wanted stronger enforcement of international law, leading the authors to conclude that today, at one of humanity's most dangerous moments, support for international law is not dying but simply waiting for the political will to rejuvenate it. In the United States, whose president has claimed that international law does not matter, 77 per cent of respondents said they would not support their government illegally invading another country, even if it claimed to be acting in the interests of the security of the American people.

And current international institutions still have enough support to underpin a renewed values-based charter. When the Universal

Declaration of Human Rights was drafted in the 1940s, experts and informed elites were consulted but not the global public. What we now have, from the World Values Survey, from Pew and from the surveys we have initiated and analysed, is a clear statement of what that public is prepared to support. As Chapter 7 showed, we have an unparalleled opportunity to underpin global order with democratic support, if active citizens in the coalition of middle powers come together to demand action.

The rule of law as the basis for stability

A further condition for a successful values-led order is that it is subject to impartial arbitration. That means we need the rule of law. But in a world no longer dominated by a single hegemon, even middle and lesser powers may be tempted to pursue their interests through force or to test the limits of international restraint. The diffusion of power, combined with the weakening of legal norms, increases the risk of conflict at all levels, and makes it even more necessary that the rule of law is upheld.

The current drift away from the rule of law can be quantified. A global decline in legal accountability and democratic standards over the past decade is documented in the World Justice Project's Rule of Law Index, Freedom House's *Freedom in the World* report, and the Economist Intelligence Unit's Democracy Index. These measures echo what we are seeing play out in the world around us today. The rule of law is being violated with impunity: recorded crimes against humanity are rising, national constitutions are being violated at the hands of corrupt elites, and modern slavery persists, but also more generally we see the increased recourse to war and unlawful conduct in war.

The UN Charter did not abolish war, but sought to confine it within strict legal and moral limits, and by the mid-twentieth century there appeared to be a hard-won consensus that war must be a last resort, authorised by legitimate authority, justified only by self-defence or the prevention of grave injustice, and conducted in a proportionate manner. Yet those limits are increasingly ignored. The principle of proportionality, codified in the Geneva Conventions, must be restored by rejecting reinterpretations that shift scrutiny away from individual acts of violence towards far less demanding assessments of the legality of overall war aims after the fact. The distinction between civilian and military targets, which has become blurred, must be re-emphasised, preventing aggressors justifying attacks on basic infrastructure and even at times schools and hospitals. Indeed, justice in war cannot be separated from justice in the decision to wage it, as Michael Walzer has argued: the moral equality of combatants requires that all parties be bound by the same rules, and that non-combatants be protected except in the most extreme and narrowly defined circumstances.[7]

Public opinion complicates this picture. Surveys suggest that many European societies are reluctant to contemplate war, even in defence of shared values. Sociologists describe Europe as a 'post-heroic' continent, self-consciously pursuing peace and individual prosperity. But merely to talk of deterrence without moral clarity about what is right and what is wrong will not bring public support. If societies are to contemplate collective defence, they must be persuaded that force is truly a last resort, grounded in just cause and constrained by law.[8]

But if the rule of law is in retreat both at home and abroad, this is driven by three converging trends that must be addressed at source. First, the rise of nationalist, authoritarian populism has recast human rights and the rule of law as obstacles to democracy rather than its foundation, while at the same time normalising the idea that law is an instrument of power rather than a restraint upon it. A sign of the deterioration is that in a Europe that has prided itself in upholding the rule of law, there are now five EU member states where, according to the 2026 report of the Civil Liberties Union for Europe, the rule of law has been eroding 'consistently and intentionally' with respect to justice, civil society, media freedom and tackling corruption.[9] Second, through digital technologies, campaigns of misinformation by extremist factions – sometimes organised by foreign powers – have eroded trust in institutions even within long-established democracies. Third, states facing acute domestic pressures have become less willing to invest political capital in defending the very international organisations tasked with peacekeeping, mediation and legal enforcement.

If the rule of law is to be revived, two false choices must first be rejected. On the one hand lies an unrealistic cosmopolitanism that often implies that Western norms are the only universal norms and the naïve assumption that naming and shaming wrongdoers, or appealing to their better nature, is enough to rebuild international law. On the other hand, a nihilistic realism reduces international relations to power alone – and treats legality as an inconvenience to be set aside whenever it conflicts with perceived national interest. Under the first approach, we run the risk of what Murray Hunt has called 'rule of law imperialism': the assumption that one historical or cultural model can be transplanted wholesale into vastly different societies. The reality is that legal traditions vary, and successful renewal of the rule of law depends on recognising this plurality, while insisting on the underlying purpose of law – to restrain arbitrary power and protect the vulnerable – and acknowledging that many minimum legal standards are widely shared. The rule of law cannot be imposed from outside, it cannot be strengthened in ungoverned or fragile contexts through military intervention, nor can it be secured solely through practical changes like building courtrooms, training judges or equipping police forces with computers and truncheons, while ignoring the underlying political economy of power.[10]

A growing body of research, including work by the Carnegie Endowment, shows that when countries abandon the rule of law, it is not because they are ignorant of legal traditions and techniques, nor too poor to afford to follow them, but because powerful interests actively undermine core legal institutions for their own gain. Corruption, the theft of assets and a history of impunity can hollow out legal systems from within. In such situations, external assistance that focuses only on capacity-building can inadvertently entrench repression rather than restrain it.[11]

Under the second approach of nihilistic realism, we risk a system in which states cherry-pick obligations, obeying rules only when convenient. This is not a defence of sovereignty but a recipe for instability. Russia's current approach illustrates the danger. By treating international law as optional and agreements as dispensable, and leveraging military technology to weaponise its assets, Russia's disregard for legal restraint has rapidly escalated into catastrophic violence. In this way the Putin regime has helped precipitate a conflict whose costs and consequences extend far beyond Ukraine.

Neither position is viable, as the UK attorney-general has recently argued.[12] However, there is, as some people have described it, a path between naïveté and nihilism: one that recognises the pursuit of national interest as legitimate, but insists that it be conducted within a framework of agreed rules. In the words of the former foreign secretary, David Lammy, this is a matter of 'advancing progressive ends by realist means'. Under this approach, international law does not negate sovereignty; it rests upon it. It is not imposed from outside, but negotiated between states that are willing to recognise their mutual dependence.[13]

This middle path depends, once again, on shifting from power to persuasion, and appealing to a values-led pragmatism. The starting point for a renewal of the rule of law must therefore be the recognition by sovereign states that shaping, upholding and complying with shared legal frameworks is in their own interests. And ultimately, this must begin at home. Nearly all sovereign states possess constitutions that commit, at least in principle, to the rule of law and human rights. These constitutional declarations provide a foundation on which to rebuild trust, but constitutions can too easily be bypassed. As with any social contract, their survival requires vigilance. Even a legal architecture that appears compelling will fail if it lacks public legitimacy. To millions of citizens, international law today seems more like an empty shell than a valued asset, honoured in textbooks but routinely overridden by the use of force abroad and violations of basic liberties at home. This perception matters; law derives its authority not merely from formal enactment, but from the belief that it serves justice and applies equally to all.

Without domestic support, international legal commitments will appear hollow. What is required is an intelligent and patient strategy beginning at home, one that accords priority to civic education, public engagement and cultural change alongside necessary reform of institutions. Crucially, people must see the rule of law not as a set of demands imposed from above, but something that protects them – a mutual agreement, grounded in shared values, that holds the powerful to account.

International law operates under similar conditions. In the absence of a global sovereign, its authority rests on *pacta sunt servanda* – the principle that agreements must be honoured. Bodies such as the International Court of Justice and the International Criminal Court embody this aspiration, but their effectiveness depends on political will. Law cannot function where promises are treated as expendable, and where international courts are regarded as external impositions rather than part of the natural evolution of justice in an interdependent world.

The task, therefore, is not to downgrade the importance of law but to reconnect it to the values that give it meaning. The law must be understood again as a restraint on the powerful and a shield for the vulnerable, for citizens within states and for smaller states within the international system. When grounded in justice and supported by public consent, it can still offer peaceful coexistence in a multipolar world.

The Atlantic Charter of 1941, at civilisation's lowest point, became a beacon for a new world because it was underpinned by a demand for the restoration, in the conduct of international affairs, of the rule of law and respect for basic human dignity. And just as the Atlantic Charter began as a bilateral agreement, but grew in only three years to encompass thirty-five states, a new like-minded statement of Principles of Cooperation is capable of attracting a similar cascade of support. So, in a world whose insecurities today have parallels with the 1940s, now is the right time to set out a new charter for a fifth world order that will uphold basic human decency.

11

RULES OF THE ROAD: A CHARTER FOR THE TWENTY-FIRST CENTURY

Words can change history. On Independence Day, 4 July, in 1962, the 175th anniversary of America's Constitutional Convention, President John F. Kennedy delivered a speech of both national and international significance in which he announced that the American Declaration of Independence, which had focused on the liberty of one nation, should now be complemented by a new Declaration of Interdependence focusing on the indivisible liberty of all citizens of the planet. In a modern, 'intercontinental' world, the United States, he said, could not secure justice, defence, prosperity or liberty on its own; it could do so only in concert with other free nations.[1]

A year later, and only months before his assassination, in a speech at the American University in Washington – the secret preparations for which were 'kept completely outside of the bureaucracy' of the White House, which saw its contents only at the last moment – he brought that Declaration to life by offering the hand of friendship to the Soviet people. 'For, in the final analysis,' he said, 'our most basic common link is that we all inhabit this small planet. We all breathe the same air. We all cherish our children's future. And we are all mortal.'[2] The unilateral initiative to ban nuclear testing that he announced that day was followed by the Partial Nuclear Test Ban Treaty, signed in Moscow on 5 August 1963 by the United States, the Soviet Union and the United Kingdom. This was Kennedy's final contribution in his desire for 'a new world of law where the strong are just, the weak secure, and the peace preserved'.[3] Today, our world is far more economically integrated, socially interconnected and interdependent than it was sixty years ago when Kennedy made his speech. But still there is no Declaration of Interdependence. So let us create one.

Our task is not to design an ideal constitution for the world from scratch, but to construct a viable framework – one that commands legitimacy, functions under multipolar conditions and endures under political pressure, all while tackling the pressing challenges of peace, development and sustainability. And building on not just Woodrow Wilson's Fourteen Points and Franklin Roosevelt's Atlantic Charter, but the United Nations Charter itself, this can best be achieved with a foundation of public support. For a new charter to earn that support, three things are essential: extensive public consultation; clarity on the domestic benefits of international cooperation; and a transparent and fair approach to sharing the burdens and benefits of global order.

As our polling has shown, under the right circumstances public opinion favours cooperation. Understandably, people see the world through the lens of their own lives, but this does not mean they are not open to international cooperation, particularly when it is shown to be in their own interest. This brings us to the second requirement for a new charter: instead of mandating international cooperation, it must explain it in terms of the domestic benefits. If, for example, we propose to transfer resources from the Global North to the Global South on the very sensible grounds that it is in all our interests to support global development and prosperity, and if we are to ask citizens in one country to make short-term sacrifices to benefit those in another, we have to be more adept at explaining how all benefit.

The idea that stability and order abroad is inseparable from cohesion and progress at home must be at the heart of a new charter. It must show how we will put into practice programmes supporting social and economic rights; rights to health, education, housing and social security; and rights to decent work, a strong supportive community and the provision of the basic necessities for life. In later chapters, I suggest what those programmes might look like. The charter itself should articulate those rights in greater detail than the Atlantic or UN charters. Doing so would give every citizen, every social movement, benchmarks to hold their government to. This is the basis of 'upwards' democratic accountability.

In that sense, rights are inseparable from democracy. We must also explain why an active participatory democracy is essential. Otherwise the quiescence and complacency of the rest of the population will allow a small minority of extremists to dominate the agenda. Democracy cannot just be a tool with which elites use the state to serve their own interests. Democracy should be how we engage with each other to ensure that, at all times, and without fear or favour, the state serves the public interest. We must not forget that democracy succeeds best when it ensures all parts of society have a say in the decisions that affect their lives. Throughout this book we have identified a missing element in our modern societies: a strong, resilient civil society. And so in the chapter on democracy we will make proposals – from civic education in our schools to citizens' juries and assemblies in our communities – to revive popular participation and reinforce democratic accountability.

This brings us to the third requirement of a new charter: transparency and accountability. The burdens and benefits in a new system must be open to public scrutiny, and governments should be held to account when they fall short. For the past century, states – and democratic publics – have been able to rely on America as the 'liberal hegemon' which has guaranteed security through NATO and ensured free navigation of the seas, while tolerating Washington's occasional tendency to bend or break the rules. The rule of law should be as it was always intended to be: a safeguard of the public interest against vested interests and a means of preventing the powerless being at the mercy of the powerful.

The charter and the domestic compact

A values-led global order and robust domestic compacts are not separate or alternative projects; they depend on each other. The most systematic attempt so far to link the local and the global has been the Sustainable Development Goals (SDGs) of 2015, and before them the Millennium Development Goals of 2000. The goals explicitly integrate economic growth with the promise of social inclusion and environmental protection. Their universality – applying to rich and poor countries alike – marks an important advance. Their weakness is a lack of clarity in how they are implemented, but they already highlight the very basic premise that none of us, and no place on earth, will be wholly safe, secure and prosperous as long as millions remain otherwise. At a national level, constitutions such as those of South Africa and India place dignity, rights and material security at their centre. Regionally, the European Union's Social Chapter demanded that economic integration be accompanied by labour protection, action to prevent discrimination and social dialogue. In both, universal values shape domestic policy. In neither case is fairness an abstraction. The challenge is in implementation: it requires tax systems seen to be just, labour markets that reward effort without exploitation, welfare systems that protect against misfortune, and public services that enable and are responsive to public participation.

Yet too often, international economic institutions have seemed to conflict with domestic compacts rather than supporting them. Polices of 'structural adjustment', fiscal austerity and deregulation were often imposed on countries by unaccountable international agencies without local consent and with little thought for the social fallout in unjustifiable levels of poverty and inequality, and this still casts a long shadow. The promised convergence did not materialise; instead, many countries became less stable and more unequal, which in turn contributed to generating populist reactions, and then democratic erosion.

For a new charter to succeed, global rules must reinforce domestic compacts rather than undermine them. Trade must support decent work. Financial integration must reduce, not increase, instability. Climate transitions must expand opportunity and ensure costs are shared fairly. And development programmes in health, education and poverty reduction must be country-owned and not imposed from outside.

Where domestic compacts are weak, so is consent for international cooperation. A global charter cannot therefore be legitimate unless it strengthens the social foundations of democratic accountability within nations. And policy alone cannot sustain domestic compacts; they must be living documents, renewed through ongoing consultation and the everyday associations of civic life. The ultimate foundation of any order, national or international, is not the words contained in the treaty or statute but the habits of cooperation learned where people actually live.

So a strong sense of belonging and community is not the enemy of internationalism, it is its precondition. Clubs, cooperatives, neighbourhood associations, religious congregations, sports teams and volunteering networks are the social infrastructure of belonging – where trust is built, differences negotiated and common purpose learned. Civic participation is about more than voting, important though that is. It is the experience of membership, taking part and making a contribution, everyday practices that show our rights are inseparable from our responsibilities.

What should be in a charter? Its substantive content

A new statement of principles must meet three tests: reaffirm the core values which underpin international cooperation – human dignity, the rule of law, democratic accountability and the sovereign equality of states; explicitly reject the idea that dividing the world into competing spheres of influence is a legitimate means of organising international order; and set out clear rules for reciprocity and burden-sharing.

To this end, I propose the following basic set of seven Principles of International Cooperation. These principles are interconnected and interdependent. Human rights – explicitly including economic and social rights as well as civic and political rights – set common goals. For sovereign states to pursue these in their own way, while retaining the confidence of the global community, they must champion the rule of law. This means ensuring transparency in decision-making while remaining accountable to their people.

Principle 1: Human dignity and the promotion and protection of human rights

We hold to the fundamental truth that every person is entitled to human dignity and full enjoyment of their human rights, and the right to develop their human capabilities to the full.

The equal and inalienable rights of every person remain the moral foundation of legitimate governance at every level. Articles 55 and 56 of the UN Charter commit states to 'universal respect for, and observance of, human rights and fundamental freedoms for all'. These principles were reaffirmed in the Universal Declaration of Human Rights in 1948 and reinforced in the Helsinki Accords under Principle VII. The 2024 Pact for the Future once again affirms that human dignity is the anchor of global cooperation. Inclusive institutions, freedom of belief and protection of minorities are universal safeguards of our common humanity.

The Atlantic Charter of 1941 committed its signatories to securing 'improved labour standards, economic advancement and social security' through international cooperation. This commitment was carried into Article 55(c) of the UN Charter, which obliges states to promote higher standards of living, full employment and conditions of economic and social progress. These principles were institutionalised through the International Labour Organization – founded in 1919 and incorporated into the UN system in 1946 – given binding legal force in the International Covenant on Economic, Social and Cultural Rights and most recently reaffirmed through Sustainable Development Goal 8 on Decent Work and Economic Growth, adopted unanimously by UN member states. We seek to redouble efforts to realise economic and social rights, the enjoyment of which is so central to citizens' perception of the legitimacy of political orders, including the global order.

Principle 2: Sovereign equality in a multipolar world

The principle of the sovereign equality of states must be the foundation of any future order and remains the cornerstone of international law.

Article 2(1) of the UN Charter affirms that the organisation 'is based on the principle of the sovereign equality of all its Members', and Article 2(4) prohibits the threat or use of force against the territorial integrity or political independence of any state. These principles were reaffirmed across Cold War divides in the Helsinki Final Act of 1975 and again in the Pact for the Future, which explicitly recognises the importance of multilateral cooperation in a multipolar world. Peaceful coexistence in an interdependent world requires dialogue, mutual respect and understanding based on recognition of legitimate differences.

In a multipolar era, sovereign equality means that power can only be legitimate if it is exercised within a shared moral and legal order. No country has the right to determine another's political, economic or security choices, and spheres of influence that undermine the independence of sovereign states have no place in the modern world. The weaponisation of trade, finance, energy or supply chains as instruments of coercion is equally incompatible with these principles, and we commit to acting together to prevent and resist it.

Sovereignty and interdependence are not opposites but, when grounded in justice and restraint, are mutually restraining.

Principle 3: Promoting the rule of law

The rule of law – predictable, impartial and equally applied – must govern relations both within and between states. No viable global order can rest on the exercise of power alone.

Legal commitments must bind the strong as well as the weak, and emergency powers must also remain subject to law. No state, however powerful, is above the law and every state, however small, should enjoy its equal protection. Where legality collapses, force fills the vacuum; where law is upheld, cooperation between states becomes possible.

The rule of law is the institutional foundation that makes power legitimate. The UN Charter's Preamble affirms faith in law as the alternative to force, while Article 1 commits members to the peaceful settlement of disputes. International adjudicatory institutions, including the International Court of Justice, were created to provide predictability in a system lacking a central authority. Subsequent UN General Assembly resolutions on the rule of law have repeatedly affirmed that legality must govern both domestic and international conduct, including during emergencies. Where legal commitments are applied selectively, or where emergency powers escape legal constraint, the result is not security but mistrust, insecurity and fragmentation.

We reaffirm our unwavering commitment to our obligations under international law, including as they relate to people affected by wars, conflicts, famines, natural disasters and oppression.

Principle 4: Collective action on shared threats to life, peace and security

All states have a responsibility to prevent war and mass harm, and advance common security. It is imperative to honour the international duty to prevent crimes against humanity, recognising a shared responsibility to address atrocities in all regions and conflicts, with no double standards.

Preventing war and mass harm has been the central purpose of the international system since 1945. Article 1(1) of the UN Charter commits states to take 'effective collective measures for the prevention and removal of threats to the peace'. This preventive logic was reinforced by the Kellogg–Briand Pact's rejection of war as an instrument of national policy, by the Helsinki Accords' emphasis on restraint, and by UN secretary-general Boutros Boutros-Ghali's Agenda for Peace, which placed preventive diplomacy and peacebuilding at the centre of multilateral action. The doctrine of the Responsibility to Protect, endorsed at the 2005 World Summit, and given legal expression in UN Security Council Resolution 1674 and the Rome Statute of the International Criminal Court, clarified that sovereignty entails responsibility. In the nuclear age, the logic of responsible protection was reinforced by the Reagan–Gorbachev principle that 'a nuclear war cannot be won and must never be fought', and later embedded in non-proliferation regimes and, most recently, in the Treaty on the Prohibition of Nuclear Weapons. The principle of common security, articulated by the Palme Commission in 1982, reinforces this logic: no nation can achieve lasting security at the expense of others.

Principle 5: Recognising the duty of states to promote active citizenship

States must create the conditions in which citizens have a say over how they are governed, with the primary form of accountability being that between the government and the governed.

Civic freedom, social cohesion and appropriate participation in how we are governed are not merely political ideals but practical foundations of a resilient society. States have a responsibility to cultivate the conditions in which participation can flourish: empowered communities, founded on protections for cultural and religious diversity, and spaces for peaceful deliberation, with democracy not imposed from above but sustained from below.

The freedom of peaceful assembly and association and the principle that the will of the people is the basis of legitimate authority are affirmed in Articles 20 and 21 of the Universal Declaration of Human Rights and given binding force through the International Covenant on Civil and Political Rights. Participation has also been recognised as a developmental imperative, most clearly in the UN Declaration on the Right to Development (1986), which affirms that people are entitled to participate actively in shaping their economic, social and political futures. The 2030 Agenda's commitment to 'peaceful, just and inclusive societies' and the Pact for the Future's emphasis on inclusive governance and social resilience reaffirm that democracy must be cultivated through strong local institutions, protected diversity and empowered civil society.

Principle 6: Equitable partnership in an interdependent world

Development is no longer peripheral but central to global legitimacy in a world marked by deep and widening inequalities. Equity between North and South, realised through country-owned, country-led programmes and reciprocity, must underpin cooperation. On this basis, interdependence becomes a foundation for partnership rather than a source of dependency. A legitimate global order should therefore be structured around reciprocity: in trade, finance, debt, technology and institutional voice. Each state 'puts in' and each 'gets back', with mutual benefits alongside mutual burden-sharing. Every state should contribute according to its means, and every state should benefit according to its needs. Without equity, an interdependent world descends into, for some, a world of domination and dictation. Widening inequalities within and between states erode social cohesion, weaken trust in institutions, and undermine the legitimacy on which cooperation depends.

Demands for development are rooted in a long tradition of collective action by developing countries. UNCTAD XV in

Bridgetown (2021) explicitly argued for transforming development models towards resilience and equality of opportunity. These themes recur in the Pact for the Future, which recognises that interdependence structured around extraction and asymmetric adjustment undermines legitimacy, whereas reciprocity transforms interdependence into partnership. True partnership, of the kind pioneered by the Accra Reset, will require capacity-building across the world, and must be underpinned by the participation of active citizens set out in Principle 5. At the heart of this partnership is investment in human capital – in people, education, health and culture – as a foundation for cooperation that delivers results.

Principle 7: Collective responsibility for shared global risks

The defining threats of the present age are global problems that require a globally coordinated response.

Pandemics, climate change, financial contagion, humanitarian disasters, irregular migration, organised crime, terrorism and the cross-border implications of transformative technologies including artificial intelligence and biotechnology do not respect borders. International cooperation on prevention, preparedness and response in each of these areas is not an act of charity, but preconditions of security, human dignity and inclusive prosperity. Shared global risks require cooperation across borders, including agreements on early warning, information-sharing and coordinated action.

Making the charter reality

How do we move this from a collection of principles to something that works in the real world? Such a charter could not be enacted through force but only through persuasion and cooperation. To succeed it would also have to fulfil some basic conditions.

Earlier charters, from the Concert of Europe of 1815 to the

Paris Charter of 1990, were Western documents, and the United Nations Charter was heavily influenced by Western thinking. A twenty-first-century charter cannot be partisan in this manner. Any charter that emerged from only one bloc, however large, would reproduce the fragmentation it seeks to overcome.

The era when the West could impose its values on international systems is long over. Climate change, pandemics, financial contagion, digital infrastructure, nuclear risk and large-scale displacement are irreducibly global in scope and nature, and their solutions must be too. And any charter which looks like a way for the powerful to impose their preferences on others will fail at birth. Multipolarity and the rising authority of the Global South means great-power domination is not only morally wrong but practically impossible. Recognising the interests and values of large, middle and small powers does not mean abandoning our principles, but it will require humility, reciprocity and genuine negotiation. To gain broad support, this charter will have to be co-authored, not merely co-signed.

Even in a deeply and unavoidably interdependent world, the nation-state is not obsolete. It is the platform upon which democracy, accountability and political legitimacy is founded and taxation, welfare and security delivered. Borders may have seemed like barriers to markets for centuries, and they can create friction, but they also mark out the lines within which the rule of law, social protection, security and democracy become possible. Any new charter must therefore recognise the importance of a positive patriotism, working with the nation-state and not around it, while rejecting divisive nationalist ideologies.

Flowing from this is subsidiarity, the idea that social and political issues should be resolved at the closest possible level to the citizen. No more global intervention than is required, but no less than is necessary. Certain challenges cannot be effectively addressed below the global level of decision-making, but there are others which cannot be solved above the national or local level.

Our past failures were often due to an inability to get this balance right. A new charter must fix this.

At the global level, certain functions are now inescapably shared: climate stability, pandemic preparedness, nuclear restraint, financial contagion, AI safety and the management of displacement. These require shared rules and shared responsibility. At the national level, democratic self-government, redistribution, public services, welfare and social protection must remain central. A new charter cannot override national democracy; it must rely upon it, while resisting both mercantilist state capitalism and exclusionary nationalism. At the local level, belonging and participation are born and come alive. This is where solidarity is learned or unlearned, and where cooperation becomes real.

A future charter cannot ignore the need to win public consent. If technocratic elites are allowed to impose their will on the rest of us, we create the conditions for populist nationalisms. International frameworks should reinforce domestic ones and not undermine them, and conditionality, imposed from above without any local engagement, must never again take precedence over national self-government.

Multipolarity is not only a term that reflects a new distribution of power; it also reflects a world in which we must recognise and respect a diverse range of values, histories and social models. There is no single global culture, or a 'flat world', nor would this be either achievable or desirable. Instead we must understand the values we have in common – these can be a moral grammar within which different political and cultural traditions can coexist, communicate and flourish. The task of a charter is not to erase difference but to build a system in which – within agreed limits of restraint, dignity and reciprocity – our diversity can flourish.

All charters set out clear powers but few have ever been able to enforce them. There are only two international bodies entrusted with powers to overrule without recourse to votes or vetoes – and both are under pressure to amend their ways of working. The World Trade Organization has an appeal system that ultimately allows its judges to overrule member countries, but despite planned reforms to prioritise negotiation, arbitration and conciliation, both China and the US are refusing to work within it. The International Criminal Court has the power to arrest, bring to trial and sentence perpetrators of crimes against humanity, but its membership is not universal. Countries including the US have refused to join, and others that were once willing to abide by its rules have either recently threatened to leave (South Africa and the Gambia) or actually done so (Burundi and the Philippines).

At the UN Security Council, it is the veto that often causes problems, allowing the exercise of authority without responsibility, in turn corroding legitimacy. Of the 124 vetoes exercised in its first twenty-five years, the Soviet Union was responsible for 112 of them. In the last twenty-five years, there have been fewer vetoes (seventy-seven) but worryingly they have been more widely spread, with the US on twenty-two, Russia on twenty, China on sixteen and the UK on six.[4] A system in which one country can block action on the gravest global risks threatens the Security Council's fundamental legitimacy. But the UN remains a vital forum, and so reform of the Security Council veto should be a priority for those seeking to renew global order. We should reconsider recent proposals such as qualified majority votes, a capacity for override from the General Assembly, or a restriction of policy areas where a veto can be exercised.

This is why it is important to be clear that a charter doesn't need a world government to implement it. What it does require is an operating system capable of authorising collective action and, where necessary, imposing sanctions without paralysing the system or relying on a dominant power to enforce them. The UN can still be part of this, but we need to think of it as more than an implementing body, but as a legitimate centre of authority:

a coordinator of action between countries and the place where countries are held accountable.

Formal endorsement of any reforms by the secretary-general and General Assembly could renew the UN itself, restoring it to the centre of a new global agenda. Effective reforms could enable more flexible and responsive forms of cooperation, better suited to today's geopolitical realities. We may not always be able to reach universal consensus, but a strong UN can ensure that disagreement does not slide into unchecked abuse of power. We should agree that a reformed United Nations is still uniquely placed to anchor the kind of initiatives proposed here. Even if, as Dag Hammarskjöld said in 1954, the UN was 'not created to bring us to heaven, but to save us from hell',[5] it still carries the best hopes of our generation and for the future.

But to focus exclusively on an institutional redesign is to miss the point. A new charter will only succeed if it works through persuasion rather than coercion. The exercise of power in a multipolar world will increasingly depend on the ability to convince rather than compel – to corral consent rather than impose compliance.

Legitimacy, reciprocity and moral credibility are therefore not decorative virtues: they are the pillars on which any new international order must stand. They are fundamental to any programme of cooperation that can deliver collective solutions on national issues like development and social justice, or global problems beyond the reach of any individual state. What that might look like – for economy and society, and for international development and the global environment – is what I will turn to next.

12

PROSPERITY: HOW WE REBUILD A FAIRER ECONOMY

The most revolutionary companies don't win through conventional means. Rather, they push the limits of what we imagine is possible. As the diffusion of AI creates new opportunities to deliver products and services in different ways, innovation will become even more critical to the next stage of our economic development.

Apple beat Nokia and other phone companies not by competing in hardware, but by redefining the phone as a pocket computer powered by brilliant software. Similarly, Tesla and BYD outpaced Ford and General Motors by reimagining the car not just as hardware, but as software. Airbnb, Netflix, Uber and Spotify stopped thinking merely of the product and instead created new platforms: Airbnb challenged Marriott and other hotel groups by turning unused homes into rentable accommodation without ever owning property or paying an annual rent; Netflix replaced Blockbuster – not by competing store to store, but by pivoting to streaming; Uber challenged taxis by turning private cars into a global transport network; Spotify succeeded over Sony by streaming music. Each showed that when it came to what the consumer was prepared to pay, access mattered more than ownership.

Through innovation, all these companies moved the goalposts. As did medical pathbreakers like the Covid vaccine, which for the first time allowed mRNA to safely instruct cells to produce viral proteins, a process which may now help us cure cancer. And new environmental technologies from carbon and methane capture, hydrogen fuel cells and biodegradable electronics, to green ammonia and even marine algae cultivation, are radically changing the way we harness sources of energy.

Innovations such as 'agentic AI systems' and 'neuromorphic chips' (that mimic brain efficiency) are not well known today, nor are quantum computing, nuclear fusion (which might itself be accelerated by AI simulations) or cell-free biomanufacturing, but breakthroughs such as these will in future be critical to delivering the higher output on which an inclusive prosperity and good public services depend, and in this new time of uncertainty, where countries feel obliged to reduce their dependency on others, give them new options for indigenous growth.

Economics dominates our everyday lives. It determines the products we consume, the homes we inhabit, the jobs we do, the jobs others do for us. It shapes the communities we live in. But in an era of hyper-individualism, we can lose sight of the inherently collaborative nature of the economy. If we want people to flourish together, the economy, from innovation to sales and after-sales services, has to be more than a collection of individuals pursuing their own interests. Nor is economics, as I have already said, merely about production, or consumption and distribution – it is an exercise in mutual cooperation to meet our shared goals. An economy founded on cooperation and mutuality is grounded in relationships, not just transactions. Our contributions and obligations to one another are what make shared opportunities possible. It is only through understanding that cooperation is the rule rather than the exception that we can successfully share knowledge, create complex products, build productive and sustainable economies, and care for the young, the vulnerable and the infirm.

People are right to be angry about the state of economic life today, and as I set out in Chapter 6, a rising sense of expectations that may always remain unfulfilled is a major force behind today's populist nationalism (and indeed left-wing populism too).

Politicians need to respond to these feelings of frustration, calling out and challenging the vested interests, the corruption, and the grotesque and inexplicable inequalities of income, wealth and power that we see in the world today.

But we also have found that populism is underpinned by a wider sense of economic malaise, an assumption that ours is a low-growth economy, which is itself undermining our political system. What I propose in this chapter, then, is a way of thinking about our economy that focuses on the importance of innovation as the driver of growth and broad-based prosperity, but also recovers ways of managing ourselves abandoned under neoliberalism. There are established traditions to build upon – Germany's regulated markets, Japan's coordinated economy and the Nordic emphasis on social investment – but all the main levers of economic policy, from industrial strategy to public investment, need to be reimagined for what they contribute to individual and collective wellbeing.

Innovation: collective genius

Innovation is the lifeblood of modern economies – the elemental force behind rising productivity and prosperity. Unlike physical goods, as Paul Romer has reminded us, ideas don't obey the law of diminishing returns.[1] One person's use of an idea doesn't prevent others from using it. Breakthroughs in one area often inspire new ideas in others. This means that innovation offers huge potential for higher growth. We still speak of innovation as the story of the lone inventor in their garage, as the one-off entrepreneurial genius with the creative and often disruptive mind. Yet innovation is inherently collaborative. Thomas Edison would not have filed more than a thousand patents without the fifty to seventy-five researchers he regularly employed at his Menlo Park laboratory.

The infrastructure for collaboration is already in place. The UK has seventeen of the world's top 100 universities, four in the top 20. If we look just at the north of England, whose cities rank among the least productive in Europe, the university system is strong, and fast-growing mid-sized firms can be found in every region, and often in our poorest communities.[2] But while universities foster collaboration, too few people from lower-income backgrounds secure places. The biggest obstacle to innovation today is not the absence of talent but the waste of it.

There are young people from disadvantaged backgrounds who could, given the chance, become successful inventors. They are our 'lost Edisons', a vast resource of untapped potential. If young people from lower-income backgrounds patented inventions at the same rate as their wealthier peers, there would, for example, be a 400 per cent rise in the number of innovations in America.[3] Unless we widen access to education and maximise incentives for innovators, we all lose out.

The challenge is therefore to take the best ideas from seminar rooms and laboratories and realise them. Models like the UK's Catapult Centres, Germany's Fraunhofer Institutes and MIT's Regional Entrepreneurship Acceleration Program show what is possible when governments, universities, corporations and entrepreneurs work together towards that goal. There are therefore two good sources for optimism: the potential of our people and the possibilities that arise from new technologies.

Modern economies grow when technology advances, investment rises and productivity improves. But this is not inevitable. After the global financial crisis, growth and innovation rates dropped sharply across the West – halving in the US and reducing UK growth by 2 percentage points a year – producing a lost decade for living standards.[4] That widespread decline was so extreme that it prompted an academic debate about whether ideas are getting harder to find,[5] as if innovation was exhausted.

But there are early signs that information technologies may be sparking a new wave of innovation and productivity growth through artificial intelligence. In the US at least, recent evidence suggests that the innovation slowdown may be reversing, driven by the rise in tech jobs and related professional services.[6] With the right incentives, innovation can spread across the economy – from smarter manufacturing and digital construction to automation that frees workers up for jobs requiring the human touch.

Commentators outside economics are right to worry about the social impact of AI and the potential threats it poses. Mass surveillance is a case in point, as demonstrated by Anthropic's recent run-in with the US government after refusing to remove safeguards from its AI model. As I write, both Anthropic and OpenAI have chosen to limit the distribution of frontier models that appear to empower people to mount highly disruptive cyber-attacks by exploiting flaws in software. The impact on the environment from the massive energy consumption required to power models is another worry, as well as the potential for chatbots to encourage harmful behaviour leading many people to feel AI is extractive not additive. A recent US report found just 18 per cent of Gen Z felt hopeful about AI.[7] However, most economists agree with Nobel laureate Philippe Aghion, who expects AI to generate modest growth – but enough to offset the past decade of stagnation.[8]

A further question mark hangs over the speed of this integration. The most important technologies often start slowly before a sudden moment of transformation. The steam engine of James Watt and the Stephensons sparked fears that horses would immediately be replaced, but to begin with it actually boosted the number of horses used in the economy – the US horse population peaked in 1910 at 20 million, five times what it had been seventy years earlier. But then came the tractor, and the number of horses plummeted to 3 million in just thirty years.[9]

We don't know yet whether AI's large language models will be more like the steam engine, sitting alongside old technology for years, or Ford's Model T and the tractor, triggering an immediate and irreversible decline in other areas. What we do know is that innovation is responsible for the 'hockey curve of growth': the massive global surge in incomes and decline in absolute poverty since 1800 after millennia when most lives were nasty, brutish and short.

The challenge, then, is not to resist new technologies but to harness and direct them for humanity's benefit. But we must examine whether innovation, instead of replacing labour, can help workers become more productive, make work more fulfilling and expand employment opportunities.

Managing disruption: direction, not drift

On the face of it, we are on the cusp of a wave of disruptive new technologies which will see both a demand for new skills and the obsolescence of old ones. Sixty per cent of American jobs today are occupations that did not exist in 1940 and this is the pattern found elsewhere across the advanced economies.[10] Millions across the world now work as full-time solar engineers, AI coders or social media influencers, while the previous legions of typists, clerks and switchboard operators have become relics.

What will these latest changes mean for the world? For a start, we can learn from the past. The Industrial Revolution delivered rising economic output but, for a hundred years, brought stagnant wages, loss of skills and poor living conditions. 'There is nothing automatic about new technologies bringing widespread prosperity,' the 2024 Nobel laureates Daron Acemoglu and Simon Johnson wrote. 'Whether they do or not is an economic, social, and political choice.'[11] And today we have two choices to make. First, there is the question of whether we can adapt to these changes to make the most of them. Can we create the right economic, social and political environment to realise the economic opportunities while securing fair outcomes for our people? More profoundly, though, where will we direct that change? It is not like a weather system that we must respond to but cannot shape. We can actively steer technological change towards human needs, as we have done recently by supporting renewable energy, rather than focusing exclusively on short-term profit. Such initiatives generate the greatest and most broad-based gains.

AI and quantum computing, robot-driven automation and new global supply chains will reshape work. But we can choose whether that is for better or worse; we can, for example, tilt the AI scales towards improving medical treatment and social care rather than, as has been happening recently, exploitation, surveillance or sexualisation. Humans bring curiosity, critical thinking and self-regulation to problems that AI's focus on probabilities and pattern recognition cannot match.[12] At its best AI can be 'Augmented Intelligence', empowering workers and extending our distinctively human capacities rather than being just another dimension of 'capital' in the production process. In retail and hospitality, handheld devices and kitchen 'co-bots' free staff to focus on service and creativity. Digital layout tools, prefabrication and augmented-reality training could make construction a high-tech, high-skill, high-wage sector. Whether we replace work or augment it is a policy choice. Public R&D grants, tax incentives and regulation should favour technologies that enhance human judgement and skill. We should fund a series of competitions, to encourage teams of innovators to address our most pressing social challenges.

The knowledge economy has the potential to emancipate and empower working people, but only if we approach it in the spirit of broad, democratic participation and experimentation.[13] The public can direct and manage how this latest disruption plays out. We do not need to be victims, subject to the whims of fate or – what may be worse – unaccountable Silicon Valley ideologues.

Work and the democratic economy

As debate rages about whether AI will destroy or enhance labour, it is important not to forget that human labour is not just a production input. It is and should be a source of creativity, pride and collaboration, as well as an opportunity to care for our fellow citizens. Yet too many workplaces are built on command and control, diminishing their employees and driving inequality.[14] A democratic economy means moving away from the corporate structures described by philosopher Elizabeth Anderson as 'private governments', wielding unchecked authority over employees.[15] Doing so can be economically efficient as well as morally right: raising productivity by liberating employees to be, at their best, creative problem solvers.

Workplaces can be improved by respecting the dignity of workers. Job satisfaction boosts productivity by 14 per cent, according to a Gallup study of over 3 million people worldwide.[16] Consider the famous 'Toyota method'. Where other production lines have treated people as cogs in the wheel, Toyota has shown how the exercise of human judgement and automation can complement each other. All workers can pause the production line at any point, and are expected to propose solutions to problems or inefficiencies immediately. Management does not see itself as issuing commands, but removing obstacles at the instigation of the workers. Trust and dignity means workers can embrace automation without fear of job loss or punishment, building on the talents that make them human rather than the mindless skills that make any of us replaceable.

Thinking of people not just as consumers but as workers and producers is what lies behind Dani Rodrik's theory of 'productivism'. Rodrik states that innovation-led growth requires experimentation and embedded collaboration between government and business, which leads to corporate success. When workers share in decision-making – as in Germany's 'co-determination' approach where workers sit on boards of directors – productivity and employment both grow, and investment can be directed towards tools which help workers rather than monitoring them.[17]

Every generation values different kinds of work in different ways. Crises like Covid showed us how much we depend on previously undervalued workers like delivery and warehouse employees. Markets can never be a perfect judge of who offers most and what we value most. Reimagining work for our generation might begin in those places where productivity is weakest, wages the lowest and corporate practices arguably the most cut-throat. One example is social care, which in the UK generates just £14 of value per hour worked, compared to £42 in manufacturing and £32 in construction. But there is nothing inevitable about low-pay, low-productivity, low-satisfaction care work. Care professionals deserve higher wages, as a matter of basic fairness, but also in recognition of their vital importance. They should also be given greater responsibility, as Wigan's pioneering 'Deal for Adult Social Care' has shown, and be supported by technologies that make their work less physically demanding and more productive. New handheld technologies could allow care workers to conduct simple medical tests such as blood pressure measurements, or provide basic triage on home visits. This would increase productivity, relieve pressure on GPs and hospitals, and crucially increase the opportunity for human interaction between care workers and those they are supporting.

In a modern and democratic economy, particularly when AI can fulfil many pattern recognition tasks but not those that depend on creativity, ingenuity or humanity, it is the things that make us distinctively human that should be put at the centre of business models. We should incentivise those that thrive on the creative and encourage workers' voices to be heard, and governments should invest in training, modular courses, incentives and safety nets that will help workers find new opportunities as our economies evolve.

The geography of contribution

Some argue that it is always most productive to concentrate wealth and talent in a few cities, and that focusing on places rather than people (helping the latter move to the former if necessary) is always inefficient. The evidence no longer supports this claim. The benefits of city scale are now offset by heavy costs: congestion, housing shortages, inequality and political backlash. The fact is that countries with greater spatial equality often grow faster. Strengthening America's second-tier cities, like Phoenix or Pittsburgh, could ease pressure on New York and San Francisco with little to no loss in productivity.[18] It makes no sense to have overcrowding, escalating house prices and the resulting inflationary pressures in one part of a country, and underemployment, labour surpluses and forced emigration in another.

There is nothing inevitable about a rise in regional economic inequalities, and many countries have avoided them in recent years. While regional inequalities have soared in the UK since the 1990s, over the same period they have remained stable in Italy and actually fallen in Germany.[19] As per Michael Porter's cluster theory, China's use of concentrations of interconnected firms in special economic zones has brought knowledge spillovers and increased productivity.[20] These examples suggest ways to rebalance our own national economy.

One approach is reforming the lower-productivity industries I mentioned earlier, which will have a greater impact on 'left behind' regions: reforming social care will boost Detroit or Manchester more than New York or London. But this may not be enough. The knowledge economy is also concentrated in a few places. Even in Nordic countries which have taken steps to equalise incomes and productivity, tech firms still cluster in a small number of neighbourhoods in Stockholm or Copenhagen.[21] This creates cultural as well as economic differences: people in these areas feel part of the future, while those elsewhere may feel left behind, regardless of their income.

That does not mean we should abandon regional rebalancing, but we should remember that recognition – voice, dignity and belonging – is as important as money in regional policy. It is about our common citizenship. Recent research in the UK has found that 30 per cent of people feel a deep sense of pride in where they live, but even then 39 per cent believe that their region or town is not reaching the potential it has to be a successful and prosperous community. This is a social and democratic problem as well as an economic challenge.[22]

Many modern constitutions put regional economic balance at their heart. Germany's Basic Law commits to 'equivalent living conditions' between regions and Australia has legislated to ensure regions can spend similar amounts on public services. A requirement to ensure equity between regions and nations should be part of every country's constitution. A truly inclusive economy recognises that every place matters, that no community is beyond renewal, and that the geography of discontent can become a geography of contribution. Regional renewal is not about nostalgia, but rather it is a strategy for national strength.

Making the case for investment

In the aftermath of neoliberalism, we need to reimagine what a democratic economy could look like, without relying just on regulation. This means considering where we focus our investment. One major analysis in the wake of the global financial crash estimated that some 85 per cent of bank credit in Western economies went on financing speculative activity rather than productive investment.[23] And, as Rachel Reeves has argued, of the £1.3 trillion lent by the banking system to the UK economy between 1997 and 2007, around 85 per cent went either to financial companies or into the property market.[24]

A more efficient economy might redirect capital towards resilience against climate change, or improving housing, digital infrastructure and care services. That means deploying what is sometimes called mission-oriented finance, where sovereign wealth funds invest in sectors of national importance. This could be supported by more effective risk-based regulation of our financial institutions,[25] and new laws to empower communities to use their local resources more efficiently.[26] Public finance can be entrepreneurial, and while markets are a valuable tool for organising productive activities, not everything can be reduced to a price. Public policy can be used not just to correct market failures, but to proactively avoid them by shaping the way markets serve the public interest.

Economic policy is not only about how we produce wealth, but about how we share it. With more and better-paid jobs across the country, fewer people and places will be left behind, and there will be less need for government to redistribute wealth. But building an economy founded on good jobs and shared prosperity will require serious investment – in infrastructure, innovation, training, transition support and the renewal of struggling regions. And when billionaires globally pay less than 0.5 per cent of their wealth in taxes, as the global tax expert Gabriel Zucman has calculated, then there is a strong case for urgently progressing negotiations at the United Nations around a fairer global tax system.

Not all spending is the same. Some is better seen as investment – laying the foundations for long-term growth, raising productivity and increasing the potential of the whole economy. Spending that helps people into decent work, spreads innovation or rebuilds local economies can, over time, pay for itself.[27]

Digital platforms generate billions by harvesting and selling user data, while contributing to social harms, from mental health problems to political polarisation. Superstar firms like Meta could help fund the social policies that address these harms, while encouraging better governance of personal data. New data cooperatives could give users more control – and potentially a stake – in how their information is used and sold. You could apply thinking similar to biotechnology, which benefits heavily from publicly funded science and genetic data donated for the common good.

More generally, automation can raise private profits while reducing public revenues from payroll taxes. Acemoglu, for example, proposes taxing firms that cut jobs while increasing profitability 1 per cent of the payroll savings they make to fund retraining.[28]

The energy transition is vital for decarbonisation, but the shift to electric vehicles risks eroding £30 billion in annual fuel duty revenues in the UK alone. Without reform, the tax system could become more regressive as wealthier EV drivers avoid tax. Road pricing – based on distance, time or congestion – could maintain revenues and promote efficiency. Quite simply, tax systems should reward what benefits the broader economy, and ensure that when public investment enables private gain, the public also shares in the rewards. This is necessary not just to raise money for public services, but to restore legitimacy. When innovation built on public investment generates private windfalls without giving back, the result is not just inequality but a collapse in trust.

The quality, resilience and fairness of an economy are not determined by fate, technology or trade alone. They are shaped by the rules we set and the institutions we build – institutions that channel investment, foster innovation and distribute opportunity. An economy is not strong just because it is growing. It is built through deliberate choices. And once we accept the need for a new political economy, our understanding of contribution, reward and responsibility changes. Capital, labour and knowledge must each serve a broader conception of the common good. Putting morality and our duties towards one another at the heart of economic policy deepens rather than diminishes the importance of reform.

If we want people to believe once again in the promise of progress, we must show that the rules of the economy serve everyone – not just the few at the frontier. The economy is a joint effort, oriented towards shared purpose, that should put markets once more at the service of society, and correct an unacceptable imbalance between the rights of a few and the rights of the many.

This is a moral project. But it is also an economic one. Because efficiency without ethics is brittle, and an economy that ignores its obligations will, in time, lose its legitimacy. We must restore the connection between freedom and fairness, growth and justice, today and tomorrow. The prize is immense: an economy that works for people, and a politics that commands trust.

13
BELONGING: HOW WE REBUILD STRONG COMMUNITIES

In 1942, three years before the guns of war fell silent, William Beveridge published his report proposing a new social contract for Britain. It was designed to show that while the world order had to be rebuilt, this had to go, as the Atlantic Charter had promised, hand in hand with a new domestic settlement.

The Beveridge Report, a 300-page official government document, was a surprise bestseller, with citizens enthusiastically queuing, even as bombs threatened to fall, on publication day. With over two thirds of a million copies sold, it was to far surpass its nearest rival in the popularity of official publications – Lord Denning's report on the Profumo affair, the government sex scandal in 1963, which sold a mere 100,000 copies.

The settlement that followed – the British National Health Service, mass secondary education, a national insurance system worthy of the name – was not charity, it was the fulfilment of a promise. 'The men and women of this country have shown by the sacrifices they are prepared to make that they are not merely soldiers in a war,' said Clement Attlee, the then-deputy prime minister. 'They are citizens of a new world.'[1]

The Beveridge social contract focused on the right to work and welfare. A new social contract must go further, focusing on not just welfare but wellbeing. Indeed, this is what Beveridge himself envisaged. In 1948, six years after his most famous report, he published a treatise on voluntary action, arguing that the burgeoning welfare state must act to complement rather than replace the vital role of strong local communities.[2]

Yet our polling shows that in twenty-first-century Britain, as in many other countries around the world, a growing number of people do not feel they belong, do not feel they count; they feel forgotten, neglected and invisible to others. In an era defined by consumerism and, more generally, by a self-interested individualism, we may have lost sight of the importance – indeed the necessity – of what I believe is the foundational element of strong, cohesive and inclusive communities: belonging. For just as we need shelter, food and warmth, we also need to belong, and to feel part of a community.

In Chapter 3, I referred to contact theory: the idea that bringing people together across lines of difference, whether religious, ethnic or ideological, reduces prejudice and increases understanding and tolerance. Over the past seventy years, hundreds of studies have shown the impact positive contact can have, and these lessons have been applied across the world to develop innovative interventions that bring different people together.[3] For example, towards the end of Sri Lanka's civil war, which arose from tensions between the Sinhalese majority and the Tamil minority, multi-ethnic sports teams helped to reduce prejudice and increase cohesion.[4]

We also know that the benefits of inter-group contact can 'generalise' to other members of the 'in-group'. During the Troubles in Northern Ireland, even indirect contact across religious lines could be significant. If a Catholic simply knew another Catholic with a Protestant friend, they were less likely to be prejudiced, and the same was true for Protestants.[5] Positive contact between the dominant group and a minority group can also lead to improved attitudes towards other groups, as was found in an eight-country study which showed that positive contact with immigrants led to improved attitudes towards LGBTQ+ and Jewish people.[6]

Earlier I suggested that the strongest communities not only have institutions that bring people together, but actively value them sufficiently to invest resources and energies into them. Yet being part of a vibrant civic life seems today to be far less important than it once was. As markets provide more and more goods and services, and when even things we once considered public goods – such as municipal swimming pools and local sports facilities or even nurseries and ante-natal classes – have become commercialised, we appear to depend less on universally available collective organisations. Put simply, this means that outside our immediate family and close friends, we appear to need each other less.

If we think of freedom in terms of our ability to choose from the widest range of consumer goods to meet our desires and appetites without having to engage with others – which would be what Michael Sandel calls a 'civic conception of freedom'[7] – then the feeling that we are on our own will surely continue to grow, as will our sense of detachment and separation from wider society. Sandel suggests that true freedom exists only when we have a meaningful say in shaping the forces that govern our collective lives. To realise that freedom we have to meet other people, and listen to and learn from each other. Then we can really debate the big questions that matter to us as citizens. Through this kind of deliberation we build a sense that we share a common life, that we are part of communities with traditions, histories, shared projects and aspirations, even if we might occasionally disagree about what this means in practice. In this sense, freedom is more than being able to make consumer choices; it is about participation in a shared civic project.

And how we build that connection with each other matters. In recent times, populist nationalists have been successful at exploiting our desire for community by creating new social groups, albeit ones where people come together around the exclusion of others. Take the example of Trump rallies in the US, often likened to carnivals more than political events.[8] They clearly create a sense of camaraderie and belonging for attendees – but it is built on division and exclusion. The polling conducted for this book shows that without contact across lines of difference, efforts to strengthen community can end up dividing us further. So when we are thinking about ways to strengthen our civic life, we must look first for opportunities for connection across lines of difference. Expanding the circle of civic-minded people into a civic majority means building relationships with people of different religions, ethnicities and ideologies.

What I propose are interventions across four areas which I believe can help expand that circle. First, and at its most basic, we need more people to be active in their communities. Second, we need civic leaders to drive change forward. Third, we need more civic spaces to bring people together. And fourth, we need to place greater emphasis on cross-cultural interaction across lines of difference.

Participation

Across the West, only around half of all citizens are members of any civic association and only a minority participate with any regularity, as we discovered in Chapter 6. This matters. The evidence shows that those who participate in a formal community organisation or club are on balance healthier and happier, and feel a greater sense of belonging.

Being a member of just one civic group cuts the likelihood of having no close friends by more than half, according to our polling. Participating in formal civic activities also provides important opportunities to develop connections with others from different backgrounds. People who don't participate at all in civic groups are three times more likely never to interact with someone of a different social class, religion or ethnicity than active community participants.

Given the many individual benefits it brings, it is striking that active citizenship is so low. However, there are systemic barriers to participation. Those working two jobs to make ends meet, single parents without childcare, or the elderly or infirm, are all less likely to have the capacity to be active in their community.

It is worth briefly reflecting on the scale of the challenge. In 2026, there are so many competing demands for attention. There is next to no barrier to taking out a phone and mindlessly scrolling for hours on end. So if we are to win that time back for in-person civic activities, then we need to ensure participation is made as easy as possible.

To encourage increased participation in civic life will require an understanding of what activities are most likely to draw people in. What I've seen work best are situations when people don't simply talk together but do things together. It's shared endeavour – repairing a roof, opening a soup kitchen – that creates the bonds that endure.

This starts with ensuring there is a vibrant civic ecosystem. Governments can support the formation and ongoing viability of groups by supporting them with civic capital funds. A good template is Denmark's Folkeoplysningsloven legislation, whereby approved civic groups receive a cash grant and ongoing municipal support to cover the costs of hiring venues. Such funds may reduce the need to charge membership fees, which can be one of the principal barriers to participation.[9]

Similar funds have proved successful on a smaller scale in the UK, the US and Canada.[10] Since 2017, Leeds City Council has offered 'Small Sparks' grants as part of its Asset-Based Community Development programme (ABCD). ABCD starts from a place of 'not what is wrong with a particular area but what is strong' and seeks to grow community spirit and improve cohesion. So-called 'community builders' are employed to map out each area's assets to find community leaders, connect people with services and support the creation of new clubs and associations that bring people of diverse backgrounds together.[11]

We must also ensure that local people are aware of what groups are available for them to join. Many neighbourhoods already have popular social media groups helping to advertise local clubs and associations. Considering my own home town, over 50,000 people – a group as big as the entire population of the town – are part of the Love Kirkcaldy! Facebook group. Civic groups of all types regularly use the platform to announce events and attract new members. And new apps, including one based in the UK,[12] are using AI to actively bring people of similar interests and causes together. While the platform connects people virtually, the hope is that this will lead to in-person meetings. For example, individuals who are interested in anything from sports to arts, culture and the environment will be connected via an AI-powered platform and encouraged to form an in-person group if one does not already exist. Of course not everyone uses social media or phone apps. If they do not already have them, local areas should create directories of clubs and associations which could be circulated, both digitally and in print, to local public spaces. In this way, care workers, health workers, social workers, teachers and other public-facing professionals can inform the people they work with what is available.

For some, the biggest barrier to becoming an active citizen may be confidence. We are in the midst of what some have called a 'friendship recession' – especially among young people.[13] Building a circle of friends can happen in a number of environments – from the workplace and parents' associations to faith groups and sports clubs – but for those who might need a formal nudge, social prescribing is one way to encourage participation. In recent years, over one million people per year in Britain have been referred to social prescribing services, which include exercise classes, gardening projects and other community organisations.[14]

In Chapter 3, I showed that some types of organisations are particularly important for strengthening our communities, namely organisations that offer 'civic opportunities' for members. For some time now, civil society organisations have been increasingly replaced by professionally run but memberless NGOs which offer few opportunities for the involvement of ordinary people.[15] We need more local civic organisations that have a strong sense of social purpose and offer members the opportunity to be active in their communities. Sports clubs, for example, can have a bigger community focus. For many in the UK, professional football teams have replaced faith groups as the institutions of greatest cultural significance, with 37 per cent of Britons saying their local club is a crucial aspect of their identity – over three times as many as attend a faith service each week.[16] This is far from unique to Britain. In Brazil, nearly 80 per cent report being active football supporters while in the US, 57 per cent of people report watching some type of sport at least once per week.[17] Sports clubs and players carry immense social power and they have great influence over fans.[18]

Many of the best-known football clubs, including Arsenal, Liverpool, Tottenham Hotspur, Glasgow Celtic and Hibernian, were founded either by churches to further the relief of poverty or loneliness, or as working men's clubs dedicated to improving the life of the local community. Indeed, the well-supported English football club Sheffield Wednesday took that name because local workers who had Wednesday afternoons off would meet to play then. Today, as money (often from abroad) dominates the game, the distance between local communities and their clubs has grown. While many clubs have foundations that carry out important community work, much more can be done to create a culture where supporting a club comes with a commitment to participating more fully in community life.

Playing in a local sports team can have far-reaching community benefits when clubs become important anchors in their communities. In almost every town and parish in Ireland, there exists a Gaelic Athletic Association (GAA) club – a total of over 2,200 clubs across the island with more than 400,000 active players, a huge proportion of the population.[19] Community values are at the centre of the GAA's mission: 'Our purpose is to promote Gaelic games, culture and lifelong participation as a community-based, volunteer-led organisation which enriches lives and communities.'[20] It is perhaps no surprise that players and members of GAA clubs tend to have prominent roles within other aspects of Irish civic life. A firm set of values means that membership comes with an obligation to give back, volunteer, respect others and be regular participants within the community.

We can also form new civic organisations with specific aims. Despite lower levels of participation, we know that people still care deeply about their local communities and have pride in their cities and towns. This suggests an opportunity to reimagine civic engagement through new organisations. The anti-racism organisation Hope Not Hate is a model here. It organises community meetings to combat the rise of extremism and division. In some areas, these meetings have blossomed into civic clubs which organise local events and publish newspapers to celebrate the positive stories of the local area.[21] Other models include Citizens UK, which has eighteen chapters across Britain, bringing together local groups to campaign for common causes, and Our Future, an innovative new charity founded in Grimsby which organises locals to collectively plan and direct investment in their area.[22] Similar programmes exist in the US such as Working Together Mississippi, which invites representatives from different religious, political and ethnic groups to join local chapters that bring people together around shared problems such as population decline in rural towns.[23]

Sometimes the purpose of groups changes. Take the Warm Welcome campaign in the UK. Its aim was simple: for those who could not afford to heat their homes in winter, heated public spaces such as cafés, libraries, church halls, community centres and sports clubs could be opened up.[24] The network was created to help those on the sharp end of the cost-of-living crisis, particularly in the energy crisis of late 2022. As one of the hardest winters in memory came to an end, the original plan was for the spaces to close. Yet something unexpected had occurred: Warm Welcome spaces had not just addressed the cost-of-living crisis, but also the growing connection crisis. They had become important meeting places for previously isolated individuals to gather and form friendships. The groups stayed open and today Warm Welcome is one of the fastest-growing and most influential charities in the UK. In the beginning the emphasis was on 'warm'. The emphasis today is on 'welcome'.

As I have said, much of the infrastructure for civic participation is already in place, and we know that people both value and desire the sense of active community that they feel is sadly lacking in our society. Putting just some of these initiatives into practice could see a real increase in civic participation, which is the first step to rebuilding our communities.

Local leaders

Without local volunteers and leaders there can be no civic life, no sports teams, no elderly groups, no youth organisations, no churches or faith groups. Every bright idea to improve a community requires the time and talents of local volunteers to make it happen. This means community champions with their feet on the ground, driving change in their area. Rebuilding our communities depends on cultivating and supporting volunteers and leaders, and inspiring a new generation to get involved and make a positive difference.

The National Council for Voluntary Organisations' Time Well Spent survey, based on 7,000 UK volunteers, found 89 per cent agreed they 'feel like I'm making a difference' through volunteering.[25] The primary motivation for first volunteering is the desire to 'improve things/help people' cited by 40 per cent of participants – far ahead of other reasons like filling spare time (31 per cent), meeting people (14 per cent) or learning new skills (13 per cent). But, alongside making a difference, the other top-ranking benefits were seen to be enjoyment (89 per cent) and personal achievement (88 per cent). We should be celebrating the many benefits that come from volunteering. From developing skills and forging meaningful connections, to boosting our physical and mental health, volunteering is among the most impactful things we can do, not only for others but for ourselves.

After a spike during Covid, volunteering rates have declined in the UK. In 2013, 27 per cent of adults in Britain formally volunteered at least once a month, but in 2024 this number was just 17 per cent, representing a drop of around 5 million.[26] In contrast, since 2021 formal volunteering in America has risen by 7 percentage points.[27] Singapore, too, has seen volunteering rates increase, thanks in part to its Corporate Volunteer Scheme allowing companies to claim a $2.50 deduction for every $1 it costs them to support employees' engagement in civic causes.

Bringing in volunteering hours as part of the formal education curriculum also looks promising. In the Canadian province of Ontario, forty hours of formal volunteering are required to graduate with a high school diploma.[28] The hope is that having experienced the benefits of volunteering, both to themselves and to their communities, young people will continue volunteering well into adulthood.

The next step up from volunteering is becoming a civic leader. These are the people in the community who make things happen – they organise, push for change, speak for their neighbours and get results. But such people are in short supply and are not evenly distributed. Too often, they're clustered in wealthier areas where people have the connections, resources and skills.[29] If we want every community to thrive, we need to grow and support local leaders in the places that need them most. I recently heard the story of an under-resourced area of the UK not drawing on all of the community funding it was entitled to. This was not due to lack of need or projects to fund; there simply were not enough community leaders to fill out the forms and send off applications.

Leadership is challenging, but training helps. The private sector spends over $60 billion annually on leadership training.[30] While expense on this scale isn't feasible in the public sector, we should be developing civic sector programmes which both support our current leaders and help identify and train the next generation. Currently, too few community leaders are being offered quality leadership training. We should fund formal training for existing local leaders in every area. As a start, a civic helpline staffed by trained professionals could be created to support community leaders with on-the-spot advice and support.

In some places, charities and institutions are already rising to this challenge. The Relationships Project led by David Robinson offers training to leaders across civic society on how positive relationships can be prioritised in their work. The Obama Foundation, as part of its mission to strengthen democracy, runs a series of community leadership programmes for young people across the US, Europe and Africa. And working globally, Theirworld has a two-year programme which provides training and networking opportunities to young activists who are campaigning to address shortfalls in global education.[31]

Recognition is also important. When I became prime minister, only 40 per cent of formal honours were awarded to local community champions. During my time in office, I advocated for this number to rise and by 2023, 70 per cent of recipients were local leaders and volunteers. More can be done to publicly celebrate community work, such as honours for groups as well as individuals, and this recognition can help encourage the next generation of leaders who can drive renewal in our communities.

Making space

Community life does not occur in a vacuum. It requires public spaces, not just virtual but physical, for people to come together on a regular basis. Connecting with others and participating in civic life is easier when there are spaces to meet that are appealing, accessible and affordable. These have been called 'third spaces' as they are neither workplaces nor home. The best of them are more than simply meeting places for different groups, they can spark new connections.

Take the example of the Sure Start programme in the UK. Initiated in 1999 to provide 'one-stop early learning shops' in disadvantaged areas, Sure Start was part of a broader architecture to improve children's life chances. This included increased child benefit, a new multi-billion-pound child tax credit, child trust funds, educational maintenance allowances, and a doubling of spending on schools, all of which were part of a comprehensive plan to abolish child poverty and empower a new generation.

By 2010 there were 3,600 Sure Start centres across the country – places where children could play, learn and make new friends. It was, for its time, probably the biggest and most successful driver of social mobility. By their teens, children from low-income families who had had access to Sure Start centres and free school meals had boosted their GCSE results by three grades. For the Sure Start generation, mental health problems decreased, juvenile delinquency fell and employment prospects were dramatically improved. One third of the upfront cost of the programme was offset by savings to the NHS through reduced hospital stays, and as research from the Institute for Fiscal Studies found, Sure Start children's centres generated £2 of financial benefits for every £1 in costs, demonstrating that if you provide a supportive environment for children in their early years and invest in their futures, the results will be transformative not just for the child, but for the wider economy.[32]

A small change can make a big and unanticipated difference. Sure Start not only provided children in their earliest and most impressionable years with transformative opportunities, but in many cases also revived local communities. Mothers met inside Sure Start centres, got to know each other, and built friendships, so that a community of Sure Start parents began to form. One mother told *The Guardian*: 'Sure Start helped [me] believe that life could be different.' While another said that 'Sure Start steadied me, held me, kept me from being lonely. It was good for me, my family and the community.'[33]

No one can doubt that parents with young children benefit from contact with other parents facing similar challenges. But what until then had been missing – and late-afternoon school-gate interactions, often brief and rushed, only touch on the problem – was a setting in which experiences can be shared, lifelong friendships can be made and vibrant communities can be built.[34] Similar outcomes have been found in the USA, with the famous example of Harlem Children's Zone.[35]

Without Sure Start centres, early childhood services in the UK have become increasingly privatised, creating 'tiers' of parents who do not interact with each other, in turn limiting the benefits that come from connecting across lines of difference. Sure Start is just one example of how investment in spaces where people meet in person to join in purposeful activities can build real community life.

Across Europe, some cities are beginning to design public spaces with connection at the forefront. In Barcelona, a city famous for its grid layout, 'superblocks' are a recent innovation in which traffic is calmed, cycling and walking are encouraged and public spaces such as parks and sports facilities are given priority. In Paris, more than 300 *rues aux écoles* (school streets) have been fully pedestrianised, giving both children a safe place to play and parents a much-appreciated opportunity to meet. In the UK, over 100 councils have supported Playing Out, a national movement of temporarily closing streets to let children play. A survey found that 94 per cent of people felt they knew their neighbours better as a result of hosting such a play street and 90 per cent felt they belonged more. For nearly 60 per cent, play streets also acted as the gateway to further involvement in other aspects of community life, from associational life to campaigns.[36]

Danish architectural policy explicitly focuses on 'putting people first'. Taking inspiration from this, the Royal Society of Arts has proposed making 'connectedness by design' a condition of any new UK government funding.[37] This is in contrast to recent UK housebuilding developments which have on average 40 per cent less green space than neighbourhoods built in the nineteenth and twentieth centuries. New developments tend to be further away from green spaces, which have also become smaller.[38] This has led to over 9 million fewer trips to green spaces every year. It is also a social access issue; those who are poorer and less educated are far less likely to have access to green spaces, a US study has found.[39]

In just a decade, UK public spending on parks and open spaces has declined by over £300 million per year in real terms. This has meant fewer parks judged to be in good condition, falling from 60 per cent to just over 40 per cent. However, communities are responding, with the creation of more than 7,000 'friends of parks' groups.[40] In many instances, these twenty-first-century civic organisations have transformed previously neglected spaces into vibrant community places. Take, for example, the Friends of Kings Norton Park in Birmingham. Years of neglect had left this local green space overgrown, underused and notable only for its high levels of anti-social behaviour. One resident described it as a place 'no one of sane mind would have been proud of, let alone visit'. But thanks to the determined work of local people, the space has been transformed and now hosts regular community events such as Parkruns and is well used by the local community.[41]

Bottom-up local activism is transforming other public assets. When Stretford Public Hall in Greater Manchester was at risk of being sold off to private developers, a group of local activists raised money through jumble sales, social nights and a grant from the council to take it into community ownership. This sense of ownership matters. Once the keys were handed over to the community, over 500 local tradespeople and volunteers helped renovate the building and today it is a community hub, home to local choirs, theatre groups, a community cinema and co-working spaces for local businesses. 'Stretford Public Hall is now more than just a building: it's a symbol of what a community can achieve when it comes together with passion, determination and a shared vision for the future,' said Annoushka Deighton, one of the founders of the project.[42] To pave the way for similar projects, communities should have first right of refusal on community assets up for sale.

Libraries are another example of crucial civic assets that can be better adapted for a new era. The important role libraries can play is well understood in Finland where they are not simply for borrowing books but are what they call 'indoor town squares'. The main library in Helsinki, named Oodi, is multipurpose – a café, a restaurant, a cinema, a recording studio and even a 'maker-space' workshop rolled into one, bringing together Finns of every class, ethnicity and generation under one shared roof. The library is used by all ages because it was designed with every generation in mind. This kind of inclusive urban design puts people first and offers opportunities for interaction across lines of difference. And, of course, the libraries retain their primary function – the average Finn borrows fifteen books per year and visits a public library nine times a year.[43] In England, less than one in three adults ever use a library after leaving school.[44] But library investment in Finland, at £50 a year per person, is four times that of the UK. It demonstrates that if public spaces and venues are of good quality, then people will use them. So rather than closing libraries, we should invest in them.*

Community is not only built in these formal spaces but also developed in the everyday routines that bring us into contact with others. School gates are already important meeting places, and other 'everyday' places could be too, such as supermarkets (the average person makes well over 200 trips to the supermarket every year), leisure centres, parks and high streets. A Dutch supermarket chain has introduced 'slow lanes' – dedicated tills for shoppers who would prefer to speak to other shoppers or the supermarket staff. They have become popular across the Netherlands and are now being introduced in other countries. Taken together, these ideas can create, renew and repurpose our spaces with the goal of encouraging social connection and community engagement.

Bridging across differences

Bringing together citizens from different parts of society takes effort. Beyond simply creating spaces where connection is possible, and may happen organically, we should not be shy about developing programmes whose explicit purpose is the forging of new connections in our communities. Increasing participation in civic life may require specially designed programmes. Young people are sadly meeting each other less than ever, and are therefore both the biggest challenge and the greatest opportunity in this area. A 2009 social experiment studied a multi-week outdoor residential programme among high school pupils. The control group comprised only white people while the treatment group was ethnically mixed. In a follow-up survey one month later, the

* The UK Labour government has recently launched the Pride in Place scheme, which will see local people in 330 disadvantaged neighbourhoods given £20 million to improve their community assets, including libraries.

white people in the mixed group expressed higher tolerance levels than the control group.[45]

Recent research has shown the benefit which contact between social classes can have for social mobility. Young people who grew up in areas where there was more interaction between income groups were found to earn £3,000 more per year as adults. This is a classic case where strengthened social connections help people do good but also do well.[46]

While schools can offer opportunities to connect within local areas, we should also recognise the potential of youth exchanges to connect people. The most famous of these is the EU's Erasmus scheme. Since it began nearly forty years ago, Erasmus has helped more than 15 million young people to visit another country in Europe.[47] Exchanges need not be international either. In Canada, for example, young people in the English-speaking provinces are offered the opportunity to visit the French-speaking provinces and vice versa.[48] In Britain, there is no similar system. It might be said that in the era of mass international travel, a young person in Dundee is as likely to visit Spain as England, Wales or Northern Ireland.

Such exchanges could be part of a new civic service initiative encouraging school leavers to become active participants and leaders in their communities. Learning from the mistakes of previous initiatives, which were criticised for their lack of uptake, participation could be opt-out rather than opt-in. Following the 'exchange', young people could be encouraged to take a six-month placement engaging in a local non-profit or civic institution. Such 6–12-month programmes currently exist in the US (AmeriCorps) and the French Service Civique, where young people are offered a small stipend to cover living costs. In the case of AmeriCorps, there is also the added incentive of a grant awarded to reduce university fees following completion. While less than 1 per cent of Americans take part in the AmeriCorps programme (again, it's an opt-in system), surveys have shown that those who do are more likely to vote, volunteer and be involved in their communities throughout their lives.[49] Another example of investments in civic life compounding over time.

The obvious issue with such programmes is cost. However, some studies have shown a long-term fiscal benefit from national service programmes if participation increases job prospects.[50] And money could be found elsewhere; for example a citizens service programme featuring a short optional military stint could allow expanding defence budgets to serve local communities.

To increase contact between different social classes, we should also encourage the development of programmes which link professional mentors with underprivileged young people preparing to leave school. A model here is a programme implemented by the Diana Award, which connects young people at risk of becoming 'NEET' (Not in Education, Employment or Training) with private-sector mentors.[51] The programme has proved very successful – not just for the mentees but also for the mentors, one of whom described it as 'quite humbling understanding some of the backgrounds and challenges that young people face . . . I think it's given me some insights and some fresh perspectives.'

It may now seem a cliché, but the diversity of our societies is truly a strength, and one which we are not making the most of. The evidence shows that bridging these differences makes us happier, more prosperous and more disposed to helping one another. It must therefore be central to any programme of community rebuilding.

Why it matters

If we cease to connect with whole swathes of our neighbourhood or with our fellow citizens, we are no longer one community but a jostling band of different, competing tribes – and we will have baked zero-sum competition into our public life. But with targeted interventions, I believe we can achieve a genuine renewal in our communities. We can find new ways of coming together, lift up and empower our leaders, reimagine our public spaces and connect across the divides in our society that others would seek to exploit. But I recognise the scale of the challenge.

Moving, as Robert Putnam has written, from an 'I' to a 'we' world may seem almost impossible.[52] But many are open to being asked to play a greater part in the life of their community, and they could become part of an extended community – part of a circle of belonging.

And changes of a similar scale have happened only recently. In the tough days of Covid, people rapidly changed their behaviour as neighbours rushed to help each other. Volunteering rates increased, neighbourhood support WhatsApp groups were created, people shopped and cooked for those who needed it, swapped numbers with neighbours, and checked in on the vulnerable. For a brief moment there was a sense of all being in this together. It proved that public-spiritedness is not an impossible dream. It may be that our civic-mindedness is latent and simply on hold, waiting to surface.

For alongside rebuilding our communities, this is about protecting the democratic system that we have all come to take for granted. Democracy is not something that happens to us, it is something we partake in. When we no longer participate, we are at risk of being left without the skills that make democracy work. The truth is that if civic life in your town is a desert, democracy from the town square to the capital of your country cannot flourish. The strength of civil society – that vast, often disorganised space between markets and governments – really does matter. This is not a new idea. Alexis de Tocqueville captured this truth nearly two centuries ago: 'Town meetings are to liberty what primary schools are to science: they bring it within the people's reach, they teach men how to use and how to enjoy it.'[53] Civic associations, he believed, were the training ground of freedom. John Stuart Mill made the same point in different language, describing such associations as 'schools of public spirit'.[54] He argued that it is through political discussion and collective action that people learn to feel empathy for their fellow citizens, and to see themselves as members of a wider political community.

So rebuilding community is not some nostalgic reinvention of the past. It is our best way of creating a better future. In a time of division, the surest defence of our values, our democracy and our wellbeing, is to renew our bonds and repair the fabric of our society. It was said that the British Empire was built on the playing fields of Eton. Today's new world may also be built on playing fields – not of a private school available to a tiny minority, but in public parks, in community centres, at new clubs and associations, and in every space where strangers choose to become neighbours. If we invest in these connections now, we can create a society where people both belong and flourish.

Our future must be built on civic strength and economic strength reinforcing one another. A strong society can both champion and set the terms for economic change, building a local consensus to meet and master the challenges we face of securing resilient, quality jobs. Without it, our political life is vulnerable to the siren call of populists, and our economic demands limited to preventing change – preserving old industries in aspic – or fulminating against the loss of high streets as people turn to online or out-of-town shopping. Even an economic upturn might not be enough to undercut the appeal of populists. Well-organised and popular civic institutions are essential if we are to manage economic change in the interests of local communities. Civic renewal through extensive devolution of power is at the heart of the recommendations of the Commission on the UK's Future set up by one UK Prime Minister, Keir Starmer, and taken forward, as I write, by his likely successor Andy Burnham. What matters is that civic revival and economic revival advance together.

14

DEMOCRACY: HOW WE PROMOTE ACTIVE CITIZENSHIP

I visited Berlin in 1990, just a few months after the Berlin Wall fell, and I could feel the excitement in the air as democracy was restored to a vast swathe of Germany. At the first Berlinale film festival to span the once-divided city, films were being shown in East Berlin venues that would have been banned outright only three months before. I was in Jakarta in 1998, meeting Indonesia's President Suharto a week before his government fell, and found him completely at a loss, unable to understand the democratic pressures – particularly from young people – behind his country's revolution. In 2012 I visited the UN peacekeeping mission in the small territory of Timor-Leste, and met the brave local leaders who had resisted both Portuguese and Indonesian colonial rule and were intent on building a democracy after years of repression.

All my life, I – and indeed most of us – have assumed the 'relentless rise' of democracy. I believed that year by year, as happened in East Germany, Indonesia and Timor-Leste, the number of democracies would steadily increase while autocracies, dynasties and theocracies would wither away. But today, 6 of the world's 8 billion people – three in every four of us – live in autocracies, under authoritarian rulers with their freedom severely restricted.[1] As a result of the stalling of democratic progress over the last fifteen years, we have returned to levels of democracy we had almost half a century ago, before what was called the 'third democratic wave' which started in Portugal, Spain and Greece.

I can track back to 1973, when I was a student, and when democratically elected President Salvador Allende was assassinated and Chile fell under the military rule of General Pinochet. I worked to help those fighting for democracy in Chile, and while years later in 2008 I was honoured to meet President Michelle Bachelet in the very building where Allende had been killed and democracy brought to a halt, I was very aware of the many nearby countries in Latin America where democracy was now under pressure. Most recently I met Muhammad Yunus of Bangladesh, who refuses to be an unelected prime minister and, modest as always, held the title of senior adviser as he oversaw his country's return to democracy.

But if I was one of many who assumed democracy was the universal idea whose time had come, recent events have forced us to re-evaluate what has to be done today to defend it. While I have had the privilege of visiting scores of countries and have been able to witness first-hand the state of democracy in many corners of the world, the meetings that I have had with leaders in Nigeria, DRC, Kenya, Tanzania, Sudan, Ethiopia, South Sudan, Mozambique, Pakistan and Afghanistan have demonstrated the challenges faced daily by those tasked with upholding democracy. Nearly 2.5 billion people – just under one in every three of us – now live in places where civic organisations are under state control or heavily censored, and where much of the public square has been shut down.[2] Indeed there are now more people (2.3 billion) living under the more extreme form of despotisms – closed autocracies – than the 2.2 billion living in electoral and liberal democracies combined.[3]

When I visited post-communist Russia, President Gorbachev had given way to President Yeltsin, who was soon to give way in turn to President Putin. It is still not clear whether Russia could have emerged as a democracy had it not suffered a brutal economic liberalisation that included the privatisation at knock-down prices of state assets. Certainly the West should have done more to bring Russia in from the cold. But by the time I met Putin at the Kremlin in 2006, his behaviour was of someone who believed that strength was all that mattered, weakness was there to be exploited, and threats were a currency to be traded. Russia had already succumbed to his authoritarian nationalism – the beginning of two decades in which he has repeatedly manipulated the constitution to extend his term in office. His licence to do so demonstrates that all previous assumptions about the triumph of democracy can no longer be sustained.

There are understandable reasons why liberal democracy – the idea of limited and fully accountable government – is vulnerable to assault: its survival requires the majority to tolerate minorities and minorities to accept majority rule, with group interests and local loyalties often overridden by a more pressing national interest. This can bring to the forefront, as William Galston puts it, destructive and dark passions – hatred, anger, resentment, revenge and the urge to dominate – which can be more powerful than 'the better angels of our nature'.[4]

Democracy can also, as he says, be undermined by 'myopia', 'naïveté' and 'parochialism', and so we have to be focused, streetwise and eternally vigilant if we are to 'shore up the norms and institutions that safeguard free societies against autocracies while doing what we can to reduce the dark passions' destructive intensity'.[5]

Even more worrying is an increasing tendency of many on the populist nationalist right to reject the very idea of democracy in favour of authoritarian and even aristocratic rule. 'I no longer believe that freedom and democracy are compatible,' the billionaire and influential Silicon Valley investor Peter Thiel has said.[6] The political theorist often cited by the MAGA movement, Patrick Deneen, has proposed an autocratic and aristocratic post-liberal future in which a self-consciously 'aristopopulist' regime, comprising a 'virtuous elite', deliberately governs for the 'common good' (defined as piety, truth, 'equitable prosperity' and good government).[7] His plan does not involve abolishing elections or representative institutions. He wants a Congress of 6,090 people, one for every 15,000 in the country, on the lines of the original Roman model. His ruling class would be given 'guardrails' derived from family and religion, but also from his new Congress. Deneen's plan combines two seeming opposites: an aristocracy brought about by his muscular populism, and then in turn, an elevation of the people by this aristocracy – a 'mixed constitution' delivering 'government by the virtuous'. It is, he says, the application of 'Machiavellian means to achieve Aristotelian ends'.[8]

Few will agree with Deneen in this, but his provocation reminds us of the uphill task democrats face. Democracy is not collapsing by accident – it is being weakened by someone else's design and it can be saved and strengthened only by our active determination to defend it. Our challenge is to understand and respond to what is less a return to the fascism or single-party dictatorships of the past, than what might be called 'competitive authoritarianism': systems in which parties still contest elections, which are seen, however, as no more than a pathway to power for elites who are servants of private interests. In this view they are no longer the means by which emerging or previously marginalised and oppressed groups are represented, or the vehicle through which those elected act for the good of all. Versions of this pattern can already be seen today on almost every continent. Perhaps most worryingly, as Nicholas Bequelin, a senior fellow at Yale Law School's Paul Tsai China Center and former regional director at Amnesty International, argues, 'the US crossing the line into the autocratic camp is a devastating blow for global governance'.[9]

Most autocracies emerge not through coups, but because elected incumbents become increasingly repressive and arbitrary. They do so by disowning previously accepted rules of the game, as has happened from India and Bangladesh to Russia and Argentina. Or they manipulate the existing rules, extending terms of office or gerrymandering constitutions, as seen in Venezuela until 2026. Much has been written by a number of commentators of how institutions are undermined: through control, for example demanding the institutions of civil society be 'approved' by central governments or subject to oppressive legal frameworks; through 'infiltration', undermining the independence of institutions through cronyism in appointments; or through what some call 'duplication', creating new and alternative government-led institutions, as in Armenia in the 1990s and Croatia after 2015. Sometimes the targeting of democratic institutions is overt and unapologetic, as in Peru where political parties were banned in 2016, and in Malawi where demonstrations were banned in 2022.[10]

Autocrats now have many ways of exerting what the National Endowment for Democracy calls 'influence', by which it means actions that manipulate, disrupt or coerce.[11] These include, it reports, the creation of pseudo-civil-society organisations as a front for their activities, the capture of institutes of learning, state control of the media, covert sabotage and downright corrupt practices, now often enabled by the accelerating use of AI and chatbots, which is making it easier than ever to generate fake news, stream self-serving propaganda and direct already vulnerable citizens into ever-narrower silos and to manipulate them.

The very existence of many civil society organisations – the associations that must be at the heart of any democratic fightback – has been under threat, not only in well-publicised cases, like Hungary until 2026, but in what is estimated to be a total of forty-one countries covering every continent: from Belarus in Europe to Tunisia in Africa, and from Peru in South America to the Philippines in Asia.[12] An international community cannot flourish as long as democracy is in retreat, and it is time to wake up to the alarming reality that we are now fighting not just for the survival of basic democratic institutions but for the values that underpin them. Our adversaries might still hold elections, but then they use them to attack protected and fundamental human rights. The task for defenders of liberal democracy is to acknowledge the electorate's frustrations with the economic and state failures of the past few decades, and show how that failure is now being exploited by the very people responsible for causing it in the first place. But, moreover, we must demonstrate the case for strengthening our democracies: to show people how they can take more control of the decisions that shape their lives.

Democracy without and within: global lessons

One way, set out powerfully by Daron Acemoglu and James Robinson in *Why Nations Fail* and *The Narrow Corridor*, is to argue the pragmatic case: that when democracy flourishes, economies do better and people are better off.[13] There is strong evidence that, in the long run, autocracy cuts sustainable growth.[14]

But even if we can show that democracy brings economic benefits, attempts from outside to promote – or more accurately impose – democracy are unlikely to succeed. In Iraq and Afghanistan, enormous investments in blood and financial resources did not produce stable liberal democracies. When the American international aid organisation USAID did its own evaluations of the long-term impacts, it concluded that democracy-building efforts from outside had, at best, a weak impact, which diminished over time.[15]

For a long time, American leaders assumed that 'gradually, the rest of the world would come to accept the basic premises of the liberal order, including democracy, free trade, and the rule of law'.[16] President Clinton tried to energise the process by bringing together a coalition of like-minded states. President George W. Bush launched a project to export democracy to the Middle East. The boldest recent attempt came from President Biden in 2021 with the Summit for Democracy. But the decision to include countries such as the Philippines, Angola, the Democratic Republic of Congo and Iraq while excluding, for example, Bangladesh and Turkey exposed how hard it now is even to define who qualifies as a 'democracy'. And as soon as the latest Middle East crisis erupted, Biden's America found itself once again having to rely on authoritarian partners such as Saudi Arabia.

'Exporting' democracy, in the sense of transplanting institutions from one country to another, simply does not work. As academics point out, the domestic conditions needed for success are hard to replicate or manufacture from the outside. They include, as commentators have suggested, a shared national narrative; a degree of ethnic, political and cultural cohesion; a home-grown grassroots constituency of people and pressure groups pushing democratic norms, practices and institutions; and usually a reasonably high level of economic development. Some past experience of pluralism and civic organisation also makes a difference.

However, this does not mean we should abandon efforts to support democracy abroad. We should do everything we can to promote democracy – but not imagine we can impose it. Instead, we should try to learn from history. We have to look at which democratic movements have failed and which have succeeded, and recent years have seen plenty of both. Take the success of the Guatemalan opposition in 2023. There, a group of political, economic and military elites attempted to rig the election and block the transfer of power after a little-known former diplomat, Bernardo Arévalo, won the presidency. They were ultimately defeated not by elite manoeuvring, but by mass mobilisation from below. Thousands of Guatemalans took to the streets over many months, demanding that senior officials resign and that the election result be respected. The opposition movement's strength lay in its ability to draw on well-organised, flexible civic organisations with nationwide networks. Between July and December 2023, marches, rallies, sit-ins and road blockades created sustained pressure. Combined with the increased attention of the international community, the cost of stealing the election became unbearable. Meanwhile in Serbia, ahead of elections in 2000, the student movement Otpor, working with the Centre for Free Elections and Democracy, registered voters, drove up turnout and monitored local voting so that when Milošević lost, they had the information at hand and could quickly mobilise supporters to defend the results.

However, this kind of non-violent social mobilisation has been successful, according to Erica Chenoweth's landmark research, in less than four out of every ten cases since 1960.[17] The Arab Spring remains the most dramatic illustration of how popular movements can be crushed by repression, while in Israel in 2023, despite one in every fourteen of the adult population demonstrating against the Netanyahu government's weakening of judicial independence, their only victory was to delay the move.

Political parties have a role to play. And confronting entrenched authoritarian regimes and the corrupt interests that support them also depends on building 'big tent' coalitions – between political parties but also more widely through popular mobilisation. Recent electoral experiences illustrate both the promise and the limits of this approach. The victories of Donald Tusk in Poland and Lula in Brazil demonstrated the power of broad coalitions. Even in India, democracy faces an uphill task because, as the writer B. R. Ambedkar argues, rigid social hierarchies and centuries of caste oppression have meant that it has always been 'only a top-dressing on an Indian soil'.[18] Although Narendra Modi remains in office, his party's dominating parliamentary majority was sharply reduced after Rahul Gandhi's nationwide campaign to rebuild the Congress party's unifying appeal across India's religious, ethnic and social divides.

In Colombia, between 2002 and 2010, popular forces and opposition parties combined to help frustrate the democratic erosion planned by President Álvaro Uribe. Even without a legislative majority, opposition parties used existing checks and balances in the legislature and the courts to back up public demands, thwarting repeated attempts to undermine judicial independence, civil society and the legislature itself. Although as we can see from current events, this was only effective for a time.

When Matthew Cleary and Aykut Öztürk compared the democratic experiences of Bolivia (2006–2019), Ecuador (2007–2017) and Thailand (early 2000s) with those of Venezuela, they found that the critical difference lay in the behaviour of the opposition.[19] In the first group of countries, proactive oppositions continuously and relentlessly resisted democratic backsliding. In Venezuela and Turkey, by contrast, opposition forces only came together decisively when it was already too late.

There is also a negative lesson here: democracies cannot be saved by adopting the tactics that authoritarians use – and here Venezuela offers a cautionary tale. The attempt to oust Hugo Chávez not by democratic resistance but through an unconstitutional coup in 2002 handed him a pretext to consolidate his control. The opposition's subsequent boycott of the 2005 elections then delivered the National Assembly into Chávez's hands. We have yet to see what will come as a result of the recent removal by armed intervention of his successor, Nicolás Maduro. And in other countries such as Turkey and El Salvador the undemocratic tactics of opposition parties have failed to halt democratic backsliding. But opposition forces in Brazil, Colombia and, most recently, Poland and Hungary have demonstrated that they can resist democratic backsliding by appealing to the courts, working through legislatures and mobilising public opinion.

Senegal recently demonstrated this through the opposition victory of the 44-year-old Bassirou Diomaye Faye as president, after two-term incumbent Macky Sall failed in his attempt to overturn term limits. And in Botswana, the Umbrella for Democratic Change – the main opposition alliance – defeated the long-ruling and increasingly abusive Botswana Democratic Party, which had held power continuously since independence. These cases reinforce a crucial lesson: resistance works best when it is early, broad-based, lawful and sustained.

We must also take social media into account. Its algorithms can intensify anger, deepen division and amplify populist autocrats, who increasingly use digital tools for surveillance and social control. 'I have come to conclude that technology broadly and the internet in particular stand out as the most salient explanations for why global populism has arisen in this particular historical period, and why it has taken the particular form that it has,' writes Francis Fukuyama in a powerful article dismissing the salience of other explanations for populism. 'In my view, it is only the rise of the internet that can explain how we can be in an existential struggle for liberal democracy, at a time in history when liberal democracy has never been as successful.'[20] We cannot doubt the importance he attaches to the popularisation of tropes, conspiracy theories and 'fake news' through social media outlets. Yet the same technologies also make it possible to spread independent information to mass audiences and to connect democratic movements across borders – taking on the role historically played by radio. During the Cold War, an estimated 17 per cent of the Soviet population tuned in to Radio Liberty.[21] Radio Free Europe's Iranian service was still reaching around 10 per cent of Iran's population until recent funding cuts, and far more among the young. At its peak in 2024, its content generated some 2.2 billion views on Instagram.[22]

It remains to be seen how effective pro-democracy strategies that combine cross-party cooperation, strategic messaging, digital mobilisation and grassroots organising will be either in the United States or across Europe.

People power

The examples above draw from many different democratic systems around the world, but there is a common thread. Larry

Kramer records many competing definitions of democracy – some rights-based, some linked to capitalism, some emphasising direct participation and others representation – but the essential common element is support for 'popular government'.[23] By this, Kramer means government by the will of the people, expressed through legal processes embedded in the system itself. It is this aspect that is now at greatest risk, especially among younger generations. Popular government requires popular support; it requires that citizens, however divided they may be on particular issues, feel that they share a common political community.

If the future of democracy depends upon popular government, then we must rebalance power away from well-funded special interests, and towards ordinary citizens. This means championing a participatory democracy, one that people are a part of – so that democracy feels like something they do, not something that is done to them.

The question naturally following on from this is: what role, and what power, do we really have as citizens? Is it rational to remain engaged when your influence seems to extend no further than a single vote every four or five years? And why bother to support democracy if, in Bernard Manin's phrase, you are treated as a member of an 'audience democracy' – a spectator rather than a participant, expected to watch politics as a performance rather than shape it as an agent of change?[24]

If we want to renew democracy, we have to answer these questions honestly, by showing that there can be a real connection between people's involvement and what actually happens; that we are all equal, with the same opportunities to participate; that there are new and better ways to engage; and – to add a crucial new argument – that all can take part directly in democratic processes, at a local and national level, that have real impact on the decisions of elected representatives.

History teaches us that ordinary citizens can hold a lot of power. Without large-scale, popular political movements, elected authoritarians, as we have suggested, are rarely defeated. This helps explain why authoritarians are so determined to narrow civic space. They fear grassroots organisations far more than they fear traditional political parties, which often continue to operate – at least formally – under illiberal rule.

Malaysia offers an instructive example. There, local organising around clean water, poor housing, schooling and the lack of public accountability led to the creation of community forums. During the 2018 elections these forums evolved from grassroots activism into a national democratic movement, becoming one of the forces behind the opposition's historic victory over a long-established and corrupt ruling party. Crucially, their legitimacy came not from ideology or charismatic national leadership, but from sustained attention to local problems – providing the basis for previously passive citizens to challenge authoritarian rule.

What both these examples suggest is the importance of what might be called a new civic dignity, based not on abstract ideas but on people's concrete worries – about jobs, housing, public safety, opportunities for their children and grandchildren. From here, broad, active national coalitions can be built around those shared concerns. One of the core lessons emerging from the cross-national work of the Democracy Hub (D-Hub), which seeks to bring together a new global community of democratic practice, is precisely this: democracy is strengthened when we respond to people's aspirations and to their specific insecurities.[25] There is emerging evidence that similar dynamics are now taking shape in parts of the West. Hyper-local mutual aid networks that formed during recent crises are, in some places, becoming hubs for the bridge-building across communities and cultures that any democratic revival will require.

But this on its own is not enough. The scaffolding of traditional politics still matters enormously. It can either frustrate local organisations or amplify their impact. Traditional forums can be for cross-perspective discussion, or they can drive polarisation. One striking finding from recent studies is that the best way to open people's minds is not to shame them or even argue with them. It's to listen to them – as Ricken Patel, co-chair of D-Hub, argues – and to ensure that people feel their concerns and aspirations are not merely registered, but genuinely understood.[26] Our formal institutions can provide space for this. The question, therefore, is how these institutions can be revitalised – indeed redesigned – to encourage deliberation and consensus-building, rather than reinforcing the rigid, national 'winner takes all' structures that currently dominate politics.

Enduring success depends on whether civic organisations can prevent, rather than intensify, polarisation. Roger Eatwell has argued that polarisation and the process of 'cumulative extremism' – by which each side feeds the radicalisation of the other – lies at the heart of the authoritarian playbook. Polarising may help win an election, but if politics becomes a war for ideological supremacy then the basis of democracy itself falls under attack. If instead we support organisations with genuinely broad-based grassroots support, Eatwell argues, we can create bonds of trust through shared action, and 'nurture a new generation of civic and political leaders rooted in the realities and aspirations of their neighbours'.[27] Put simply, the civic leaders we need today are bridge builders rather than just firebrands. And the civic institutions we need are ones that will restore the centrality of the ordinary citizen.

Deliberative governance through citizens' assemblies represents one of the most important breakthroughs in democratic practice of recent decades. Properly designed, such assemblies suggest a new democratic system which could give people power to influence politics, justice and government funding in areas that influence their lives. This could be a counterweight to partisan politics and a vital new centre of democratic life – linking the public directly to those in power and showing how common ground can be found.

A citizens' assembly gives participants the opportunity to

access balanced information, interrogate witnesses, deliberate on competing choices and – crucially – seek consensus. They are not only a way of loosening the grip of political parties and special interests over public debate; they also recognise the value that is added when citizens themselves engage directly in shaping policy and law. Most importantly, they can help rebuild the broken connection between what the public wants and what the public actually sees delivered.

Across every continent, from citizens' assemblies to policy juries and independent citizen reviews, ordinary people are now coming together to consider public issues far from the overheated divisiveness of party politics. *Noema* editor Nathan Gardels described them as non-partisan 'islands of goodwill' emerging inside fractured political systems.[28] What they point towards is not the replacement of representative democracy, but its renewal through participation.

Making a difference

Does this make any real difference? Before examining the full range of participatory models, we should note that this is not an abstract debate. The evidence suggests that when people become more closely involved in their own democracy, outcomes improve. Deliberative processes have led to mobile phones being banned in Belgian schools; to new social housing being built in Paris; to changes in transport policy and tourism regulation in Barcelona; and to shaping the legal framework for Uber in Taiwan. They have improved nursing recruitment in Belgium, transferred responsibility for allocating a €30 million public budget in Barcelona directly to citizens, and shaped wildfire and earthquake prevention strategies in California.

In some cases, deliberation has brought about changes even at the constitutional and societal level, sometimes connected to referendums.[29] In Ireland, citizens' deliberation transformed the politics of abortion and same-sex marriage.[30] In Japan, it shaped decisions on pension reform and nuclear power. In Mongolia in 2017 it influenced reforms to the powers of the president and prime minister and the method of their election. In Bulgaria, it shifted opinion on the longstanding segregation of Roma children in education. In all of these cases, what began as an apparently fixed public position was transformed through a process of questioning, gathering evidence and collective reasoning.

One of the most striking demonstrations of this effect came from the large-scale American deliberative project convened by Jim Fishkin in 2021, which brought together 1,000 randomly selected citizens for structured discussion across the country. The result saw significant shifts in opinion towards stronger collective action on seventy-two major policy proposals across climate and energy. A group of Americans from across different states, parties, age groups and income levels came together in support of substantial reductions in greenhouse gas emissions. Participants even agreed on a bipartisan framework to give long-term predictability to public and private investment in the energy transition, while assisting workers and regions dependent on fossil fuels.

Fishkin's broader conclusion, set out in his book *Can Deliberation Cure the Ills of Democracy?*, is that polarisation is often far less established than it appears.[31] In his 'America in One Room' forum, Republicans frequently moved significantly towards positions initially associated with Democrats, and Democrats sometimes moved just as far in the opposite direction. He also found evidence that while politicians tend to look at policy in the short term, public deliberation can extend these timelines and strengthen concern for long-term consequences.

Taiwan provides one of the most advanced real-world examples. Its national platform now engages thousands of citizens across more than two dozen major policy issues, with over 80 per cent of deliberations leading directly to government action.[32] Citizens submit statements about a policy question, which other citizens then vote to agree or disagree with. Software called Polis then maps these responses to identify where broad agreement exists across otherwise divided groups. Rather than allowing direct argument or reply, the platform is designed to identify shared views rather than focusing on disagreement. Resulting areas of agreement are compiled into a report put directly to the relevant minister, who is expected to respond publicly to each point. As Taiwan's first digital minister put it, this is 'a way for government to work with the people, not just for the people'.[33] Extreme positions consistently fall to the margins, while consensus views accumulate in the middle.

Engaged California, an attempt at governing with the people not just for them, is an initiative in participation without populism, making California the largest political jurisdiction in the world to attempt online citizens' deliberation at scale.[34] The project has three permanent aims: to allow policymakers to listen, to allow citizens to be heard, and to allow citizens to connect with one another in a time when civic life is fragmenting. Alongside existing instruments of direct democracy – ballots, referendums and recall – it is now becoming part of the state's formal decision-making process. Its first major use, responding to the 2025 firestorms, generated nineteen citizen-backed recovery recommendations by the end of that year, with public support for each tracked online through AI-enabled visual mapping of the emerging consensus.[35]

Paris offers another model, this time a standing, reconvened citizens' assembly. Its randomly selected 100-member assembly has successfully proposed major environmental and housing reforms and now operates under a rule requiring legislators not only to hear its conclusions but to act on them within a defined timeframe. As a result, the city's first 'citizen bill', tackling Paris's twin problems of homelessness and vacant properties, has already been enacted. As Claudia Chwalisz of Democracy Next has argued, the principle now established is that 'consensus should be sought', and that when it is reached through fair processes, governments have a duty to respond.[36]

Other institutional innovations point in the same direction. In Mongolia, citizen deliberation is required for any change to the constitution. In Ostbelgien, the German-speaking region of Belgium, a permanent citizens' assembly operates through rotating random selection: each year 1,500 residents are invited at random, from whom thirty are randomly selected to deliberate over several months. Government is now formally required to consider how to implement their recommendations.

None of this, however, means that small citizens' assemblies should become a substitute for wider civic education and public debate. Fishkin himself warned against using mini-publics as a shortcut to bypass mass engagement, and cautioned against institutionalising small assemblies at the expense of a broader public sphere. So the central question is not whether deliberation works – it does – but how widely it can be extended.

Crafting a shared democratic story

Together, what these experiments show is the need for citizens to have a voice sufficiently powerful to challenge the dominance of wealth and vested interests at the top of society. This points away from what might be called a 'thin' democracy – one in which citizens participate passively and episodically – and towards a 'thicker' form that is not just about voting but actively contributing, and not just at election time. Far from undermining representative democracy, such participatory institutions strengthen it by improving the range of opinion and the depth of experiences that can contribute to the decisions made by elected representatives.

The proposals examined in this chapter are a response to the collapse of trust in our democracies. Any democratic process must include clear safeguards for balance, objectivity and impartiality, and citizens' assemblies and citizens' juries must not become vehicles for pressure groups to entrench their own views. But when processes of decision-making are made transparent and fair, the public can appreciate that fellow citizens coming together in assemblies, juries or community meetings are interrogating the best available evidence, questioning experts directly and reaching carefully reasoned conclusions through dialogue. Even if these new institutions do nothing more than weaken the grip of fake news, algorithmic echo chambers and prejudiced online silos, they will already be performing a vital democratic function by changing the terms of public debate itself.

But we will not defeat anti-democratic populism simply by fact-checking it, as if making a better set of statistics available to the public can by itself change the direction of travel. Nor will a random scattering of assemblies reverse decades of civic decay. The bigger prize is something more fundamental: a shared democratic story that emerges from what we feel must change as a result of our everyday struggles – the cost of living, the state of schools and health services, the condition of high streets, our children's futures. This may enable us to believe once more in the power of collective engagement to exercise meaningful control over the decisions that shape our lives. So it makes sense to encourage far more frequent, informal and in-person civic gatherings that restore the idea of a public square. Where this is not possible physically, digital tools – such as California's online town halls – can help recreate deliberation at scale. What matters is that democracy comes to feel less like a single vote or an occasional protest, and more like a continuous practice of listening, debating and deciding together.

Democracy survives and endures when citizens are willing to defend its principles by withdrawing support from leaders who violate them. It survives when people are prepared to speak up against self-serving elites, rather than retreating into resignation or cynicism. From mass mobilisation to stop an authoritarian takeover in South Korea to resistance to democratic backsliding even in European Union countries, from coalitions against autocracy in India to civil society movements in Latin America, we see expressions of a deeper claim than simply a protest against an autocratic leader or an undemocratic policy. We see ordinary people refuse to surrender ownership of their political systems. Only recently we saw Italian citizens, driven by a surge in young voters, reject an attempt to politicise the judiciary through a popular vote, despite the ongoing political popularity of the far right.

What unites the most successful of these movements is not just ideology, but solidarity in action to address grievances that can be named, debated and acted on together. They will normally have forged new alliances across class, age, religion, ethnicity and region. And in doing so, they will have renewed the possibility of democracy, even in societies that seemed locked into cycles of backsliding and rising authoritarianism.

This brings us back to the core argument of this chapter. The two preceding chapters showed how rebuilding the economy and restoring social cohesion are essential to cutting off the demand for populist nationalism at its source. This chapter has shown that those two pillars are still not themselves enough to ensure lasting progress without a democratic renewal to match them.

The various experiments underway across the world do not offer a single blueprint, but together they point in the same direction: towards a form of popular government that is once again animated by the will, the voice and the dignity of ordinary people. The real test of success, therefore, is not simply whether more people tell pollsters that they 'support democracy', or even whether turnout ticks up at the next election – important as both would be. The deeper test, as our polling has shown, is whether millions more people are actively engaged in shaping the civic life of their communities, and working together across lines of difference.

And that should begin with civic education – not necessarily one that over-moralises about 'the virtues', but one that both teaches students, in Jefferson's words, 'to recognise ambition in all its shapes' and demonstrates that there is something worth fighting for beyond ourselves. School – the one institution that at some point everyone attends – should be, as James Traub describes it, 'the cradle of citizenship', and yet, as the need for civic education has risen, it has been sidelined to the point of there being, as he reports, discomfort about using the language of virtue and not even common criteria for evaluating truth.[37] This must change.

If democracy is to flourish again in what is now an authoritarian age, it will not be because it was imposed from above or imported from abroad. It will be because it was rebuilt from within – patiently and collectively, even imperfectly – by citizens who once again came to see it not as a remote, out-of-touch system that governs them, but as a shared enterprise that belongs to all of us. In this digital age, the active and engaged citizen matters more than ever.

15

SOLIDARITY: DEVELOPMENT WITHOUT DEPENDENCE

On a single day in September 2025, two gatherings took place within a few blocks of each other in New York. At the United Nations, President Trump delivered a tirade lasting nearly two hours that declared an end to America's support for the liberal world order. A few streets away, at the headquarters of the Rockefeller Foundation, a smaller but historically more consequential meeting was underway. African leaders had assembled to announce the Reset: a wholly new approach to development, and a transformation in the way the continent's 1.5 billion people would, in future, receive healthcare.

The contrast between the two events could not have been starker. One was the sound of the old order collapsing. The other was the first signal of what might replace it.

I have made more visits to African countries than all the US presidents of the past 100 years combined, not only in my capacity as a government minister but as a UN envoy and a WHO ambassador. Over those years I have witnessed both the scale of the continent's challenges and the extraordinary determination of its people to overcome them. In Tanzania I watched doctors and nurses battling to end the scourge of tuberculosis in young children. In Kenya I met schoolchildren classified as HIV/AIDS orphans or half-orphans, depending on the health condition of their parents. In Nigeria I saw how dilapidated school buildings put young girls' health at risk. In 2012, the founder of the World Wide Web, Tim Berners-Lee, and I visited Ethiopia to observe how new technology could open up education for blind pupils who did not even have access to Braille. In Mozambique I visited health clinics without even the most basic funding. In the new state of South Sudan, and then in Sudan, I met young mothers whose health indicators lagged far behind their European counterparts. And in South Africa, Nelson Mandela showed me his foundation's efforts to fund what even one of Africa's wealthiest countries still lacked: children's hospitals.

From its history of dependency and neglect – most recently demonstrated by the global disparity of access to the Covid-19 vaccine – a new resolve has grown across Africa that has been vigorously expressed in my recent meetings. 'Never again,' said African leaders, as they planned locally based vaccine manufacturing plants for the continent. The Reset, launched that day in New York, takes that resolve further still. It breaks the Global South's dependency on the Global North with a clear announcement of future self-reliance and self-sufficiency: Africa's healthcare will no longer be franchised out to external agencies. Instead, services will be delivered by local providers, according to local priorities, and funded increasingly through local revenues. Africa will build its own capacity to deliver healthcare, free from dependence on external control.

While in the years after the millennium Africa's health sector recorded impressive progress in maternal and child health and in addressing HIV, malaria and tuberculosis, the gap in life expectancy between sub-Saharan Africa and Europe remains stark: sixty-four years against eighty-two. Infant mortality in Africa per 1,000 live births stands at seventy-two compared to just four in Europe. Maternal mortality in sub-Saharan Africa, at 575 per 100,000, though down 40 per cent since 2000, remains more than forty times higher than the European figure of thirteen per 100,000. Some 67 per cent of all people living with HIV are in sub-Saharan Africa, which still accounts for between 60 and 70 per cent of new infections and AIDS deaths worldwide, and 95 per cent of global malaria deaths and new cases occur in Africa. One reason for all this is that health spending per capita across most of the continent ranges from just $50 to $250 a year – compared with $3,000 to $7,000 across Europe and around $13,000 in the United States.[1]

The lessons African leaders have learned is that progress is possible, but to achieve it they should move beyond donor-driven projects run from the outside towards country-owned and country-led systems – built on local initiative and local decision-making as countries take control of their own health futures. This is not simply a change in how healthcare – or indeed development more broadly – is organised. It is a change in who holds power: a new global order with self-reliance and mutual benefit at its core. And it is a change that has to take place, at a time when the costs of a fragmenting, more protectionist world bear heavily on poorer countries. Extreme fragmentation could leave countries up to 12 per cent poorer. Lower-income countries together hold just 1 per cent of global reserves, while the IMF resources that they might have to rely on amount to less than 1 per cent of the value of the world economy. Those facts mean further defaults may be on their way, which have historically meant a 30 per cent rise in poverty for a decade and a 13 per cent rise in infant mortality.[2] What is more, because of the greater share taken up by food and fuel in household incomes, these countries have been characterised in this decade by extreme uncertainty, at the sharp end of the persistent shocks that have upended growth in the world economy.

And so to address these challenges, I set out in this chapter the kind of compact for development that can replace the old donor–recipient relationships, as the old paternalism and hierarchies give way to an equal partnership between Global North and Global South in which a renewed commitment to shared economic growth drives development and development, in turn, drives growth.

The poverty problem

No one should forget the huge progress made in the quarter-century after 1990. Life expectancy in the poorest countries rose by nine years;[3] child mortality was halved;[4] primary school enrolment nearly doubled;[5] HIV was brought under control; polio was virtually eradicated; extreme poverty fell from nearly 50 per cent of the global population to 10 per cent; and especially because of advances in Asia, the global population of middle-class individuals with an income of more than $10 a day has grown to 3.6 billion.[6] Since 2000, more than half of low-income countries have now reached lower-middle-income status, like Bangladesh, and a few such as Indonesia have achieved middle-income status.

But in recent years progress has slowed, and in some areas reversed. In 2025, 838 million people were living in extreme poverty – up from 712 million in 2022[7]* – and more than 600 million will still be in extreme poverty by 2030, half of them children, and more than half of them in sub-Saharan Africa, where hunger is also increasing. By 2030, on current trends, 300 million people will be officially on the edge of starvation. The first Sustainable Development Goal (SDG) was, boldly, to 'end poverty in all its forms, everywhere'.[8] Yet children, who make up only around 30 per cent of the world's total population, account for over 50 per cent of those living on less than $3 a day,[9] with three out of every four of them growing up in sub-Saharan Africa.† Six hundred million Africans live without electricity.[10] A decade after it was

* According to the World Bank's $2.15-per-day poverty measure.

† Even though the number of children in extreme poverty has fallen by around 100 million over the past decade, the need is still vast. If we use the higher, more realistic poverty threshold of $8.30 a day – which is more relevant in middle-income countries – the number rises to 1.4 billion, or nearly 66 per cent of all children worldwide. While this is down from 73 per cent a decade earlier, it is still far too high. The global gains in reducing poverty also mask stark differences between regions. In India, the proportion of children living in extreme poverty fell from more than 25 per cent to just over 5 per cent between 2011 and 2022. Across south Asia, rates declined from around 25 per cent to 6 per cent.

signed, SDG 6, universal access to basic public services, is already sixty years behind schedule globally,[11] and in fragile states is not likely be achieved for 240 years. Collectively, rich countries spend around one quarter of their GDP on social protection, with welfare available to almost all citizens. but even after progress over the last decade,[12] 42 per cent of residents in lower-middle-income countries and 25 per cent in low-income countries – 2 billion of our fellow citizens – have no protection at all.[13]

Thirty-nine of the world's poorest states are in sub-Saharan Africa, and of them thirty-three are affected by conflict. Thirty-one of these countries have per capita annual incomes below $1,315 – around $3 per person daily. In total, twenty-two low-income countries with growing populations are the most reliant on low-productivity subsistence farming, less able to benefit from trade, more dependent on now-shrinking aid budgets and thus poorly equipped to follow the typical modernising path of export-led, low-cost manufacturing that has transformed much of Asia.[14]

The state of aid

It is over half a century since the Pearson Report called for developed economies to transfer 0.7 per cent of their national income to the developing world[15] – and a quarter of a century since 189 countries and every international institution signed up to the United Nations' Millennium Development Goals, which were to become the Sustainable Development Goals. I was a member of a UK government which helped negotiate $200 billion in debt relief and planned an increase in development assistance from 0.26 per cent of GDP in 1997 to, eventually, the 0.7 per cent recommended by Pearson. But with only one third of the SDG targets for 2030 on track and progress on others requiring a rescue plan involving a huge investment – public and private – of more than $4 trillion a year,[16] the whole global financial architecture has been officially deemed by the UN to be 'entirely unfit for purpose in a world characterized by unrelenting climate change, increasing systemic risks, extreme inequality, entrenched gender bias, highly integrated financial markets vulnerable to cross-border contagion, and dramatic demographic, technological, economic, and geopolitical change'.[17]

But even while the need continues to grow, the aid money is drying up. In 2024, twenty-two of the thirty-three members of the OECD's Development Assistance Committee slashed their official aid budgets and in 2025 the seventeen largest donors cut future contributions by 30 per cent. Only four countries now meet the 0.7 per cent UN target,[18] with the result that in the humanitarian disaster in Gaza, around 30 per cent of the one million people left there had no access to food at all,[19] even after the ceasefire.

At the same time, other potential sources of funding for development have also been decreasing. Foreign direct investment into emerging markets and developing economies has fallen to just 2 per cent of global flows – less than half its peak before the financial crisis[20] – and with debt levels in low-income countries now at an eighteen-year high, more than half of those countries are in, or at high risk of, debt distress. Today two thirds of external public and publicly guaranteed debt in emerging markets is now owed to private entities; much of it is Chinese debt, a dramatic turnaround from just two decades ago when the main creditors were the advanced economies and the multilateral institutions. Only four countries (Chad, Ethiopia, Ghana and Zambia) have secured relief under the G20's Common Framework,[21] and as concessional finance – loans offered below market rates – dries up, more governments have turned to collateralised loans: opaque deals made 'under the counter' and off the balance sheet that are now pushing debt burdens toward unpayable levels.[22] Without far greater transparency, and restructuring, this crisis will deepen further. Four in every ten developing countries – nearly half of them in Africa – now spend 10 per cent or more of government revenues simply servicing their debts. In 2024, sub-Saharan African countries alone spent around $163 billion on 2024 debt repayments that could otherwise have been invested in children, education and health.[23]

A new model for development

'Now is the time for transformation that is owned and driven by Africa,' writes Mavis Owusu-Gyamfi, an African leading voice.[24] She seeks a turnaround from the traditional donor–recipient relationships to development without domination: an equal partnership between North and South which guarantees the South strategic autonomy and ensures, in both North and South, fairness and reciprocity in economic relationships. Underlying such a 'North–South Compact for Development' should be a fresh distinction drawn between what is necessary for development and what is necessary for the delivery of global public goods, the latter of which are in everyone's interests and should no longer be a charge on aid budgets, but seen for what they are: a shared responsibility, recognising that if the North did nothing to help the South, carbon emissions would worsen everywhere, public health crises would increase worldwide, and migration flows would grow at an even faster rate than in recent years.

In a new compact, decisions and programmes must first come under local control by local people, rather than being monopolised by external agencies. Furthermore, while aid flows will remain critical in the transition to a new relationship, economic development is the key to the Global South's future and that means reforms to what are currently Northern-imposed policies regulating trade, financial flows, technology and migration. All have a substantial spillover effect on the South, and decisions by the IMF, the World Bank, the WTO, the UN or the G20 have to fully take into account the interests of those with the greatest development needs.

The third requirement is to move from the ad hoc piecemeal

funding of development to a system of equitable burden-sharing, based on each country's capacity to contribute. Most of all, this should underpin a humanitarian aid system whereby, instead of passing the begging bowl round – usually too late after a crisis hits – contributions are provided on a predictable basis by those most able to afford it, as happens for UN peacekeeping.

The fourth stipulation is that we set out the responsibilities of each partner in development, with agreed procedures for accountability and audit, to ensure that the right to direct funds locally is matched by the responsibility to use funds well. For in a world where needs vastly exceed available resources, effectiveness and efficiency must necessarily become a central focus for allocating and deploying development funding.

If a new model for development is going to work, we need to build a new architecture on the lines of the Reset mentioned above – not just for health but for trade, education and humanitarian aid – that will respect the Global South's desire for and right to self-government.

Education: the key to development

Global education is facing a double crisis: declining funding and declining school attendance, with absenteeism rising by 10 per cent in the last year alone,[25] taking us further away than ever from achieving the 2030 goal of universal education. At least 260 million school-age children will not go to school today or any day. And as teacher numbers fall and class sizes grow, another 290 million pupils are experiencing a decline in the quality of their education so that even at the age of ten, seven out of ten children in low- and middle-income countries are still unable to read.[26] There is a good reason why. Not only did total global education spending per child stagnate in the last decade but it is now falling, with education aid itself expected to be down by 25 per cent by 2027, the steepest decline since the 1990s.[27]

With competing priorities in health, climate and poverty reduction, ministers are retreating from the modest benchmarks of allocating 4 per cent of GDP and 15 per cent of public spending to education. The backlog in necessary investment is now so great that to catch up, Global South countries would need to allocate education more than 10 per cent of their national income. It is a shortfall which imaginative initiatives like the recent Côte d'Ivoire debt swap can reduce but not eliminate.

And yet there is a strong case for seeing educational spend – and school meals for children – as the best form of investment a country can make. Differences in levels of investment in human capital are proved to be the primary driver of wealth disparity between high- and low-income nations. Worldwide, each additional year of schooling increases an individual's future earnings by about 10 per cent.[28*] Focusing on improving teaching quality through proper training, rigorous assessment and effective feedback can make a significant difference in pupil outcomes at minimal cost. Just 2 per cent of children under five in sub-Saharan Africa are growing up with three or more children's books in their homes but pre-school education comprises just 1 per cent of education budgets.[29] We need the determined focus on early learning that Chile's outstandingly successful Chile Crece Contigo programme offers from the first prenatal appointment.[30]

AI cannot and should not replace teachers, but it can augment their work, and as Kenya's use of AI has shown it can offer a cost-effective route to monitor school performance and free up teachers to individually mentor their pupils. An after-school programme on these lines in Edo, Nigeria, delivered improvements in six weeks that would normally take 1½–2 years of conventional

---

* When I chaired the Education Commission some years ago, we found that in order to achieve the SDG of quality universal education within this generation, lower-middle-income countries needed to spend 8.5 per cent of GDP, while low-income countries needed to spend up to 11.8 per cent.

schooling.[31] Kenya's Tusome project, a pilot scheme to improve literacy, reduced the number of non-readers by half within two years, showing the benefit of supporting locally run initiatives.[32] As with health, education must transition from its high dependency on external agencies to greater local control, with new international funding focused on building up the home-grown capacity to achieve this.

Enrolment in higher education in the Global South increased by 91 per cent in the first two decades of this century and in sub-Saharan Africa by 125 per cent, thanks in part to impressive initiatives such as the Nelson Mandela Extranet programme, a peer-to-peer certificate initiative, which has reached over 600,000 young people and is on course to reach a further 2 million over the next five years. But still, while Africa is home to 25 per cent of the world's 16–25-year-olds, it has just 6 per cent of the world's students, and only 9 per cent of African 18–23-year-olds are enrolled in university, against the global average of 38 per cent. This is partly because further education is too expensive for many in Africa. In sub-Saharan Africa overall, every student costs the equivalent of 30 per cent of GDP per capita, and as much as 48 per cent in South Africa.[33] These costs mean that we must find new ways of financing further education – by online learning or preferably with hybrid courses, mixing in-person and online teaching. Some initiatives are leading the way, like the Maharishi Invincibility Institute, which champions free tertiary education programmes in the Global South and under whose 'earn and learn' programme students split their time between classrooms and work placements.[34]

So the Global South cannot just import the old model of tertiary education from the North. A modular system, fashioned locally – which may be online, in situ or a mix of the two – may be the way forward if we are to adequately bridge the gap between the needs of a growing youth population and an education system struggling to meet them.

Trade, employment and growth

If low- and lower-middle-income countries are to finance education, health and anti-poverty programmes, their economies need to grow faster – and again, this cannot be achieved through aid. 'We need to stop just pulling people out of the river,' Desmond Tutu explained. 'We need to go upstream and find out why they're falling in.'[35] But despite having nearly 20 per cent of the world's population, Africa accounts for just 3 per cent of global economic activity and 2 per cent of world trade, and receives less than 1 per cent of private capital investment.[36]

The Global South, including some of the poorest states in Africa, is richly endowed, with 30 per cent of the world's critical materials and metallic resources.[37] Its other great resource is its people; if it can mobilise this successfully, its youthful population can offer a demographic dividend that is no longer available to many of the advanced economies. But low levels of investment, poor productivity, technological backwardness and educational underachievement, combined with rising debt, demographic pressure and climate risks, create a low- and middle-income trap from which too many countries cannot escape. For every two people that joined the working-age population of the Democratic Republic of Congo, Nigeria or Ethiopia before 2020, only one ever gained employment, according to Bloomberg Economics analysis of International Labour Organization figures.[38]

But if the traditional route out of low-income status for developing countries, to focus on industrialising in order to export goods, has been narrowing as a result of labour-replacing automation and the reshoring of manufacturing, a vastly different way of creating jobs has to be devised in its place. Some countries like India, Singapore and the Philippines have created productive, globally competitive, tradable services in the way Japan, South Korea and then China did for manufacturing. And the 1.2 billion young people competing for only 400 million jobs[39] will now have to look to those technologically advanced firms that can develop an export trade in services or in goods consumed locally, and to those small and medium-sized companies making productivity-enhancing investments, not least in the green economy. The World Bank's 2024–33 strategy has zeroed in on a shift from low-productivity agriculture to increased productivity in all sectors, including farming. It hopes to achieve this by working towards more adult men gaining formal jobs, more girls leaving school with qualifications, and more women in the workforce in general.

But while the Global South's path to prosperity will be different from that previously followed by the Global North, low rates of economic growth are not just an African story but a problem in much of both the Global North and South. The post-war order sought to reconcile an open international economy with domestic social contracts promising full employment, welfare and stability, in which governments strived to join the global economy without making sacrifices at home.[40] This had its weaknesses. The world that globalisation forged was not the 'flat' landscape predicted, but an environment where the most important players still went their own way. The institutions it created initially prevented the law of the jungle, but as we have seen they have since been hollowed out. And the promise – that growth would be broadly shared, opportunities expanded and democracy strengthened – is no longer believed. In particular the North's response to the failures of globalisation – homeshoring, friendshoring and bans on export–import technology and investment – has made it all the harder to achieve what was once the common objective of a balanced global economy.

Exposing what he calls the 'developmental trilemma', Dani Rodrik has argued that we may not be able to achieve all three of the central priorities of our era: enabling development in the Global South, advancing global decarbonisation and restoring middle-class prosperity in the West. All three are essential, but in practice, pushing forward on any two can risk abandoning the third. Rich countries' strategies to rebuild domestic manufacturing and resilience may narrow the opportunity for lower-income countries to industrialise through export-led growth. And aggressive climate policies such as carbon border adjustment mechanisms could further constrain countries still reliant on fossil fuels. These tensions are real but not insurmountable. The question is whether we can design a new multilateralism that builds agreements on free and fair trade around new industrial, employment and innovation policies at home that do not sabotage cooperation abroad.

To simply throw away the benefits of our global trading system would be 'suicide in a fit of insanity'. Even as it struggles the World Trade Organization retains 160 members who account for 98 per cent of global trade, most of whom still trade openly and free from tariffs, even if many non-tariff barriers remain. Rebuilding the global system without destroying its gains demands a different kind of 'embedded liberalism' for the twenty-first century,[41] one that comprehensively addresses today's structural challenges – in particular the threats to secure employment, what some people are referring to as the four Ds (decarbonisation, digitalisation, demographic change and declining incomes from work), amid rising domestic inequalities within countries. For most countries in the Global South as well as the Global North, a broad-based prosperity can best be achieved by guiding technological change, incentivising new investment and revitalising those communities that have been left out and left behind. And that means supporting domestic industrial policies tied to environmental sustainability while avoiding the temptations to enter a self-defeating spiral of protectionism. Ursula von der Leyen, president of the European Commission, recently proposed joint negotiations between the EU and the Indo-Pacific states (mostly through the CPTPP trade bloc),[42] which together account for more than half of the world's economic activity, with a view to 'redesigning' the WTO to 'show the world that free trade with a large number of countries is possible on a rules-based foundation'. This could include guaranteeing mutual investment rights, binding mechanisms for settling trade disputes and even pooling liquidity to respond to financial shocks.[43]

Our common and shared interests, North and South, are such that any new approach must extend beyond trade and include managing volatile financial flows and raising global growth, not least by addressing the structural imbalances that no single country can resolve acting on their own. China saves too much and consumes too little (household consumption is only 40 per cent of GDP), Europe saves too much and invests too little, and America saves too little and absorbs too much, sustained by the dollar's reserve-currency role and the rest of the world's appetite for safe dollar assets. Only coordinated action by the major economies – to simultaneously boost Chinese consumption, European investment and American exports – can remove the underlying sources of global instability and boost global growth. The IMF was designed for a world of episodic, country-specific crises rather than today's structural imbalances and systemic risks. A global growth compact could work to address imbalances, and to support countries exposed to global shocks by reducing the need for countries to build up precautionary reserves beyond what is reasonable.[44]

And coordinated global action should support the Global South directly. Elite corruption, capital flight and tax avoidance cost African countries around $90 billion a year to illicit financial flows, far more than the $60 billion they receive in aid.[45] Only a tiny fraction of investment from large institutional investors like pension funds currently goes to low- and middle-income countries. Shifting even a small share of those flows towards productive investment in these countries would materially improve development outcomes.

Ultimately, the test of any reformed global framework is an improvement in the lives of ordinary people in North and South alike. Solidarity at home and abroad need not be seen as at odds with each other – but, rather, as mutually reinforcing pillars of a stable, just and sustainable global economy.

Humanitarian aid and its challenge

Even if growth resumes, trade flows pick up and overall poverty is reduced, there will always be humanitarian crises which will overwhelm individual governments and cannot be addressed without the world coming together to demand international collaboration and assistance. According to Tufts University estimates, annual deaths from hunger since 2020 have stood at between 200,000 and 300,000, many of these occurring in Yemen and Ethiopia. While this is less than a third of the average of 928,000 a year between 1870 and 1970, it is a significant and worrying increase from the post-1980 annual average of 75,000. When famine hits, the problem is always the same, as we have seen recently, from devastating floods in Pakistan, Libya and Mozambique, to the displacement of people from wars in Ukraine, Gaza, Sudan, Myanmar and the DRC. But it is not a lack of food worldwide that is the real problem but the lack of political will to ensure people receive it.[46]

While until recently humanitarian aid was consistently reaching over 100 million people annually, preventing famines for example in the Horn of Africa and the Sahel, the discouraging news is that we are currently meeting less than half of the global need and that, while demand is increasing, aid is decreasing. As I write, half the population in Sudan alone – nearly 25 million people – are experiencing acute food insecurity, with a record high of 638,000 facing catastrophic hunger,[47] and it is estimated that the numbers of people who are facing acute food insecurity worldwide could rise from 318 million to 363 million during 2026.

Humanitarian aid is the closest thing we have to a global safety net, and at a time when poverty, war and climate change threaten to unravel the fragile gains made over recent decades, the need for it is more urgent than ever. Yet the system is in such disrepair that the UN's incoming emergency relief coordinator, Tom Fletcher, has described it as 'under-financed, over-stretched, and under assault'[48] – a system that is broken, recreates the dependent relationships that we pledged to abolish and marginalises the Global South.

As with health and education, the reform of humanitarian aid requires the direct involvement of local organisations, who are best placed to identify and address needs in their own communities. But these local organisations, best at operating on the front line, currently receive barely 1 per cent of humanitarian funding. Instead two thirds of funding goes to a 'dense mesh' of UN agencies and international NGOs which are managed from outside.

Aware of these shortfalls, aid originations agreed a 'Grand Bargain' in 2016, committing, first, to make humanitarian support 'as local as possible, as international as necessary'; second, to shift to predictable multi-year financing; third, to expand 'anticipatory aid' to pre-empt disasters; and fourth, to end the humanitarian–development divide and replace it with a joint, more integrated, multi-year approach to both the assessment of needs and the delivery of support.[49] The Grand Bargain's initial target was for 25 per cent of aid to be delivered locally, but none of their targets have been met, so the first recommendation I have is to channel more humanitarian aid through local agencies. That will avoid money being wasted in transit and lives being lost from decisions made at a distance.

This ties in to our aim of increasing anticipatory aid. Contrary to the perception created by media coverage, most humanitarian crises can be anticipated, and they lend themselves to early, locally led preventive action. Climate-related events such as droughts and floods can often be prepared for in advance. In Bangladesh, for example, delivering cash to vulnerable households prior to a flooding forecast enabled families to feed their children and avoid having to sell their household goods to survive – a striking demonstration of how advance action can avert long-term harm.

Often humanitarian emergencies can last for years, although most aid involves short-term, reactive funding in the immediate aftermath. Instead, we need predictable, multi-year financing geared towards crisis prevention. So, a further recommendation is that humanitarian support should shift towards building resilience, by working to integrate humanitarian finance with long-term development finance.

'Resilience' in this context has many different connotations. At its most basic level it means enabling people to withstand, manage and recover from shocks without having to resort to coping strategies that hurt them in the longer term. Consider the families on the front line of the climate crisis. Farmers in countries like Somalia and Ethiopia are extraordinarily innovative and resilient. They are used to managing droughts and dealing with uncertain rainfall. In Bangladesh and Pakistan, the management of floods is built into livelihood systems and risk management strategies. But what happens when more protracted and severe droughts and more intensive floods overwhelm traditional coping mechanisms?

In 2022, large parts of Pakistan recorded record-breaking floods, with some provinces receiving seven to eight times their average rainfall. More than 33 million people were affected, with 17 million homes destroyed and $2.5 billion in food crops lost. In this case, World Weather Attribution analysis estimates that global warming increased the intensity of rainfall by 50–75 per cent.[50] Climate events like this are overwhelming traditional coping mechanisms, forcing families to sell productive assets, skip already inadequate meals, and take children out of school and put them into work.[51]

Humanitarian responses will never be enough to address the challenges posed by the climate crisis. Too little aid invariably arrives too late, but there is a tried and tested alternative. Adaptive safety nets, as they are called, can be put in place in advance so that when crisis strikes, the most vulnerable can be quickly identified and reached with the cash they need to access food and avoid being forced into distress sales.

The idea that a safety net infrastructure cannot be created in countries affected by conflict, and the wider governance challenges that accompany humanitarian disaster, is profoundly misplaced. In the Sahel, an adaptive safety net programme now reaches over 1.2 million people across countries including Mali, Senegal, Burkina Faso and Niger. The Productive Safety Net Programme in Ethiopia is a public works programme that employs the rural poor during droughts.[52] The Hunger Safety Net Programme in Kenya provides regular cash transfers that automatically expand when, as during the 2021–2 drought, advances were triggered.[53]

These models provide governments and donors with a ready-made platform to expand their safety net programmes. New technologies like mobile banking are making it dramatically easier, cheaper and more efficient to target and reach people affected by climate shocks and other events, and offer the potential to deliver at speed and scale. So my final recommendation is that governments step up their efforts to extend the reach and increase the effectiveness of safety net coverage – which means that more aid should be delivered as cash, giving people in crisis the dignity of choice. Transportation costs and logistics alone account for two thirds of the cost of delivering US food aid. Yet while the share of humanitarian aid provided in cash to local organisations has doubled in a decade, the increase is only from 4 per cent to 8 per cent, far short of the 25 per cent target set in the Grand Bargain.[54]

Humanitarian workers in the UN and the NGO community already do an extraordinary job. They save and rebuild lives, they are often on the front lines of humanitarian disasters, and they respond with moral urgency when help is most needed. Those providing long-term development finance generate fewer headlines, but their work too also saves lives and helps create pathways out of poverty.

How do we pay for it?

Fair burden-sharing is essential if our aim is a world in which no country needs aid. The current system, which relies less on guaranteed contributions and more on voluntary donations, is uncertain and arbitrary. In addition the resources allocated by the World Bank to low- and middle-income countries are now equivalent to just 0.1 per cent of global GDP – the smallest commitment in its history, even as development needs have grown sharply. Multilateral development banks as a whole now provide loans equivalent to just 0.35 per cent of developing countries' national incomes, down from 0.5 per cent in the 1990s.[55] All this means that there is still no reliable global financial safety net or insurance system: even currency swaps are restricted to favoured allies, and concessional lending is not always available even to countries facing shocks that are no fault of their own.

In the absence of reform, countries feel they have no choice but to turn to bilateral deals that deepen dependence without delivering structural transformation. A reformed multilateral system, built on fair financing and shared decision-making, offers a better path to a world where countries finance their own development via growth, investment and trade. Supporting the transition to autonomy should therefore be the priority in international funding – the aim being financing the transition to services delivered by local providers, for local people, which will be funded in time through local taxes.

Tobacco, alcohol and sugary products already cause over 10 million deaths worldwide each year.[56] A 50 per cent increase in tobacco prices could raise $2.1 trillion for low- and middle-income countries over five years, while saving 50 million lives over half a century. Forty-three African countries have now imposed solidarity levies on tobacco products, with some of the proceeds allocated to public health, and a smaller number have targeted alcohol and sugar.[57]

What we now require is the application of the principle that already finances UN peacekeeping, almost half of the WHO's budget, and payments to the World Bank and IMF. It is not unreasonable to argue that all the richest countries which pay too little now should agree a formula by which they contribute fairly. Allocations could be adjusted to account for the benefits a country gains from the global system – from the resumption of trade to the privileges of world leadership. Permanent membership of the UN Security Council, the G20 or the boards of the IMF, the World Bank and the Financial Stability Board could trigger higher contribution levels. Floors and ceilings could be revisited, especially those limiting payments from countries with per capita wealth well above global averages. Models like the EU's allocation formulas or the UK's Barnett formula, which adjust resources in line with population shifts, could be adapted for global public goods.

To make the most of these resources, we must show clear value for money. That means adopting the best ways not just of spending money but of raising it. The use of guarantees – still underutilised in development – can unlock vast amounts of private and multilateral finance. A $100 billion package of guarantees, paired with $20 billion in paid-in capital, could unlock $500 billion in development finance. A small amount of grant aid could 'buy down' interest rates, bringing repayment terms close to those of the best concessional loans. The International Finance Facility for Education (IFFEd) has created over $1 billion in education resources from just $40 million in cash and $230 million in guarantees.[58] The Innovative Finance Facility for Climate in Asia and the Pacific (IF-CAP) uses $3 billion in guarantees to create up to $15 billion for climate adaptation and mitigation to respond to climate issues – a $1-in, $5-out ratio.[59] The World Bank's new Portfolio Guarantee Programme estimates that $5 billion in guarantees could generate $30 billion in lending over a decade, funding girls' education, climate adaptation and healthcare.[60] The health partnership Gavi's vaccine bonds, repaid over thirty years by the richest countries, have already raised nearly $10 billion to vaccinate 500 million children.[61]

Guarantees can work for climate finance, for education and for health – including unlocking capital for the private sector arm of Gavi, which already has a credit rating. By pooling guarantees through multilateral institutions, advanced economies can leverage their creditworthiness to draw in private capital. Used imaginatively, and with reforms to international governance, these tools will make scarce aid budgets go further.

The lesson to the Global South is clear: progress is possible, but only if reform moves beyond donor-driven projects and towards country-led systems built around local initiatives.

In the 1770s, while the British Government was desperately trying to hold onto America, over five hundred loyal British subjects in New York drafted and signed what was called a 'Declaration of Dependence', pledging undying loyalty to the British crown.[62] But it proved no match for the idealistic and forward-looking Declaration of Independence that captured the hearts and minds of the majority of the American population. A similar lesson is having to be learned today by the Global North about the aspirations of the Global South. Just as the American citizens of the late eighteenth century could no longer tolerate a dependency relationship that subjugated America, and just as it became impossible for the British to defend it, so too the Global South will no longer accept that its future lies in being dependent on the Global North. The Accra Accord, highlighted at the opening of the chapter, which points a way forward by emphasising home-grown leadership and the building of domestic capacity, has shown that progress is possible. This, as we will find in the next chapter, is also a way forward when we address the existential problem of climate change.

16

OUR SHARED WORLD: A SUSTAINABLE FUTURE

Wildfires, storms, floods, record-breaking heatwaves and droughts are what some now call 'the new normal'. With disruption to lives and livelihoods from California to Bangladesh, from Greece to Guatemala, that go far beyond unusual weather patterns, neither the wealthiest nor the poorest are immune. But how nations deal with this existential problem of climate change has been a source of controversy from the first successful agreement on climate at what was called the Conference of the Parties (COP) at Kyoto in 1997.

My own experience of the COP process revolved around the fifteenth COP at Copenhagen in December 2009, when, fresh from what seemed a successful April G20 summit, aimed at preventing a recession from becoming a depression, there were high expectations of success. An agreement between the UK and the US secretary of state, Hillary Clinton, prior to the summit, that a $100 billion-a-year global climate fund be constituted to support developing countries and island states, seemed to signal that major progress could be made.

When 195 countries sat down together at an event that required a unanimous declaration, the only way forward was to convene an informal executive comprising around twenty leading countries from the Global North and South.

The proceedings of the informal executive descended into

farce when, after Germany's chancellor, Angela Merkel, proposed that the rich countries would unilaterally cut carbon emissions by half by 2050, the Chinese ambassador, standing in for his premier, refused this Western offer. He did so on the grounds that while China was not yet a high-income country it would be by 2050. His stance so angered one prime minister sitting close to him that I feared the event would end in physical blows.

A face-saving compromise had to be reached. President Obama made a side agreement with the Global South. They agreed only to greater transparency in each country's reporting of what they were doing to cut emissions. Far from solving the problem of ever-rising carbon emissions, the summit managed to set back the cause of tackling them.

Copenhagen came six years before the successful Paris accord and the last three relatively unsuccessful COPs. At the 2015 UN Climate Change Conference in Paris, governments had agreed that to sustain a liveable planet, they should aim to restrict global warming to 1.5°C above pre-industrial levels, or at least 'well below 2°C'. It was a moment of rare consensus – a shared acknowledgement that doing nothing would cost far more than tackling the problem. But since then, as progress has slowed and as droughts, floods and fires have become more frequent, more severe and more life-threatening, climate change has started to impinge on our everyday lives as much as murderous wars, job-destroying recessions and other human and natural disasters.

As we can see from the events of COP15, this is not just an environmental crisis, it is a political one. It is the ultimate test of whether a new global order, based on the aspirations of a civic-minded majority, can achieve more and work better than the current war of words between rival blocs. If the world cannot work together on an existential threat that recognises no borders and spares no nation, then the promise of any renewed international settlement will ring hollow. But the potential is there for action on climate to become the bridgehead for new forms of cooperation and collective action.

The difficulties in reaching agreement since the Paris summit show that the institutions we built for an earlier era are struggling to keep pace with the scale, speed and geography of the crisis we face. For even as summits bring forward pledges, and markets signal risk, emissions continue to rise, and communities across the world are already being forced to adapt.

The question this chapter asks, therefore, is not primarily technological. We already know much of what needs to be done, and in many cases have the means to achieve it. The question is whether we can assemble the political and – critically – the financial coalitions capable of acting at scale.

Tipping points and the human toll

Demand for fossil fuels and energy is at record levels – not least because of the energy needs of AI data centres.[1] As was heard at COP30 in Brazil, current projections suggest global temperature increase will reach around 2°C by 2100,[2] even if governments meet all their current commitments. If countries carry on as is, that figure will rise to over 3°C. Even the most optimistic reading, therefore, leaves us missing our own targets.

The financial cost of this is rising exponentially. The amounts being paid out for damage caused by floods, droughts and fires are beginning to reach what Canadian prime minister Mark Carney called a 'tragedy of the horizon', exceeding what insurance companies and governments can absorb.[3] The human consequences are starker still, with living standards and life expectancies being affected. Since 2020, 4 million Somalis have been internally displaced by drought, floods and conflict-driven insecurity,[4] and in Pakistan 8 million people were forced from their homes by the 2022 floods.[5] Climate is becoming a driver not only of migration but of political fragility and, in parts of Africa and Asia, of inter-state conflict.[6] As former US treasury secretary Hank Paulson's institute has identified in a new report,[7] biodiversity loss is accelerating, compounding the risks to food systems, water security and livelihoods and creating what scientists now call 'climate tipping points'[8] which could be reached before 2100.[9]

Increasing carbon emissions will also increase the death toll. Eighty-three million excess deaths will occur between 2020 and 2100 if emissions stay at 2020 levels, according to Daniel Bressler's calculations of the 'mortality cost' of carbon.[10] Between 2030 and 2050, droughts, floods and fires, malnutrition, malaria, diarrhoea and other conditions caused by excessive heat will cause around 250,000 additional deaths each year, according to the World Health Organization. The costs, reflected in both increased insecurities and injustices that hit the poorest hardest, can be counted not only in degrees of warming or percentage points of GDP, but in homes lost, communities displaced and lives cut short.

A breakthrough in possibility: technology has moved faster than politics

For all the accumulating tragedies, the past decade has also delivered something close to an economic and technological breakthrough. Cost reductions for renewables have been almost unprecedented – with wind, solar and battery storage down 90 per cent since 2010. Green energies that once required heavy subsidy are now, in many places, simply the cheapest option.[11] The technological advances behind this have also created a new geography of energy. A world 'solar belt' in sunnier climes could see energy costs from solar power fall by half by 2050, while a corresponding 'wind belt', including countries such as the UK, Canada and Germany, could achieve the same as smart grids and battery storage improve. Energy abundance, not scarcity, is becoming a realistic prospect.

As market logic shifts in favour of decarbonisation, and as we start to benefit from new advances in areas like quantum computing and nuclear fusion, the old trade-off between prosperity and sustainability could become a thing of the past. Advances in electrification are already providing the conditions for decarbonisation well beyond the electricity sector. According to the International Energy Agency (IEA), by 2030 we could deliver more than 80 per cent of the reductions needed to reach 1.5°C by electrifying transport, heating and manufacturing, increasing the share of renewable energy in electricity generation, and improving energy efficiency. After 2023's COP28 agreed to triple renewable energy capacity by 2030 to at least 11,000 gigawatts, 2024 saw 585 gigawatts of renewables installed across the world, accounting for an astonishing 92.5 per cent of additions to global power capacity.[12] As a result, clean power now accounts for more than 40 per cent of global electricity generation.[13] In 2024, 17 million electric cars were sold, more than 20 per cent of all cars sold that year, and despite a recent slowdown in the West, the share of EVs in car sales is set to surpass 40 per cent in 2030, replacing, according to the IEA, an estimated 5 million barrels of oil a day.[14]

And yet these extraordinary advances cannot mask the fact that fossil fuels still account for around 90 per cent of CO_2 emissions and roughly 80 per cent of the global energy mix.[15] According to the IEA's baseline scenario, fossil fuel use as a percentage of total energy demand is only predicted to fall to 58 per cent by 2050, far from the 10 per cent envisaged in its net zero scenario.[16] Here lies the paradox that we have to confront. While huge advances have been made in reducing the cost of renewables, we have yet to find a way of converting these cost savings into the massive investment needed in every continent of the world. We have the technologies. We know the economics increasingly favour them. But we have not bridged the gap between what is technically feasible and what is politically deliverable. And while technology has raced ahead, politics has moved in the opposite direction.

Why cooperation is failing: protectionism, energy security and the limits of COP

As we have discussed, the old world order was founded on American hegemony, and ran on an energy system based on fossil fuels and an open multilateral trading and financing regime. All three are now under strain at precisely the moment when tackling climate change requires deeper cross-border cooperation. And while all countries need to invest more, the impact of lower-cost energy can only be unlocked by making investment capital more accessible in the places where emissions will rise fastest and investment is most needed: the industrialising Global South. Recent increases in protectionism are making this harder, not only by reducing cooperation on international investment, but also as countries prioritise their own energy security. For years, the discussion of energy revolved around prices and how cheap they could be, but now it is more about resilience and control.

Europe, for example, has taken the short-term option of buying more expensive liquefied natural gas from America as it diversifies away from Russia. More broadly, a hundred or so countries have refocused on their national industrial policies, protecting their resources, building domestic capacity and competing for technological advantage. There is, paradoxically, some climate logic to this. Fossil-fuel-importing nations, which represent 74 per cent of the world's population, have a strong incentive to reduce their dependence on volatile supplies from abroad. Indeed, according to the energy think tank Ember, 'replacing imported fossil fuels using three key levers – electric vehicles, heat pumps and renewables – can cut net fossil fuel imports by 70%, [. . .] saving $1.3 trillion globally each year'.[17] Energy independence and decarbonisation can align.

But growing rivalry between the major powers not only complicates cooperation but sets it back. Instead of pooling resources, governments are competing, hedging and protecting their own interests. Even on climate, where multilateralism seems the commonsense response, we are seeing fragmentation.

Three scenarios: risks of the great power trap

How, then, is the energy transition likely to unfold in a world that is characterised more by rivalry than trust? Three scenarios for the future of climate action, set out in Harvard's Project on Climate Agreement, capture this dilemma[18] – although none offers a stable or satisfactory path to the level of cooperation we need.

The first scenario, a policy of 'competitive cooperation', assumes that the major blocs – the European Union, the United States and China – continue to race one another in clean technology and green industrial policy. The EU extends its influence through its Global Gateway and Clean Trade and Investment partnerships, the United States through the Development Finance Corporation and China through the Belt and Road Initiative. In this scenario heightened competition fragments supply chains, driving up costs, but national industrial strategies help drive down the cost of renewables – by a projected 80 per cent in solar, 73 per cent in offshore wind, 57 per cent in onshore wind and 80 per cent in electric batteries.[19] Progress continues, but through rivalry rather than any shared purpose.

For a time, this scenario looked plausible. Competition can spur innovation. And there is a logic to each bloc seeking energy independence while simultaneously accelerating the shift away from fossil fuels. But this balance has been undermined by the sharp turn in US policy, with Trump's America actively reversing course on climate diplomacy. At the United Nations, the president dismissed climate change as 'the greatest con job ever perpetrated on the world', described renewable energy as a 'scam' and derided Europe's green energy ideas as 'suicidal'. Meanwhile, as legal and political pushback has intensified in America, Republican-led states such as Tennessee have prompted withdrawals by asset managers from ESG (Environmental, Social and Governance) coalitions like the Net Zero Asset Managers Initiative. BlackRock, the world's largest asset manager and once a corporate leader in championing climate action, announced its exit in 2025.[20] The symbolism is hard to miss: capital markets, too, are succumbing to the pressures of politics.

The second scenario therefore is climate activism without America, where China and the EU step into the leadership vacuum. On the surface, Europe in particular is well placed to do so. The EU is on track to meet its 2030 target of a 55 per cent emissions reduction compared to 1990 levels and has added a commitment to a 90 per cent net greenhouse gas reduction by 2040.[21*] To reinforce this, the European Commission has introduced the Clean Industrial Deal, aimed at 'lowering energy prices, creating high-quality jobs and the right conditions for companies to thrive', supported by the Net Zero Industry Act and Affordable Energy Action Plans. Nuclear power is expanding again in France, Hungary, the Netherlands, Poland, Romania, Slovakia, Sweden and the UK. European banks are adjusting too: Danske Bank has slashed over 1,700 fossil fuel companies from its investable portfolio,[22] while Commerzbank has set aside €270 million in provisions tied to climate-related risks and US tariffs.[23] And regulators increasingly require climate risk assessments.[24]

Yet, despite gaining some advantage from being a first mover, Europe has become dependent on Chinese imports for many clean technologies. Domestic resentment about costs and subsidies has been fuelling far-right, anti-environment populism. And while the EU continues to set ambitious targets, it cannot agree on the

---

* Investments in clean energy manufacturing more than doubled between 2022 and 2023, driven particularly by batteries. By 2024, nearly half of the EU's electricity came from renewables, while coal had fallen to just 10 per cent of the electricity mix. According to the IEA, clean energy accounted for nearly one third of GDP growth in 2023. After China, Europe is now second in the world for solar panels, wind power and electric vehicle sales – and is the region with the highest share of GDP growth attributable to clean energy, higher even than China.

action needed to deliver them. The introduction of the new EU-wide emissions trading system, ETS2, has already been pushed back from 2027 to 2028. If protectionism in Europe intensifies, China could respond with export controls on rare earths and critical components, raising prices and slowing the energy transition.

That brings us to the third scenario: China as the dominant climate power. And here the scale of China's energy transition is undeniable; it is responsible for over 30 per cent of global CO_2 emissions, so decisions made in Beijing will have the single largest impact on the global trajectory. China may yet surprise us by offering what the Harvard study calls 'a hopeful, if geopolitically unorthodox, path for global decarbonisation'.[25]

Today nearly three quarters of all large-scale solar and wind projects under construction worldwide are being built in China. It has increased its share of global solar manufacturing to over 80 per cent of world production.[26] It manufactures over 75 per cent of the world's batteries, and over 65 per cent of its wind turbines. It accounts for around 70 per cent of global EV production and 65 per cent of sales, with nearly half of all vehicles bought in China in 2024 being electric.[27] Its dominance also extends into the minerals underpinning the transition to renewable energy. China controls, on average, two thirds of global processing and refining output for lithium, graphite, cobalt, nickel, copper and rare earth elements. With the surge in renewable installations, China's emissions fell 1.6 per cent year-on-year in the first quarter of 2025.[28] If reductions continue, China could become the de facto climate leader of the world.

But here, too, there are limits. Modelling by the Centre for Research on Energy and Clean Air suggests China could achieve a 30 per cent reduction in emissions by 2035, yet it faces major challenges, including its continued reliance on coal, and its problems with grid integration and energy storage.[29] China's official target – to reduce greenhouse gases by between 7 and 10 per cent by 2035 – has disappointed many in its lack of ambition. And anti-dumping claims multiply, asserting that China undercuts competitors through subsidies, technology practices or deals that favour Chinese jobs.

Taken together, the three scenarios outlined share a common weakness: overreliance on one country or continent. Whether this is America, China or Europe, it risks the weaponisation of resources, turning supply chains into vulnerabilities. Sanctions, bans and retaliatory controls could all slow trade in renewables, raise costs and delay decarbonisation for everyone. This makes energy transition a hostage to great-power politics, with every election, every trade dispute, every diplomatic incident becoming a climate risk.

Which is why we must look beyond the great powers on both climate change and security. If superpower cooperation becomes ever more fraught, the greatest loser will be the regions lagging furthest behind – the Global South outside China. It is essential that we look at new ways of securing progress – through coalitions that do not depend on a single power, but can be led by those willing to act. The test, then, is whether a different kind of alignment is possible: not a China–America bipolar world or a bloc-led order, but a broader political and financial coalition made up of those who cannot afford failure.

The fourth scenario: a coalition of the responsible

The Harvard study authors conclude that 'real-world developments will likely mix elements from all three scenarios [. . .] with no single outcome unfolding in a linear way'. But there is a fourth scenario. If major powers turn inward, the Global South will lose access to the finance it needs for cheaper, more sustainable energy. The answer is a coalition of the willing – governments ready to act, states and regions where popular demand is strong, private manufacturers making breakthroughs, financial institutions willing to share risks, international financial institutions with existing mandates, and a civil society pushing for change. As in the wider charter I have proposed, this coalition does not exclude America or China, but neither does it wait for them. It will instead rely on five major participants.

First, Europe. Our surveys of international opinion show that today Europe is trusted more than America and far more than China to take on critical global issues, and that people look to Europe to take a lead. It has already begun to do so, negotiating tentative agreements with China, and with strong leadership credibility across Africa, Latin America and the rest of Asia. Already security dependent on America and trade dependent on China, Europe cannot afford to be energy dependent on Russia or the Middle East. It therefore has perhaps the most to gain from expanding non-fossil fuel technologies and industries. If its vehicle and manufacturing sectors can complete the green transition, Europe's pivotal role in wind power, hydrogen and battery production means it could benefit industrially as well as environmentally.

Second, Asia itself. While we have seen how decisive China's investments already are, other Asian powers including India and Indonesia have become increasingly aware of the economic and social threat that climate change poses. India, facing excessively high temperatures and mounting climate pressures, will play an increasingly important role despite its net zero target currently being set on the distant horizon of 2070. As part of a broader coalition, its shift to renewables could be transformative, not only for its own citizens but for regional supply chains and technology diffusion.

Third, and perhaps unexpectedly, the United States beyond Washington. Nearly half of America's states, representing around two thirds of US economic output, remain committed to climate action. They are an important counterweight to federal climate denial policies and are powerful in their own right. Working with city-regions across the world – from Sydney to Seoul to Seattle, from Chicago to Copenhagen to Cape Town – they form a powerful network with substantial political and economic clout. If the federal government hesitates, cities and states can still build standards, markets and partnerships that keep the transition moving.

Fourth, businesses, particularly through their innovation. The private sector has already driven major breakthroughs in battery storage, nuclear fusion, AI-driven innovation, green steel and cement, methane reduction, landscape restoration and green shipping corridors. These are not just theoretical possibilities but represent current and ongoing areas of investment and experimentation. Firms have strong incentives to reduce costs, secure supply chains and capture new markets, and we are finding that where political rhetoric cools, commercial logic often steps up.

Fifth, finance. The financial sector – from pension funds to multilateral banks – can determine whether projects live or die. When financial institutions and multilateral development banks work together to reduce investment risk, they can operate at a scale that public budgets cannot. Public–private partnerships, government guarantees and innovative mechanisms can make existing technologies financially viable. A measure of the problem is that UK pension funds allocate just 0.5 per cent of their assets under management to the emerging markets and developing countries where the need is greatest.[30] These same countries can help address this by working to improve their investment environments. Investor objections include policy inconsistencies, poor regulation, lack of transparency and political instability. These are often overstated, and should be tackled head-on.

And finally, let us not underestimate the importance of citizens themselves. As our polling has revealed, millions of people in every part of the world see the benefits of cooperation, and reject a 'my tribe first and only' approach to global problems – including the environment. Active citizens are at the heart of this fourth scenario: embracing new technologies, utilising their power as consumers and investors, pushing their governments and peers to go faster and changing their own behaviour to reduce emissions. Who do you bank with? Where is your pension invested?

Legitimacy matters, and it comes from us, the citizens. Without it, even the best-designed policies falter.

When taken together, a different picture of the international order of the future emerges. Not a single leader imposing rules, but a dense web of states, regions, companies, financial institutions and citizens capable of acting in concert. A plurilateral, multi-stakeholder system that has the collective power to mobilise capital, share risks and spread innovation even when the great powers disagree.

Even in our darkest moments, progress has been possible. Over the last thirty years the world has repaired the ozone layer through sustained cooperation. And most recently, in June 2025, despite protectionist pressures, countries agreed a global treaty on marine biodiversity and conservation in our seas, hailed by Greenpeace as 'the biggest conservation victory ever'. These successes remind us that a call to work together is not utopian; it has precedent.

The decisive partner: winning the Global South

The real test of such a coalition lies in what happens across the Global South. If the energy transition stalls there, it stalls everywhere. If it succeeds there, global emissions fall decisively.

This is not just a moral argument, but an economic and demographic one. For it is here that the majority of increased energy demand will come in future years, and here that the battle for the future will be won or lost. And yet energy consumption in these economies starts from a strikingly low base. Across Africa, Latin America and south-east Asia, energy demand per person is only 32 gigajoules per year, less than 20 per cent of their counterparts in the Global North.[31] This is not least because one in ten of the world's citizens still lack access to electricity, the majority of them in the South. For many communities, the transition is not about replacing one energy source with another, but about gaining reliable power for the first time.

Across the Global South there is therefore immense potential demand for cheap renewable energy. Some middle-income countries are already overtaking the Global North in their share of solar and wind in electricity generation.[32] Indonesia is using its nickel resources to develop EV and battery supply chains. Morocco is trying to become a green hydrogen supplier on Europe's doorstep. With the right finance and technology, many other countries could also leapfrog the old world of energy to arrive at clean energy systems.

But the worldwide distribution of investment tells us a different story. Between them, the emerging and developing economies account for less than 5 per cent of the market value of clean energy technologies generated today, and their share of clean energy investment stands at just 15 per cent of the global total.[33] The skewed nature of global investment means that countries such as Brazil, India and Pakistan are not meeting the rising demand for energy by producing their own renewables at scale, but are among the top importers of Chinese solar panels.

In other words, the places where energy demand is rising fastest and where emissions trajectories will be determined are precisely those where capital is scarcest and borrowing costs are highest. As Dani Rodrik has argued, in the race to secure an energy transition, countries outside the Global South may end up denying it the capital and technology it needs, and with it the chance to build local jobs and industries. This is already a reality for many countries deprived of energy investment. High upfront costs mean that even the technologies that are cheapest over their lifetime can appear unaffordable to poorer countries. Sub-Saharan Africa gives us the clearest example: despite being one of the regions most suited to solar-generated energy, it suffers from chronically low levels of investment. Today, with 15 per cent of the world's population, Africa accounts for a meagre 1.5 per cent of renewable generation. Across the Global South what is missing is affordable, patient capital and the confidence among governments, multilateral development banks and investors that projects will be viable.

Any workable coalition, therefore, must treat these countries not as aid recipients or passive beneficiaries, but as equal partners in a new generation of investment and growth. If the new order cannot channel investment to where it is most needed, it will fail us, not just strategically but morally. But if we can reduce the cost of capital, share risks, and build credible country platforms for investment, then the Global South can become the engine of the energy transition.

How do we pay for it? De-risking and benefit-sharing at scale

While the decisive theatre is the Global South, and the decisive constraint is finance, all developing countries also have a role to play. They must redirect existing energy subsidies away from fossil fuels and towards renewables. They must take the lead in promoting credible country platforms such as those already existing in southern Africa, Senegal, Indonesia and Vietnam that combine climate ambition with green industrial policy.

But these domestic efforts can only succeed if we also extend access to international finance. What the Global South needs above all is investment in adaptation to new energy systems and climate impacts. With the lowest historical carbon footprint in the world, it has less need for mitigation to unwind past emissions – where finance has been more available but less useful – than for adaptation to deal with present and future shocks. Since the first COPs in the 1990s, climate agreements have been underpinned by the principle of 'common but differentiated responsibilities': the idea that while all countries must act, those with the greatest historical responsibility and greatest capacity must do more. It follows that finance for mitigation and adaptation should flow from the major emitters in the North to those countries in the South now suffering most acutely from droughts, floods and fires.

The record here is poor. In Copenhagen in 2009, COP15 saw developed countries commit to providing $100 billion annually for mitigation and adaptation. That target was not met until 2024, and even then, more than 70 per cent of this was loans, largely directed to middle-income countries and focused on mitigation, when the greatest need was – and remains – for grants to low-income countries for adaptation. In that year, low-income countries received less than one tenth – just $11 billion – of the $116 billion in reported climate finance.

Private investors are currently penalised by rules that treat developing-world investments as far riskier than they actually are. Capital charges sit at 13 per cent when a fair assessment of actual default rates would put them at 4 per cent. And insurance companies shut themselves out of these markets almost entirely. If we can change this, Europe's thirty-five largest asset owners could, according to expert advice, double their investment in the Global South, creating an annual flow of around $120 billion over five years – equivalent to the entire annual investment of the World Bank Group.[34]

At the most recent COP, a new global climate finance goal of $300 billion a year by 2035 was agreed. But UNCTAD estimates developing countries' actual needs are far greater – around $900 billion a year now, rising to $1.46 trillion by 2030, roughly three to five times the new target. A Loss and Damage Fund has also been established, but as of mid-2025 only $768 million had been pledged.[35] Worse still, while from Copenhagen onward the commitment of the Global North was that climate finance would be 'new and additional' to existing aid, what support there is for climate is in fact coming at the expense of health, education and anti-poverty programmes. If aid budgets continue to fall, countries will face an unenviable choice between relieving immediate human need and investing in long-term climate resilience.

The better way forward is fair burden-sharing. Contributions should be allocated based on historical and current emissions, population size and GDP per capita. The Overseas Development Institute has developed an equitable burden-sharing model that starkly contrasts with current practice.[36] The gap between what countries should contribute and what they actually do is striking. Norway, France, Germany and Sweden are each contributing well above their fair share – in Norway's case, by nearly three times. Japan and the Netherlands are also paying more than their share. But the United States, which has by far the largest fair-share obligation of any country at $44.6 billion, contributed only $14.4 billion in 2022. Australia, Portugal and Greece also fall well short. The United Kingdom, despite its historical role in driving the climate agenda, contributed only 68 per cent of its fair share, and Italy, Canada and Spain all sit at between 58 and 72 per cent. And according to the Centre for Global Development, China's global share should be 5 per cent now and 10 per cent by 2030, while the Gulf States' share should be 4 per cent rising to 7 per cent.[37]

Short of a comprehensive burden-sharing agreement, one idea is for the wealthiest petrostates to accept a voluntary levy on oil and gas export revenues. This would redirect the windfall gains from high fossil fuel prices towards energy-importing countries whose energy payments have often funded these windfalls. In a similar vein, the Global Solidarity Levies Task Force, co-chaired by Barbados, France and Kenya, has proposed an oil extraction levy that could raise around $85 billion annually, alongside an expanded civil aviation levy, building on schemes introduced by France and the UK in 2005, with the potential to raise €147 billion a year.[38]

None of this, however, will be sufficient unless public finance can be deployed more effectively to mobilise private capital at scale. Climate already accounts for more than one dollar in three committed by the World Bank. At COP29 in Baku, multilateral development banks (MDBs) promised lower-middle-income countries $120 billion a year by 2030, alongside efforts to mobilise an additional $65 billion from the private sector.[39] Even so, MDBs will need increased capital if they are to meet climate objectives while sustaining their core anti-poverty missions. Reforming the World Bank's Capital Adequacy Framework could unlock up to $357 billion in additional headroom if agreed by the United States. But by leveraging public money more aggressively to crowd in private finance, this figure could rise further to $500 billion a year.[40]

The idea of 'de-risking' private investment has been around for a decade, since the UN-led Addis Ababa declaration 'From Billions to Trillions'. Yet the results have been disappointing. One estimate suggests that each dollar invested by MDBs and development finance institutions mobilises just 75 cents in private finance for developing countries, and only 37 cents for low-income countries.[41] Public–private partnerships, once promoted as the preferred model for infrastructure finance, peaked at $158 billion in 2012 and had fallen to $86 billion by 2024. Today the private sector funds only around 13 per cent of infrastructure financing in low- and middle-income countries.[42]

And the financing conditions are harsh. The cost of debt for private renewable-energy projects in poorer countries can reach up to 25 per cent, and even then projects often require publicly financed power purchase agreements, price guarantees, subsidies and co-financing. A World Bank study found that solar projects in lower-income countries – among the most profitable technologies over their lifetime – required around $2 in subsidies to attract just $1 in private investment.

Some barriers are now being addressed. Currency risk, a major deterrent, features prominently in the 'G20 Roadmap towards Better, Bigger and More Effective MDBs', which proposes expanded foreign-exchange hedging and other instruments.[43] The 'Healthy Debt on a Healthy Planet' report has proposed a special purpose vehicle to issue green bonds for emerging and developing economies, backed by future development assistance commitments from advanced economies.[44] Drawing inspiration from the

International Finance Facility for Immunisation, such bonds could achieve AAA ratings if debt-servicing costs were underwritten by donor countries.

But the most promising opportunity lies in combining loans and grants with guarantees from the world's richest countries. This approach, pioneered by the Asian Development Bank and now extended through the World Bank's Portfolio Guarantee Platform, could be worth $20 billion annually by 2030.[45] A $1 billion guarantee matched with $200 million in grants can create close to $5 billion in resources, allowing adaptation and transition investments to be front-loaded rather than delayed. This is what economic cooperation looks like in practice: using public balance sheets strategically to unlock private capital, sharing risk across borders, and lowering the cost of capital where it matters most.

There may yet be a climate recession, particularly in America. But the initiatives set out in this chapter give cause for hope. Progress will be faster and fairer if we can persuade the West, China and the United States to work together. Crucially, this approach does not assume that the US will always have a veto, nor does it accept a permanent division between the Global North and South. Instead, it seeks to reformulate that relationship on the basis of mutual interest.

The public is already ahead of its governments. Across the polling set out in this book, majorities in the Global North and South alike say they want their countries to cooperate on climate, even if at some cost to themselves. That sentiment is a precious resource, providing the constituency on which the essential financing mechanisms set out in this chapter ultimately depend. Leaders like Mia Mottley of Barbados are charting a way forward, but those governments that treat climate as a zero-sum contest are misreading the people for whom they claim to speak. The future of the planet may turn less on what the powerful are forced to concede than on what the many are prepared to support.

CONCLUSION

THE POWER OF HOPE

Even the most successful can have blind spots, whatever their wealth, power or standing in other respects. John Pierpont Morgan became the most famous banker in America when he bought out Andrew Carnegie to become the owner of a virtual monopoly with US Steel. He had initially backed Thomas Edison. But when Edison asked Morgan to sponsor his invention of electricity, Morgan turned him down. Edison had to find his own way to success, and when it came to understanding the importance of the most important invention of its time, Morgan was shown to have a blind spot.

But so too did Edison. An established multimillionaire in his own right, he was about to appoint one Henry Ford as his general manager, but Edison insisted Ford abandon his idea of developing and popularising the internal combustion engine. Now, because Edison had a blind spot when it came to the most important manufacturing breakthrough of his time, Ford had to make his own way, setting up his own companies, the first of which failed, but eventually succeeding in shifting the world from horse-drawn transport to motors.

But Ford was not immune to misjudgement, either. Having become the most famous industrialist in the world, he now sought a career in politics and in 1918, he resolved to stand for the US Senate. He believed he could win in Michigan, where he employed thousands of workers whom he expected to vote for him, but he refused to canvass or deliver any public speeches, thinking it would be enough simply to claim his opponent was corrupt. He held antisemitic and racist views that he believed were no disqualification. But his fatal mistake was to reckon he could get away without punishment for his fickleness in changing party midway through the campaign, from Republican to Democrat. He lost, showing himself to be not so different from Morgan and Edison.

And he was not alone among the great figures of that era in misjudging what mattered most. It was President Woodrow Wilson who advised Ford to change parties in midstream. As the First World War came to a conclusion, Wilson drew up the plan for a League of Nations – a proposal that, had it succeeded, might have changed the course of the twentieth century. But when it came to the Senate vote on joining, Wilson refused to accept the amendments proposed by more sceptical senators; too proud to modify his own proposals, he could not bring himself to compromise. His proposal was defeated, his plan collapsed and – in part because the United States never joined – the League of Nations was doomed to failure. Wilson's blind spot was that while he willed the end, he was too dogmatic to achieve it.

These were some of the most brilliant people of their age, and none of them had perfect insight about their own futures. Although times have changed, we should be open to the possibility that we have a blind spot of our own. We talk a great deal about hope but appear to put little faith in it actually inspiring the change we need. Instead, we British pride ourselves on being pragmatic, are suspicious of lofty ideals, often look askance at dreamers, worship at the feet of the empiricist and, as a result, play down the importance of hope. We tend to reject grand visions, and are more likely to tell people that if they have visions they should, as Helmut Schmidt, the former German chancellor, used to say, see an eye doctor. But it is time to recognise this blind spot for what it is: a barrier to a hopeful future.

What our polling tells us

I opened this book by talking about what is wrong with our world – highlighting the crises that have come to define our times. In this moment, when the global order is breaking up and civic life is breaking down, and when right-wing populists and ethno-nationalists have been setting the pace in elections across the world, it can be difficult to find cause for hope. Populist nationalists offer a form of politics which thrives on economic disappointment and social division. Because this is their route to winning support, it is of course not in their interest to fix these underlying problems. Their electoral standing is best served not by building communities but by dividing them: turning neighbour against neighbour, nation against nation, insider against outsider. Their aim is not to expand the circle of belonging but to narrow it. Rarely have so few done so much damage across so many countries. We need to reject their kind of poison, casting it out of the body politic.

Fortunately, as our surveys show, only a minority of the global population – less than one in every four – see the world as a struggle between an 'us' and a 'them', whether the others be foreigners or immigrants or 'global elites'. That minority tend to be zero-sum in their mindset, believing they – and their own country – can only do well if others do badly. But they are also least likely to be involved in their communities and, for that reason, they might be best described, to recoin a phrase, not as 'citizens of somewhere' but as 'citizens of nowhere'.

But most people do not think of the world in those adversarial terms. In Chapter 6 we identified two groups: a civic-minded majority who represent 75 per cent of the population within whom there is a civic core of around 28 per cent. People in this core are actively engaged in their communities, and generally positive-sum rather than zero-sum in their thinking. They are most likely to interact with people across ethnic and religious divides, and resist the appeal of populist nationalism.

Almost all of the broader group of 75 per cent, even the civic core, are frustrated by the failure of the system to deliver for them and their communities, and, outside the civic core, some could be attracted to a populist nationalist message. Indeed, it is how this group respond that will determine what happens to the populist nationalist upsurge that we are witnessing today but also whether civic life flourishes or fragments in the years to come. For they form a very large group of men and women who, in the right circumstances, are willing to cooperate across divides, have some sense that their lives are bound up with the lives of others and are open to working with others including those of different ethnic, religious or social backgrounds.

We see that in areas where economic change is happening and people feel left behind, and where civic institutions are weak and inward looking, populist nationalism will tend to thrive. But in areas where economic change is happening, broad-based membership of strong outward-looking civic institutions can resist the appeal of populist nationalism, though in the longer term a plan for economic renewal is also required. The polling evidence shows, as I have explained in Chapter 6, that the simple act of bringing people together across social and other divides in schools, workplaces, neighbourhood groups and voluntary associations reduces populist nationalist voting as well as making for stronger inclusive communities. Building greater trust within your neighbourhood, which itself evolves through everyday interactions, reduces populist nationalist voting further. When backed up by economic policies that address financial insecurity and can shift the national mood from economic pessimism to optimism, an even greater reduction in support for populist nationalist parties will occur. If these conditions are met, our preliminary conclusions are that the populist nationalist vote share could fall by between 15 and 20 percentage points. If none of these changes take place, then populist nationalist parties will continue to enjoy support and may see an increase in it. But if these changes we have outlined were to happen across the West, and we saw both economic and civic renewal, then this will reverse almost in its entirety the populist nationalist wave of the last decade, and make it difficult if not impossible for such parties to form governments.

And there is a thread that links what we do locally in our own communities to what happens in the wider world. We know that global events, from Covid to conflict in the Middle East and Ukraine, can directly affect the lives of people not just in the biggest and richest cities but in the tiniest communities in some of the most remote corners of the earth. The very same pressures that have caused the breakdown of the world order put pressure on family finances everywhere and make everyday life in every community more difficult. And recent events have brought home just how much the weaponisation of even one geographic choke point – the Strait of Hormuz – can disrupt the daily lives of ordinary citizens across the entire world.

But what we have also found in our surveys of global public opinion is that men and women who are involved in the everyday life of their own communities, regularly talking to and meeting with fellow citizens across ethnic, religious and other lines of difference, are the very people who are also most likely to favour cooperation across borders. It is they who are far more open to countries working with each other, not just for their own personal benefit but for the common good. So while the influence of events may be easily tracked from the global to the local, the influence of the general public can also be tracked – from the local to the global, starting from their involvement in their own neighbourhoods and extending to their support for cooperation across borders. The path between the global and the local is a two-way street. So, as the table below shows for a group of ten developed democracies we have surveyed in our data, the people who are most active in their community and connect most often across lines of difference are also those who resist populist nationalism and are most likely to support international cooperation. Conversely, those who see the world as a struggle between an 'us' and a 'them' are less likely to be actively involved locally, less likely to meet people of different backgrounds and more likely to support populist nationalists and reject international cooperation across borders.

But people cannot be expected to think of themselves as global citizens unless they first experience what it is like to be a citizen at home. In our polling, those in, for example, the US, the UK, France, Spain and Germany who are civic to their core are at least 20 percentage points more likely to favour international cooperation. And if we could, according to an additional survey, shift people from feeling no sense of belonging to feeling even 'a little' sense of belonging, support for international cooperation would rise from 53 per cent to nearly 75 per cent.

What we have discovered is that there is no way out of the global breakdown that does not challenge us to repair broken communities, starting at home – and that means strengthening local institutions, and not just offering greater economic and social security, but creating the conditions in which people can learn to negotiate through and live with their differences, and come to see cooperation across past divides as something worthwhile and even beneficial. Building stronger local communities means that as people develop habits of cooperation and show empathy towards one another, they become, as we have found, more supportive of cooperation abroad.

Nationalism at home will translate into a lack of internationalism abroad. But reaching out a helping hand within your own community makes you more likely to extend the hand of friendship across borders.

		% of population	% active citizens	% diverse connections (daily)	% diverse connections (monthly)	% high tolerance	% don't feel they belong	% populist nationalist voteshare	% support international cooperation
US	Civic core	26	64	42	86	87	15	26	70
	Civic-minded majority	66	62	37	83	83	20	36	63
	Us vs Them	34	47	27	68	59	30	45	50
UK	Civic core	28	69	40	87	88	17	12	61
	Civic-minded majority	75	55	33	77	76	22	18	53
	Us vs Them	25	41	25	62	60	44	38	40
France	Civic core	25	56	30	80	85	23	16	58
	Civic-minded majority	66	53	26	74	77	26	24	51
	Us vs Them	34	34	21	56	53	39	41	35
Australia	Civic core	28	72	33	84	87	12	2	60
	Civic-minded majority	76	62	31	83	80	20	5	53
	Us vs Them	24	53	27	71	69	29	18	43
Canada	Civic core	30	60	36	86	87	17	0.5	62
	Civic-minded majority	75	53	33	80	76	22	0.7	55
	Us vs Them	25	43	32	71	65	38	1.5	42
Germany	Civic core	30	55	35	77	85	23	8	67
	Civic-minded majority	74	50	31	76	75	26	13	59
	Us vs Them	26	43	32	66	55	40	39	43
New Zealand	Civic core	28	69	38	85	88	14	3	59
	Civic-minded majority	66	66	37	84	83	17	6	54
	Us vs Them	34	56	31	78	69	26	11	49
Poland	Civic core	29	52	25	60	81	22	19	66
	Civic-minded majority	70	49	23	58	71	22	23	57
	Us vs Them	30	43	23	47	58	31	35	39
Spain	Civic core	28	60	41	79	86	14	7	65
	Civic-minded majority	68	55	34	77	80	17	13	58
	Us vs Them	32	47	28	68	59	26	21	43
Sweden	Civic core	32	68	31	78	88	16	9	64
	Civic-minded majority	77	65	29	76	76	21	15	59
	Us vs Them	23	56	26	63	58	35	33	49

Note: As set out in Chapter 6, the civic core is defined as those who hold above-country-average positive-sum views across economic and cultural issues we tested – trade, inequality, technology, migration and multiculturalism. The civic-minded majority are those who hold substantially (0.5 SD) above-average positive-sum views on either economic or cultural dimensions. Those who are 'Us vs Them' are substantially more zero-sum on average across both economic and cultural dimensions. 'Diverse connections' refers to those who say they interact with someone from a different class, religion or ethnicity at least daily or monthly. 'Active citizens' refers to those who say they are members of at least one civic institution or association, such as a sports club, church, trade union or political party. 'Don't feel they belong' refers to those who say it's not true they feel like they are part of a community where they belong.

What it means for our world order

A new world order for the twenty-first century cannot be built in the manner of the nineteenth and twentieth centuries – by diplomatic elites balancing their power and doing so behind closed doors with the public reduced to the role of bystanders, mere watchers on the shore. That is because no order that values human rights, the rule of law and democratic accountability can be built, let alone endure, without the support of an active, engaged citizenry. One that recognises that, regardless of our differences, we must find a way to live together. And we must strive to do so, because if we do not act, populist nationalists will impose upon us their vision of an adversarial world where we are at war with each other.

Indeed, the way forward is best described in terms used by Adam Smith and mentioned in the introduction: circles of empathy, starting with an inner circle, the intense loyalties you feel for your family and friends, to the rather less intense but still discernible empathy you might feel towards an outer circle of people who share the city, country and planet with you. If he is right, the distinction that is often drawn between people 'over here' and people 'over there' is not so deep nor so engrained that it excludes empathy for strangers.

Indeed, our empathy is like the flame of a candle. It burns brightest for those closest. But even at a distance, and even if it is reduced to a flicker of light, and especially when it is not alone but joined by dozens or hundreds or thousands of others, it can still light up the world. And the good news is, human warmth is not a finite resource. Your love for family and friends does not entail your freezing out everyone else.

It can often lead you to show concern for people you have never met and never will. Like the love defined in the New Testament letter to the Corinthians, our empathy need not always be 'self-seeking' nor 'dishonour others' nor be 'boastful' nor 'delight in evil' but be 'kind to others'.

We can imagine a better world as an ever-widening circle of people open to cooperating with others. Sometimes, it is true, this is only because it is in our direct interest to work together, but often it is because, as our surveys show, we come to appreciate the overall benefits of cooperation – or because we simply believe in helping people in need. In each case, we can think of ourselves as part of a nation of 'belongers', active citizens, engaged, or ready or willing to be engaged, in the life of our own communities.

And so there is no road to the future that does not run through strong, resilient local communities. The more people participate in activities in their own neighbourhoods, the stronger and more cohesive their communities become, the more powerful is the resistance to extremism, and the more willing people are to consider cooperation across frontiers.

Shaping the policy outcomes

At heart, the issue is not just why countries have left so many behind, but why so many have left the life of their communities. Yet an active citizenship is the beating heart of a healthy democracy. We cannot succeed as democratic societies unless we learn to live together once again in vibrant communities.

It may be that we have forgotten why civic strength is important. 'Each new need immediately awakens the idea of association,' wrote Alexis de Tocqueville two hundred years ago,[1] showing us that if we are not to cede control to vested interests, and if we are, as Robert Bellah and colleagues have said, 'to humanize the market and the administrative state', we need strong and vibrant civic associations.[2] 'The art of association becomes,' says de Tocqueville, 'the mother of action, studied and applied by all.'

And a vibrant civic life is essential for a strong public square. Democracy is an ideal that can be made real only if we realise the idea that we must share in common association and endeavour at every level of our lives. Everyday clubs and societies, said Tocqueville, teach people how to participate democratically. 'Civil associations,' he said, 'facilitate political association.'[3]

Yet we have for too long been too indifferent to our civic institutions and too complacent about the resilience of our democracy, so that civic cohesion and even democracy itself are now at risk. We have assumed that passive citizenship is as good as active citizenship; that public service is what someone else does and not an obligation on all good people; and that politics can be a spectator sport, to be treated with cynicism in the belief that those who seek power are out only for themselves.

What has gone wrong?

We were right, in the name of equality, to dispense – as we did most of all from the 1960s onwards – with the deference of the past, and we were right to reject the old hierarchies under which decisions were made for us but not by us. But we threw the baby out with the bathwater: in the pursuit of individual autonomy and personal liberation, we undervalued the importance of the obligations we owe to each other, and the result is what Bellah and colleagues called the 'sickness' of an excessive individualism, which discourages 'the habits of the heart' – reciprocity, a commitment to the common good and participation in public life – upon which a strong society and a healthy democracy are founded.[4]

So we have to remind people that, again to quote de Tocqueville, 'the only way opinions and ideas can be renewed, hearts enlarged, and human minds developed, is through the reciprocal influence of men upon each other', and that citizenship is exercised not just by voting, but by building associations, organisations and institutions where people meet, talk to each other, interact with others of different faiths, ideologies and ethnicities, and seek to find common ground.[5]

A community cannot flourish with a sedentary, sit-it-out population who consider inactivity, passivity and disengagement the norm. It is only when strangers become neighbours, neighbours become citizens and citizens become active citizens that we create strong communities.

And it is when people start to see the school, the hospital, the library and the civic centre in their area not just as 'my school, my hospital, my library and my civic centre' but as 'our school, our hospital, our library and our civic centre' that communities are built and last.

And a democracy cannot succeed when millions are sitting on the sidelines, assuming that standing back is more worthy of praise than ever coming forward. A democracy cannot succeed if the professionalisation of politicians at a national level destroys participation at a local level and politics becomes a dirty word. If the once vibrant clubs and political organisations become hollowed-out empty shells, and if, as a result, the public square is abandoned to cranks, fanatics and extremists who rush in to fill the vacuum left by the withdrawal of mainstream opinion from public life.

True citizenship consists not only in the occasional casting of a ballot paper but in the constant and rewarding participation of and with fellow citizens in common cause, day in and day out, across the span of our communities. And to put it simply, the enduring fabric of democracy is not a single thread – a vote on polling day – but a rich tapestry of engagement in a shared and larger life, lived together day after day, week after week, with our friends and fellow citizens.

Democracy can once again flourish – and be free of demagoguery – if, at its centre, are active citizens participating in civic associations within a culture that encourages engagement, responsibility and accountability.

What do we do?

Stronger communities will not be delivered by an edict from Whitehall, a decree from the Élysée or a Truth Social post from the Oval Office. Political leaders can enable, support and sponsor community change – but change cannot come without local leadership. It is active citizens, local community leaders, who will start to turn the tide.

You, the reader, are not a spectator to history. You are a participant.

You may think that, if you care about economic justice or worry about a conflict far away, the only ways you can make a difference are by writing to a newspaper or your MP, organising local solidarity campaigns with the like-minded, or raising funds for national and international charities. But that undervalues one of the most important roles you can play: rebuilding civic connections not just with people like you, but with people who are not like you – those who may not share the same background or values. If you do not build those connections, no one else will. A civic majority already exists but today lies dormant. It is time to awaken it – to herald the dawn of the active citizen, with all that the potential citizens working together can unleash.

Failure to act is not an option, nor can what we propose take second place to other political objectives. Rebuilding our civic life must become the central mission of our time. And we must not let our blind spot cause us to miss this moment. We must mobilise hope.

Why hope?

History is full of turning points, but sometimes, most recently the Arab Spring of 2011, it fails to turn. Other moments (1789, 1815, 1917–18, 1945) marked the start of something new, a turning from darkness towards hope.

In 1946, in a war-ravaged Paris, as millions were camping out in the ruins of Europe, Simone de Beauvoir, Jean-Paul Sartre, Arthur Koestler, André Malraux and Albert Camus got together. Camus is said to have posed a question to his existentialist colleagues: 'Didn't we get it all wrong when we said there were no such things as moral values?' And his answer to his own question was, 'If we were to admit this to be the case, would that not be the beginning of hope?'[6] As we stand at another critical historical juncture, as one world order is giving way to another – and, as in the 1940s, not quietly but violently – we are once again in need to take heed of Camus's statement of hope.

Invariably, at moments of crisis, the world's greatest writers and thinkers have found inspiration in the very idea of hope. 'Man needs, for his happiness, not only the enjoyment of this or that, but hope,' wrote Bertrand Russell. 'It is not a finished Utopia that we ought to desire, but a world where imagination and hope are alive and active.'[7] And hope is a motivator, a driver towards action; it is what makes us get up in the morning, why we bring children into the world, why we work hard for all manner of causes, strive for qualifications, start businesses and give to charity. Hope alone explains why so many of us are determined to make our mark on the world and leave it a better place. But, as a cursory history of literature also tells us, the power of hope cannot easily be conveyed through cold impersonal sentences that do not inspire. People don't think in abstractions. We must tell stories – not trite tales full of superficial platitudes, but ones that illuminate what it means to hope, and that enable us to imagine a different, better future.

Both literature and history have always given me an abundance of these stories. As I have discovered from a host of writers, literature persistently returns to a handful of standard themes that are ultimately founded on hope: the quest (Homer's *Odyssey* or J. R. R. Tolkien's *Lord of the Rings*); the 'rags to riches' progression from no one to someone (Charles Dickens's *David Copperfield*, George Bernard Shaw's *Pygmalion* or F. Scott Fitzgerald's *The Great Gatsby*); the triumph over something monstrous (Jonathan Swift's *Gulliver's Travels*); the banishing of evil (John Bunyan's *The Pilgrim's Progress*, C. S. Lewis's Chronicles of Narnia or Philip Pullman's His

Dark Materials series); and, also, the hope (but often fear too) that comes with rapid change, from a stranger arriving in town (Robert Browning's 'The Pied Piper of Hamelin' and many Western films) to someone leaving to seek a better future (John Steinbeck's *The Grapes of Wrath* and, with more success, Maya Angelou's *I Know Why the Caged Bird Sings*). These stories of hope that have influenced me that envisage a better future can inspire, but stories are also bridges, between those with something to give and those who assume they have nothing to offer; they can connect those who have and those who have not, whether that be material help or hope.

As I found in the mining communities that I was privileged to represent for a third of a century, the hope of a better future was the building block of communities, far more so than mere bricks and mortar. One of the schools in my local area had the motto 'Rise to the light', a signal that education would help the sons and daughters of miners escape the dangers of digging for coal. Hope carries the prospect of a positive future around which people can come together. But if we are to persuade people again that a better future can be built, we have first to show that there are grounds for hope. And I believe that, despite what can feel like a constant onslaught of bad news, there is good cause to hope for the future. In fact it is now, when things seem at their darkest, that we need it most. In *Man's Search for Meaning*, drawn from his experience of humanity at its very lowest ebb – his fight for survival in a 1940s Nazi concentration camp – Viktor Frankl observed that for people under enormous pressure 'hope is not a luxury – it is a lifeline'.[8]

Today, we need that lifeline. We need the extraordinary and transformative power of hope. As Helen Keller wrote, 'Hope sees the invisible, feels the intangible, and achieves the impossible.'[9]

Hope is not optimism

I am not proposing we simply sit back and wait for hope to bear fruit. Let us not confuse hope with optimism, which is a general sense that things may change for the better, a sentiment more akin to wishful thinking. Hope, by contrast, is muscular and demanding. During the Second World War the phrase 'coming in on a wing and a prayer' was coined, then immortalised in the 1942 film *Flying Tigers*, the story of a fatally damaged aircraft limping home, the crew desperate to survive, but with nothing to hold on to but their prayers and their faith in fortune favouring the brave. Hope does not come in on a wing and a prayer. It has little time for good luck, or fortune, but it creates its own agency. Hope contains an imperative to act; it demands a positive rather than passive engagement with the world – not to assume that things will work out for you, but to ensure that you will work things out. It is this kind of hope, the hope that President Kennedy had for the future, that led the great poet Robert Frost, who was reading his poem 'The Gift Outright' at the president's inauguration, to change his original wording about the America that 'would become' to the America that 'will become'.[10] As the late Jonathan Sacks, perhaps the most impressive writer on the distinction between optimism and hope, wrote, 'Optimism is the belief that the world is changing for the better. Hope is the belief that, together, we can make the world better.'[11]

So if someone is optimistic, it is a far less reliable predictor of their willingness to take action than to be filled with hope – and it offers far weaker outcomes. When confronted with a task, those with high hopes of a specific outcome will, according to research studies, persist longer, endure more, sideline any distractions, be more innovative and generally show far more resolve than those who say they are optimistic but may lack a clear purpose. Hope marries a goal with the desire to make that future outcome a reality. Change-makers will not just believe in a goal, but will make the mental effort to achieve it. We will not always succeed but will learn even if we falter. In his study of the American civil rights movement, *Shattered Dreams, Infinite Hope: A Tragic Vision of the Civil Rights Movement*, and of its disappointments – mobility for black people was often not people moving upwards but people moving 'from a smaller ghetto to a larger one' – Brandon Terry talks of a tragic hope, which, even if unrealised, nonetheless 'affirms the resilience and responsibility of moral agency rather than resignation. Unfulfilled hopes are not failures but the inevitable companions of a relentless pursuit of justice. These disappointments are not a verdict on the futility of struggle but a summons to press forward.'

And, as with the civil rights movements, change-makers rarely act alone. Building a future that is truly different and better takes more than seeing hope as no more than pursuit of personal goals. It demands a more collective and relational idea of hope, in which we imagine working together. It is not as individuals that we will bring about change, but as a society – as a people organised in strong communities and building collective institutions that amplify not just one voice but many.

A revolution of values

So if mobilising the power of hope through an active citizenship is the indispensable building block of the good society, this starts with, and cannot succeed without, a shared sense of basic human decency. It arises from a commonsense view that while human beings can be aggressive, appetitive, competitive and self-interested, we can also be cooperative, altruistic, empathetic and understanding of others. 'The mechanism that makes us the kindest species also makes us the cruellest species on the planet,' historian Rutger Bregman has written, while proposing the 'radical idea' that 'most people, deep down, are pretty decent'.[12]

In a follow-up survey to our world opinion poll, we put that contention to you, the general public – and you agreed. When we asked people in the United Kingdom whether they agree or disagree with the statement 'Most people are basically good and want to do the right thing', the vast majority (79 per cent) strongly agreed or somewhat agreed, with only 17 per cent 'somewhat' in disagreement and 4 per cent strongly so. In America the results were similar.

But what do we mean by 'decent'? On one level it can mean simply being compassionate and kind to others, but on a deeper level it is a more complex and hardworking emotion: empathy – our ability to stand in other people's shoes and our capacity to see other people as they see us. We might argue this is the very thing that sets us apart as a species. Looking again at Adam Smith's expanding circles of empathy, as our proximity lessens, empathy weakens – but it still persists. And, crucially, the empathy felt towards the inner circle does not preclude the empathy felt for the outer circle.

How do we turn this empathy into something practical? Robert Putnam's work on social capital focuses on the networks that connect people. A central part of his story is set around something that we talk about less and less, but which has the power to turn intangible empathy into something we can hold and implement practically: a set of shared values. This, too, is based in an innate human decency. In his 'I Have a Dream' speech Martin Luther King linked the human disposition to act with decency to the pursuit of the moral imperatives of justice and brotherhood, urging a 'revolution of values' to give priority to the needs of people over materialism, racism and militarism.[13] Is it possible to rediscover a solid base of values, founded in the idea of empathy for and obligation to each other, that people can embrace as essential to the building of social capital?[14]

Writing around the same time as Putnam, Robert Bellah and his co-authors termed these norms 'the habits of the heart . . . the commitments that tie people together in community'. These are, they wrote, 'the moral understandings, civic commitments, and social practices – such as family life, civic engagement, and respect for others – that sustain democracy and the common good'. Encouraging a strong sense of duty, they said, would 'prevent extreme individualism from eroding community bonds'.[15]

The key lesson here is that without active and engaged citizens who feel some sense of duty towards each other, even strong and heartfelt feelings of compassion and empathy will not secure positive change. Decency may provide an ethical imperative in favour of justice and brotherhood, and even fuel anger against injustices, but it needs to be underpinned by that strong sense of social obligation to deliver real progress. Compassion, it has been said, awakens our senses, but hope emerges through the wilful choice to act out of duty, often no matter the odds. Both are needed: decency and duty, compassion and commitment, must go hand in hand. Because while what people feel matters, what people do matters more.

If an innate empathy provides the emotional spark, it risks burnout unless we take deliberate steps towards active engagement in making change happen. In terms of how this plays out on the ground, Putnam offered a number of recommendations that we discussed earlier. He proposed that people be incentivised to join clubs and be trained to become community leaders. He also called on governments to play their part by addressing economic and social inequalities and encouraging participation to revive the public square. But, looking back on this half-century of investigating public opinion, he highlighted one overriding conclusion: we had to rediscover a sense of social obligation. 'What stands upstream of all these other trends is morality . . . A sense that we're all in this together and that we have obligations to other people. Now, suddenly, I'm no longer the social scientist, I'm a preacher. I'm trying to say, we're not going to fix polarisation, inequality, social isolation until, first of all, we start feeling we have an obligation to care for other people.'[16]

This is not a view bound to any particular political party. If Putnam reached his conclusion from a progressive standpoint, a similar conclusion has been reached by many from the right, including its pre-eminent contemporary philosopher, Patrick Deneen, whose main theme is that the 'desiring individual' has to give ground to the socially responsible citizen.[17] Coming from a different but related perspective, on the collapse of culture, Olivier Roy calls for a cultural revival grounded in a stronger sense of what we owe to each other. Roy is sceptical that society can be held together by formal rules alone, in the absence of support for deeper shared virtues. His concern is that shared frameworks of meaning are 'collapsing, coming unstuck', generating what he calls 'tremendous moral-ism', but not 'deeper, shared moral substance'. We have, he argues, lost an ethical basis for advancing justice and wisdom. 'What is questionable, ultimately,' he concludes, is 'whether explicit norms are sufficient in themselves for society to function'. To sustain society he calls for a rediscovery of deeper moral meaning and shared virtue,[18] one not tied to political groups or national interests – all of which can, he says, be subject to corrupting forces – but to a far more fundamental shared humanity. 'Our civilisation is founded on greed and fear, but in the lives of common men the greed and fear are mysteriously transmuted into something noble,' wrote George Orwell.[19] 'If you had asked me what I was fighting for,' he wrote in 1936 after signing up for the Spanish Civil War, 'I should have answered: "Common decency".'[20] In his commentary on 1930s Britain, *The Road to Wigan Pier*, Orwell urges us to start from what he calls the 'native decency of the common man', the innate moral goodness in ordinary people that for too long has been 'stifled by elites, poverty, and power structures but is rooted in fairness, generosity, and self-respect'.[21]

Can we make a difference?

Human decency begins within the individual. It takes the decisive intervention of your own willpower to turn that human decency into practical change.

The power to take this first step, therefore, lies with you. And that power stands apart from external events. 'Forces beyond your control can take away everything you possess except one thing, your freedom to choose how you will respond,' said Viktor Frankl, declaring that 'the last of the human freedoms [is] to choose one's attitude'.[22]

Change can, therefore, begin with just one person moved to action. Think of Emily Dickinson, writing not of a life of gestures towards the totality of mankind, but in discrete acts of targeted kindness towards individuals:

> If I can stop one Heart from breaking
> I shall not live in vain
> If I can ease one Life the Aching
> Or cool one Pain[23]

And again, it seems that most of us feel this. The last section of our polling, and what has perhaps given us our most revealing findings, focused on people's deeper feeling about the future – and in particular their aspirations and their hopes. We asked in our poll, 'Do you believe ordinary people can make a difference in solving big challenges like climate change and inequality?' In a world where solutions seem to elude even our most brilliant and committed leaders, the response was perhaps surprising. By a large majority, two to one, 57 per cent of you said that said yes, you could make a difference. Of the remainder, 15 per cent did not express an opinion and only 28 per cent said no.[24]

It might begin within ourselves, but this desire to make a difference most commonly manifests itself in engaging in something larger than ourselves. And it may just start with ideas, with wanting to take a moral stance against injustice or to change the power imbalances in society, but the results are often practical. The desire to make a difference is, according to our polling, the biggest driving force leading to volunteering and active engagement in your local community. It trumps self-interest, enjoyment and a desire for personal development – although it also almost always delivers all three. 'Duty' can seem a somewhat joyless word, but enjoyment and fulfilment often are derived from the knowledge that you are making a difference.

People don't just believe in our duty to act as individuals: our polling also found that we want to believe in the overall goodness of our neighbours. Overwhelmingly, we feel that as a community we can and do come together when needed. In the UK and the USA we asked, 'In times of crisis (e.g. pandemic, natural disaster), do you believe most people in your community pull together or look out for themselves?' And in the UK we found that 42 per cent believe people will always pull together, and 28 per cent believe that they will do so in the right circumstances. Fewer than a quarter (23 per cent) believe people just look out for themselves. The picture is not dissimilar to that in America, where 39 per cent believe we will always pull together and 20 per cent say people will just look out for themselves, while 33 per cent say it depends on the circumstances.

A similar picture emerges when we look at what people think of relationships further afield. People's sense of responsibility does not, as we might have feared, stop at the front door or the city wall. When we asked whether we have a shared responsibility to others, even to people we do not know in other countries, there was, again, a positive answer – 72 per cent of UK respondents agreed, 20 per cent 'strongly' and 52 per cent 'somewhat', with only 22 per cent 'somewhat' disagreeing and a mere 6 per cent in total disagreement. Take America and once more the picture is not so different: 58 per cent 'strongly' or 'somewhat' agree on their responsibility to others while only 14 per cent 'strongly' or 'somewhat' disagree, with 22 per cent neither agreeing or disagreeing.[25]

This confirms that the majority of people do not themselves see an unbridgeable divide between 'us' and 'them' and between those 'over here' and those 'over there', even if levels of intensity are different between empathy towards people at home and people far from home. A clear majority – even those who say things are not currently working well – want our society to prosper locally and globally,[26] and are willing to pull together to make this happen. And this starts with our individual human agency, turning a laudable but often ineffective display of compassion into a determined hope, ensuring that change is not something that happens to us, it is what we make happen.

A call to action

It is this combination of goal-directed hope ('We must change'), decency ('I want to help') and willpower ('We will not give up') that will build the better future we want to see. People sense we are at a turning point, and if we have a clear idea what a good world, a fair and just world, would look like, we also know what we have to do to realise it. Asked in our poll whether you think it is still possible to build a better future for the next generation, 73 per cent across the UK said you believed so – 24 per cent definitely believed we could build that better future for the generation to come and 49 per cent thought it was 'probable'. Americans are even more optimistic, with 34 per cent 'definitely' believing a better future is possible and 40 per cent thinking it 'probable'.[27] And this optimism is cross-party, with 34 per cent of Democrats and 45 per cent of Republicans 'definitely' agreeing we can build a better future.

There is of course a gap that we need to bridge between people saying they want to build a better future and doing enough to bring it about. But we also know you can learn to be a good citizen. From the return of civic education to the encouragement of youth community service, we can not only encourage but educate ourselves and others to believe in our own agency. You have already begun that process – by reading this book, by what you choose to do next.

As we have explored over the course of this book, the ripple effects from the decisions of individuals can change the world.

And for those of us who believe in that change, who believe in hope – starting at home, and spreading out across the world – remember, we are in the vast majority. If, as we have found, only 4 per cent believe they have no responsibilities to people in their own communities at home and only 6 per cent believe they have none to their fellow human beings far from home, then the world looks more open to cooperation than most people might believe.

If we can find hope in the sentiments expressed by the majority of people across the world, we can also find seeds of it in what is already happening. In these pages I have had to paint a picture of a world where wars are devastating hitherto peaceful communities, where children are dying because humanitarian support has been pulled away, and where human rights laws are being systematically and increasingly violated. But we can also bear witness to the power of hope: in the populist pressures for democracy in a South Korea that ousted a president hell-bent on martial law; in India's diverse coalition of parties turning back the tide of sectarian and authoritarian one-man rule; in the Brazilian people and their judiciary who stood firm in the face of a rejected president attempting to organise a coup; in Hungary where a civic revival has been the inspiration for removing an ever more dictatorial leader; and in the Philippines, where journalists whom their former President Duterte put in prison will soon be reporting on his trial before the International Criminal Court for crimes against humanity.

We are already building a new world. This new order will not be built in a month or a year, it will not be quick or easy, but it can be built brick by brick. And it can be done, because, while the situation is perilous, we are not powerless. The hope for a better future requires boldness, a firmness of action, a forthrightness in taking on our adversaries, a persistence in calling for wrongs to be righted. 'You cannot swim for new horizons,' William Faulkner wrote, 'until you have courage to lose sight of the shore.'[28] That means standing up to prejudice, discrimination and the suppression of freedoms. It means championing an inclusive politics of belonging at a local level. It means getting the balance right between the individual autonomy we all seek and the obligations we know in our hearts we have a duty to discharge to others. We all have it within us to rise to this challenge – beginning at home.

The message of this book is that we will never come together as citizens of our world if we are not prepared to come together as citizens in our local communities. It is our coming together, from different backgrounds and perspectives, answering a shared call to action founded on a strong belief in something bigger than ourselves, that will ultimately unlock change for good. If we cannot feel empathy towards people of different backgrounds at home, we will be unlikely to feel empathy for people far from home – and only you can make that difference in your community.

The stakes are high. The only way to save our democracy is by turning passive citizens into active citizens. Right now, community appears dormant and the public square looks empty, waiting for the only people who can make them come alive – ourselves. I have spent much of my life close to the centre of national and international politics, trying to push back against entrenched interests through decisions that I hoped would change our societies for the better. It is only recently that I have come to the conclusion I should have reached years ago: that the best and perhaps the only way to start change is to start with our own lives and in our own local communities. For if we are to build a new world order, one that includes and embraces all of humanity, it will not start from politicians making decisions from on high, from communiqués or conventions, or from councils or conferences. It will start with me and you. A future worthy of our best ideals calls on us to summon up the best in ourselves. The future starts with us and it is ours to shape.

ACKNOWLEDGEMENTS

As I complete my writing, the Gulf is in flames. The outcome of the Israeli–Iranian–American confrontation is unclear. Already rising inflation, rationing and the pressures of debt are destabilising governments across the world. If this set of crises, the biggest disruption of energy markets in history and the biggest interference in global supply chains in peacetime, continues, the world could be heading for a new recession with all the implications that this threat to living standards entails for the popularity of governments, the spread of protests and the survival of regimes.

Amid this ever-changing landscape, I've tried to separate the major trends which will continue to shape our world for years to come from events which will come and go. And in doing so, I've drawn on the expertise and support of many people; indeed my repeated requests for advice and questions may have strained many friendships. To all of those named, and for those too many in number who remain unnamed, I am grateful.

The two themes of the book – economic decline and civic decline, or what people talk of as a broken economy and a broken society – involved detailed polling as well as more general research, and this was led by Dan Turner, Peter Tompkins and Matt Chennells.

The book's writing coincided with the months running up to the birth of the twins born to Dan and his wife Anna. Dan, who is a researcher at King's College London and a non-resident scholar and Steel fellow at the University of Southern California's Schaeffer Institute for Public Policy and Government Service, is a polymath whose range of knowledge and insights extends far beyond his professional expertise as an economist. His thinking has been central to all the chapters, which cover the changes in the world economy and order and their relevance to a new economic policy for the advanced economies and for the Global South. As the book was being sent to the publishers, the twins, Phoebe and James, arrived 45 seconds apart. If this book conveys anything that endures, it is my hopes for the best future for them and all children and young people.

Also a non-resident scholar and Steel fellow at the University of Southern California Schaeffer Institute is Peter Tompkins, who has worked with me on so many projects before this one. Peter has been involved directly in every part of the book's compilation. He shares a long-term interest in what is happening to our civic life and in particular how hard-pressed communities that are in danger of being left behind can be strengthened and become more cohesive. His research and insights were fundamental not just to the arguments put forward in the two chapters on community, but much else too.

The polling was led by Matt Chennells of Focaldata, who, with James Kanagasooriam and James Alster, has been responsible for compiling and assessing the results from public opinion in forty countries, from which we have drawn our arguments.

As always, Ross Christie has been vital in providing invaluable suggestions, introducing new evidence of substance and painstakingly checking references. At Save the Children and in his work for the UN, Kevin Watkins has been a leader in international development, and after conversations also with the head of OCHA, Tom Fletcher, I have drawn on their proposals for a reform of the humanitarian aid system. I'm grateful to Carmel Nolan for her pre-eminent skills in managing our communications, for advising on how we present our arguments and for much more. Reid Lidow provided support and advice on early drafts.

I have been assisted in the editing by the excellent work of Christopher O'Neil, who joined our office more recently, and Nathan Jones. Asad Jamal has been a constant source of ideas and support. I am also grateful to Ajaz Ahmed and his team at Studio.One for their inspirational design expertise.

Murray Hunt, Andrew Puddephatt and Daniella Lock are experts on the rule of law, human rights, democracy and more generally on the state of the international order. I've drawn heavily on their comments for the chapters which cover democracy and the rule of law. I'm grateful to Lea Kaspar, who has recently joined the work we are doing on international cooperation. As part of that work I have also benefited from conversations with Pedro Sánchez, Mark Carney, Keir Starmer, Richard Hermer, Mia Mottley, former President Obasanjo and others. In this context, advice from John Bew, David Muir and Andrew Thompson has been gratefully received, although none of them or anyone other than myself bears any responsibility for any errors of fact or judgement, or, indeed, for the conclusions I have drawn.

Ricken Patel is running a major project with the Open Society Foundation on the revival of democracy, and his comments have been central to some of the recommendations I make. I have benefited from the advice of two environmental experts, Andrew Steer and Michael Jacobs; as well as Arian Marti; and from Liesbet Steer and Justin van Fleet's work on global education. Michael Wills, Wilf Stevenson and Nick Butler have been helpful, as always, in commenting on sections of writing through this book. I am grateful to David Sainsbury, Gary Lubner, Joe Burns and Stuart Roden for their support of Labour and progressive policies. While not part of this latest project, I have, as ever, been grateful for discussions I have had with the novelist and medic Dr Colin Currie CBE.

A few years ago, during Covid, I had the benefits of conversations online with Mohamed El-Erian and Michael Spence, two of the most intelligent and insightful people with whom I have had the privilege of working. Together, we produced the book *Permacrisis*. Their wealth of experience has been invaluable.

I am particularly grateful to the Rockefeller Foundation for sponsoring research which has been important to the compilation of the chapters on international collaboration. I am also grateful to Professor Steve Lamy, with whom I have shared a series of lectures in recent years, and to Larry Kramer for hosting a civil-society seminar at LSE.

Equally, the University of Southern California Leonard D. Schaeffer Institute for Public Policy and Government Service has been responsible for supporting the research into civil society that has yielded not only surprising results but a significant set of insights into how civic society can be rebuilt, under the leadership of Dana Goldman and Leonard Schaeffer himself. As part of the newly created Center for Civic Society I look forward to the Schaeffer Institute publishing more of our background work, and the more detailed model explaining how we relate the rise of populist nationalism to the economic and civic decline that we are seeing in many former industrial communities.

As always, I am thankful to Mary Bailey and Gil McNeil, who run our office so well, and I want to acknowledge the support I receive when in the public eye by the team from the Metropolitan Police.

Hope is at the centre of this book, and I cite a number of writers who have inspired me; they are referenced in the text at various times. I've drawn on the journalistic and literary talents of friends of mine, such as Bob Shrum, whose range of experience and expertise in public life extends over more than half a century. He and his wife Marylouise Oates have always been great friends. I have benefited too from conversations with Jonathan Freedland, whose own writing I admire greatly and who has always been an inspiration to me. And of course I want to thank all those I have worked with in Kirkcaldy and Fife over many years – all too many to mention – whose commitment as community leaders of local civic organisations to building a strong community has been the inspiration for this book.

The editors I've worked with from Simon & Schuster – Kris Doyle, Kat Ailes and Jonathan Wadman – have not only provided expert advice and given me the benefit of their great organisational skills, but I've also had to draw on that very special characteristic they have had in dealing with me: patience. No project of this scale could have been possible without the encouragement and support of Jonny Geller and his excellent team at Curtis Brown.

My two brothers, John and Andrew, and their wives, Angela and Clare, and families have always given me great encouragement and help. And as this project ended, we all managed to celebrate a landmark birthday as a family who have always supported each other. When I say we have always supported each other I have to confess that it has almost invariably been them supporting me. I can never repay the debt I owe to them, nor to Sarah and my own children. They have made enormous sacrifices to help me at a time when they are all so busy with their own projects. They are always willing to help, while also keeping me sane by sharing their own interests, far removed from global politics – whether literature or football.

NOTES

PREFACE

1 Chrystia Freeland, 'The Great Capitulation is over. What will take its place?', *New York Times* (25 February 2026), https://www.nytimes.com/2026/02/25/opinion/trump-europe-civil-society.html
2 Danny Quah, 'The Global Economy's Shifting Centre of Gravity', *Global Policy*, Vol. 2, No. 1 (2011), pp. 3–9.
3 Trang Nguyen, 'Coming Home to Witness the Rise of the East', Lee Kuan Yew School of Public Policy (16 April 2018), https://lkyspp.nus.edu.sg/cag/news/details/coming-home-to-witness-the-rise-of-the-east
4 Julie Ray and Anita Pugliese, 'Desire to migrate remains at record high', Gallup (31 October 2024), https://news.gallup.com/poll/652748/desire-migrate-remains-record-high.aspx

INTRODUCTION

1 Hal Brands, 'Three Scenarios for a Post-Trump World', *Foreign Policy* (23 March 2026), https://foreignpolicy.com/2026/03/23/post-trump-world-order-cold-war-spheres-of-influence/
2 Daniel W. Drezner, 'This time is different: why US foreign policy will never recover', *Foreign Affairs* (May/June 2019), https://www.foreignaffairs.com/united-states/time-different
3 Shiro Armstrong and Danny Quah, 'Economics for the Global Economic Order: The Tragedy of Epic Fail Equilibria', Lee Kuan Yew School of Public Policy (October 2023), available at https://www.dannyquah.com/working-papers/2023-10-Shiro.Armstrong-Danny.Quah-Economics-Global-Economic-Order-Epic-Fail/

4 Danny Quah, 'Correlated Trade and Geopolitics Driving a Fractured World Order', in Lili Yan Ing and Dani Rodrik (eds), *The New Global Economic Order* (Abingdon: Routledge, 2025).

5 'The high cost of global economic fragmentation', *IMF Blog* (28 August 2023), https://www.imf.org/en/blogs/articles/2023/08/28/the-high-cost-of-global-economic-fragmentation

6 'New data shows conflict at historic high as US signals retreat from world stage', Peace Research Institute Oslo (9 June 2025), https://www.prio.org/news/3616

7 Xinhua, 'Xi-Trump meeting charts course for constructive strategic stability in China-U.S. ties', gov.cn (17 May 2026), https://english.www.gov.cn/news/202605/17/content_WS6a09c2d0c6d00ca5f9a0b04a.html

8 Matthew Levitt, 'Will Iran turn to terrorism?', *Foreign Affairs* (24 March 2026), http://foreignaffairs.com/iran/will-iran-turn-terrorism

9 David Goodhart, *The Road to Somewhere: The Populist Revolt and the Future of Politics* (London: Hurst & Co, 2017).

10 Eleanor Roosevelt, 'Where Do Universal Human Rights Begin?', presented at the United Nations Commission on Human Rights, 27 March 1958.

11 Kofi Annan Foundation, 'Champions for Peace', https://www.kofiannanfoundation.org/youth-peace/champions-for-peace/

12 Thomas Jefferson, letter to Richard Price (8 January 1789).

13 Abraham Lincoln, letter to the editor of the *Sangamo Journal* (13 June 1836).

14 John F. Kennedy, remarks at Vanderbilt University, 18 May 1963.

15 Larry Summers, quoted in Niall Ferguson, 'Trends are bad, events are worse, but "trevents" may surprise us', Bloomberg (2 October 2022), https://www.bloomberg.com/opinion/articles/2022-10-02/niall-ferguson-trevents-predict-future-of-economies-and-geopolitics

1: THE RISE AND FALL OF FOUR WORLD ORDERS

1 Julian Borger, Dan Sabbagh and Andrew Roth, 'Donald Trump says "a whole civilisation will die" if Iran ignores demands', *The Guardian* (7 April 2026), https://www.theguardian.com/world/2026/apr/07/israel-warns-iran-lives-at-risk-if-they-use-trains-trump-deadline

2 Robert Tait, '"A litany of lies": Trump's rambling primetime Iran address sparks backlash', *The Guardian* (2 April 2026), https://www.theguardian.com/us-news/2026/apr/02/trump-iran-war-address-backlash

3 Maya Yang, '"I don't need international law": Trump says power constrained only by "my own morality"', *The Guardian* (8 January 2026), https://www.theguardian.com/us-news/2026/jan/08/trump-power-international-law

4 Stephen Collinson, 'Trump's new US mission statement: Strength, force, power', CNN (6 January 2026), https://edition.cnn.com/2026/01/06/politics/trump-greenland-venezuela-colombia-miller-analysis

5 James Traub, 'Zero-Sum Nation', Substack (26 May 2025), https://jamestraub.substack.com/p/zero-sum-nation?
6 Rosa Brooks, 'The End of Morality', *Foreign Policy* (15 June 2026).
7 TOI Staff, 'Netanyahu transcript: "We have to be more powerful than the barbarians, or they will crash our gates, destroy our societies"', *Times of Israel* (20 March 2026), https://www.timesofisrael.com/netanyahu-transcript-we-have-to-be-more-powerful-than-the-barbarians-or-they-will-crash-our-gates-destroy-our-societies/
8 Jacob Siegel, 'Bibi's "Bismarck" speech', *The Tablet* (31 August 2018), https://www.tabletmag.com/sections/news/articles/bibis-bismarck-speech
9 Otto von Bismarck, speech in the Prussian House of Representatives, 30 September 1862.
10 Giovanni Arrighi, *The Long Twentieth Century: Money, Power, and the Origins of Our Times*, new edition (London: Verso, 2009).
11 'President Woodrow Wilson's 14 Points (1918)', National Archives (USA) (February 2022), https://www.archives.gov/milestone-documents/president-woodrow-wilsons-14-points
12 Woodrow Wilson, address to the United States Senate, 22 January 1917.
13 Harry S. Truman, 'The President's Farewell Address to the American People' (15 January 1953), transcript available at https://www.trumanlibrary.gov/library/public-papers/378/presidents-farewell-address-american-people
14 Townsend Hoopes and Douglas Brinkley, *FDR and the Creation of the UN* (New Haven, CT, and London: Yale University Press, 1997).
15 Charter of the United Nations, Chapter VII, Article 43, 'Action with Respect to Threats to the Peace, Breaches of the Peace, and Acts of Aggression'. See https://legal.un.org/repertory/art43.shtml (accessed 23 April 2026).
16 George Bush, 'Address Before a Joint Session of the Congress on the Cessation of the Persian Gulf Conflict' (6 March 1991), American Presidency Project, https://www.presidency.ucsb.edu/documents/address-before-joint-session-the-congress-the-cessation-the-persian-gulf-conflict
17 See Francis Fukuyama, 'The End of History?', *National Interest* (Summer 1989), pp. 3–18; Francis Fukuyama, *The End of History and the Last Man* (New York: Free Press, 1992).
18 'Conference on Security and Co-operation in Europe: Final Act' (1975), available at https://www.osce.org/sites/default/files/f/documents/5/c/39501-1.pdf
19 For figures see UN Trade and Development website at https://unctad.org/topic/investment/world-investment-report
20 Daron Acemoglu, David Autor, David Dorn, Gordon H. Hanson and Brendan Price, 'Import Competition and the Great US Employment Sag of the 2000s', *Journal of Labor Economics*, Vol. 34, No. S1 (2016), pp. S141–S198.
21 Branko Milanovic, *Global Inequality: A New Approach for the Age of Globalization* (Cambridge, MA: Belknap Press, 2016).

22 David Autor, David Dorn, Gordon Hanson and Kaveh Majlesi, 'Importing Political Polarization? The Electoral Consequences of Rising Trade Exposure', *American Economic Review*, Vol. 110, No. 10 (2020), pp. 3139–83.

2: A FIFTH WORLD ORDER?

1 James Callaghan, interviewed by Peter Hennessy, 1988, quoted in *The Human Button*, BBC Radio 4 (2 December 2008).

2 John F. Kennedy, press conference, 21 March 1963, in which he warned of the prospect of fifteen to twenty or even twenty-five nuclear-weapon states within two decades. See *Public Papers of the Presidents of the United States: John F. Kennedy* (1963), p. 281, https://www.govinfo.gov/app/details/PPP-1963-book1

3 Rafael Grossi, interview with the *Daily Telegraph*, 20 April 2026, as reported in: Dominic Nicholls, 'World faces nuclear arms race, UN atomic chief warns', *Daily Telegraph* (20 April 2026).

4 Kenneth Payne, 'AI Arms and Influence: Frontier Models Exhibit Sophisticated Reasoning in Simulated Nuclear Crises', arXiv 2620:14740 (February 2026), arxiv.org/abs/2602.14740

5 'Closer than Ever: It Is Now 89 Seconds to Midnight', *Bulletin of the Atomic Scientists* (28 January 2025), thebulletin.org/doomsday-clock/2025-statement/; 'It Is Now 85 Seconds to Midnight', *Bulletin of the Atomic Scientists* (27 January 2026), thebulletin.org/doomsday-clock/2026-statement/

6 *The Security We Need: Rebalancing Military Spending for a Sustainable and Peaceful Future* (New York: United Nations, 2025), https://disarmament.unoda.org/en/milex-sdg-report/report-secretary-general-global-impact-increasing-military-expenditure-sdgs

7 *Democracy Report 2025: 25 Years of Autocratization – Democracy Trumped?*, V-Dem Institute (March 2025), https://www.v-dem.net/documents/54/v-dem-dr-2025-lowres-v1.pdf

8 Ibid.

9 *Freedom in The World 2024: The Mounting Damage of Flawed Elections and Armed Conflict*, Freedom House (February 2024), https://freedomhouse.org/sites/default/files/2024-02/FIW-2024-DigitalBooklet.pdf

10 Milan W. Svolik, 'Polarization versus Democracy', *Journal of Democracy*, Vol. 30, No. 3 (2019), pp. 20–32.

11 'Separation of powers under attack in 45 countries', Verisk Maplecroft, 17 November 2021, https://www.maplecroft.com/insights/analysis/2021/hro-2021/separation-of-powers-under-attack-in-45-countries/

12 See https://monitor.civicus.org/globalfindings-2025/innumbers/ (accessed 17 March 2026).

13 Oona A. Hathaway and Scott J. Shapiro, 'Might unmakes right: the

catastrophic collapse of norms against the use of force', *Foreign Affairs* (July/August 2025), https://www.foreignaffairs.com/united-states/might-unmakes-right-hathaway-shapiro

14 'Global Trends: Forced Displacement in 2024', UNHCR (June 2025), https://www.unhcr.org/sites/default/files/2025-06/global-trends-report-2024.pdf

15 For further information see https://ucdp.uu.se/

16 United Nations General Assembly, *2005 World Summit Outcome*, A/RES/60/1 (24 October 2005), paragraphs 138–40.

17 Independent International Commission on Kosovo, *The Kosovo Report: Conflict, International Response, Lessons Learned* (Oxford: Oxford University Press, 2000).

18 Kofi Annan, address to the UN General Assembly, 20 September 1999. Reproduced in Kofi Annan, *We the Peoples: The Role of the United Nations in the 21st Century* (New York: United Nations, 2000).

19 Odd Arne Westad, *The Coming Storm: Power, Conflict and Warnings from History* (London: Allen Lane, 2026).

20 'Convention for the Amelioration of the Condition of the Wounded in Armies in the Field. Geneva, 22 August 1864', available at https://ihl-databases.icrc.org/en/ihl-treaties/gc-1864 (accessed 17 March 2026).

21 'The Geneva Conventions and their Commentaries', ICRC, https://www.icrc.org/en/law-and-policy/geneva-conventions-and-their-commentaries (accessed 17 March 2026).

22 'Convention (IV) Respecting the Laws and Customs of War on Land and Its Annex: Regulations Concerning the Laws and Customs of War on Land. The Hague, 18 October 1907', available at https://ihl-databases.icrc.org/en/ihl-treaties/hague-conv-iv-1907 (accessed 17 March 2026).

23 'Convention (II) with Respect to the Laws and Customs of War on Land and Its Annex: Regulations Concerning the Laws and Customs of War on Land. The Hague, 29 July 1899', available at https://ihl-databases.icrc.org/en/ihl-treaties/hague-conv-ii-1899 (accessed 17 March 2026).

24 'Declaration Renouncing the Use, in Time of War, of Explosive Projectiles Under 400 Grammes Weight. Saint Petersburg, 29 November / 11 December 1868', available at https://ihl-databases.icrc.org/en/ihl-treaties/st-petersburg-decl-1868 (accessed 17 March 2026).

25 'Protocol for the Prohibition of the Use of Asphyxiating, Poisonous or Other Gases, and of Bacteriological Methods of Warfare. Geneva, 17 June 1925', available at https://ihl-databases.icrc.org/en/ihl-treaties/geneva-gas-prot-1925 (accessed 17 March 2026).

26 'Convention on the Prohibition of the Use, Stockpiling, Production and Transfer of Anti-Personnel Mines and on Their Destruction. Oslo, 18 September 1997', available at https://legal.un.org/avl/ha/cpusptam/cpusptam.html (accessed 17 March 2026).

27 'General Treaty for the Renunciation of War (Kellogg–Briand Pact), Paris, 27

August 1928', available at https://www.iilj.org/wp-content/uploads/2016/08/General-Treaty-for-the-Renunciation-of-War-Kellogg-Briand-Pact.pdf (accessed 17 March 2026).

28 David Smith, '"A very dangerous person": alarm as Pete Hegseth revels in carnage of Iran war', *The Guardian* (8 March 2026), https://www.theguardian.com/us-news/2026/mar/08/pete-hegseth-pentagon-trump-iran

29 Peter Beaumont, 'Is the US committing war crimes by targeting Iran's civilian infrastructure?', *The Guardian* (3 April 2026), https://www.theguardian.com/law/2026/apr/03/us-war-crimes-iran-civilian-infrastructure-international-law-school-strike

30 'Wars on women escalate as global conflicts reach record highs', UN Women (20 October 2025), https://www.unwomen.org/en/news-stories/press-release/2025/10/wars-on-women-escalate-as-global-conflicts-reach-record-highs

31 'Impact of Armed Conflict on Children: Report of the Expert of the Secretary-General, Ms. Graça Machel, Submitted Pursuant to General Assembly Resolution 48/157', United Nations, A/51/306 (August 1996), available at https://docs.un.org/en/A/51/306

32 'Protecting Children in Armed Conflict: Executive Summary', Theirworld (September 2020), https://resourcecentre.savethechildren.net/pdf/protectingchildren-summary.pdf

33 See https://asp.icc-cpi.int/states-parties

34 Magdalena Del Valle, 'Trump heads to UN gathering facing billions in unpaid dues', Bloomberg UK (22 September 2025), bloomberg.com/news/articles/2025-09-22/trump-heads-to-annual-un-meeting-facing-billions-in-unpaid-dues

35 Philippe Sands, 'Trump and his ilk imagine a world without international law – but they will not achieve it', *The Guardian* (19 November 2025), https://www.theguardian.com/commentisfree/2025/nov/19/international-law-assault-rules-destruction-trump

36 Harold Hongju Koh, 'One Hundred Days of Lawlessness', Project Syndicate (2 May 2025), https://www.project-syndicate.org/onpoint/trump-100-days-of-lawlessness-what-to-do-about-it-by-harold-hongju-koh-2025-05

37 Ibid.

38 Kate Cronin-Furman, *Hypocrisy and Human Rights: Resisting Accountability for Mass Atrocities* (Ithaca, NY, and London: Cornell University Press, 2022).

39 Cyril Ramaphosa, Anwar Ibrahim, Gustavo Petro and Varsha Gandikota-Nellutla, 'Israel's actions strike at the foundations of international law', *Foreign Policy* (25 February 2025), https://foreignpolicy.com/2025/02/25/israel-war-crimes-trump-international-criminal-court/

40 Nadeen Ebrahim, 'Biden snubbed by Middle East allies as Arab world seethes over Gaza hospital blast', CNN (19 October 2023), https://edition.cnn.com/2023/10/18/middleeast/arab-allies-snub-biden-gaza-mime-intl

41 Viktor Orbán, speech at the 25th Bálványos Summer Free University and Student Camp, Băile Tuşnad, Romania, 26 July 2014. Official English translation published by the Hungarian Prime Minister's Office: https://2015-2019.kormany.hu/en/the-prime-minister/the-prime-minister-s-speeches/prime-minister-viktor-orban-s-speech-at-the-25th-balvanyos-summer-free-university-and-student-camp

42 See https://sdgs.un.org/goals

43 See https://unfccc.int/process-and-meetings/the-paris-agreement

44 'National Security Strategy of the United States of America', President of the United States (November 2025), https://www.whitehouse.gov/wp-content/uploads/2025/12/2025-National-Security-Strategy.pdf

45 Ivo Daalder, 'The problem with Trump's oil obsession', *Politico* (8 January 2026), https://www.politico.eu/article/the-problem-with-donald-trump-oil-obsession-venezuela/

46 Jacob Magid, 'Full text: Charter of Trump's Board of Peace', *Times of Israel* (20 January 2026), https://www.timesofisrael.com/full-text-charter-of-trumps-board-of-peace/

47 'National Security Strategy of the United States of America', President of the United States (November 2025).

48 Gary Gensler, Simon Johnson, Ugo Panizza and Beatrice Weder di Mauro, *The Economic Consequences of The Second Trump Administration: A Preliminary Assessment*, rev. ed. (Paris and London: CEPR Press, 2025).

49 Kenneth N. Waltz. 'The United States: Alone in the World' in *Imbalance of Power: US Hegemony and International Order*, edited by I. William Zartman (Boulder, CO: Lynne Rienner, 2009).

50 Andreas Kluth, 'America First is quickly becoming America Alone', Bloomberg (12 February 2025), https://www.bloomberg.com/opinion/articles/2025-02-12/america-first-is-quickly-becoming-america-alone

3: THE BREAKDOWN OF COMMUNITY?

1 Martin Sharkey, 'Kirkcaldy: linoleum capital of the world', BBC News (21 May 2018), https://www.bbc.co.uk/news/uk-scotland-edinburgh-east-fife-44128557

2 David McCrone, *Changing Scotland Society, Politics and Identity* (Edinburgh: Edinburgh University Press, 2025).

3 Robert D. Putnam, and Shaylyn Romney Garrett, *The Upswing: How America Came Together a Century Ago and How We Can Do It Again* (New York: Simon & Schuster, 2020).

4 Martin Sandbu, *The Economy of Belonging; A Radical Plan to Win Back the Left Behind and Achieve Prosperity for All* (Princeton, NJ: Princeton University Press, 2020), p. 51.

5 'National Accounts at a Glance', Office for National Statistics (30 October 2020), https://www.ons.gov.uk/economy/grossdomesticproductgdp/compendium/unitedkingdomnationalaccountsthebluebook/2020/nationalaccountsataglance

6 Brian Abel-Smith and Peter Townsend, *The Poor and the Poorest: A New Analysis of the Ministry of Labour's Family Expenditure Surveys of 1953–54 and 1960* (London: Bell, 1965); 'Gross Domestic Product: Year on Year Growth: CVM SA %', Office for National Statistics (12 February 2026), https://www.ons.gov.uk/economy/grossdomesticproductgdp/timeseries/ihyp/pn2

7 'Long-Term Trends in UK Employment: 1861 to 2018', Office for National Statistics (29 April 2019), https://www.ons.gov.uk/economy/nationalaccounts/uksectoraccounts/compendium/economicreview/april2019/longtermtrendsinukemployment1861to2018

8 McCrone, *Changing Scotland Society, Politics and Identity.*

9 David Perfect, *Gender Pay Gaps*, Equality and Human Rights Commission (2011), https://www.equalityhumanrights.com/sites/default/files/briefing-paper-2-gender-pay-gap-0.pdf

10 See https://www.fifepits.co.uk/starter/east/pits/s/pit-6.htm?

11 'The Heritage of Marmoleum', Forbo Flooring Systems website, https://www.forbo.com/flooring/en-uk/inspiration-references/making-spaces-into-places-blog/the-heritage-of-marmoleum/p85so5? (accessed 18 March 2026).

12 McCrone, *Changing Scotland Society, Politics and Identity.*

13 Steve Fothergill and Tony Gore, 'The Implications for Employment of the Shift to High-Value Manufacturing', Government Office for Science (October 2013), https://assets.publishing.service.gov.uk/media/5a7c5f2840f0b626628ab985/ep9-shift-to-high-value-manufacturing-implications.pdf

14 'Seafield Colliery Roof Fall – Kirkcaldy – 1973', Northern Mine Research Society, https://nmrs.org.uk/mines-map/accidents-disasters/fife/seafield-colliery-roof-fall-kirkcaldy-1973/ (accessed 18 March 2026).

15 Ewan Gibbs, *Coal Country: The Meaning and Memory of Deindustrialization in Postwar Scotland* (London: University of London Press, 2001).

16 Nicola Newson, 'Trade Unions: Members and Relations with the Government', House of Lords Library (29 June 2023), https://lordslibrary.parliament.uk/trade-unions-members-and-relations-with-the-government/

17 'Trade Union Statistics', Department for Business and Trade and Department for Business, Energy & Industrial Strategy (22 May 2025), https://www.gov.uk/government/collections/trade-union-statistics

18 Joanne Macaulay, 'Hundreds of churches will have to close, says Kirk', BBC News (20 May 2023), https://www.bbc.co.uk/news/uk-scotland-65645891

19 'History', The WI website, https://www.thewi.org.uk/about-us/history-of-the-wi (accessed 18 March 2026).

20 Zara Healy, '"Very chill": the changing face of working men's clubs', BBC News (23 December 2024), https://www.bbc.co.uk/news/articles/cql5endrz5no

21 Jonny Gordon-Farleigh, 'More than a Century of Community Wealth – the History and Future of Britain's Social Clubs', Resilience (20 November 2024), https://www.resilience.org/stories/2024-11-20/more-than-a-century-of-community-wealth-the-history-future-of-britains-social-clubs/

22 Julia Kollewe, 'Number of pubs in England and Wales falls below 39,000 for first time', *The Guardian* (30 December 2024), https://www.theguardian.com/business/2024/dec/30/number-of-pubs-in-england-and-wales-falls-below-39000-for-first-time

23 'Community Life Survey 2023/24: Volunteering and Charitable Giving', *GOV.UK* (2024), https://www.gov.uk/government/statistics/community-life-survey-202324-annual-publication/community-life-survey-202324-volunteering-and-charitable-giving

24 'Brits spend more time on their mobiles than watching TV set for the first time', IPA (25 June 2025), https://ipa.co.uk/news/touchpoints-2025

25 Allan Crow, 'Kirkcaldy funding: 700 views in MP's survey as priorities for Lang Toun are revealed', *Fife Today* (22 September 2025), https://www.fifetoday.co.uk/news/people/kirkcaldy-funding-700-views-in-mps-survey-as-priorities-for-lang-toun-are-revealed-5329329

26 'This Place Matters: Reimagining Community Cohesion in Britain', UCL Policy Lab (July 2025), https://www.ucl.ac.uk/policy-lab/sites/policy-lab/files/this-place-matters-ucl-citizens-mic-july-2025.pdf

27 Lara Spirit, 'Even David Lammy fears Labour has lost its grip on London', *The Times* (3 April 2026), https://www.thetimes.com/uk/politics/article/keir-starmer-may-local-elections-labour-latest-8nvk8h9pr

28 Andrew Dugan, 'Over 1 in 5 people worldwide feel lonely a lot', Gallup (10 July 2024), https://news.gallup.com/poll/646718/people-worldwide-feel-lonely-lot.aspx

29 Kathryn Armstrong and Bernd Debusmann Jr, 'US Surgeon General Vivek Murthy recounts bout of profound loneliness', BBC News (2 May 2023), https://www.bbc.co.uk/news/world-us-canada-65461723

30 Michele M. Kroll, 'Prolonged social isolation and loneliness are equivalent to smoking 15 cigarettes a day', University of New Hampshire (2 May 2022), https://extension.unh.edu/blog/2022/05/prolonged-social-isolation-loneliness-are-equivalent-smoking-15-cigarettes-day#

31 John T. Cacioppo, Mary Elizabeth Hughes, Linda J. Waite, Louise C. Hawkley and Ronald A. Thisted, 'Loneliness as a Specific Risk Factor for Depressive Symptoms: Cross-sectional and Longitudinal Analyses', *Psychology and Aging*, Vol. 21, No. 1 (2006), pp. 140–51.

32 Delaney Peterson, Matthijs Rooduijn, Frederic R. Hopp, Gijs Schumacher and Bert N. Bakker, 'Loneliness Is Positively Associated with Populist Radical Right Support', *Social Science & Medicine*, Vol. 366 (2025), article 117676.

33 'New Strategy and Council of Europe Action Plan for Social Cohesion',

Council of Europe (7 July 2010), https://www.coe.int/t/dg3/socialpolicies/socialcohesiondev/source/2010strategy-actionplan-socialcohesion.pdf

34 Paula Surridge, 'Labour wins big but the UK's electoral system is creaking', *The Guardian* (5 July 2024), https://www.theguardian.com/politics/article/2024/jul/05/labour-wins-big-uk-electoral-system-creaking

35 Felix Butzlaff and Michael Deflorian, 'Direct Social Action beyond Party Politics: How New Subjectivities Change the Idea of Social Transformation', *Political Research Exchange*, Vol. 3 (2021), article 1896343.

36 Jeffrey M. Jones, 'New high of 45% in US identify as political independents', Gallup (12 January 2026), https://news.gallup.com/poll/700499/new-high-identify-political-independents.aspx

37 Jessica Murray, 'Class no longer main dividing line in UK politics, survey shows', *The Guardian* (25 June 2025), https://www.theguardian.com/politics/2025/jun/25/class-age-education-dividing-lines-uk-politics-electoral-reform

38 James Kanagasooriam and Elizabeth Simon, 'Red Wall: The Definitive Description', *Political Insight*, Volume 12, Issue 3 (2021). See: https://journals.sagepub.com/doi/10.1177/20419058211045127

39 James Blagden and François Valentin, '2023 Social Fabric Index', Onward (2 May 2023), https://ukonward.com/reports/2023-social-fabric-index/

40 Lainey Newman and Theda Skocpol, *Rust Belt Union Blues: Why Working-Class Voters Are Turning Away from the Democratic Party* (New York: Columbia University Press, 2023).

41 Newman and Skocpol, *Rust Belt Union Blues*.

42 Alexis de Tocqueville, *Democracy in America* (Ware: Wordsworth Classics, 1998).

43 Hahrie Han, *How Organizations Develop Activists: Civic Associations and Leadership in the 21st Century* (New York: Oxford University Press, 2014).

44 Milan de Vries, Jae Yeon Kim and Hahrie Han, 'The unequal landscape of civic opportunity in America', *Nature Human Behaviour*, Vol. 8 (2024), pp. 256–63.

45 Franklin Foer, 'The Death of the Public Square', *The Atlantic* (6 June 2018), https://www.theatlantic.com/ideas/archive/2018/07/the-death-of-the-public-square/564506/

46 Noreena Hertz, *The Lonely Century: A Call to Reconnect* (London: Sceptre, 2020).

47 Jamie Gollings and Niamh O'Regan, 'No news is bad news: The hidden threat of unchecked local misinformation', Social Market Foundation (8 June 2026), https://www.smf.co.uk/wp-content/uploads/2026/06/No-news-is-bad-news-June-2026-correct.pdf

48 Matteo Cinelli, Gianmarco De Francisci Morales, Alessandro Galeazzi, Walter Quattrociocchi and Michele Starnini, 'The Echo Chamber Effect on Social Media', *Proceedings of the National Academy of Sciences of the United States of America*, Vol. 118, No. 9 (2021), article e2023301118.

49 Andrés Rodríguez-Pose, 'The Rise of Populism and the Revenge of the Places That Don't Matter', *LSE Public Policy Review*, Vol. 1, No. 1 (2020), article 4.

4: NEOLIBERALISM: FREE FOR ALL, BUT NOT FAIR FOR ALL?

1 'Changes in the Economy since the 1970s', Office for National Statistics (September 2019), https://www.ons.gov.uk/economy/economicoutputandproductivity/output/articles/ changesintheeconomysincethe1970s/2019-09-02

2 OECD, *Retaining Talent at All Ages* (Paris: OECD Publishing, 2023).

3 Rebecca Montacute and Carl Cullinane, '25 Years of University Access: How Access to Higher Education Has Changed over Time', Sutton Trust (October 2023), https://www.suttontrust.com/wp-content/uploads/2023/10/25-Years-of-University-Access.pdf

4 Richard Blundell, Monica Costa Dias, Robert Joyce and Agnes Norris Keiller, 'What Has Been Happening to Career Progression?', Institute for Fiscal Studies (July 2020), https://ifs.org.uk/publications/what-has-been-happening-career-progression

5 Pippa Norris and Ronald Inglehart, *Cultural Backlash: Trump, Brexit, and Authoritarian Populism* (Cambridge: Cambridge University Press 2019).

6 'Inequality – Bridging the Divide', United Nations (23 October 2025), https://www.un.org/en/un75/inequality-bridging-divide

7 Herbert Kitschelt and Anthony J. McGann, *The Radical Right in Western Europe: A Comparative Analysis* (Ann Arbor: University of Michigan Press, 1997).

8 Jon Alexander, *Citizens: Why the Key to Fixing Everything Is All of Us* (Kingston upon Thames: Canbury Press, 2022).

9 Branko Milanovic, *Global Inequality: A New Approach for the Age of Globalization* (Cambridge, MA: Belknap Press, 2016).

10 Mia Gray and Anna Barford, 'The Depths of the Cuts: The Uneven Geography of Local Government Austerity', *Cambridge Journal of Regions, Economy and Society*, Vol. 11, No. 3 (2018), pp. 541–63.

11 Thiemo Fetzer, 'Did Austerity Cause Brexit?', *American Economic Review*, Vol. 109, No. 11 (2019), pp. 3849–86.

12 Eleonora Alabrese, Jacob Edenhofer, Thiemo Fetzer and Shizhuo Wang, 'From Local to National: Austerity, Immigration and Support for UKIP', UK in a Changing Europe (5 November 2024), https://ukandeu.ac.uk/from-local-to-national-austerity-immigration-and-support-for-ukip/

13 Minouche Shafik, *What We Owe Each Other: A New Social Contract* (London: Bodley Head, 2021).

14 Mark Weisbrot, 'We're all Keynesians – again', *The Guardian* (25 January 2008), https://www.theguardian.com/commentisfree/2008/jan/25/wereallkeynesiansagain

15 Gary Gerstle, *The Rise and Fall of the Neoliberal Order: America and the World in the Free Market Era* (New York: Oxford University Press, 2022).

16 Ibid., p. 140.

17 Wendy Brown, *Undoing the Demos: Neoliberalism's Stealth Revolution* (New York: Zone, 2015).

18 Lionel Robbins, *An Essay on the Nature and Significance of Economic Science* (London: Macmillan, 1932).

19 Michael J. Sandel, *What Money Can't Buy: The Moral Limits of Markets* (London: Penguin, 2013).

20 Robert F. Kennedy, speech at the University of Kansas, 18 March 1968, transcript available at https://www.jfklibrary.org/learn/about-jfk/the-kennedy-family/robert-f-kennedy/robert-f-kennedy-speeches/remarks-at-the-university-of-kansas-march-18-1968

21 Jan De Loecker, Jan Eeckhout and Gabriel Unger, 'The Rise of Market Power and the Macroeconomic Implications,' *Quarterly Journal of Economics*, Vol. 135, No. 2 (2020), pp. 561–644.

22 Jan De Loecker, Frederik Obermeier and John Van Reenen, 'Firms and Inequality,' *Quarterly Journal of Economics* 135, No. 1 (2020): 1–51.

23 Anna Stansbury and Lawrence H. Summers, 'The Declining Worker Power Hypothesis: An Explanation for the Recent Evolution of the American Economy', Brookings Institution (2020), https://www.brookings.edu/wp-content/uploads/2020/12/StansburySummers-Final-web.pdf

24 'New employment protections will improve workers' wellbeing, but won't make any difference to economic growth', Resolution Foundation (3 July 2025), https://www.resolutionfoundation.org/press-releases/new-employment-protections-will-improve-workers-wellbeing-but-wont-make-any-difference-to-economic-growth/

25 Paul Gomberg, *How to Make Opportunity Equal: Race and Contributive Justice* (Malden, MA: Wiley-Blackwell, 2007).

26 Jakob Deutloff, Hermann Held and Timothy Lenton, 'High Probability of Triggering Climate Tipping Points under Current Policies Modestly Amplified by Amazon Dieback and Permafrost Thaw', *Earth System Dynamics*, Vol. 16, No. 2 (2025), pp. 565–83.

27 Hannah Ritchie and Fiona Spooner, 'The 2024 Living Planet Index reports a 73 per cent average decline in wildlife populations – what's changed since the last report?' Our World in Data (10 October 2024), https://ourworldindata.org/2024-living-planet-index

28 Thomas Piketty, *Capital in the Twenty-First Century* (Cambridge, MA: Belknap Press, 2014); Emmanuel Saez and Gabriel Zucman, *The Triumph of Injustice: How the Rich Dodge Taxes and How to Make Them Pay* (New York: W. W. Norton, 2019); Milanovic, *Global Inequality*.

29 Raj Chetty, Nathaniel Hendren, Patrick Kline and Emmanuel Saez, 'Where Is the Land of Opportunity? The Geography of Intergenerational Mobility in the United States', *Quarterly Journal of Economics*, Vol. 129, No. 4 (2014), pp. 1553–623.

30 Tom Calver, 'Cynical Americans Are Starting to Sound Rather British', *The Times* (24 April 2026).

31 Larry Kramer, 'Beyond Neoliberalism: The Problem and Possibilities for Rethinking Political Economy', Hewlett Foundation (April 2018), available at

https://www.law.nyu.edu/sites/default/files/Beyond%20Neoliberalism%20by%20Larry%20Kramer.pdf

32 Daniel Kahneman and Angus Deaton, 'High Income Improves Evaluation of Life but Not Emotional Well-Being', *Proceedings of the National Academy of Sciences*, Vol. 107, No. 38 (2010), pp. 16489–93.

33 'Omnia debita solventur?', Deutsche Bank (22 October 2025), https://www.dbresearch.com/PROD/IE-PROD/PDFVIEWER.calias?pdfViewerPdfUrl=PROD0000000000606735&rwnode=REPORT

34 Bank for International Settlements, *Annual Economic Report* (June 2025), https://www.bis.org/publ/arpdf/ar2025e.pdf

35 Data compiled by Angus Maddison, University of Groningen. For further information see https://www.rug.nl/ggdc/historicaldevelopment/maddison/

36 Seth G. Benzell, Laurence J. Kotlikoff, Maria Kazakova, Guillermo Lagarda, Kristina Nesterova, Victor Yifan Ye and Andrey Zubarev, 'The Future of Global Economic Power' (17 December 2023), https://kotlikoff.net/wp-content/uploads/2023/12/The-Future-of-Global-Economic-Power-12-17-23.pdf

37 All statistics from UNCTAD.

38 Benzell et al., 'The Future of Global Economic Power'.

39 McKinsey Global Institute, 'Asia's Future Is Now', McKinsey & Company (14 July 2019), https://www.mckinsey.com/featured-insights/asia-pacific/asias-future-is-now

40 Calculated from IMF Direction of Trade Statistics for 2023.

41 Liu Yang, 'China–EU trade surges 19.9 per cent in Jan–Feb, underscoring resilience and complementarity amid global turmoil: Chinese expert', *Global Times* (10 March 2026), https://www.globaltimes.cn/page/202603/1356703.shtml

42 US Census Bureau, US International Trade in Goods and Services.

43 Thilo Hanemann, Daniel H. Rosen, Mark Witzke, Steve Bennion and Emma Smith, 'Two-Way Street: US–China Investment Trends – 2021 Update', Rhodium Group (19 May 2021), https://rhg.com/research/twowaystreet-2021/

44 Hongrun Li, 'China's Export Shift from the US to Europe and Southeast Asia', The Diplomatic Affairs (23 June 2025), https://www.thediplomaticaffairs.com/2025/06/23/chinas-export-shift-from-the-u-s-to-europe-and-southeast-asia/

45 'China is trying to win over Africa in the global trade war', *The Economist* (19 June 2025), https://www.economist.com/middle-east-and-africa/2025/06/19/china-is-trying-to-win-over-africa-in-the-global-trade-war

46 Antonio Gramsci, *Selections from the Prison Notebooks of Antonio Gramsci* (New York: International Publishers, 1971).

47 Joseph S. Nye Jr. 'Soft Power and Public Diplomacy Revisited', *The Hague Journal of Diplomacy*, Vol. 14, No. 1–2 (2019), pp. 7–20; Joseph S. Nye Jr, *Soft Power: The Means to Success in World Politics* (New York: PublicAffairs, 2009).

48 'Global Soft Power Index 2025', Brand Finance, https://brandirectory.com/softpower (accessed 19 March 2026).

49 Konrad Jagodzinski, 'Global Soft Power Index 2025: The Shifting Balance of Global Soft Power', Brand Finance (20 February 2025), https://brandfinance.com/insights/global-soft-power-index-2025-the-shifting-balance-of-global-soft-power; *Democracy Perception Index 2025*, Nira Data (2025), https://www.niradata.com/dpi

50 'Concept Paper on the Global Governance Initiative', Ministry of Foreign Affairs, People's Republic of China (1 September 2005), https://www.fmprc.gov.cn/eng/xw/wjbxw/202509/t20250901-11699912.html

5: NATIONALISM: THE DOMINANT IDEOLOGY OF THE AGE?

1 'S8-Episode 7: Unleashing Hidden Talent', *Awake at Night* podcast, United Nations (22 December 2023), https://www.un.org/en/node/213006

2 Anna Gross, Lucy Fisher, David Sheppard and Amy Mackinnon, 'US government to fund Maga-aligned think-tanks and charities in Europe', *Financial Times* (5 February 2026), https://www.ft.com/content/f8696da1-5fe6-4218-be9c-5309bd9a6ae5

3 Marshall McLuhan, *Understanding Media: The Extensions of Man* (New York: McGraw-Hill, 1964).

4 E. J. Hobsbawm, *Nations and Nationalism Since 1780: Programme, Myth, Reality*, 2nd ed. (Cambridge: Cambridge University Press, 1992), p. 191.

5 Ernest Gellner, *Nations and Nationalism* (Oxford: Blackwell, 1983).

6 George Orwell, 'Notes on Nationalism', *Polemic* (October 1945). Also see https://www.orwellfoundation.com/the-orwell-foundation/orwell/essays-and-other-works/notes-on-nationalism/

7 Francis Fukuyama, *Identity: The Demands for Dignity and the Politics of Resentment* (New York: Farrar, Straus & Giroux, 2018).

8 Robert D. Kaplan, *The Revenge of Geography: What the Map Tells Us About Coming Conflicts and the Battle Against Fate* (New York: Random House, 2012).

9 'Europe "no longer at peace" with Russia, says Germany's Merz', Reuters (29 September 2025), https://www.reuters.com/world/europe-no-longer-peace-with-russia-says-germanys-merz-2025-09-29/

10 Moira Fagan and Jacob Poushter, 'NATO Seen Favorably Across Member States', Pew Research Center (9 February 2020), https://www.pewresearch.org/global/2020/02/09/nato-seen-favorably-across-member-states/

11 Yuval Noah Harari, 'Welcome to the liberal buffet', *Financial Times* (27 April 2019), https://www.ft.com/content/bcd4f5ce-65ae-11e9-b809-6f0d2f5705f6

12 James Walston, 'Introduction: Italy's 150th Anniversary', *Bulletin of Italian Politics*, Vol. 3, No. 2 (2011), pp. 217–24.

13 JD Vance (@JDVance), 'During my senate campaign in 2022, I met a

Ukrainian-American man in NE Ohio', X (15 September 15 2023), https://x.com/JDVance/status/1894484552120148063

14 Ian Ward, 'The online right's favorite nativist slogan is gaining traction in the real world', *Politico* (31 July 2025), https://www.politico.com/news/magazine/2025/07/31/heritage-american-jd-vance-online-right-phrase-00481724

15 Marco Rubio, 'Secretary of State Marco Rubio at the Munich Security Conference', US Department of State (14 February 2026), https://www.state.gov/releases/office-of-the-spokesperson/2026/02/secretary-of-state-marco-rubio-at-the-munich-security-conference

16 Stephen Holmes, 'Rubio's silk-stocking diplomacy', *Project Syndicate* (15 February 2026). https://www.project-syndicate.org/commentary/rubio-munich-security-speech-sugar-coated-jd-vance-racism-by-stephen-holmes-2026-02

17 Stewart Patrick, 'What happened to "the West"?', *Foreign Affairs* (18 September 2025), https://www.foreignaffairs.com/united-states/what-happened-west

18 See e.g. Zhang Weiwei, *The China Wave: Rise of a Civilizational State* (Hackensack, NJ: World Century, 2012).

19 Helena Rosenblatt, *The Lost History of Liberalism: From Ancient Rome to the Twenty-First Century* (Princeton, NJ: Princeton University Press, 2018).

20 Ronald Dworkin, 'Liberalism', in *Public and Private Morality*, ed. Stuart Hampshire (Cambridge: Cambridge University Press, 1978), pp. 113–43.

21 See Timothy Garton Ash, *Homelands: A Personal History of Europe* (London: Bodley Head, 2023).

22 Adrian Wooldridge, *Centrists of the World, Unite!: The Lost Genius of Liberalism.* (London: Allen Lane, 2023).

23 Andreas Wimmer, 'States of war', *Foreign Affairs* (7 November 2013), https://www.foreignaffairs.com/articles/africa/2013-11-07/states-war

24 Andreas Wimmer, *Nation Building: Why Some Countries Come Together While Others Fall Apart* (Princeton, NJ: Princeton University Press, 2018).

25 This account of Belgian nationalism is also drawn from Wimmer, *Nation Building.*

26 Charles Taylor, 'The Politics of Recognition', in *Multiculturalism: Examining the Politics of Recognition*, ed. Amy Gutmann (Princeton, NJ: Princeton University Press, 1994).

27 Jürgen Habermas, 'Citizenship and National Identity', in *Between Facts and Norms: Contributions to a Discourse Theory of Law and Democracy* (Cambridge, MA: MIT Press, 1996).

28 UCDP/PRIO Armed Conflict Dataset, https://ucdp.uu.se/downloads/

6: WHAT THE PUBLIC SAY (1): UNDERSTANDING THE ROOTS OF POPULIST NATIONALISM

1 Chris Clarke, 'Notes on Trust (1)', *Parables*, Substack (8 June 2026), https://parables.substack.com/p/notes-on-trust-1

2 Pippa Norris and Ronald Inglehart, *Cultural Backlash: Trump, Brexit, and Authoritarian Populism* (Cambridge: Cambridge University Press, 2019).
3 R. D. Putnam, *Bowling Alone: The Collapse and Revival of American Community* (New York: Simon & Schuster, 2000).
4 Francis Fukuyama, 'It's the internet, stupid', *Persuasion* (2 October 2025), https://www.persuasion.community/p/its-the-internet-stupid

7: WHAT THE PUBLIC SAY (2): LINKING THE LOCAL TO THE GLOBAL

1 Thomas Jefferson, letter to James Madison (6 September 1789), transcript available at Founders Online, National Archives (USA), https://founders.archives.gov/documents/Madison/01-12-02-0248
2 Kwame Anthony Appiah, *The Ethics of Identity* (Princeton, NJ: Princeton University Press, 2005).

8: INTERDEPENDENCE: UNDERSTANDING OUR CONNECTED WORLD

1 *Being There*, directed by Hal Ashby (Lorimar Productions, 1979), starring Peter Sellers as Gardiner.
2 The passage appears in James Stockinger, 'Locke and Rousseau: Human nature, human citizenship and human work', unpublished PhD thesis, University of California, Berkeley (1990), cited in Robert Bellah, Richard Madsen, William Sullivan, Ann Swidler and Steven Tipton, *The Good Society* (New York: Vintage, 1992).
3 'Driving over the Peak, or a False Summit? – Speech by Alan Taylor', Bank of England (14 January 2026), https://www.bankofengland.co.uk/-/media/boe/files/speech/2026/speech-by-alan-taylor-at-national-university-of-singapore.pdf
4 'Trade Openness over Time, World', Our World in Data, https://ourworldindata.org/grapher/globalization-over-5-centuries (accessed 21 March 2026).
5 Philip R. Lane and Gian Maria Milesi-Ferretti, 'The External Wealth of Nations Revisited: International Financial Integration in the Aftermath of the Global Financial Crisis', *IMF Economic Review*, Vol. 66, No. 1 (2018), pp. 189–222.
6 Danny Quah, 'Inadvertent Cooperation in a G-minus World', Lee Kuan Yew School of Public Policy (November 2025), available at https://www.dannyquah.com/Storage/2025.11-Danny.Quah-Inadvertent-Cooperation-G-minus-deck.pdf
7 Don Herzog, *Sovereignty RIP* (New Haven, CT, and London: Yale University Press, 2020).

8 Alexander Stubb, *The Triangle of Power: Rebalancing the New World Order* (Hull: Biteback, 2026).

9 'Davos 2026: Special Address by Mark Carney, Prime Minister of Canada', World Economic Forum (20 January 2026), https://www.weforum.org/stories/2026/01/davos-2026-special-address-by-mark-carney-prime-minister-of-canada/

10 Christopher Sabatini and Lydia Lysard, 'Understanding and Improving Sanctions Today', Chatham House (July 2025), https://www.chathamhouse.org/2025/07/understanding-and-improving-sanctions-today; Global Trade Alert data, available at https://globaltradealert.org/data-center

11 John G. Ikenberry, *After Victory: Institutions, Strategic Restraint, and the Rebuilding of Order after Major Wars*, New Edition, Princeton University Press, 2001.

12 Arnold Wolfers, *Discord and Collaboration: Essays on International Politics* (Baltimore: Johns Hopkins University Press, 1962).

13 Stephen M. Walt, 'The predatory hegemon: how Trump wields American power', *Foreign Affairs* (March/April 2026), https://www.foreignaffairs.com/united-states/predatory-hegemon-walt

14 Edward Fishman, *Chokepoints: How the Global Economy Became a Weapon of War* (London: Elliott & Thompson, 2025).

15 Scott Bessent, US Treasury Secretary, 'Remarks from Secretary of the Treasury Scott Bessent at The Economic Club of New York's America 250 Gala Dinner: American Economic Statecraft in the 21st Century', US Department of the Treasury (23 June 2026), https://home.treasury.gov/news/press-releases/sb0539; discussed further in Mohamed El-Erian, 'America Was Being Played. The Bessent Doctrine Says Those Days Are Over', *New York Times*, 7 July 2026.

16 Helen Clark and Ellen Johnson Sirleaf, 'The new age of resource competition needs transparency', *Project Syndicate* (27 February 2026), https://www.project-syndicate.org/commentary/global-resource-competition-demands-transparency-democratic-accountability-by-helen-clark-and-ellen-johnson-sirleaf-2026-02

17 Jonathan Haskel and Stian Westlake, *Capitalism without Capital: The Rise of the Intangible Economy* (Princeton, NJ: Princeton University Press, 2017).

18 'The nightmare scenario for global trade', *The Economist* (27 March 2026), https://www.economist.com/interactive/briefing/2026/03/27/the-nightmare-scenario-for-global-trade

19 Justin Harper, 'Suez blockage is holding up $9.6bn of goods a day', BBC News (26 March 2021), https://www.bbc.co.uk/news/business-56533250

20 United Nations, *2024 Review of Maritime Transport: Navigating Maritime Chokepoints* (New York: United Nations, 2024).

21 *World Energy Outlook 2025*, International Energy Agency (November 2025), https://www.iea.org/reports/world-energy-outlook-2025

22 Jason Bordoff and Meghan L. O'Sullivan, 'The new energy order', *Foreign*

Affairs (July/August 2022), https://www.foreignaffairs.com/articles/energy/2022-06-07/markets-new-energy-order

23 Tatiana Mitrova and Anne-Sophie Corbeau, 'The EU in a petrostates and electrostates world', *National Interest* (19 December 2025), https://nationalinterest.org/blog/energy-world/the-eu-in-a-petrostates-and-electrostates-world

24 Martin Sandbu, 'It is time for Europe to weaponise its chokepoints', *Financial Times* (22 February 2026), https://www.ft.com/content/b92fd917-9f1b-4393-b96d-6d22ba757c72?syn-25a6b1a6=1

25 Edward Fishman, 'How to Fight an Economic War: A Field Manual for a Ruptured World', *Foreign Affairs* (21 April 2026), https://www.foreignaffairs.com/united-states/how-fight-economic-war-fishman

26 Joint Committee on the National Security Strategy, *Subsea Telecommunications Cables: Resilience and Crisis Preparedness*, First Report of Session 2024–26, HC 723 / HL Paper 179 (19 September 2025), https://committees.parliament.uk/publications/49566/documents/264088/default/

27 Anthony Cuthbertson, 'Elon Musk now controls two thirds of satellites as 10,000th Starlink launches', *The Independent* (21 October 2025), https://www.independent.co.uk/space/elon-musk-starlink-satellites-spacex-b2848690.html

28 Ibid.

29 'Davos 2026: Special Address by Mark Carney'.

30 'Canadian International Merchandise Trade Web Application', Government of Canada, https://www150.statcan.gc.ca/n1/pub/71-607-x/71-607-x2021004-eng.htm (accessed 21 March 2026).

31 'Davos 2026: Special Address by Mark Carney'.

32 Blaise Metreweli, speech at MI6, 15 December 2025, transcript available at https://www.gov.uk/government/speeches/speech-by-blaise-metreweli-chief-of-sis-15-december-2025

33 Nelson Rockefeller, quoted in Jeffrey Whyte, 'A new geography of defense: The birth of psychological warfare', *Political Geography* (2018), 67, pp. 32-45.

34 Walt, 'The predatory hegemon'.

35 Ibid.

36 Craig Singleton, 'Welcome to the Era of Mutually Assured Disruption', *Foreign Policy* (17 October 2025), https://foreignpolicy.com/2025/10/17/us-china-trump-xi-trade-summit-conflict/

37 Amanda Taub, 'How good intentions helped pave Trump's road to Iran', *New York Times* (7 March 2026), https://www.nytimes.com/2026/03/07/world/middleeast/trump-iran-human-rights-international-law.html

38 Mark Carney, Address to the Australian Parliament, 5 March 2026.

39 Eswar S. Prasad, *The Doom Loop: Why the World Economic Order Is Spiraling into Disorder* (New York: Basic Venture, 2026).

9: POWER: THE MAKING OF A MULTIPOLAR WORLD

1 Marco Rubio, interview with Megyn Kelly, *The Megyn Kelly Show* (30 January 2025), transcript available at https://www.state.gov/secretary-marco-rubio-with-megyn-kelly-of-the-megyn-kelly-show

2 Zaki Laïdi, 'The spheres-of-influence illusion', *Project Syndicate* (13 March 2026), https://www.project-syndicate.org/onpoint/carving-up-world-into-spheres-of-influence-will-not-bring-stability-by-zaki-laidi-2026-03

3 Ray Dalio, 'The big thing: we are in a world war that isn't going to end anytime soon', LinkedIn (7 April 2026), https://www.linkedin.com/pulse/big-thing-we-world-war-isnt-going-end-anytime-soon-ray-dalio-sbrqe

4 Alexander Stubb, *The Triangle of Power: Rebalancing the New World Order* (Hull: Biteback, 2026).

5 'National Security Strategy of the United States of America', President of the United States (November 2025), https://www.whitehouse.gov/wp-content/uploads/2025/12/2025-National-Security-Strategy.pdf

6 Donald Trump, press conference at Mar-a-Lago, Palm Beach, Florida (3 January 2026), reported in, among others, PBS *NewsHour*; see https://www.pbs.org/newshour/politics/how-the-monroe-doctrine-factors-into-the-u-s-arrest-of-venezuelas-maduro

7 'US needs Greenland for purpose of national security, says Trump ahead of talks', ABC News (14 January 2026), https://www.abc.net.au/news/2026-01-14/trump-says-us-needs-greenland-for-purpose-of-national-security/106229044

8 Edward Luce, 'Trump is not just sinking in the Gulf', *Financial Times* (31 March 2026), https://www.ft.com/content/1a36ccb1-0100-44eb-97ac-d1f50c6d23f4?syn-25a6b1a6=1

9 Meghann Myers, '"Make Europe Great Again" and more from a longer version of the National Security Strategy', *Defense One* (10 December 2025), https://www.defenseone.com/policy/2025/12/make-europe-great-again-and-more-longer-version-national-security-strategy/410038/

10 Cited in Myers, '"Make Europe Great Again" and more'.

11 Stephen M. Walt, 'The predatory hegemon: how Trump wields American power', *Foreign Affairs* (March/April 2026), https://www.foreignaffairs.com/united-states/predatory-hegemon-walt

12 Daron Acemoglu, 'The war on Iran and the war on Anthropic', *Project Syndicate* (2 March 2026), https://www.project-syndicate.org/commentary/trump-war-on-iran-and-anthropic-shed-rules-and-constraints-by-daron-acemoglu-2026-03

13 Ron Suskind, 'Faith, certainty and the presidency of George W. Bush', *New York Times Magazine* (17 October 2004), https://www.nytimes.com/2004/10/17/magazine/faith-certainty-and-the-presidency-of-george-w-bush.html

14 Barry R. Posen, 'Emerging Multipolarity: Why Should We Care?', *Current History*, Vol. 108, No. 721 (2009), pp. 347–52.

15 Michael Beckley, 'The Middle Power Delusion: Not Choosing Is Not an Option', *Foreign Affairs* (25 May 2026), https://www.foreignaffairs.com/united-states/middle-power-delusion
16 Zheng Wang, 'The G-2 Reality: America and China Cannot Dominate or Exclude Each Other', *Foreign Affairs* (26 May 2026), https://www.foreignaffairs.com/united-states/g-2-reality
17 Xinhua, 'Xi-Trump meeting charts course for constructive strategic stability in China-U.S. ties'
18 'Article by Vladimir Putin "On the Historical Unity of Russians and Ukrainians"', President of Russia website (12 July 2021), http://en.kremlin.ru/events/president/news/66181
19 Mihir Sharma, 'How India can supercharge its development', *Foreign Affairs* (2026).
20 Devesh Kapur and Arvind Subramanian, *A Sixth of Humanity: Independent India's Development Odyssey* (New Delhi: HarperCollins India, 2025).
21 TOI Business Desk, 'EAM Jaishankar calls for "hedge, de-risk, diversify" strategy amid Iran War', *Times of India* (4 April 2026), https://timesofindia.indiatimes.com/business/india-business/india-solidly-through-global-shocks-eam-jaishankar-calls-for-hedge-de-risk-diversify-strategy-amid-iran-war/articleshow/130016331.cms
22 S. Jaishankar, *The India Way: Strategies for an Uncertain World* (New Delhi: HarperCollins India, 2020).
23 Valentina Romei, 'Is the US economy outperforming Europe?', *Financial Times* (28 December 2023), https://www.ft.com/content/27e41599-3b8f-4c7a-877b-8ac1d443021f?syn-25a6b1a6=1
24 'Address by Mr Draghi – Presentation of the Report on the Future of European Competitiveness – European Parliament – Strasbourg' (17 September 2024), https://commission.europa.eu/document/download/fcbc7ada-213b-4679-83f7-69a4c2127a25-en
25 Frances Burwell and Kenneth Propp, 'Digital sovereignty: Europe's declaration of independence?', Atlantic Council (14 January 2026), https://www.atlanticcouncil.org/in-depth-research-reports/report/digital-sovereignty-europes-declaration-of-independence/?utm-source=substack&utm-medium=ema
26 Dan Baer and Erik Brown, 'Unstrategic ambiguity: Trump's erratic approach leaves Europe guessing', Carnegie Russia Eurasia Center (7 April 2026), https://carnegieendowment.org/russia-eurasia/research/2026/04/unstrategic-ambiguity-trumps-erratic-approach-leaves-europe-guessing
27 'Initiative for Europe, Speech by M. Emmanuel Macron, President of the French Republic' (26 September 2017), https://www.diplomatie.gouv.fr/IMG/pdf/english-version-transcript---initiative-for-europe---speech-by-the-president-of-the-french-republic-cle8de628.pdf
28 Timothy Garton Ash, Ivan Krastev and Mark Leonard, 'Alone in a Trumpian

World: The EU and Global Public Opinion after the US Elections', European Council on Foreign Relations (January 2025), https://ecfr.eu/publication/alone-in-a-trumpian-world-the-eu-and-global-public-opinion-after-the-us-elections/

29 Speech by President von der Leyen at the EU Ambassadors Conference 2026: https://ec.europa.eu/commission/presscorner/detail/da/speech-26-576

30 Robert Shrimsley, 'Strategic supplication is Europe's only Trump policy', *Financial Times* (8 January 2026), https://www.ft.com/content/1439dce5-00a5-4010-bd9a-385a918bac1b

31 Paul-Henri Spaak, prime minister of Belgium, 1938–9, 1946 and 1947–9. See Giles Merritt, *Slippery Slope: Europe's Troubled Future* (Oxford: Oxford University Press, 2016).

32 'The quest for prosperity', *The Economist* (15 March 2007), https://www.economist.com/special-report/2007/03/17/the-quest-for-prosperity

33 Christopher S. Chivvis, 'America needs an alliance audit', *Foreign Affairs* (25 February 2026), https://www.foreignaffairs.com/united-states/america-needs-alliance-audit

34 Peter J. Katzenstein and Lucia A. Seybert (eds.), *Protean Power: Exploring the Uncertain and Unexpected in World Politics* (Cambridge: Cambridge University Press, 2018).

35 Daron Acemoglu and James A. Robinson, *The Narrow Corridor: States, Societies, and the Fate of Liberty* (London: Penguin, 2019).

36 Garton Ash et al., 'Alone in a Trumpian World: The EU and Global Public Opinion after the US Elections'.

37 C. Raja Mohan, 'The multipolar delusion', *Foreign Affairs* (March/April 2026), https://www.foreignaffairs.com/united-states/multipolar-delusion-mohan

38 Tobias Bunde, Sophie Eisentraut and Leonard Schütte (eds.), *Multipolarization: Munich Security Report 2025* (February 2025), https://securityconference.org/assets/02-Dokumente/01-Publikationen/2025/MSR-2025/Multipolarization--Munich-Security-Report-2025.pdf

39 Michael Beckley, 'The Middle Power Delusion', *Foreign Affairs* (May/June 2026), https://www.foreignaffairs.com/united-states/middle-power-delusion

40 Ibid.

41 Armen Sarkissian, *The Small States Club: How Small Smart States Can Save the World* (London: Hurst Publishers, 2023).

42 Convention on the Prohibition of the Use, Stockpiling, Production and Transfer of Anti-Personnel Mines and on their Destruction (18 September 1997), available at https://legal.un.org/avl/ha/cpusptam/cpusptam.html

43 *Rome Statute of the International Criminal Court*, International Criminal Court (2021), https://www.icc-cpi.int/sites/default/files/2024-05/Rome-Statute-eng.pdf

44 For further information see https://isa.int/

45 See https://wtoplurilaterals.info/plural-initiative/the-mpia/

46 Stubb, *The Triangle of Power*.

47 Anne-Marie Slaughter, *The Chessboard and the Web: Strategies of Connection in a Networked World* (New Haven, CT: Yale University Press, 2017).

48 'The world is in a new age of variable geometry, says Mark Carney', *The Economist* (12 November 2025), https://www.economist.com/the-world-ahead/2025/11/12/the-world-is-in-a-new-age-of-variable-geometry-says-mark-carney

49 Penny Wong, 'UN at 80: Shaping our future together conference United Nations association of Australia', Australian Minister for Foreign Affairs website (22 October 2025), https://www.foreignminister.gov.au/minister/penny-wong/speech/un-80-shaping-our-future-together-conference-united-nations-association-australia

50 Gayle Markovitz and Kate Whiting, 'What Is "Minilateralism" and Why Is It on the Rise?', World Economic Forum (16 January 2026), https://www.weforum.org/stories/2026/01/minilateralism-and-will-2026-be-the-year-size-doesnt-matter/

10: COOPERATION: PRINCIPLES TO UNDERPIN A NEW WORLD ORDER

1 The Atlantic Charter (14 August 1941), available at https://avalon.law.yale.edu/wwii/atlantic.asp

2 Michael Ignatieff, *Human Rights as Politics and Idolatry* (Princeton, NJ: Princeton University Press, 2001).

3 Sandra Fredman, 'Challenging the Divide: Socio-economic Rights as Human Rights', in *Comparative Human Rights Law* (Oxford: Oxford University Press, 2018), ch. 3.

4 Jeff King, *Judging Social Rights* (Cambridge: Cambridge University Press, 2012).

5 John Gray, 'Why I am not a post-liberal', *New Statesman* (18 October 2025), https://www.newstatesman.com/ideas/2025/10/how-to-save-british-liberalism

6 Federica Du Pasquier, 'Not Dead Yet: International Law in an Age of Uncertainty', Lex International (2025), https://lexinternational.org/wp-content/uploads/2025/12/IL-Report-Digital-Final.pdf

7 Michael Walzer, *Just and Unjust Wars: A Moral Argument with Historical Illustrations*, 3rd edition (New York: Basic, 2000).

8 'Fewer people are willing to fight for their country compared to ten years ago', Gallup International (25 March 2024), https://www.gallup-international.com/survey-results-and-news/survey-result/fewer-people-are-willing-to-fight-for-their-country-compared-to-ten-years-ago

9 'Liberties Rule of Law Report 2026', Civil Liberties Union for Europe (2026), https://www.liberties.eu/f/wtaqoq

10 Murray Hunt, 'Supercharging UK Support to the Rule of Law Abroad', Foreign Policy Centre (19 October 2021), https://fpc.org.uk/supercharging-uk-support-to-the-rule-of-law-abroad

11 Rachel Kleinfeld, 'How to Advance the Rule of Law Abroad', Carnegie Endowment for International Peace (4 September 2013), https://carnegieendowment.org/posts/2013/09/how-to-advance-the-rule-of-law-abroad

12 Richard Hermer KC, 'Attorney General's Harry Street Lecture speech' (24 March 2026), https://www.gov.uk/government/speeches/attorney-generals-harry-street-lecture-speech

13 Michael Cross, 'Hermer: No pick and mix on international law', *Law Society Gazette* (30 May 2025), https://www.lawgazette.co.uk/news/hermer-no-pick-and-mix-on-international-law/5123435.article

11: RULES OF THE ROAD: A CHARTER FOR THE TWENTY-FIRST CENTURY

1 John F. Kennedy, 'Address at Independence Hall, Philadelphia, Pennsylvania, July 4, 1962', in *Public Papers of the Presidents of the United States: John F. Kennedy, 1962* (Washington, DC: United States Government Printing Office, 1963), item 278, available at the John F. Kennedy Presidential Library and Museum, www.jfklibrary.org.

2 John F. Kennedy, 'Commencement Address at American University, Washington, DC, June 10, 1963', in *Public Papers of the Presidents of the United States: John F. Kennedy, 1963* (Washington, DC: United States Government Printing Office, 1964), item 232, available at the John F. Kennedy Presidential Library and Museum, www.jfklibrary.org.

3 'Inaugural Address, January 20, 1961', John F. Kennedy Presidential Library and Museum, https://www.jfklibrary.org/archives/other-resources/john-f-kennedy-speeches/inaugural-address-19610120

4 'Security Council Data – Vetoes since 1946', United Nations Peace Security Data Hub, https://psdata.un.org/dataset/DPPA-SCVETOES

5 Dag Hammarskjöld, address at the University of California Convocation, Berkeley (13 May 1954), transcript available at https://digitallibrary.un.org/record/1291161

12: PROSPERITY: HOW WE REBUILD A FAIRER ECONOMY

1 Paul M. Romer, 'Endogenous Technological Change', *Journal of Political Economy*, Vol. 98, No. 5, Pt 2 (1990), pp. S71–S102.

2 Saul Klein, 'Amid the economic gloom, the UK's tech firms give us a reason to

celebrate', *The Observer* (18 December 2025), https://observer.co.uk/news/science-technology/article/amid-economic-gloom-the-uks-stable-of-innovative-tech-firms-is-reason-to-celebrate

3 Alex Bell, Raj Chetty, Xavier Jaravel, Neviana Petkova and John Van Reenen, 'Who Becomes an Inventor in America? The Importance of Exposure to Innovation', *Quarterly Journal of Economics*, Vol. 134, No. 2 (2019), pp. 647–713.

4 John Fernald and Robert Inklaar, 'The UK Productivity "Puzzle" in an International Comparative Perspective', Federal Reserve Bank of San Francisco (March 2022), https://www.frbsf.org/wp-content/uploads/sites/4/wp2022-07.pdf

5 Nicholas Bloom, Charles I. Jones, John Van Reenen and Michael Webb (2017), 'Are Ideas Getting Harder to Find?', *American Economic Review*, Vol. 110, No. 4 (2020), pp. 1104–44.

6 David J. Deming, Christopher Ong and Lawrence H. Summers, 'Technological Disruption in the Labor Market', NBER (January 2025), nber.org/papers/w33323

7 Gallup, Walton Family Foundation and GSV Ventures, *The AI Paradox: More Exposure, Less Confidence Among Gen Z* (2026).

8 Philippe Aghion and Simon Bunel, 'AI and Growth: Where Do We Stand?', Federal Reserve Bank of San Francisco (June 2024), https://www.frbsf.org/wp-content/uploads/AI-and-Growth-Aghion-Bunel.pdf

9 Claudia Goldin and Lawrence F. Katz, *The Race between Education and Technology* (Cambridge, MA: Harvard University Press, 2009).

10 David Autor, Caroline Chin and Anna Salomons, 'New Frontiers: The Origins and Content of New Work, 1940–2018', NBER (August 2022), https://www.nber.org/papers/w30389

11 Daron Acemoglu and Simon Johnson, *Power and Progress: Our Thousand-Year Struggle over Technology and Prosperity* (New York, PublicAffairs, 2023).

12 Pablo Pena, 'The Human Edge', *F&D Magazine* (December 2025), https://www.imf.org/en/publications/fandd/issues/2025/12/the-human-edge-pablo-pena

13 Roberto M. Unger, *The Knowledge Economy* (London: Verso, 2019).

14 Dani Rodrik and Stefanie Stantcheva, 'A Policy Matrix for Inclusive Prosperity', NBER (April 2021), https://www.nber.org/papers/w28736

15 Elizabeth Anderson, *Private Government: How Employers Rule Our Lives (and Why We Don't Talk about It)* (Princeton, NJ: Princeton University Press, 2017).

16 James K. Harter, Corey E. Tatel, Sangeeta Agrawal, Anthony Blue, Stephanie K. Plowman, Jim Asplund, Sabrina Yu and Andy Kemp, 'The Relationship between Engagement at Work and Organizational Outcomes', Gallup (May 2024), https://www.gallup.com/workplace/321725/gallup-q12-meta-analysis-report.aspx

17 Simon Jäger, Shakked Noy and Benjamin Schoefer, 'What Does Codetermination Do?', NBER (June 2021), https://www.nber.org/papers/w28921

18 Pablo D. Fajgelbaum and Cecile Gaubert, 'Optimal Spatial Policies', NBER (February 2025), https://www.nber.org/papers/w33493

19 Anna Stansbury, Dan Turner and Ed Balls, 'Tackling the UK's Regional Economic Inequality: Binding Constraints and Avenues for Policy Intervention', *Contemporary Social Science*, Vol. 18, No. 3–4 (2023), pp. 318–56.

20 Michael E. Porter, 'Clusters and the New Economics of Competition', *Harvard Business Review* (November–December 1998), https://hbr.org/1998/11/clusters-and-the-new-economics-of-competition

21 Jane Gingrich, 'Regional Inequality and the Knowledge Economy: North America and Europe', *Journal of European Social Policy*, Vol. 35, No. 3 (2025), pp. 264–79.

22 Will Jennings, 'Perspectives on Place: What the English Think about Their Local Area', University of Southampton, https://www.southampton.ac.uk/leaf-content/uploads/jennings-2026-perspectives-on-place-what-the-english-think-about-their-local-area.pdf

23 Adair Turner, 'Overt Monetary Financing – dangerous drug or miracle medicine?', *Positive Money* (7 September 2015), https://positivemoney.org/uk/archive/qe-for-people-dangerous-drug-or-miracle-medicine-lord-adair-turner/

24 Rachel Reeves, *The Everyday Economy* (2018), https://www.rachelreevesmp.co.uk/wp-content/uploads/sites/96/2020/09/374425087-Rachel-Reeves-The-Everyday-Economy-1.pdf

25 Mariana Mazzucato and Henry Lishi Li, 'The Entrepreneurial State and Public Options: Socialising Risks and Rewards', UCL Institute for Innovation and Public Purpose (2020), https://discovery.ucl.ac.uk/id/eprint/10196907/1/Mazzucato-final-the-entrepreneurial-state-and-public-options.pdf

26 Elinor Ostrom, *Governing the Commons: The Evolution of Institutions for Collective Action* (Cambridge: Cambridge University Press, 2015).

27 Nathaniel Hendren and Ben Sprung-Keyser, 'The Case for Using the MVPF in Empirical Welfare Analysis', NBER (May 2022), https://www.nber.org/papers/w30029

28 Acemoglu and Johnson, *Power and Progress*.

13: BELONGING: HOW WE REBUILD STRONG COMMUNITIES

1 Clement Attlee, speech to the Labour Party conference, 1942.

2 William Beveridge, *Voluntary Action: A Report on Methods of Social Advance* (London: George Allen & Unwin, 1948).

3 Thomas F. Pettigrew and Linda R. Tropp, 'A Meta-analytic Test of Intergroup Contact Theory', *Journal of Personality and Social Psychology*, Vol. 90, No. 5 (2006), pp. 751–83.

4 Nico Schulenkorf, 'Sport Events and Ethnic Reconciliation: Attempting to Create Social Change between Sinhalese, Tamil and Muslim Sportspeople in War-Torn Sri Lanka', *International Review for the Sociology of Sport*, Vol. 45, No. 3 (2010), pp. 273–94.

5 Stefania Paolini, Miles Hewstone, Ed Cairns and Alberto Voci, 'Effects of Direct and Indirect Cross-Group Friendships on Judgments of Catholics and Protestants in Northern Ireland: The Mediating Role of an Anxiety-Reduction Mechanism', *Personality and Social Psychology Bulletin*, Vol. 30, No. 6 (2004), pp. 770–86.

6 Katharina Schmid, Miles Hewstone, Beate Küpper, Andreas Zick and Ulrich Wagner, 'Secondary Transfer Effects of Intergroup Contact: A Cross-National Comparison in Europe', *Social Psychology Quarterly*, Vol. 75, No. 1 (2012), pp. 28–51.

7 Michael Sandel, *Democracy's Discontent: America in Search of a Public Philosophy* (Cambridge, MA: Belknap Press, 1996).

8 Jen Golbeck, 'I've traveled across the country to attend Trump rallies. Here's what you won't see on TV', *HuffPost* (13 September 2024), https://www.huffpost.com/entry/donald-trump-rallies-mainstream-media-n-66e07063e4b0f6ea72e2b59c

9 '"Learning to Participate" through Formal, Non-formal and Informal Learning', European Commission Youth Wiki (13 March 2026), https://national-policies.eacea.ec.europa.eu/youthwiki/chapters/denmark/57-learning-to-participate-through-formal-non-formal-and-informal-learning

10 Mandy Wilson, Ellie Munro, Angela Ellis Paine, Rob Macmillan, Peter Wells and Angus McCabe, 'Understanding Success in Big Local: Our Bigger Story – The Longitudinal Multimedia Evaluation of the Big Local Programme', Sheffield Hallam University (July 2024), https://ourbiggerstory.com/wp-content/uploads/2025/03/Our-Bigger-Study-What-is-Success.pdf; 'America's Future Starts with Local Communities', Trust for Civic Life, https://trustforciviclife.org; 'About the Canada Service Corps', Government of Canada (29 July 2024), https://www.canada.ca/en/services/youth/canada-service-corps/about.html

11 Lisa Keenan and Mick Ward, 'Asset-Based Approaches in Local Authorities: The Leeds Experience', Local Government Association, local.gov.uk/asset-based-approaches-local-authorities-leeds-experience (accessed 25 March 2026).

12 'Neya: Oxford's Local Connection App', https://www.joinneya.com

13 Carolyn Bruckmann, 'The Friendship Recession: The Lost Art of Connecting', Harvard Kennedy School (February 2025) https://www.happiness.hks.harvard.edu/february-2025-issue/the-friendship-recession-the-lost-art-of-connecting

14 Feifei Bu, Alexandra Burton, Naomi Launders, Amy E. Taylor, Alvin Richards-Belle, Stephanie Tierney, David Osborn and Daisy Fancourt, 'National Roll-Out of Social Prescribing in England's Primary Care System: A Longitudinal Observational Study Using Clinical Practice Research Datalink Data', *Lancet Public Health*, Vol. 10, No. 11 (2025), pp. e903–e911.

15 Skocpol, Theda. *Diminished Democracy: From Membership to Management in American Civic Life* (Norman: University of Oklahoma Press, 2003).

16 Jake Puddle, *Shared Goals: The Power of Football Clubs to Connect Diverse*

Communities, British Future (May 2024), https://www.britishfuture.org/wp-content/uploads/2024/05/British-Future-Shared-Goals.pdf

17 Frankie Karrer, 'Streaming Sports Viewership is a Growth Opportunity', MNTN Research (19 April 2022), https://research.mountain.com/insights/streaming-sports-viewership-is-a-growth-opportunity/

18 Ian Taylor and Karen Dobres, 'Sports Clubs and Social Impact', Government Outcomes Lab (1 November 2023), https://golab.bsg.ox.ac.uk/community/blogs/sports-clubs-and-social-impact/

19 'What is the GAA?', Government of Ireland, https://www.ireland.ie/en/gaa/what-is-the-gaa/ (accessed June 2026); Indecon International Economic and Strategic Consultants, 'Assessment of Economic and Social Impacts of Inter-County Gaelic Football, Camogie and Hurling Players in Ireland: Final Report', submitted to the Gaelic Players Association (December 2024), https://www.gaelicplayers.com/wp-content/uploads/2025/02/Indecon-Report-on-the-Economic-and-Social-Impact-of-GPA-players-FINAL-19.12.2024-1.pdf.

20 'GAA Purpose, Vision and Values', GAA, https://www.gaa.ie/the-gaa/administration (accessed 27 April 2026).

21 'The Story of HOPE not Hate's Communities Work', HOPE not Hate, https://hopenothate.org.uk/the-story-of-hope-not-hates-communities-work/ (accessed 25 March 2026).

22 'Our Wins', Citizens UK, https://www.citizensuk.org/campaigns/campaign-wins/ (accessed 25 March 2026).

23 'Working Together Mississippi', Trust for Civic Life, https://trustforciviclife.org/grantees/working-together-mississippi/ (accessed 25 March 2026)

24 'The Warm Welcome Story', Warm Welcome, https://www.warmwelcome.uk/about-us (accessed 25 March 2026).

25 Rei Kanemura, Amy McGarvey and Alex Farrow, 'Time Well Spent 2023: A National Survey on the Volunteer Experience', NCVO (June 2023), https://www.ncvo.org.uk/news-and-insights/news-index/time-well-spent-2023/

26 Emily Harle, 'Volunteering rates rise but remain far below pre-pandemic levels, research shows', *Third Sector* (10 December 2025), https://www.thirdsector.co.uk/volunteering-rates-rise-remain-far-below-pre-pandemic-levels-research-shows/volunteering/article/1942736

27 Megan Brenan, 'Volunteerism has recovered from pandemic low', Gallup News (21 January 2026), https://news.gallup.com/poll/701204/volunteerism-recovered-pandemic-low.aspx

28 'Get Your High School Volunteer Hours', Ontario (26 June 2025), https://www.ontario.ca/page/get-your-high-school-volunteer-hours

29 Simon Jeffrey, 'Introduction', in *Delivering Change: City Partnerships and Public Assets*, Centre for Cities (19 June 2017), https://www.centreforcities.org/reader/delivering-change-city-partnerships-make-public-assets/introduction/

30 Ayse Yemiscigil, Dana H. Born and Horace Ling, 'What Makes Leadership Development Programs Succeed?', *Harvard Business Review* (28 February 2023), https://hbr.org/2023/02/what-makes-leadership-development-programs-succeed
31 'Global Youth Ambassadors', Theirworld, https://theirworld.org/projects/global-youth-ambassadors/ (accessed 25 March 2026).
32 Pedro Carneiro, Sarah Cattan, Gabriella Conti, Claire Crawford, Christine Farquharson and Nick Ridpath, *The Short- and Medium-Term Effects of Sure Start on Children's Outcomes*, Institute for Fiscal Studies (May 2025), https://ifs.org.uk/publications/short-and-medium-term-effects-sure-start-childrens-outcomes
33 Sally Weale, '"Gift of hope and confidence": parents recall how Sure Start was a lifeline', *The Guardian* (10 April 2024), https://www.theguardian.com/society/2024/apr/10/sure-start-centres-early-years-support-families (accessed 19 February 2026).
34 Ibid.
35 Paul Tough, *Whatever It Takes: Geoffrey Canada's Quest to Change Harlem and America* (Boston, MA: Houghton Mifflin, 2008).
36 'Play Streets: Community Impact', Playing Out (2022), https://playingout.net/wp-content/uploads/2022/12/Play-Streets-Community-Impact-Infographic.pdf
37 'Friends with Benefits: How Diverse Social Connections Drive Economic Mobility', RSA (3 December 2025), https://www.thersa.org/wp-content/uploads/2025/11/Revealing-Social-Capital-Report-Final-The-RSA.pdf
38 Alex Chapman, 'Exposed: The Collapse of Green Space Provision in England and Wales', New Economics Foundation (3 May 2022), https://neweconomics.org/2022/05/exposed-the-collapse-of-green-space-provision-in-england-and-wales
39 Lorien Nesbitt, Michael J. Meitner, Cynthia Girling, Stephen R. J. Sheppard and Yuhao Lu, 'Who Has Access to Urban Vegetation? A Spatial Analysis of Distributional Green Equity in 10 US Cities', *Landscape and Urban Planning*, Vol. 181 (2019), pp. 51–79.
40 'Grassroots Action Manifesto', Parks Community, https://parkscommunity.org.uk/grassroots-action-manifesto/ (accessed 25 March 2026).
41 J. Woodward, J. South and R. Julian, 'Exploring the Role of Friends of Parks Groups in Improving Urban Green Spaces for Health. And the Potential Impact on Inequalities: A Multiple Case-Study Design' (2024), available at https://eprints.leedsbeckett.ac.uk/id/eprint/11376/
42 Annoushka Deighton, 'A Hall, a Home, a Movement' in *Stories from Community Britain*, Co-operative Party (February 2025), p. 12, https://party.coop/wp-content/blogs.dir/5/files/2025/02/Stories-from-Community-Britain-Pages.pdf
43 Oliver Moody, 'Finland proposes a very novel idea – invest in the public library', *The Times* (20 June 2025), https://www.thetimes.com/world/europe/article/finland-proposes-a-very-novel-idea-invest-in-the-public-library-q6s2tpp5d
44 'Facts and Figures', Libraries Connected, https://www.librariesconnected.org.uk/facts-and-figures (accessed 25 March 2026).

45 Donald P. Green and Janelle S. Wong, 'Tolerance and the Contact Hypothesis: A Field Experiment', in *The Political Psychology of Democratic Citizenship*, ed. Eugene Borgida, Christopher M. Federico and John L. Sullivan (New York: Oxford University Press, 2009), pp. 228–46.
46 Green and Wong, 'Tolerance and the Contact Hypothesis'.
47 'Marking 37 Years of Erasmus+: Key Numbers and Achievements', Erasmus+ (17 June 2024), https://erasmus-plus.ec.europa.eu/news/marking-37-years-of-erasmus-key-numbers-and-achievements
48 'Youth Exchanges Canada – Exchanges Canada', Government of Canada (18 July 2024), https://www.canada.ca/en/canadian-heritage/services/funding/exchanges-canada/youth-exchanges.html
49 Andrea K. Finlay, Constance Flanagan and Laura Wray-Lake, 'Civic Engagement Patterns and Transitions over 8 Years: The AmeriCorps National Study', *Developmental Psychology*, Vol. 47, No. 6 (2011), pp. 1728–43.
50 Clive Belfield, 'The Economic Value of National Service', Voices for National Service (September 2013), https://voicesforservice.org/wp-content/uploads/2016/03/Sep19-Econ-Value-National-Service-2.pdf
51 'The Diana Award Mentoring Programme', Diana Award, https://diana-award.org.uk/our-programmes-and-initiatives/mentoring (accessed 25 March 2026).
52 Robert Putnam, *The Upswing: How We Came Together a Century Ago and How We Can Do It Again* (London: Swift Press, 2020).
53 Alexis de Tocqueville, *Democracy in America*, trans. Gerald Bevan (London: Penguin, [1835–40] 2003).
54 John Stuart Mill, 'Considerations on Representative Government' (1861), in *On Liberty and Other Essays*, ed. John Gray (Oxford: Oxford University Press, 1991).

14: DEMOCRACY: HOW WE PROMOTE ACTIVE CITIZENSHIP

1 Only 7 per cent of the world population (0.6 billion) live in liberal democracies. Staffan I. Lindberg (ed.), *Democracy Report 2026: Unraveling the Democratic Era?*, V-Dem Institute (2026), https://www.v-dem.net/documents/75/V-Dem-Institute-Democracy-Report-2026-lowres.pdf
2 Staffan I. Lindberg (ed.), *Democracy Report 2024: Democracy Winning and Losing at the Ballot*, V-Dem Institute (2024), https://www.v-dem.net/documents/43/v-dem-dr2024-lowres.pdf
3 Lindberg, *Democracy Report 2026*.
4 William A. Galston, *Anger, Fear, Domination: Dark Passions and the Power of Political Speech* (New Haven, CT: Yale University Press, 2025).
5 Ibid.
6 Peter Thiel, 'The Education of a Libertarian', *Cato Unbound* (13 April 2009), https://www.cato-unbound.org/2009/04/13/peter-thiel/education-libertarian/

7 Patrick J. Deneen, *Regime Change: Toward a Postliberal Future* (New York: Sentinel, 2023).

8 Ibid.

9 David Pilling, 'Autocrats behaving badly: Donald Trump emboldens global strongmen', *Financial Times* (30 March 2025), https://www.ft.com/content/15cc7dc7-c78a-42c8-b166-29755836335a

10 Joep van Lit and Carolien van Ham, 'The Would-Be Autocrats' Toolkit: What Do Incumbents Do When They Undermine Democracy?', *European Political Science Review*, Vol. 18, No. 1 (2026), pp. 138–57 – a systematic analysis of incumbent-led democratic recession, identifying legal/incremental undermining of democratic institutions (executive aggrandisement, legislative manipulation, control of electoral systems).

11 Juan Pablo Cardenal, Jacek Kucharczyk, Grigorij Mesežnikov and Gabriela Pleschová, *Sharp Power: Rising Authoritarian Influence*, National Endowment for Democracy (December 2017), https://www.ned.org/wp-content/uploads/2017/12/Sharp-Power-Rising-Authoritarian-Influence-Full-Report.pdf

12 'In Numbers', Civicus Monitor, https://monitor.civicus.org/globalfindings-2024/innumbers/ (accessed 25 March 2026).

13 Daron Acemoglu and James A. Robinson, *Why Nations Fail: The Origins of Power, Prosperity, and Poverty* (London: Profile, 2012); Daron Acemoglu and James A. Robinson, *The Narrow Corridor: States, Societies and the Fate of Liberty* (London: Penguin, 2019).

14 Alberto Alesina's work from the mid-1990s showed that political instability is associated with lower economic growth. A 2000 study by Shang-Jin Wei suggested that inconsistency in the operation of the law fosters corruption and disinvestment – a conclusion echoed by Mary Hallward-Driemeier, Gita Khun-Jush and Lant Pritchett in their aptly titled 'Deals versus Rules: Policy Implementation Uncertainty and Why Firms Hate It' (NBER, May 2010), https://www.nber.org/papers/w16001

15 'Worldwide Audit of USAID's Democracy and Governance Activities', USAID (30 March 2009), https://oig.usaid.gov/sites/default/files/2018-06/9-000-09-005-p.pdf.

16 Rebecca Lissner and Mira Rapp-Hooper, *An Open World: How America Can Win the Contest for Twenty-First-Century Order* (New Haven, CT: Yale University Press, 2020).

17 Erica Chenoweth and Maria J. Stephan, *Why Civil Resistance Works: The Strategic Logic of Nonviolent Conflict* (New York: Columbia University Press, 2011).

18 Valerian Rodrigues (ed.), *The Essential Writings of B.R. Ambedkar* (Oxford: Oxford University Press, 2004).

19 Matthew R. Cleary and Aykut Öztürk, 'When Does Backsliding Lead to Breakdown? Uncertainty and Opposition Strategies in Democracies at Risk', *Perspectives on Politics*, Vol. 20, No. 1 (2022), pp. 205–21.

20 Francis Fukuyama, 'It's the internet, stupid', *Persuasion* (2 October 2025), https://www.persuasion.community/p/its-the-internet-stupid

21 Arch Puddington, *Broadcasting Freedom: The Cold War Triumph of Radio Free Europe and Radio Liberty* (Lexington: University Press of Kentucky, 2000), pp. 285–7.

22 Radio Free Europe/Radio Liberty, *Annual Report 2024* (Prague: RFE/RL, 2024).

23 'What is needed is hard thinking', LSE (15 October 2024), https://www.lse.ac.uk/news/latest-news-from-lse/j-october-2024/kramer-lecture.

24 Bernard Manin, *The Principles of Representative Government* (Cambridge: Cambridge University Press, 1997), pp. 218–34.

25 See https://dhub.org

26 Ricken Patel, 'Democratic Populism and Human Politics' (31 January 2025), https://www.rickenpatel.net/post/democratic-populism-and-human-politics

27 Roger Eatwell, 'Community Cohesion and Cumulative Extremism in Contemporary Britain', *Political Quarterly*, Vol. 77, No. 2 (2006), pp. 204–16.

28 Nathan Gardels, 'How to soul-search as a losing party', *Noema* (22 November 2024), https://www.noemamag.com/how-to-soul-search-as-a-losing-party/

29 OECD, *Innovative Citizen Participation and New Democratic Institutions: Catching the Deliberative Wave* (Paris: OECD Publishing, 2020).

30 David M. Farrell, Jane Suiter and Clodagh Harris, '"Systematizing" Constitutional Deliberation: The 2016–18 Citizens' Assembly in Ireland', *Irish Political Studies*, Vol. 34, No. 1 (2019), pp. 113–23.

31 James S. Fishkin, *Can Deliberation Cure the Ills of Democracy?* (Oxford: Oxford University Press, 2025).

32 Divya Siddarth and Audrey Tang, 'How Taiwan Is Crowdsourcing Its Way to a More Deliberative Democracy', *MIT Technology Review*, 21 August 2018.

33 Suzanne Bearne, 'Taiwan's digital minister on how technology can revitalise democracy', *The Guardian*, 27 September 2020.

34 Eric Johnson, 'Engaged California aims for "rough consensus"', *California Local* (3 March 2025), https://californialocal.com/localnews/statewide/ca/article/show/331879-engaged-california-aims-for-rough-consensus/

35 'LA aligns on recovery plans', Engaged California, https://engaged.ca.gov/lafires-recovery/action-plan/ (accessed 25 March 2026).

36 Laura Giesen, 'DemocracyNext: replacing elections with deliberation', Democracy Technologies (20 September 2022), https://democracy-technologies.org/participation/democracynext-deliberation/

37 James Traub, *The Cradle of Citizenship* (W. W. Norton & Co., 2026).

15: SOLIDARITY: DEVELOPMENT WITHOUT DEPENDENCE

1 World Bank, *World Development Indicators*, https://datatopics.worldbank.org/world-development-indicators/; *Trends in Maternal Mortality 2000 to 2020*, World Health Organization (2023), https://iris.who.int/server/api/core/bitstreams/c3957b94-cdd5-47d7-85f8-6202be229f8e/content; *Atlas of African*

Health Statistics 2022, World Health Organization (2022), https://iris.who.int/server/api/core/bitstreams/23fc9653-c200-4c36-8e19-e8623cb58656/content

2 Kristalina Georgieva, 'The price of fragmentation', *Foreign Affairs* (September/October 2023), https://www.foreignaffairs.com/united-states/price-fragmentation-global-economy-shock

3 'Life expectancy rising, but UN report shows "major" rich–poor longevity divide persists', United Nations, https://social.desa.un.org/sdn/news/life-expectancy-rising-but-un-report-shows-major-rich-poor-longevity-divide-persists (accessed 25 March 2026).

4 'Child Mortality and Causes of Death', World Health Organization, https://www.who.int/data/gho/data/themes/topics/topic-details/GHO/child-mortality-and-causes-of-death (accessed 25 March 2026).

5 Esteban Ortiz-Ospina, 'A century of progress in access to primary education', Our World in Data (31 October 2025), https://ourworldindata.org/data-insights/a-century-of-progress-in-access-to-primary-education

6 'The Emergence of the Middle Class: An Emerging-Country Phenomenon', CaixaBank (September 2019), https://www.caixabankresearch.com/sites/default/files/content/file/2019/09/im-1909-35-36-dossier-4-en.pdf

7 Samuel Kofi Tetteh Baah, Elizabeth Foster, Dean Mitchell Jolliffe, Christoph Lakner and Gabriel Lara Ibarra, 'The World Bank's new global poverty lines in 2021 prices', *Data Blog*, World Bank (9 June 2025), https://blogs.worldbank.org/en/opendata/the-world-bank-s-new-global-poverty-lines-in-2021-prices; R. Andres Castaneda Aguilar, Carolina Diaz-Bonilla, Christoph Lakner, Minh Cong Nguyen, Martha Viveros and Samuel Kofi Tetteh Baah, 'September 2024 global poverty update from the World Bank: revised estimates up to 2024', *Data Blog*, World Bank (20 September 2024), https://blogs.worldbank.org/en/opendata/september-2024-global-poverty-update-from-the-world-bank--revise

8 'Goal 1: End Poverty in All Its Forms Everywhere', Sustainable Development Goals, https://www.un.org/sustainabledevelopment/poverty/ (accessed 25 March 2026).

9 Gabriel Lara Ibarra, Daylan Salmeron Gomez, Solrun Engilbertsdottir, Carolina Diaz-Bonilla, Enrique Delamonica and Jennifer Yablonski, 'Children in Monetary Poor Households: Global, Regional, and Select National Trends in the Progress against Child Poverty', World Bank Group (September 2025), https://documents1.worldbank.org/curated/en/099151009052581696/pdf/IDU-439588fb-b2c2-4d7f-941b-90275692e782.pdf

10 Oyeniyi Abe and Victor Azubike, '600 million Africans don't have electricity – the green energy transition must start with them', *The Conversation* (27 January 2025), https://theconversation.com/600-million-africans-dont-have-electricity-the-green-energy-transition-must-start-with-them-245282

11 Natalie Kenway, 'Achieving SDGs "62 years behind schedule"', *PA Future* (11 September 2020), https://future.portfolio-adviser.com/achieving-sdgs-62-years-behind-schedule/

12 Ibid.

13 *State of Social Protection Report 2025: The 2-Billion-Person Challenge*, World Bank Group (2025), https://openknowledge.worldbank.org/server/api/core/bitstreams/3a191516-270b-40c9-acdf-79e3f382c708/content

14 World Bank, *Global Economic Prospects* (January 2025), http://hdl.handle.net/10986/42452

15 Lester B. Pearson, *Partners in Development: Report of the Commission on International Development* (New York: Commission on International Development, 1969).

16 Vibhu Mishra, 'UN warns of $4 trillion shortfall threatening global development goals', United Nations (28 April 2025), https://news.un.org/en/story/2025/04/1162671

17 'Reforms to the International Financial Infrastructure', United Nations (May 2023), https://www.un.org/sites/un2.un.org/files/our-common-agenda-policy-brief-international-finance-architecture-en.pdf

18 Justin Yifu Lin and Yan Wang, 'Development finance must shift away from aid', *Project Syndicate* (31 October 2025), https://www.project-syndicate.org/commentary/developing-countries-must-reduce-foreign-aid-dependence-by-justin-yifu-lin-and-yan-wang-2025-10

19 Maia Davies, 'Almost a third of people in Gaza not eating for days, UN food programme warns', BBC News (25 July 2025), https://www.bbc.co.uk/news/articles/ckgjg81qqwvo

20 'FDI flows to developing economies drop to lowest level since 2005', World Bank Group (16 June 2025), https://www.worldbank.org/en/news/press-release/2025/06/16/foreign-direct-investment-in-retreat

21 'Navigating the Debt Crisis: Reforming the Common Framework for African Countries', United Nations Development Programme (August 2025), https://www.undp.org/sites/g/files/zskgke326/files/2025-08/undp-working-paper-series-navigating-the-debt-crisis-7-aug-2025.pdf

22 'Radical [Debt] Transparency', World Bank Group (2025), https://documents1.worldbank.org/curated/en/099439106192540687/pdf/IDU-a86e3bb4-3446-4716-9131-085141b81950.pdf

23 Marina Zucker-Marques, Riccardo D'orsi, Kamal Ramburuth, Patrick Njoroge and Kevin Gallagher, 'Diverting Development: The G20 and External Debt Service Burden in Africa', Institute for Economic Justice (April 2025), https://www.bu.edu/gdp/files/2025/05/IEJ-G20-Diverting-Dev-Prospects-1.pdf

24 Mavis Owusu-Gyamfi, 'I went into last week's The World Bank Group/International Monetary Fund Spring meetings feeling uncertain', LinkedIn (May 2025), https://www.linkedin.com/posts/mavis-owusu-gyamfi-i-went-into-last-weeks-the-world-bankinternational-activity-7323327965142921216-DhSS/

25 For further information see 'Key Effectiveness Messages for the 4th International Conference on Financing for Development (FfD4)', Global Partnership for Effective Development Co-operation (22 November 2024), https://www.effectivecooperation.org/effectiveness-messages-ffd4

26 'What is learning poverty?', World Bank Group (28 April 2021), https://www.worldbank.org/en/topic/education/brief/what-is-learning-poverty

27 'Aid to Education: Time for Tough Decisions', UNESCO (June 2025), https://unesdoc.unesco.org/ark:/48223/pf0000394153

28 Claudio E. Montenegro and Harry Anthony Patrinos, 'A Data Set of Comparable Estimates of the Private Rate of Return to Schooling in the World, 1970–2014', *International Journal of Manpower*, Vol. 44, No. 6 (2023), pp. 1248–68.

29 'What is learning poverty?', World Bank Group.

30 '10 Years of Chile Grows with You (Chile Crece Contigo): Key Components and Lessons Learned for the Setting Up of Comprehensive Child Development Support Systems', World Bank (July 2018), https://documents1.worldbank.org/curated/en/992351537159031673/pdf/129940-WP-PUBLIC-Chile-Crece-Contigo-10-años-FINAL-July-2018.pdf

31 Martín De Simone, Federico Tiberti, Maria Barron Rodriguez, Federico Manolio, Wuraola Mosuro and Eliot Jolomi Dikoru, 'From Chalkboards to Chatbots: Evaluating the Impact of Generative AI on Learning Outcomes in Nigeria', World Bank Group (May 2025), https://documents1.worldbank.org/curated/en/099548105192529324/pdf/IDU-c09f40d8-9ff8-42dc-b315-591157499be7.pdf

32 Noam Angrist, David K. Evans, Deon Filmer, Rachel Glennerster, F. Halsey Rogers and Shwetlena Sabarwal, 'How to Improve Education Outcomes Most Efficiently? A Comparison of 150 Interventions Using the New Learning-Adjusted Years of Schooling Metric', World Bank Group (October 2020), https://openknowledge.worldbank.org/server/api/core/bitstreams/0e25e5c2-23e8-42b2-bb35-36d03aa60a66/content

33 'Government Expenditure per Student, Tertiary (% of GDP per Capita)', World Bank Group, https://data.worldbank.org/indicator/SE.XPD.TERT.PC.ZS?locations=A4 (accessed 26 March 2026).

34 For further information see https://maharishiinstitute.org/

35 Bono, 'A clenched fist and an open hand: lessons learned from Desmond Tutu', *Time* (31 December 2021), https://time.com/6132224/desmond-tutu-bono/

36 'The future of Africa will be shaped by investment rather than aid', *The Economist* (19 March 2026), https://www.economist.com/international/2026/03/19/the-future-of-africa-will-be-shaped-by-investment-rather-than-aid

37 'Africa's critical mineral resources, a boon for intra-African trade and regional integration', United Nations Economic Commission for Africa (22 December 2024), https://www.uneca.org/stories/africa%E2%80%99s-critical-mineral-resources%2C-a-boon-for-intra-african-trade-and-regional-integration

38 Michael Cohen, Nduka Orjinmo, Yvonne Mhango, Tom Fevrier, Peter Martin and Michael J. Kavanagh, 'Africa will need 1 million jobs by the end of the century. Where will it find them?', Bloomberg (13 November 2025), https://www.bloomberg.com/graphics/2025-africa-population-jobs/

39 'Jobs and Growth Overview', World Bank Group (8 August 2025), https://www.worldbank.org/en/topic/jobsandgrowth/overview

40 John Gerard Ruggie, 'International Regimes, Transactions, and Change: Embedded Liberalism in the Postwar Economic Order', *International Organization*, Vol. 36, No. 2 (1982), pp. 379-415.
41 Ruggie, 'International Regimes, Transactions, and Change'.
42 Tim Ross, Camille Gus, Gabriel Gavin and Clea Caulcutt, 'EU leaders try to out-bully Trump, floating world trade club without US', *Politico* (27 June 2025), https://www.politico.eu/article/eu-leaders-donald-trump-us-trade-tariffs-ursula-von-der-leyen/
43 Ibid.
44 United Nations, Report of the Commission of Experts of the President of the United Nations General Assembly on Reforms of the International Monetary and Financial System, UN (New York, September 2009).
45 UNCTAD, 'Tackling Illicit Financial Flows for Sustainable Development in Africa', UNCTAD Economic Development in Africa Report 2020 (September 2020), https://unctad.org/publication/economic-development-africa-report-2020
46 David Pilling, 'Global famine deaths rise as leaders use food as a weapon', *Financial Times* (25 August 2025), https://www.ft.com/content/a8f68db8-c083-491d-aa07-9273c4afd177
47 'Sudan faces worsening humanitarian catastrophe as famine and conflict escalate: UN experts', United Nations (14 April 2025), https://www.ohchr.org/en/press-releases/2025/04/sudan-faces-worsening-humanitarian-catastrophe-famine-and-conflict-escalate
48 Pilling, 'Global famine deaths rise as leaders use food as a weapon'; 'Tom Fletcher's commitment to the humanitarian community', United Nations Office for the Coordination of Humanitarian Affairs (18 November 2024), https://www.unocha.org/news/tom-fletchers-commitment-humanitarian-community . In 2023, the last year for which full accounts are available, the UN Appeal aimed to mobilise $54 billion – a 25 per cent increase on 2022 – to reach 230 million people. But even as both the people in need and cost estimates had to be revised upward, funding went down and less than half of the original $54 billion requested was raised. The same fate befell the World Food Programme, which recorded the largest shortfall in its sixty-year history, prompting cuts in over half its operations.
49 Veronique Barbelet, 'As Local as Possible, as International as Necessary: Understanding Capacity and Complementarity in Humanitarian Action', ODI Global (26 November 2018), https://odi.org/en/publications/as-local-as-possible-as-international-as-necessary-understanding-capacity-and-complementarity-in-humanitarian-action/
50 'Climate change likely increased extreme monsoon rainfall, flooding highly vulnerable communities in Pakistan', World Weather Attribution (14 September 2022), https://www.worldweatherattribution.org/climate-change-likely-increased-extreme-monsoon-rainfall-flooding-highly-vulnerable-communities-in-pakistan/

51 Stephane Hallegatte, Mook Bangalore, Laura Bonzanigo, Marianne Fay, Tamaro Kane, Ulf Narloch, Julie Rozenberg, David Treguer and Adrien Vogt-Schilb, *Shock Waves Managing the Impacts of Climate Change on Poverty* (Washington, DC: World Bank, 2016).

52 For further information see 'Sahel Adaptive Social Protection Program', World Bank Group, https://www.worldbank.org/en/programs/sahel-adaptive-social-protection-program-trust-fund (accessed 26 March 2026).

53 For further information see 'HSNP', National Drought Management Authority, https://ndma.go.ke/hunger-safety-net-programme-hsnp/ (accessed 26 March 2026).

54 'Falling Short? Humanitarian Funding and Reform', Development Initiatives (October 2024), https://devinit.org/files/documents/1506/falling-short-humanitarian-funding-and-reform.pdf

55 'Strengthening Multilateral Development Banks: The Triple Agenda', G20 2023 India (27 September 2023), https://www.g20.in/content/dam/gtwenty/gtwenty-new/document/Cover%20with%20Inside%20page%204%20oct.pdf

56 Rachel Nugent, 'Tobacco, Alcohol, and Sugary Beverages in Low- and Middle-Income Countries: Harms, Consumption and Costs', Bloomberg Task Force on Fiscal Policy for Health (March 2018).

57 Juliet Nabyonga-Orem, Christmal D. Christmals, Kingsley F. Addai, Kasonde Mwinga, Diane Karenzi-Muhongerwa, Sylvia Namuli and James A. Asamani, 'The Nature and Contribution of Innovative Health Financing Mechanisms in the WHO African Region: A Scoping Review', *Journal of Global Health* (15 November 2023), https://jogh.org/2023/jogh-13-04153

58 For further information see https://iff-education.org/how-does-it-work/

59 'ADB announces IF-CAP, new program to accelerate billions in climate change financing', Asian Development Bank (2 May 2023), https://www.adb.org/news/adb-announces-if-cap-new-program-accelerate-billions-climate-change-financing

60 'World Bank announces new steps to add billions in financial capacity', World Bank Group (17 July 2023), https://www.worldbank.org/en/news/factsheet/2023/07/17/world-bank-announces-new-steps-to-add-billions-in-financial-capacity

61 For further information see https://www.gavi.org/investing-gavi/innovative-financing/iffim

62 Sandra McNamara, 'The Loyalist Declaration of Dependence, 1776', *Journal of the American Revolution* (20 December 2018), https://allthingsliberty.com/2018/12/the-loyalist-declaration-of-dependence-of-1776/

16: OUR SHARED WORLD: A SUSTAINABLE FUTURE

1 'Global Energy Review 2025: CO_2 Emissions', International Energy Agency (2025), iea.org/reports/global-energy-review-2025/co2-emissions; 'Growth in

global energy demand surged in 2024 to almost twice its recent average', International Energy Agency (24 March 2025), iea.org/news/growth-in-global-energy-demand-surged-in-2024-to-almost-twice-its-recent-average

2 'CAT Thermometer', Climate Action Tracker (November 2025), climateactiontracker.org/global/cat-thermometer/

3 Mark Carney, 'Breaking the Tragedy of the Horizon: Climate Change and Financial Stability', speech at Lloyd's of London, 29 September 2015, transcript available at https://www.bankofengland.co.uk/-/media/boe/files/speech/2015/breaking-the-tragedy-of-the-horizon-climate-change-and-financial-stability.pdf (Carney was governor of the Bank of England when he gave this speech.)

4 'Somalia', European Civil Protection and Humanitarian Aid Operations, European Commission (26 February 2026), https://civil-protection-humanitarian-aid.ec.europa.eu/where/africa/somalia-en

5 '2022 Pakistan floods: 1,700 killed and millions affected', British Red Cross, https://www.redcross.org.uk/stories/disasters-and-emergencies/world/climate-change-and-pakistan-flooding-affecting-millions (accessed 26 March 2026).

6 Cristina Cattaneo and Timothy Foreman, 'Climate Change, International Migration, and Interstate Conflicts', *Ecological Economics*, Vol. 211 (2023), article no. 107890.

7 Andrew Deutz, Geoffrey M. Heal, Rose Niu, Eric Swanson, Terry Townshend, Zhu Li, Alejandro Delmar, Alqayam Meghji, Suresh A. Sethi and John Tobin-de la Puente, *Financing Nature: Closing the Global Biodiversity Financing Gap*, Paulson Institute, Nature Conservancy and Cornell Atkinson Center for Sustainability (2020), https://www.paulsoninstitute.org/wp-content/uploads/2020/10/FINANCING-NATURE-Full-Report-Final-with-endorsements-101420.pdf

8 'Understanding Climate Tipping Points', European Space Agency (7 December 2023), https://www.esa.int/Applications/Observing-the-Earth/Space-for-our-climate/Understanding-climate-tipping-points

9 Andrew Moseman, 'Will climate feedback loops push us past a "point of no return"?', MIT Climate Portal (4 October 2022), https://climate.mit.edu/ask-mit/will-climate-feedback-loops-push-us-past-point-no-return

10 R. Daniel Bressler, 'The Mortality Cost of Carbon', *Nature Communications*, Vol. 12 (2021), article no. 4467.

11 The United Nations calculate that 90 per cent of newly installed renewable energy is cheaper than fossil fuels, and the International Energy Agency recorded $2.2 trillion of global investment in clean energy in 2025 – twice that for fossil fuels. 'World Energy Investment 2024: Overview and Key Findings', International Energy Agency (6 June 2024), https://www.iea.org/reports/world-energy-investment-2024/overview-and-key-findings

12 'IRENA: 5 key facts behind a record-breaking year', KeyFacts Energy (21 April 2025), https://keyfactsenergy.com/news/31017/view/

13 Euan Graham and Nicolas Fulghum, 'Global Electricity Review 2025', Ember (8 April 2025), https://ember-energy.org/app/uploads/2025/04/Report-Global-Electricity-Review-2025.pdf

14 'Global EV Outlook 2025: Expanding Sales in Diverse Markets', International Energy Agency (July 2025), https://iea.blob.core.windows.net/assets/7ea38b60-3033-42a6-9589-71134f4229f4/GlobalEVOutlook2025.pdf

15 'Causes and Effects of Climate Change', United Nations, https://www.un.org/en/climatechange/science/causes-effects-climate-change (accessed 26 March 2026).

16 'World Energy Outlook 2024', International Energy Agency (July 2024), https://iea.blob.core.windows.net/assets/140a0470-5b90-4922-a0e9-838b3ac6918c/WorldEnergyOutlook2024.pdf

17 Kingsmill Bond, Sam Butler-Sloss and Daan Walter, 'Energy Security in an Insecure World The New Electrotech Strategy', Ember (April 2025), https://ember-energy.org/app/uploads/2025/04/Slidepack-Energy-Security-in-an-Insecure-World.pdf

18 Michael A. Mehling, 'In the Vortex of Great Power Competition: Climate, Trade, and Geostrategic Rivalry in US–China–EU Relations', Harvard Project on Climate Agreements (March 2025), https://www.belfercenter.org/sites/default/files/2025-03/harvard-project-mehling-climate-trade-250322.pdf

19 Kingsmill Bond and Sam Butler-Sloss, 'The Renewable Revolution: It's Exponential, Global, and This Decade', RMI (June 2023), https://rmi.org/wp-content/uploads/dlm-uploads/2023/06/rmi-renewable-revolution.pdf

20 'Excerpt from letter to clients on BlackRock's decision to leave NZAM', BlackRock (9 January 2025), https://www.blackrock.com/corporate/newsroom/announcement/blackrock-withdraws-from-nzam

21 'EU's Climate Law presents a new way to get to 2040', European Commission (2 July 2025), https://ec.europa.eu/commission/presscorner/detail/en/ip-25-1687

22 Frances Schwartzkopff and Evelina Youcefi, 'Danske Bank cuts fossil-fuel exposure from its investments', Bloomberg (12 August 2025), https://www.bloomberg.com/news/articles/2025-08-12/danske-bank-cuts-fossil-fuel-exposure-from-its-investments

23 Frances Schwartzkopff and Arno Schuetze, 'Commerzbank sets aside $313 million for tariff, climate risks', Bloomberg (6 August 2025), https://www.bloomberg.com/news/articles/2025-08-06/commerzbank-sets-aside-313-million-for-tariff-climate-risks

24 Frances Schwartzkopff, 'Fund managers to get new risk management tool – ESG Investing', Bloomberg (12 August 2025), https://www.bloomberg.com/news/articles/2025-08-12/fund-managers-to-get-new-risk-management-tool-esg-investing

25 Michael A. Mehling, 'In the Vortex of Great Power Competition: Climate, Trade, and Geostrategic Rivalry in U.S.–China–EU Relations', *Harvard Project*

on Climate Agreements (March 2025), https://www.belfercenter.org/sites/default/files/2025-03/harvard-project-mehling-climate-trade-250322.pdf

26 International Energy Authority, 'Special Report on Solar PV Global Supply Chains', International Energy Agency (August 2022), https://iea.blob.core.windows.net/assets/d2ee601d-6b1a-4cd2-a0e8-db02dc64332c/SpecialReportonSolarPVGlobalSupplyChains.pdf

27 International Energy Authority, 'Global EV Outlook 2025' Expanding sales in diverse markets (July 2025), https://iea.blob.core.windows.net/assets/7ea38b60-3033-42a6-9589-71134f4229f4/GlobalEVOutlook2025.pdf

28 Lauri Myllyvirta, 'Analysis: Clean energy just put China's CO2 emissions into reverse for the first time', CarbonBrief (15 May 2025), https://www.carbonbrief.org/analysis-clean-energy-just-put-chinas-co2-emissions-into-reverse-for-first-time/

29 Centre for Research on Energy and Clean Air (CREA), 'China's clean energy trends could cut emissions by 30% in 2035 if sustained: A Scorecard for China's New Climate Targets', CREA (3 October 2024), https://energyandcleanair.org/wp/wp-content/uploads/2024/10/CREA-China-Scorecard-New-climate-targets-10.2024.pdf

30 Samantha Attridge, Bianca Getzel et al., 'The cost of caution: rethinking UK pension funds' approach to emerging markets', IPE (14 June 2024), https://www.ipe.com/comment/viewpoint-the-cost-of-caution/10073893.article

31 Vikram Singh and Kingsmill Bond, 'Powering Up the Global South: The Cleantech Path to Growth', RMI (October 2024), https://rmi.org/wp-content/uploads/dlm-uploads/2024/10/Powering-up-the-global-south.pdf

32 Ibid.

33 'World Energy Investment 2024', International Energy Agency (June 2024), https://iea.blob.core.windows.net/assets/60fcd1dd-d112-469b-87de-20d39227df3d/WorldEnergyInvestment2024.pdf

34 Samantha Attridge, 'Resetting the Private Capital Mobilisation Narrative: From Rhetoric to Reality', Elcano Royal Institute, ARI 47/2025, (27 March 2025), https://www.realinstitutoelcano.org/en/analyses/resetting-the-private-capital-mobilisation-narrative-from-rhetoric-to-reality/

35 Charles Kenny, 'The Crisis of Climate and Development Finance', Center for Global Development (27 May 2025), https://www.cgdev.org/publication/crisis-climate-and-development-finance

36 Laetitia Pettinotti, Sarah Colenbrander and, Tony Mwenda Kamninga, 'A Fair Share of Climate Finance? The Collective Aspects of the New Collective Quantified Goal', ODI Global (3 September 2024), https://odi.org/en/publications/a-fair-share-of-climate-finance-the-collective-aspects-of-the-ncqg/

37 Jonathan Beynon and Edward Wickstead, 'Climate Finance: Fair Shares Revisited', Center for Global Development, (31 May 2024), https://www.cgdev.org/publication/climate-finance-fair-shares-revisited

38 For further information see: https://solidaritylevies.org/; Luan Santos, Michael Jakob, Jonathan Gardiner, Flora Dicke and Benjamin Görlach,

'International Oil Extraction Levy: Design Recommendations and Impact Analysis', Ecologic Institute (27 June 2025), https://www.ecologic.eu/sites/default/files/publication/2025/International-Oil-Extraction-Levy-50209.pdf

39 World Bank, 'Climate Finance', World Bank Group (12 November 2024), https://www.worldbank.org/en/news/factsheet/2024/11/12/climate-finance

40 Lawrence Summers and N. K. Singh, 'The G20 Independent Expert Group Report Card on Strengthening Multilateral Development Banks: An Incomplete Grade' (October 2024), https://www.cgdev.org/sites/default/files/2024-10/IEG-report-triple-agenda-report-card-oct2024.pdf

41 Charles Kenny, 'The Crisis of Climate and Development Finance', Center for Global Development (27 May 2025), https://www.cgdev.org/publication/crisis-climate-and-development-finance.

42 Ibid.

43 G20, 4th Finance Ministers and Central Bank Governors (FMCBG) Meeting: 'G20 Roadmap towards Better, Bigger and More Effective MDBs', G20 Brasil 2024 (October 2024), https://coebank.org/documents/1724/G20-Roadmap-towards-better-bigger-and-more-effective-MDBs-T69DXmX.pdf https://coebank.org/documents/1577/G20-Roadmap-towards-better-bigger-and-more-effective-MDBs-q3jhd4A.pdf

44 Expert Review on Debt, Nature and Climate, 'Healthy Debt on a Healthy Planet: Towards a Virtuous Circle of Sovereign Debt, Nature and Climate Resilience', Expert Review on Debt, Nature and Climate (April 2025), https://d1leqfwiwfltz5.cloudfront.net/documents/ERDNC-Final-Report---Digital-W0AyK1T.pdf

45 World Bank, 'World Bank Group Guarantee Platform', World Bank Group (March 2025), https://www.worldbank.org/en/about/unit/brief/guarantees-platform

CONCLUSION: THE POWER OF HOPE

1 Alexis de Tocqueville, *Democracy in America*, trans. James T. Schleifer, ed. Eduardo Nolla (Indianapolis: Liberty Fund, 2012), Vol. II.

2 Robert N. Bellah, Richard Madsen, William M. Sullivan, Ann Swidler and Steven M. Tipton, *Habits of the Heart: Individualism and Commitment in American Life* (University of California Press, 1985; updated edition 1996).

3 de Tocqueville, *Democracy in America*.

4 Bellah et al., *Habits of the Heart*.

5 de Tocqueville, *Democracy in America*.

6 Albert Camus, quoted in Olivier Todd, *Albert Camus: A Life* (London: Chatto & Windus, 1997).

7 Bertrand Russell, *Political Ideals* (Nottingham: Spokesman, [1917] 2007), p. 19.

8 Viktor E. Frankl, *Man's Search for Meaning: The Classic Tribute to Hope from the Holocaust* (London: Penguin, 2004).

9 Helen Keller quoted in William R. Miller, *8 Ways to Hope: Charting a Path through Uncertain Times* (New York: Guilford Press, 2024), p. 115.
10 Ernst Bloch, *The Principle of Hope*, 3 vols (Cambridge, MA: MIT Press, 1995).
11 Jonathan Sacks, *To Heal a Fractured World: The Ethics of Responsibility* (London: Bloomsbury, 2006), p. 166. Also see https://rabbisacks.org/quotes/optimism-and-hope/ (accessed 27 March 2026).
12 Rutger Bregman, *Humankind: A Hopeful History* (London: Bloomsbury, 2020).
13 See 'Read Martin Luther King Jr's "I Have a Dream" speech in its entirety', NPR (16 January 2023), https://www.npr.org/2010/01/18/122701268/i-have-a-dream-speech-in-its-entirety
14 Robert D. Putnam, *Bowling Alone: The Collapse and Revival of American Community* (New York: Simon & Schuster, 2000).
15 Robert N. Bellah, *Habits of the Heart: Individualism and Commitment in American Life*, new ed. (Berkeley: University of California Press, 2007).
16 Putnam, *Bowling Alone*.
17 Patrick J. Deneen, *Why Liberalism Failed* (New Haven, CT: Yale University Press, 2018).
18 Olivier Roy, *The Crisis of Culture: Identity Politics and the Empire of Norms* (New York: Oxford University Press, 2023).
19 George Orwell, *Keep the Aspidistra Flying* (London: Penguin, [1936] 2000).
20 George Orwell, *Homage to Catalonia* (London: Penguin, [1938] 2000).
21 George Orwell, *The Road to Wigan Pier* (London: Penguin, [1937] 2001).
22 Frankl, *Man's Search For Meaning*.
23 Emily Dickinson, 'If I Can Stop One Heart from Breaking', in *Further Poems of Emily Dickinson* (Boston: Little, Brown, 1929).
24 Online polling by Focaldata. N=1,120 UK NatRep, 18+. fieldwork: 28–29 July 2025.
25 Ibid.
26 Ibid.
27 Ibid.
28 William Faulkner, *Three Famous Short Novels: Spotted Horses, Old Man, The Bear* (London, Vintage, [1961] 2011).

INDEX